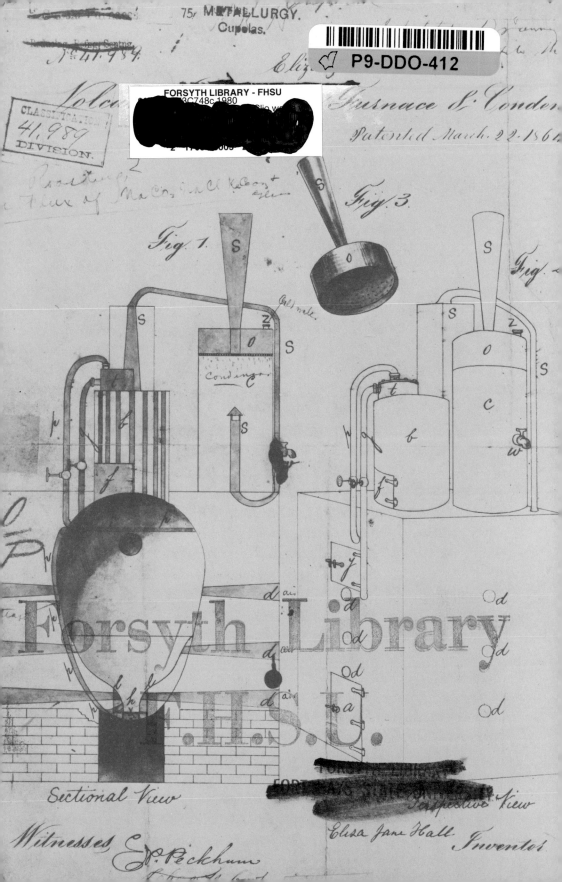

*Studies in the History
of American Women*

THE HERITAGE OF THE PAST
IS THE SEED THAT BRINGS FORTH
THE HARVEST OF THE FUTURE

Statue at the portals of the National Archives.

Clio Was a Woman

STUDIES IN THE HISTORY OF AMERICAN WOMEN

edited by Mabel E. Deutrich
and Virginia C. Purdy

HOWARD UNIVERSITY PRESS
WASHINGTON, D.C.
1980

This Special Edition
published by Howard University Press for the
National Archives Trust Fund Board
National Archives and Records Service
General Services Administration
Washington, D.C.

Printed in the United States of America.

Library of Congress Cataloging in Publication Data

Conference on Women's History, Washington, D.C.,
   1976.
   Clio was a woman.

   (National Archives conferences; v. 16)
   Includes bibliographies and index.
   1. Women — United States — History — Congresses. 2. Women — United States — History — Sources — Congresses. I. Deutrich, Mabel E. II. Purdy, Virginia C. III. Title. II. Series: United States. National Archives and Records Service. National Archives conferences; v. 16.
   HQ1410.C65   1976   301.42'2'0973   79-15336
   ISBN 0-88258-077-9

NATIONAL ARCHIVES CONFERENCES

VOLUME 16

Papers and Proceedings of the Conference on Women's History

April 22-23, 1976
The National Archives Building
Washington, D.C.

PREFACE

This volume contains the papers prepared for the Conference on Women's History held at the National Archives on April 22-23, 1976.

The National Archives and Records Service, a part of the General Services Administration, administers the permanently valuable, noncurrent records of the federal government. These archival holdings date from the days of the Continental Congresses to the present.

Among the one million three hundred thousand cubic feet of records now constituting the National Archives of the United States are hallowed documents such as the Declaration of Independence, the Constitution, and the Bill of Rights. Most of the archives, however, whether in the National Archives building, the regional archives branches, or the presidential libraries, are less dramatic. They are preserved because of their continuing practical utility for the ordinary processes of government, for the establishment and protection of individual rights, and for their value in documenting our nation's history.

Since 1967 the National Archives and Records Service has held a series of conferences for the exchange of ideas and information between archivists and researchers. These conferences are designed to inform scholars about the wealth of useful research materials available in the National Archives, and also to provide an opportunity for researchers to suggest ways in which their use of these records could be facilitated. The papers of each conference are published in the belief that this exchange of ideas and information should be preserved and made available in printed form.

In the summer of 1974, about a dozen historians wrote to the National Archives suggesting that women's history be the subject of a conference. It was also suggested that the National Archives mount a major exhibit relating to women and publish a guide to research on women's history.

Plans were already underway for an exhibit commemorating both the International Women's Year and the Bicentennial. Titled "Her Infinite Variety: A 200-Year Record of America's Women," the exhibit was on display in the main exhibition hall of the Archives Building from July 1975 to February 1976.

The proposals for a conference and a guide were initially rejected. A little later, however, they were referred to Mabel E. Deutrich, who had demonstrated her interest in the status of women by serving for many years on the women's committee of the General Services Administration. In addition, she was the first chairwoman of the Society of American Archivists' Committee on the Status of Women and, in this capacity, prepared a comprehensive report on women in the archival profession. Her enthusiastic support for the proposals contributed to the decision to implement them. She was immediately designated director of the conference. Virginia C. Purdy was appointed women's history specialist in January 1976 to prepare a guide to resources in the National Archives relating to American women. Deutrich is assistant archivist of the United States for the National Archives. She and Virginia Purdy are coeditors of this volume.

JAMES B. RHOADS
Archivist of the United States

CONTENTS

xii   CONTENTS

LIST OF ILLUSTRATIONS

Picture credits: Unless otherwise noted, the illustrations reproduced in this volume are from National Archives records and are identified by record group or file number.

INTRODUCTION

There are four large statues at the portals of the National Archives Building — two at the Pennsylvania Avenue entrance and two at the Constitution Avenue entrance. Two of the statues, one at each entrance, are of women. At the Pennsylvania Avenue side there is a woman with an open book on her lap. At the base of the statue is the following inscription: "What is past is prologue." The woman's statue at the Constitution Avenue entrance is a mother with her small child. On its base are the lines "The heritage of the past is the seed that brings forth the harvest of the future."

One might surmise that the fact that two of the four statues are of women meant that the creators of the National Archives recognized that we live in a "people's world" instead of a "men's world." Unfortunately this is not true. A dozen years before the National Archives was established, Arthur M. Schlesinger, Sr., began an essay on "The Role of Women in American History" with the challenging assertion that:

> an examination of the standard histories of the United States and of the history textbooks in use in our schools raises the pertinent question whether women ever made any contributions to American national progress that are worthy of record. If the silence of the historians is taken to mean anything, it would appear that one-half of our population have been negligible factors in our country's history.[1]

In 1971 Janice Law Trecker, after examining over a dozen of the most popular United States history textbooks, found women still treated as "supplementary material." In commenting on the textbooks, she stated:

> Based on the information in these commonly-used high school texts, one might summarize the history and contributions of the American woman as follows: Women arrived in 1619 (a curious choice if meant to be their first acquaintance with the new world). They held the Seneca Falls Convention on Women's Rights in 1848. During the rest of the nineteenth century, they participated in reform movements, chiefly temperance, and were exploited in factories. In [1920] they were given the vote. They joined the armed forces for the first time during the Second World War and thereafter have enjoyed the good life in America. Add the names of the women who are invariably mentioned: Harriet Beecher Stowe, Jane Addams, Dorothea Dix, and Frances Perkins, with perhaps Susan B. Anthony, Elizabeth Cady

Stanton and, almost as frequently, Carry Nation, and you have the basic "text."[2]

The picture painted by Schlesinger in 1922 and Trecker in 1971 is hardly of a "people's world." In the mid-1960s, however, "a resurgent women's movement began to call attention to the curious invisibility of women in American history, and by the beginning of the 70s an increasing number of scholars were embarking upon research in the field, and organizing courses in women's history."[3]

The National Archives and Records Service was in tune with the scholarly community. In 1972 the National Historical Publications and Records Commission named a special advisory committee to make recommendations concerning the editing and publishing of papers of women. The committee recommended the papers of some ninety women and women's organizations. The committee's report was accepted by the commission. Five resulting, on-going publications are the Jane Addams papers, the National Women's Trade Union League of America and papers of its principal leaders, the Emily Howland papers, the M. Carey Thomas papers, and the Mary Boykin Chesnut 1861-64 diary. Certain women were excluded from the committee listing because their papers are included in larger enterprises. The Abigail Adams papers, for example, are part of the papers of the Adams family. The John Hope papers project has been renamed the John and Lugenia Burns Hope papers to reflect the significance of a remarkable woman in her own right.

Several articles relating to women have been published in *Prologue: The Journal of the National Archives*. One issue, Winter 1973, was devoted exclusively to women.

"Her Infinite Variety: A 200-Year Record of America's Women" was the title of an exhibit at the National Archives commemorating both the International Women's Year and the Bicentennial. The exhibit examined the roles of women at home, at work, as reformers, in wartime, and in public life. It attracted a great deal of favorable attention. First Lady Betty Ford attended the opening of the exhibition on July 10, 1975.

When, in the summer of 1974, members of the Committee on Women Historians of the American Historical Association requested the National Archives to facilitate research in women's history by holding a conference and preparing a guide to source materials, it responded again. Normally for the topics selected for the series of National Archives conferences, there are many sizable blocks of records relating to them. In the case of women's history there are only two, and both of them relatively recent, and by National Archives standards, rather small — records of the Women's Bureau and records of the Children's Bureau. Important as these two record groups are, they do not constitute a sizable enough quantity of records to serve as a basis of a conference. Furthermore, they pertain only to the last sixty years.

Upon a little reflection, however, the National Archives realized that it was precisely because there are no sizable blocks of records relating predominantly to women that it must hold a conference and prepare a guide to point out some of the many nuggets of information and stimulate their use. Although the National Archives holdings, with some minor exceptions, are restricted to records of the federal government, there are not many facets in our lives that are not somehow impinged upon by the federal government. This has become increasingly true over the years. But even in the infant days of our nation, the federal government had direct contacts with the people. To name a few, censuses were taken, wars were fought, patents were granted, justice was administered, and public lands were granted. It is true that for this period there are many more references to men, but the diligent searcher will find information relating to some women.

The Civil War forced women from all walks of life into new tasks and occupations. Large numbers of women entered into paid employment. They were needed to make clothing, bullets, and other items needed by the soldiers; to nurse and care for the sick and wounded; and to cook and to wash clothes for the army. Some women served as scouts and spies; still others worked for the federal government, as copyists and trimmers of paper money. During each of the succeeding wars, many more new and broader vistas were opened to women.

Clearly the National Archives had an obligation to point to the treasure troves in its possession. But after having come to this realization, it was faced with the problem of selecting topics. Because the federal government is involved in endless ways with its citizens, including the women, the number of possible topics was great. It was necessary, of course, to have one paper relating to our holdings in general. Then, although the main purpose of the National Archives conferences is to make known the resources in the National Archives, the planners felt it was also necessary to have a paper describing the important survey of women's history sources in various repositories that is being carried out by the University of Minnesota. Because of the countless subjects and the desire to show the diversity of National Archives records relating to women, a chronological approach was used for most of the remaining sessions. Thus there were sessions on ''Women in the Pre-Federal Period,'' ''Emergence of the New Nation,'' ''World War I and the Great Depression,'' and ''The Impact of World War II on Sex Roles.'' To provide variety and interest to the program, instead of having a traditional keynote address, it was decided to open the conference with a dialog between two leading historians in the field of women's history. Again, partly for variety but very importantly to point to the rich audiovisual resources of the National Archives, one session, ''American Women Through the Camera's Eye,'' consisted of a slide show of pictures with appropriate commentaries and background music. There was a session relating to ''Two First Ladies'' — Edith Bolling Wilson and Eleanor Roosevelt. Finally there was a wrap-up session entitled ''Retrospect and Prospect.''

The papers in this volume are those which were delivered at the conference in the National Archives on April 22-23, 1976. They appear in the order in which they were originally presented. Following all of the sessions except the slide show and the final or wrap-up session, there were comments or questions from other conference participants; these have been summarized and follow the dialog and papers of each chapter. Obviously, a conference such as this one, and the publication of the proceedings cannot be accomplished without the assistance of a great number of people. The director, first of all, is indebted to the Archivist of the United States James B. Rhoads, without whose support, financial and otherwise, the conference and this volume could not have materialized. The director is also grateful to the program participants, particularly Anne F. Scott, Eleanor F. Straub, and James E. O'Neill who served as informal program advisers. Special thanks go to Elsie Freivogel who not only served as an informal program adviser, but as conference coordinator she and her secretary, Marie Howard, took care of the myriad arrangements necessary for any conference. Gloratene Jones assisted the director in making contacts with program participants. Much credit, especially for this volume, belongs to Virginia C. Purdy. After her appointment as women's history specialist in January 1976, she relieved the director of many of the "last minute" responsibilities relating to the conference, and she is coeditor of this volume.

Finally, my thanks go to Betty Cooks who edited the copy and to Bettye Jo Grier and Roberta Hailstalk who typed womanfully on the final manuscript.

MABEL E. DEUTRICH
Conference Director

NOTES

1. Arthur M. Schlesinger, "The Role of Women in American History," *New Viewpoints in American History* (New York: Macmillan, 1935), p. 126.
2. Janice Law Trecker, "Women in U.S. History High School Textbooks," *Social Education* 35, no. 3 (March 1971): 252.
3. Anne F. Scott, "Women in American Life," *The Reinterpretation of American History and Culture,* eds., William H. Cartwright and Richard L. Watson, Jr. (Washington, D.C.: National Council for the Social Studies, 1973), p. 151.

*Studies in the History
of American Women*

Official objections to employing women clerks in the Patent Office, 1855. In the early 1850s the Patent Office took the innovative step of employing Clara Barton and two other women as clerk copyists, much to the dismay of Robert McClelland who became secretary of the Department of the Interior in 1855. The secretary wrote, "I have no objection to the employment of females in the Patent Office, or any other of the Bureaus of the Department, in the performance of such duties as they are competent to discharge, and which may be executed by them at their private residences, but there is such an obvious impropriety in the mixing of the sexes within the walls of a public office, that I determined to arrest the practice . . ."

Women had worked for the federal government and its predecessors in various capacities from the time that Mary Katharine Goddard became postmistress in Baltimore in 1775. Other women were employed in the Philadelphia Mint about 1800, and somewhat later women were performing certain types of light shop work in the Bureau of Engraving and Printing. Several Women's Bureau *bulletins* have dealt with women in the federal service. (See Appendix.)

The Hon. Robert McClelland could not foresee that the three clerk coypists he was trying to displace were the foremothers of a federal white collar work force that would include about six hundred and fifty thousand "females" by the mid 1970s.

(R. McClelland to Hon. Alex De Witt, September 27, 1855, Letters Sent, Vol. I, Patents and Miscellaneous Division, Records of the Office of the Secretary of the Interior, RG 48.)

WHAT WE WISH WE KNEW ABOUT WOMEN: A DIALOG

Anne F. Scott and William H. Chafe

DUKE UNIVERSITY

SCOTT: In persuading the National Archives that a dialog was a more appropriate beginning for the Women's History Conference than the traditional keynote address, we were taking the word "keynote" very literally. That is to say, we are well aware that the enormous amount of energy and imagination that is being displayed by the practitioners of women's history throughout the country is not yet matched by the kind of clarity of definition or firmness of conceptualization that we hope the field will ultimately attain.

It seemed to us, therefore, that a conference of this kind was a tremendous opportunity for an exchange of ideas, for inquiry, and for opening up lines of communication. We expect to learn as much as anybody else.

It was only after the decision was made to open the conference with a dialog that we realized that there was something appropriate about having a member of either gender represented. Who knows, we might have slightly different angles of vision.

CHAFE: At the risk of sacrificing some of the informality that we hope to maintain, we decided that it might be helpful to provide you with an idea of what we will cover in this dialog.

The first thing we will discuss is that age-old question of what women's history is, and why we study it. Second, we thought it would be helpful to address ourselves to some of the major conceptual difficulties or problems that we see in the study of women's history. Third, we want to identify one or two research problems that we believe are particularly significant. And fourth, we want, at least, to raise the question of methodology and how we might proceed to address these questions. We have not, in our discussion, planned to deal extensively with the issue of sources. Since most of the papers in this volume will deal with that in depth, we thought we might better concentrate on these first four areas.

And so on that basis we will begin . . .

SCOTT: That is our road map. You can tell at the end of our discussion whether we have managed to stay with it.

I don't suppose there is anybody working in our field who hasn't many times faced the question from colleagues, from students, occasionally even from newspaper reporters. "What is women's history, and why do you want to study it?" Or the even more devastating question, "Is there any?" So first of all, I tried to develop a definition that would be broad enough for everyone. It is something like this: Women's history is the study of the life experiences, the activities, the values, the functions, the relationships, the common problems, the consciousness, the life cycle of women — as these have changed over time in different times and places in different groups — studied from the point of view of the women themselves. Within that broad definition, everybody has to find a focus — the part of the elephant that he or she really wants to take hold of.

I have been changing my mind about this over a period of about twenty years, but right now I am particularly interested in the way women have functioned in social institutions, particularly those of their own construction, and secondly, in the study of women's cultural values, which are often very different from the values of men in the same groups at the same time. I am convinced that when the attempted reconstruction of the social reality of the past deals only with men, it is incomplete and therefore inevitably incorrect. Social history without women is like somebody playing a piano concerto with only the left hand.

You have a different formulation, I think, of where you would take hold of the elephant.

CHAFE: Nothing that I will say is in conflict with what you've said. I especially think that it is important to deal with the question of women's history as a very basic part of social history.

There have, in the past, been tendencies to define women's history as "contributors' history," focusing on famous women, or as "protest history," focusing exclusively on protest activity. Such a definition tends to ignore the complexity and richness of women's history as an integral part of the entire fabric of society and as a vehicle for giving us insight into how society has functioned.

It seems to me that the American society is organized around three principal reference points — sex, race, and class. If that in fact is true, then clearly women's history provides a basic way of getting an insight into the way in which society has operated over time.

Women's history provides us with the opportunity to examine a pattern of experience in which 51 percent of the population participates. It also gives us extremely important insight into the everyday process of life in all spheres. In addition, looking at the society from the perspective of that 51 percent, we have a very valuable vantage point from which to study the structures of society, the institutions of society, how power is distributed, how roles are allocated, what values are held by which people, and how those values are acted upon. In this sense, women's history has the possibility of giving us a fundamental insight into how the status quo is perpetuated, how social control operates, and what some of the preconditions might be for social change.

Finally, it's important that we recognize the extent to which sex is a variable, intersecting with race and class as variables, and thereby creating both the opportunity and the challenge of seeing how women of different classes and different races share common experiences based upon their sex and, on the other hand, the extent to which they have different experiences based upon their distinctive races and classes.

SCOTT: In a sense, your definition leads into what we said would be next on the map: conceptualization. Because that is your conceptualization for the moment. I spent forty-five minutes arguing with my husband about what conceptualization means, and finally I retreated to a less controversial term: organizing ideas.

Clearly we are in need of organizing ideas. We are piling up data everywhere we look. I looked at the program for the Berkshire Conference,[1] for example, and was astonished at the variety of topics being presented. And your students, my students, students all over the place are accumulating materials. But if we're going to make use of them, we must develop some ways of organizing the data so that it will begin to tell us something.

As I said earlier, I'm interested right now in the way women function in institutions. Maybe I can do better with a "for instance" than I can with an abstract definition. Let me take the example of work, which is an institution.

I ask my students to define work, and they say it's something you hate to do. I reply, "Do you really mean that?" And they think awhile and then they say, "Well no, it's something you like to do."

It's interesting how much trouble we have when we try to define something we are so familiar with.

And yet we know that work is central to human life. Studs Terkel in the beginning of his book[2] quotes William Faulkner as saying "You can't eat for eight hours a day, and you can't make love for eight hours a day, and you can't drink for eight hours a day. The only thing you can do for eight hours a day is work, and that's the source of all our troubles."

I have lately found it useful to try to find out how women have felt about work, the kinds of work they are willing to do, what they think is worth the effort, all the changes in work patterns that have occurred and how women have defined success for themselves, as opposed to how they define success for their husbands. In different times and places and different ethnic communities *success* means different things.

For whom are women willing to work? Who gets the fruits of their labor? How does work of various kinds affect a woman's self-image? How does it affect child rearing? How does it affect parent-child and husband-wife relationships? How does women's work affect the way the society is structured at any given time? How does it affect the rapidity of the economic development?

In other words, I guess I'm splitting that well worn and not very well defined concept of the Protestant ethic into sex genders. I don't believe that men and women have always shared the same attitudes about work. It's a big jump, when you start to think of it, from Benjamin Rush in 1796 saying "Everybody knows that in a country like this, women have got to be trained to work if the family is to survive," to Thorstein Veblen in 1896 saying "Everybody knows that the way a man shows the world that he has succeeded is by keeping his wife in complete idleness." Both statements, of course, are male observations, but I think they are clues to a dramatic change in certain middle-class values.

Once you begin to look at women's work from as many different points of view as you possibly can, you begin to see a pattern of relationships. For example, women's work, I would assert, shaped the development of the textile industry and the garment industry in this country. The nature and definition of women's work contributed to the survival of the first generation of immigrant families. What women were willing to do contributed to the formation of stable black families after Reconstruction. It was a concept of work which gave rise to the development of higher education for women in the late nineteenth century. I think women's work had dramatic effects upon family structure in the 1920s and 30s. I would even go so far as to make a hypothesis that one of the contributing factors to the relative lack of pain in the recent recession is the widespread existence of the two-income family.

For that last observation, I do not have any data. That's just a "for instance." But these are examples of what I mean by taking a concept and a cultural value and trying to trace out all its implications.

I know that every time I say these things, you have some astringent comments.

CHAFE: No, I don't. Not at all. The conceptual problem that I guess bothers me or occupies me most is the very basic problem of how we define group behavior when we talk about women as a group.

What are we talking about? Are we talking about a form of group behavior in which women are acting self-consciously as a collective whole, or are we talking about behavior in which women are functioning or acting similarly as individuals but without necessarily having a sense of doing so because of their collective identity? To put it another way, when we talk about group behavior, is our definition of a group a function of our position as observers, or is it a function of the participants' sense of acting as a group self-consciously?

That is a difficult problem to deal with. As I have tried to grapple with it, I have thought of a very crude typology that I'd just like to share with you for your reaction.

Dividing behavior into two basic forms, we might call one "aggregate be-havior" and the other "collective behavior." There would be four stages here.

The first stage of aggregate behavior might occur in a situation where women do similar things as individuals but without necessarily having a sense that they are doing these things because they are women, or because the things they are doing are part of women's role. For example, 95 percent of colonial women probably kept poultry. I wonder though whether it's necessarily true that they did so with a sense that this was part of woman's place or woman's role, even though it is important that we know retrospectively that such work was in fact an activity that most women did.

The second stage of aggregate behavior would be a situation in which women acted from an implicit or explicit sense that what they were doing was part of woman's role, and was expected of women, for example, cooking food for a sick neighbor. This kind of activity would be associated with woman's role, but would be done as an individual, maybe in response to that role, but not necessarily as a collective activity.

The third stage is what we might call a form of collective behavior, where women unite on the basis of their sex and on the basis of a perception of goals and aspirations or values associated with being female, so that their activities are noted in a collective sense of identity and purpose. Here for example, the women's club movement, women's missionary societies, and social welfare activities all would provide examples. The interesting thing here is that this would be collective behavior, self-consciously engaged in, but without necessarily being in opposition to the prevailing cultural definition of a woman's place.

And finally, of course, there would be the collective behavior that we associate with protest activity where once again women would unite to behave, to act self-consciously on the basis of a stated set of goals, but in this case in opposition to the status quo and in challenge to traditional attitudes. Here, or course, most manifestations of feminism would be examples. I'm not sure whether this typology makes sense, but I'm pretty sure that the problem of what we mean when we talk about group behavior is one that women's historians have to grapple with if our work is to have the coherence and precision that it needs.

SCOTT: My intuitive way of judging something like that is to say, "How many examples can I think of?" For instance, it would be disingenuous of me to claim I've never heard you say this before. But every time I hear it I think of more examples.

It's always been disconcerting to me in my own life when something I thought of is later described by the historians as a trend. I find that my own behavior, for example, as a young person in college and afterward has been neatly categorized by the sociologists, and I did just what I was supposed to do. But this experience also provides useful insight for a historian.

One of the "for instances" that leaps into my mind is really a contemporary example with which the historian of the year 2000 will have to grapple, a development that we see among our own students. Among women who are highly educated, or are in the process of accumulating higher education, and who come from upper-middle-class families, we see a dramatic change in the value attached to child-bearing and to marriage itself.

When I first began teaching at Duke University in 1960, there was something known as the "senior panic." That happened when one was going to graduate without an engagement ring. But nowadays, senior women come around to see me and sort of say, "Well, you know, I'm only doing this because my parents insist," or find other excuses for why they are engaged.

That is a dramatic change in values that has happened over a period of fourteen or fifteen years among a certain group in the population, each of whom thinks she thought it up. And later on it will be described as aggregate behavior.

CHAFE: That's true.

SCOTT: It belongs in your typology about level two, doesn't it?

CHAFE: Yes, I guess so. Some of it is probably collective too.

SCOTT: Some of it is collective because the young women talk to each other and reinforce one another. But it's not an organized antimarriage protest movement.

CHAFE: Yes. But there is a fascinating question there, one that needs to be considered.

SCOTT: Also when we talked about this before, you had the notion of the multiplier effect. That is how a value change like this will spread through the population. And one thing we thought about was that this will of course change the whole nature of the economy. If these women are not marrying, not having children, what are they going to do then? It's certainly going to change the whole nature of public school education as the number of first graders diminishes dramatically. Doubtless there will be many other changes that we have not yet thought of.

CHAFE: Yes. I think it will create some of the most basic social value questions for the next twenty years.

SCOTT: Not to mention the effect on the male psyche.

CHAFE: Right. One other conceptual question that we had thought about, particularly in terms of differentiation, is the basic problem — which I think is more American than European — of how we deal with the differences by class, culture, and race among women.

If we just look at the immigrant experience in the early twentieth century, and the extent to which people from twenty or thirty different cultures and ethnic groups came into the society, and if we see how heterogeneous America remains despite the old melting pot idea, we must also address the question of where those distinctions of race, class, and ethnicity come in, and where the commonality of the female experience transcends those differences. I'm not quite sure how one gets at that. But one of the things that we might do is to look at an analogy of women as a minority group, comparable to an ethnic group, and to ask to what extent women as a group have the same experiences or institutions as different ethnic groups?

For example, can we say that women as an entire group have a separate culture? That is a basic problem that I think we will be coming back to. Can we say that they have a distinctive language? Can we say that there is a set of institutions that keep their community together and provide a rallying point? To what extent can we talk about a ghetto existence among women? This idea sounds not terribly relevant, but if you think of the single-sex college or of suburbia, in some ways you are talking about situations which have some of the same characteristics as ethnic ghettos. And finally, to what extent do women have a transmission of a cultural heritage from woman to woman which is similar to the transmission of an ethnic heritage from generation to generation?

Now all of these parallels may in fact not hold, but by asking the questions, I think we can address the problem of whether or not the commonality is greater than the diversity. And we might come to the point of talking about separate female cultures or languages or institutions within each ethnic class and racial group, which would then provide another basis from which to generalize.

SCOTT: You know another "for instance" just popped into mind. I can't resist remembering an Italian community that we lived in where the woman who worked for us spoke standard Italian to us but spoke the dialect at home and managed to make this transition all the time. In a way women do that. We speak our own language and then we speak the general language, and that's why the men don't know that we have our own language.

Anyway, the next point on your road map is that we were going to discuss areas in women's history where research might be very productive. It is presumptuous, in a way, for us to think we can say "this is where it ought to go." Again, I think of the program for the Berkshire Conference in June, with its enormous array of subjects that interest people, not to mention all the other areas of inquiry that people are investigating. I suppose one could take a sort of Adam Smithian view: let every historian do what serves his or her best interest, and some invisible hand will bring it all together into a nice whole.

But I don't think it works that way. I think we can look across into other fields of history and see why this kind of fragmentation means that you just get more fragmentation. So some of us at least are playing around with the vision of some collective research, collective in the sense that we have a huge problem, and different people take hold of different parts of it with some agreement about what they are going to look for, and with some idea of how they are going to put the pieces together.

I keep coming back to my favorite topic: institutional structures. Women have been adept at structuring institutions. This is one of the best kept secrets in American history. And they structure them for dual purposes. The overt purpose is education or philanthropy or reform, or building an art museum, or starting something like the juvenile protection agency or the Freedmen's Bureau, and so on and on endlessly. But there's also the covert purpose, which is to form an acceptable framework in which women can have a public life. This has been going on for a long time, certainly as far back as Joanna Graham in 1797 with her group for the care of poor widows and orphans in New York. And yet there are very, very few careful studies of particular women's institutions. Louise Young's massive work on the League of Women Voters and Nancy Schrom Dye's work on the Women's Trade Union League are exceptions. I have heard rumors that someone out in Evanston is finally getting hold of the Women's Christian Temperance Union (WCTU) papers. Also, there is Allen Davis's work on the settlement houses. But I think we have a vast untouched field here that is going to require the work of many people to put the pieces together.

The other example that I'd like to put before you is in line with the notion that you touched on when you mentioned the possibility of a female subculture, that is, a collective study of single-sex institutions. The women's colleges are only the most obvious place to begin. There are many other single-sex institutions, so many that it will take a number of scholars to work out parallel studies in order to find out how they function internally, or what effect they have on the women who participate in them. How do these single-sex institutions change self-images as compared to institutions in which both men and women participate, and how have they changed over time, or how has woman's role changed over time, partly as a result of such institutions?

Now I know you have another typology to come along with here.

CHAFE: No, but I think that the institutional question is very important, not only on a public basis, but on the basis of what we might refer to as private or informal institutions. It has always seemed to me that the church is not only an extremely important institution for many communities, but has been a major focus of women's activities, and that the church group, although an informal institution, is nevertheless a crucial activity in which women come together and have an opportunity to share things, share confidences, share aggression, and share humor in ways that are not provided for in their families perhaps. And there are many examples of these kinds of informal institutions — the day care cooperatives, coffee clubs, play groups, as well as church activities.

One of the things we might look at, in considering these more informal institutions, is the idea that they may serve as survival mechanisms, picking up that notion from the studies that have been done of slave culture in the antebellum period. We might also think about the extent to which these manifestations of separate group activity are essential to maintaining stability and sanity in a situation that is otherwise oppressive.

If we look at it in that sense, then I think these informal institutions become interesting examples which cut two ways. They are both instruments of social control and potential instruments of social change. They are instruments of control to the extent that they provide a safety valve for expression of things between women that cannot be expressed in another context. They also become vehicles of social change at the point where a collective sense of anger develops. This anger may find expression in opposition, for example, to a decision by a Baptist Board of Deacons — all male — that the women's club is going to have its budget cut or something like that, or that someone is going to take over auditing the books who is not a female. And at that point there might be a rebellion.

I know you have an example of this out of your own research in the Methodist records.

SCOTT: Well, there's a real case in the Methodist church when the women had organized their missionary society, and as soon as its treasury reached — I've forgotten what the figure was, but let's say half a million dollars — the men said, "Oh that's too much money for women to handle; we will take it over."

That led to a revolt. One woman actually resigned from the church, although she did not give up being a missionary. She said she would be a missionary at large, thank you very much, but she wanted nothing more to do with the Methodist church.

I'm interested in the things you have brought up — these informal groups; but they take you into the problem of methodology because when you want to study an organization that has minutes and records and so on, you know where to start, even though there may be lots of things you wish you knew but that aren't there. But when you talk about these informal groupings, which are so important, then the question of how to find out about them comes right at the top of the list.

And of course we said we were going to discuss methodology. I don't suppose it is any different from any other field of history, but we find over and over again that no one methodology is adequate.

I had a memo from a fellow historian the other day who asked about a group that she hoped to start in our neighborhood. And she said, "Do you use any methodology?" I thought that was an odd way to use the word because obviously the minute you put pen to paper you are using *some* kind of method.

But the traditional business of searching sources and narrative presentations takes us just so far. People have been experimenting with statistics and sometimes making giant leaps between what the statistics seem to indicate and what they say they prove. Then there's oral history, which you and a lot of other people are now developing as a very useful tool. Demographic analysis also lends itself to some giant leaps of the imagination. One of the questions that bothers me is how any one person is going to become competent enough to use these analyses, or even competent enough to work with other specialists.

CHAFE: I think that everything that we have touched upon so far points to how complex the strategies for dealing with many of these questions will be, and how necessary it will be to take risks and to step out of the traditional historian's mold and ask for help, engaging in interdisciplinary activity with persons from other disciplines.

Oral history is a very valuable additional technique for getting at some of these questions, particularly where one is dealing with groups of people who have not left behind written records. These would include particularly immigrant and working-class women who have not for the most part left behind diaries or other records.

The problem with oral history is that too many people see it as a panacea. And it's not a panacea; it is only as good as the research design that is behind it and the skill of preparation in its use. It's really not going to do us much good to go to Florence Lusemb and ask her what it was like to march in the suffrage parade in 1918. What we really need to do is to go beyond that and start asking a whole variety of other questions. Her answers then might lead up to that question but should also describe that network of causes and relationships that have created that particular moment in time that brings us to her in the first place. And so I think oral history is very advantageous if used with a sense of its limitations.

One of the things that strikes me as being most valuable is the participant-observer technique used by anthropologists. Some of you may know of Carol Stack's book called *All Our Kin,* which is a participant-observer's study of black family networks in a Mississippi River town. One of the things that her methodology shows is how effectively one can use anthropological techniques to get inside some of these informal institutions. Some of these crucial internal networks have a lot to do with the development of group sensibility and group protest, but we can't really get at them through traditional historical techniques. I think literature is another example of that kind of network.

We can learn more about using the material manifestations of culture, by which I mean such things as houses — how houses are designed, what kind of tools people used, what kind of toys they played with, their clothing, the church rituals, all those kinds of things. We need to draw upon indirect kinds of evidence.

I also think we must take advantage in a productive way of quantification, of age cohort analysis, and of intergenerational mobility studies. But in doing that, we have to keep in mind those crucial questions of culture, of values, and of socialization because statistics alone — just like oral history alone — really are not going to tell us very much.

I think that the study of women's history faces a magnificent challenge to break new ground in cross-disciplinary kinds of endeavors; it can therefore lead the way methodologically as well as substantively toward transforming the profession of history, making it both more adequate and more accurate.

SCOTT: There are two things that come to my mind. First of all, can the participant-observer technique possibly be used retrospectively, or is it only useful to create a record for the historian of the future?

CHAFE: Well, Carol Stack's work can be examined as both evidence of what was happening in 1972 and as a suggestion of what might have been happening eighty years ago. Obviously time and circumstances change the particular patterns of interaction that are formed, but I believe a cautious observer can identify similarities over time in the way people of a specific culture respond to each other in similar situations. Especially in family and cultural patterns there is a good possibility of tracing continuity over time. Stack's work on the black family, for example, bears a remarkable similarity to some of the patterns of the eighteenth and nineteenth centuries found by Herbert Gutman, particularly in terms of extended and informal kinship systems.

SCOTT: Well, I wish I thought that. I would like to have been a participant-observer at the WCTU convention in Atlanta in 1896 when Frances Willard said, "If this be socialism, make the most of it." What was going on in Atlanta in 1896? In the WCTU? But I cannot relive the past.

The other thing I want to ask is this: From Herodotus to Woodward and Bernstein there has been a kind of rule of thumb that says that two or three independent sources must say the same thing before you believe it. Now what are the oral historian's criteria? Do you have any such rule of thumb?

CHAFE: Ideally, you do need two or three independent sources, but at the very least, the piece of evidence should fit so well into the pattern of evidence from other sources that it would meet any standard of reasonable judgment.

SCOTT: One big question with oral history is that you know that you are getting somebody's retrospective perception; how do you evaluate it?

We edit our past all the time. How can you cope with that? I keep a journal. I go back and I read what I really said at some past time. And then I think about what I believe I meant, and they have little relation to each other. Every time I rewrite the past I make myself look better.

Do you have any way to minimize this problem?

CHAFE: Only by so immersing yourself in the written sources and in the corollary evidence, that by the time you ask a question of the source, you have a fairly good sense of whether the answer fits into the context which you have concluded in your own mind was apparent from the other sources.

It's a very touch-and-go thing. That is why I think we have to be careful about using oral history, and why in many instances it becomes a dangerous source if used as an answer in itself.

SCOTT: You can see we can go on like this forever — and we will.

A great benefit of a collection like this one is a broadening of our lines of communication. One of the most exciting things to me about women's history as it has come into being in the last seven or eight years, has been the high level of real community among the scholars, that is, the absence of parochial jealousy. Nobody is going around holding her fact to her bosom for fear someone else might publish it. There is an extraordinary willingness to share ideas, sources, leads, and papers.

One final comment: I hope that now that historians of women are approaching respectability, we will not lose the excellent characteristics that we enjoyed when we were poor and unknown.

NOTES

1. Third Berkshire Conference on the History of Women, 9-11 June 1976, Bryn Mawr College, Bryn Mawr, Pennsylvania.
2. Studs [Louis] Terkel, *Working* (New York: Pantheon Books, 1974), p. 11.

DISCUSSION SUMMARY

Iris Stevenson of Santa Rosa College in California opened the discussion by referring to Anne Scott's comment about the current phenomenon of upper middle-class women going into graduate study instead of marrying and raising families. In California, she noted, there seem to be large numbers of working-class women beginning graduate study, often after marriage. She wondered if this was a purely West Coast trend because of free higher educational institutions in that region, or if working-class women in the East and South were also combining graduate study with marriage and family.

Scott said that beyond the census data that show the constantly rising age of marriage she had only impressionistic data to support her observation. William Chafe noted that three-quarters of all college graduates come from families in the upper 40 to 50 percent economic brackets, and that it is from this group that graduate students must come. Therefore he believed that most graduate students everywhere would have to be classified as middle class. Scott suggested that some social historian should study the effect of free public higher education in California on that state's culture.

Lillian Anthony-Welch from the University of Nebraska pointed out that some of the suggestions made in the keynote dialog could only be carried out by an "interdisciplinarian"; yet many university graduate schools do not pursue an interdisciplinary approach. Chafe responded that only a small part of women's history requires an interdisciplinary treatment, and that he believed that the willingness to share among scholars in women's studies might offer one solution. He suggested that networks of sociologists, economists, political scientists, and others might be developed. All participants need not be engaged in research; some might be only advisers.

On the other hand, Scott felt that historians who are training graduate students should try to "make life better for them than it was for us." Faculty should take the initiative in organizing graduate history programs to include at least one or two other disciplines, particularly demography and statistics.

Anthony-Welch's second point was to encourage practitioners of oral history to support their work by using novels, other literature, and music. In her studies of black women she found that the blues and the spirituals were very helpful. Sometimes when she was having difficulty with an interview she would remember, "Bessie Smith sang it, then it was all right."

Khin Khin Jensen, now at Augsburg College in Minneapolis but a native of Burma, made a plea that women's historians practice empathy with their subjects when they adopt the anthropologist's observation-participation technique. In the

15

part of the world where she comes from, she said, "anthropologists have played havoc with history" and have been excluded from some countries. Chafe commented that anthropologists themselves are rejecting traditional methods and insisting on studies based upon an understanding of a people's history instead of emphasizing only the present kinship structure, etc. However, he thought it was extremely difficult to go into a community to study it without being offensive. Scott suggested training students to be participant-observers in the groups of which they are a part where they will be less disruptive than outsiders. She has had interesting outcomes from having students write papers called "Three Generations of Women in My Family." Even these generated some friction, but in most cases they led the students undertaking them to an enormously increasing sensitivity to what goes on within their own families.

The technique can also be applied to other institutions to which we belong, she said. "I would give a good deal if I had had the sense to be making notes in the board meetings of the National League of Women Voters in the 1940s," she added. "I bet there are some other people who would give a good deal if I had, too."

Mary Hargreaves of the University of Kentucky was interested in Chafe's reference to informal institutional pressures, but questioned whether they were an agency of revolt. She recalled that between 1940 and 1960 the informal institution was a strong restraint against women's employment. Chafe replied that he had not intended to indicate that such institutions were always agencies of revolt, that he felt that they were just as often agencies of control. In fact, he said, it is difficult to identify the process through which an informal group changes from an agency of control to one of protest. The historian usually has to start with the active protest and work backwards. To illustrate the unpredictability of informal groups, Scott recalled what Tocqueville has said of voluntary associations, that when people get together you never know what they will talk about. She was also reminded of an old southern minister who opposed separate prayer meetings for women saying, "Who knows what they will pray for?" Choosing an illustration from her own experience she said that the informal neighborhood association used to say to her, "How can you neglect you children?" Then there was a critical attitude shift toward censure of the woman who did nothing but look after her children.

Pauline Mahon Stetson, a student in women's studies at the George Washington University, Washington, D.C., remarked that the relation of Catholic nuns to the feminist movement would make a fruitful subject for research.

An interdisciplinary approach to the study of women's history would be greatly facilitated, suggested Deborah Hood of the University of Pennsylvania, if there were some sort of central referral service so that a scholar could learn about other researchers working in fields closely related to his own. Scott thought that this was an excellent idea, one that could be implemented by a journal like *Signs* of which Catherine R. Stimpson is editor. Husband-wife research teams were also mentioned as a type of cooperative research where the skills and knowledge of one complemented the talents of the other.

From Jean Fagan Yellin of the English Department at Pace University came a comment on the complexity of making comparative studies of, for example, black and white women at a given time. She noted that in the United States in 1876 such a study would involve considering southern and northern white women, freedwomen in the South and free black women in the North, and their interrelationships. She considered the task overwhelming and sought advice. Chafe again suggested cooperation among scholars, such as those working on immigrants, or Jewish women. In any event, he warned that it is important to avoid generalizing about middle-class white women and applying those generalizations to all other women.

Finally, Carol Srole from the University of California at Los Angeles reported that a feminist theory study group at UCLA was applying Chafe's typology of aggregate behavior and suggested that he might want to determine at what point in both individual and aggregate behavior women become feminists. She recommended that conferees keep in mind Chafe's four categories as they listened to the papers presented during the conference.

I

HISTORY RESOURCES RELATING TO WOMEN

INTRODUCTION

Clarke A. Chambers

This chapter deals with archives and records, the resources for the study of history relating to women. Putting first things first, I think we need to formulate questions before we go to the past, and the keynote dialog essentially directed and opened up questions to which historians must be sensitive. And then, of course, we must have the documents – the primary materials – before we can even begin to answer the multitude of questions that we must address.

In any new field of historical investigation, whatever it may be, first comes the task of identifying, locating, and learning how to use new kinds of material, learning how to find materials that are buried in disguise in old and regular kinds of records that we are accustomed to using. This has been especially true of all the fields of social history as they have broken away in such exciting ways in the last ten, fifteen, or twenty years: immigration history and black history, the history of the poor, history from the bottom up, as we call it colloquially. Certainly it is true of women's history.

When I began my own studies in the field of social welfare history some fifteen years ago, that was the first problem; there were no records, or very few, in traditional depositories or historical research centers. There were a few exceptions, but I was finding that the materials were buried in back rooms, offices, attics. Any new field, as it breaks away, faces that problem, and it is that large problem that we will address in this chapter.

Our first two authors considered the need for interdisciplinary work in many areas. The most basic requirement for such work has often been evaded and ignored, and that is the need for communication between historians and people who are curators of manuscripts or preservers of archival records.

The study of women's history, then, has to ask new questions, and certainly it has to seek out new evidence or evidence buried in unexpected places. The authors of the two papers that compose this chapter are engaged in precisely that kind of function: opening up manuscripts and archives collections for the use of all historians of women. The first is Andrea Hinding, director of the Women's History Sources Survey about which she has written for this volume. She also carries many other professional responsibilities. As archivists and historians must be, she is versatile. Virginia Purdy, women's history specialist at the National Archives, has also written about her current work. People who work in local and state records, as I did very briefly at one point in my early career, often spoke of "early settlers," and Virginia Purdy was an "early settler" in bridging lines between history, archiving and curation, because she has worked in the academic and museum worlds as well as in archives. Her M.A. thesis dealt with married women's property rights, a subject not many scholars were interested in at the time she wrote it. It is particularly that kind of bridging that makes me rejoice.

AN ABUNDANCE OF RICHES: THE WOMEN'S HISTORY SOURCES SURVEY

Andrea Hinding

With funds provided by the National Endowment for the Humanities (NEH) and the University of Minnesota, the Social Welfare History Archives is conducting a nationwide survey of archives and manuscripts repositories for unpublished sources documenting the history of women in the United States from the colonial period to the present. The Women's History Sources Survey (WHSS) will result — the gods willing and some brave publisher permitting — in a multi-volume reference work, a guide that will expand the possibilities for research on women's lives and roles.

The survey is not an attempt to acquire new sources. WHSS does not seek, for example, to rescue decaying court records from the basements of old court houses — although it inevitably will find and rescue a few records — nor will the survey take Aunt Mary's diaries from her attic and place them in a suitable repository. Rather, WHSS seeks to report the existence of manuscripts collections and record groups already in repositories that are regularly open to researchers.

The WHSS was first proposed by a group of historians, led by Mary Maples Dunn, Carl Degler, Janet Wilson James, Gerda Lerner, and Anne Firor Scott, who urged the Organization of American Historians (OAH) to include in its 1972 program a session on archives and manuscripts sources for studying women's history. The response of those attending the OAH session and the increasing number of scholars and graduate students specializing in the field led Rockefeller Foundation staff members Peter Wood and Jane Allen to convene a women's history conference in June 1972 for historians, archivists, and graduate students in the field. After two days of discussions at foundation offices in New York City, conference participants created a list of priorities for women's history, one of the principal among them being the need to advance bibliographic control over the primary sources that are essential for research in women's history and women's studies.

Clarke A. Chambers (codirector of the survey and director of the Social Welfare History Archives) and I were invited by the group of historians who had planned the OAH session to submit a proposal for a nationwide survey of women's history sources to the NEH. Although the first proposal was rejected, the NEH staff encouraged resubmission of the proposal in modified form. With assistance from Simone Reagor (then staff member of NEH's research grants division and now its chief) and others, the survey proposal was rewritten and submitted again. On March 31, 1975, the NEH announced it would join the University of Minnesota in funding the survey.

When the WHSS staff[1] began work in spring 1975, the first task was to create a mailing list of repositories and historical agencies that might have pertinent records. No one had such a "union" list — indeed no one knew even approximately how many hundreds or thousands of repositories existed in the United States — but estimates by experts suggested there might be six thousand repositories. With assistance from the American Association for State and Local History and the staff of the National Historical Publications and Records Commission[2], the WHSS staff compiled an initial mailing list of nearly ten thousand repositories. Even that promised to be smaller than the total number of repositories, however, for a two-year intensive survey of Illinois sources for women's history being conducted at the University of Illinois Chicago Circle Library by Mary Lynn McCree, Mary Ritzenthaler, and Virginia Stewart yielded fifty names that had not been uncovered by any other organization.

In March 1976, the WHSS staff sent a letter to each of the ten thousand repositories identified, introducing the survey and asking each respondent to complete and return the business reply card that had been enclosed with the letter. The reply card asked for a repository address correction, if necessary; the name of the person reporting; whether the repository had archives and manuscripts collections; and, if so, approximately how many pertained to women's history as described in the introductory letter. As of this meeting more than three thousand repositories have responded, and follow-up efforts to increase the number of responses are underway.

At the same time the mailing list was being compiled, the WHSS staff devised a questionnaire repositories could use to report collections, plus a set of criteria to assist archivists and manuscripts curators in determining which collections were suitable for inclusion in the survey.

While designing the questionnaire, the WHSS staff continually weighed the amount of information researchers and archivists would want to have about a collection, considering as well the possibility that a questionnaire seeking detailed information might discourage many respondents — those in large repositories with

Women's History Sources Survey Questionnaire. (Back and front of a single page.)

6(a) *Dates of birth and death or of founding*

6(b) *Occupation or chief activity*

6(c) *Types of materials*

6(d) *Description of collection*

WOMEN'S HISTORY SOURCES SURVEY QUESTIONNAIRE

Please complete a questionnaire for each collection containing material pertaining to women. Refer to accompanying "Instructions" and "Criteria for Inclusion" as necessary.

REPOSITORY

PERSON REPORTING

1. Collection title

2. Inclusive dates

3. Size of collection

   In addition, report the number of microfilm and tape reels or microfiche cards, if any.

4. Is the collection open for use at present?

   _____ Yes.

   _____ Yes, but access is restricted (See "Instructions").

   _____ No.

5. Is a description or guide to the collection available?

   _____ No guide is available.

   _____ Unpublished guide is available in the repository.

   _____ Published guide is available (Please give full citation):

6. Contents (Respond on reverse side)

   (a) Give the *birth and death dates* of the individual or the *founding date* (if known) of the organization around which the collection is formed.

   (b) Describe the *occupation or chief activity* of the individual, family, organization, or institution around which the collection is formed.

   (c) List the *types of materials* included, e.g., correspondence, diaries, financial records, minutes, scrapbooks, photographs, oral history tapes and transcripts, etc.

   (d) *Describe the collection*, especially as it pertains to women's lives and roles. Please highlight those individuals, organizations, events, topics, or other aspects of the collection that seem significant.

Office use	
REP #	
Coll #	

hundreds of collections to report as well as respondents in smaller repositories with fewer collections but even more limited resources to employ. In its final form the questionnaire asked for what seemed minimal information: the name of the collection; its location, size, and inclusive dates; whether there were restrictions on use; and whether the repository had finding aids to facilitate utilization of the collection. The questionnaire also invited respondents to further describe the collection by giving the birth and death dates of the individual or the founding date of the organization around which the collection was formed; describe the occupation or chief activity of the individual, family, organization, or institution around which the collection was formed; list types of materials in the collection; and describe the collection content, especially as it pertains to women's history. In all cases librarians, archivists, and manuscripts curators were urged to use their knowledge of their own collections to determine what to emphasize and report.

If designing a questionnaire to elicit the greatest possible amount of information without discouraging or confusing respondents was difficult, the question of what ought to be included in the survey was then even thornier. Because women comprise half the human race, they appear "organically" in most manuscripts collections and in the records of virtually all organizations and institutions. Does that mean, as one University of Minnesota colleague asked, that *every* collection is a "women's" collection?

Answering the colleague's question risked opening a Pandora's box of historiographic and philosophical questions the WHSS staff was reluctant to face. The staff finally decided to use a general criterion ("That the collections contain material by women or about women's lives and roles") illustrated by sample collections typically falling into one of seven categories:

1. Papers of a woman, e.g., Jane Addams;

2. Records of a women's organization or group, e.g., League of Women Voters of New Hampshire;

3. Records of an organization, institution, or movement in which women played a significant part, e.g., Amalgamated Clothing Workers of America;

4. Records of an organization, institution, or movement that significantly affected women, e.g., Birth Control Federation of America;

5. Groups of materials assembled by a collector or repository around a theme or a type of records that relate to women ("artificial" collections), e.g., autograph letters of California suffrage leaders;

6. Papers of a family, e.g., Adams Family; and

7. Collections with "hidden" women, that is collections that contain significant or extensive material about women but whose title or main emphases may not indicate the presence of such material, e.g., records of the Bureau of Indian Affairs in the National Archives.

Again archivists were also urged to use their judgment in deciding which collections or record groups to report.

Much effort was invested in writing the questionnaire and the criteria for determining whether a collection should be included in the survey, because most of the work must be done by the repositories themselves. Those repositories that return business reply cards indicating they have collections pertaining to women's history were sent questionnaires and "criteria for inclusion" and asked to complete one questionnaire for each collection or record group that meets the criteria outlined. When repositories returned completed questionaires, the WHSS staff prepared collection descriptions from them and returned the draft descriptions to repositories so that errors can be corrected before the guide is published.

Knowing, however, that pressures of limited staff and resources would prevent many repositories from participating in the survey, WHSS also provided funds to employ twenty fieldworkers to visit selected repositories in all regions of the country, either to survey the collections themselves or to convince repository staffs of the significance of the survey and the desirability of their reporting their own collections. In a test of the potential efficacy of fieldwork techniques, Mary Ostling, a graduate student in American history at the University of Minnesota, visited more than two dozen repositories in Minnesota, North Dakota, and South Dakota during the summer of 1975. The experiment demonstrated the importance of employing fieldworkers not only to report collections where repository staffs were unable to do so but also to explain in person the importance of participation in projects to report holdings in subject areas.

The title of this paper, "An Abundance of Riches," was chosen particularly because it seems the best way to characterize the Women's History Sources Survey. "Abundance" refers first of all to the archives and manuscripts sources themselves. If women have been excluded from written history, as so often has been observed, it is not because the primary sources to document their past did not exist. Already the response to preliminary mailings indicates that there are thousands of collections in repositories, many of which are little-known or used and rarely reported in national guides to sources (e.g., the *National Union Catalog of Manuscript Collections* or the Hamer *Guide*). The WHSS staff hopes to report more than twenty thousand collections in its published guide, but believes that ten times that number may be housed in archives across the country.

"Abundance" also describes the support given the survey by many persons associated with it. The NEH staff offered not only money but intelligent advice and help in drafting the proposal and in the survey's initial stages. Frank B. Evans and Elsie Freivogel, staff members of the National Archives and Records Service, encouraged the codirectors to attempt the project and provided invaluable assistance in planning the survey. The group of historians responsible for the 1972 OAH session on sources continued to lend support and many have joined the WHSS Advisory Board, which consists of archivists Maxine B. Clapp, University of Minnesota; Lynn B. Donovan, California Historical Society; Elsie Freivogel, National Archives and Records Service; Frank B. Evans, now with United Nations

Educational, Scientific, and Cultural Organization (UNESCO) in Paris; Lucile M. Kane, Minnesota Historical Society; and Dorothy Porter, Howard University; and of historians Carl Degler, Stanford University; Janet Wilson James, Boston College; Gerda Lerner, Sarah Lawrence College; Anne Firor Scott, Duke University; and Joan Hoff Wilson, University of California at Sacramento.

An "abundance of riches" refers also to the benefits to be derived from the survey. For the field of women's history, the survey promises increased bibliographic control over the primary sources that are essential to the creation of new knowledge and perspectives about women. It assures for historians in other fields the chance to know and use collections not previously described in national or even local guides to sources. Urban historians, historians of race and class and region, and demographers and biographers, as well as scholars in the fields of literature, political science, law, sociology, and American studies will also find significant new material to support their studies.

The survey also promises to help archivists understand better the nature and possibilities of sources for women's history. One archivist wrote, for example, that her initial reaction to the March 1976 letter describing the survey was that her institution had no such collections; after reflection, however, she said she realized that several of her collections did contain material giving important information on the roles women had played in her institution. Her response, which is typical of many received, suggests that as archivists consider whether they have collections to report, they may become more sensitive to other potential sources of information for researchers. This process of reflection may cause researchers to discover collections and record groups that provide better documentation for the roles women have played in institutions, movements, and geographical areas.

WHSS communication with so many archives and manuscripts repositories also promises to benefit those guiding the archives profession in its increasingly active role of preserving the nation's collective memory. Survey results thus far strongly indicate that the archives profession is not a singular profession with a shared vocabulary and experience; the problems of crossing the barriers between archivists and manuscripts curators, between the volunteers who staff most local historical agencies and the directors of large university research centers are formidable. The survey reaffirms the existence of a problem that many have discussed but not acted to correct: that a great percentage of the nation's primary sources are housed in less than satisfactory conditions and in the custody of volunteers and others with less formal training than might be desired. If primary sources are to be preserved adequately, some attention must be paid to the differing needs and resources of such repositories and to the problem of providing assistance in the training of thousands of custodians so that they can best meet their responsibilities.

The survey also suggests to those concerned about the status and role of women in contemporary society that although women may have come a long way since the nineteenth century, there is a great distance yet to travel. At times the WHSS staff had difficulty explaining to some repositories what was meant by a women's collection; a number responded indignantly that there was no sexism in their organization. "Around here," one correspondent claimed, "women are generally still regarded as human beings, not as some rare endangered species, subject to specialized study apart from history in general." The response, though more clever than many, was typical of a resistance to — or even resentment of — a project devoted to women.

Finally, "abundance" refers to the generosity of archivists, manuscripts curators, and librarians, some of whom have asked their already overburdened staff to report nearly five hundred collections. Equally encouraging are the responses from those who clearly are volunteers or amateurs — those who approach archives and manuscripts from the "bottom up." They too have eagerly answered form letters, often with notes written with elderly, shaky hands, to say how pleased they are to cooperate. Because more than 10 percent have taken the time to write special notes or comments on the business reply cards, the WHSS staff is making a special effort to reply in kind, for we find that even in a project of this size, there is definitely a place for the personal.

Before the survey is completed in 1977 and the guide to women's history sources is published in 1978, many different people will have cooperated in what Anne Firor Scott has called "a grand manuscripts search." Still more will share in the rewards.

NOTES

1. In addition to codirectors Chambers and Hinding, the WHSS staff consists of Ames S. Bower, editor; Anna Glover and Wendy S. Larson, secretaries; Doris L. Lunden, administrative assistant; and, Linda Ziemer, student assistant. David Klaassen and Cheryl Peters, Social Welfare History Archives staff members, are adjunct members of the WHSS staff. The publisher is R.R. Bowker.
2. The staff of the National Historical Publications and Records Commission was preparing the *Directory of Archives and Manuscript Repositories in the United States* (Washington, D.C.: National Archives and Records Service, 1978).

National Archives publications. The staff of the National Archives makes every effort to inform researchers about its holdings. For many record groups and parts of record groups there are published inventories describing the records of a particular agency or office down to the filing unit level. Special lists go into more detail, sometimes calling attention even to single documents of a particular type or relating to a special topic. A limited supply of these publications is available for single copy distribution to institutions and scholars without charge as long as they are in print. The *Select List of Publications of the National Archives and Records Service* pictured above at the top of the grouping contains information about these, as well as about other finding aids such as the *Guide to the National Archives of the United States,* subject guides, and proceedings of National Archives conferences, all of which are for sale from the Government Printing Office or private publishers.

Many records in the National Archives have been microfilmed; for some microfilm publications, descriptive pamphlets have been prepared. The catalog of *National Archives Microfilm Publications* is a listing of all records on microfilm, the number of reels in each publication, and the availability of descriptive pamphlets.

Prologue: The Journal of the National Archives, appears quarterly and contains scholarly articles based largely on research in the National Archives and notes about new accessions of records and services available from the agency.

The *Select List of Publications,* the *National Archives Microfilm Publications,* and information about subscriptions to *Prologue* may be obtained by writing to the Publications Sales Branch (NEPS), National Archives and Records Service (GSA), Washington, D.C. 20408.

NATIONAL ARCHIVES RESOURCES FOR RESEARCH IN THE HISTORY OF AMERICAN WOMEN

Virginia C. Purdy

We have been told from childhood that the American government is a government "of the people, by the people, for the people." When we consider that an increasing percentage of "the people" is female, it is obvious that the records of the federal government are bound to contain a great deal of material relating to American women.

It is generally thought, however, that in these records, for the most part, women are sunk forever in statistical anonymity, poor faceless creatures lost in columns of figures. They have, according to this view, risen to the surface occasionally when they were making nuisances of themselves by signing petitions for reform legislation or insisting upon what they chose to call their "rights." It is the purpose of this paper to point out that this is not so, that there are rich lodes of original materials pertaining to women's history in the National Archives.

There are two keys that every researcher must have if he or she is to open the door of the National Archives to find materials on any subject. The first is the fact that its holdings consist primarily of the records of the federal government. The second is the knowledge that government archives are arranged according to the agency of government that created them. In the National Archives the records of a single agency or bureau are called a record group. No matter what subject a scholar is researching — whether it be women, warblers, or wood pulp — the questions that must be asked are these: Did the federal government concern itself with this subject? If so, what agency or bureau carried out that concern? The answers to these questions, and sometimes the aid of a good archivist, will often lead to fruitful searches in the appropriate record groups.

31

For example, let us consider the career of Amelia Earhart. All of her pioneering aviation activities were under private auspices, the last tragic round-the-world flight a project of Purdue University. The National Archives would, therefore, seem to be a poor hunting ground for source materials about Amelia Earhart. But look a little closer.

In May 1932 she became the first woman to fly across the Atlantic alone. Congress awarded her the Distinguished Flying Cross for this achievement. She was thereafter called as an expert witness on aeronautical matters in hearings before committees of both houses of Congress. Hence, there are documents in the records of the Senate and the House dealing with her work.[1]

The Department of State first became concerned with Earhart because she made this first trans-Atlantic flight without checking with them. She should have asked the department to secure permissions for landings and overflights in foreign countries. Her failure to do so caused a flurry of memorandums within the department. At the same time, American diplomats abroad reported their participation in the gala celebrations held in her honor in Brussels and Paris. The chargé d'affaires in Paris sent newspaper clippings and a copy of a speech he had made at one of the Earhart dinners. "Miss Earhart," he had said, "you have invaded the realm of the gods. You have mounted to Olympus and snatched the thunderbolt from Jupiter and handed it to Juno."[2]

In the Department of Commerce the Bureau of Air Commerce enjoyed Earhart's reflected glory when she returned to the United States. The records show that Secretary of Commerce Daniel C. Roper was also moved to eloquence by the feat of this charming young woman. "Miss Earhart has settled for all time," he wrote, "the question as to whether the woman can equal, and even exceed, man in the air. I congratulate her and womankind . . . ."[3] The director of the bureau received and dutifully filed invitations and programs for Amelia Earhart celebrations across the country in honor of not only this 1932 flight but of others. Every time she made a new international flight, there was a new round of dinners. If Earhart ate half the items on those elaborate menus, it's a wonder she could still get into a cockpit.

When we come to a study of Earhart's last flight, we find that at least sixteen government agencies, bureaus, or offices had a part in either the preparations for the flight or the search for her and her navigator after their Lockheed Electra disappeared over the Pacific Ocean in July 1937. The records relating to Earhart were not kept in all cases, but there is documentation of her career in at least fifteen record groups.

Earhart's husband, George Palmer Putnam, took care of all arrangements for what would be her last flight. This time, international protocol was not neglected, and the Department of State was asked to secure the necessary permissions for landings and overflights.[4] The Bureau of Air Commerce checked facilities at landing fields in remote areas where refueling stops would be necessary.[5] The Navy's Hydrographic Office supplied maps and charts of the proposed routes.[6] The Federal Communications Commission supplied information about the radio equipment in Earhart's plane.[7] The most careful planning was necessary for the long flight across the Pacific. One stop was planned for refueling and possible plane repairs at Howland Island, a tiny dot in the Pacific midway between Hawaii and New Guinea. The island was administered by the Office of Territories of the Department of the Interior. Its field representatives in Honolulu cooperated with the Coast Guard to see that the fuel supplied by Standard Oil was delivered to the island.[8] Along the vast stretches of open water that the Electra had to traverse, U.S. Navy and Coast Guard vessels would be standing by. There is correspondence about all these details in the records of most of the participating agencies.

On March 17, 1937, Earhart and a crew of three flew to Hawaii, heading west on the first leg of the round-the-world flight. On take off from Luke Field for the second leg of the flight, she crashed but was unhurt. Immediately army mechanics undertook to dismantle the plane and get it back to the United States for repairs. In the records of the U.S. Army Overseas Operations and Commands there is a fifty-six-page account of the proceedings of the officers who investigated the crash.[9]

Most of the original preparations for the flight had to be repeated before Earhart once more set out in June. This time she flew east with a crew of only one, her navigator Frederick Noonan. We all know the tragic ending at least in outline. The plane disappeared while it was headed for Howland Island. From this point on in the account, the records proliferate.

In Coast Guard records, the drama is starkly delineated in terse messages sent and received and in the log of the Coast Guard cutter *Itasca* as ships and planes combed the area where Earhart's plane was believed to have gone down.[10] The General Records of the Department of the Navy include a ninety-four page "Report of Earhart Search by U.S. Navy and U.S. Coast Guard, July 2-13, 1937,"[11] and the deck logs of the U.S.S. *Colorado, Ontario,* and *Swan* in the Records of the Bureau of Naval Personnel describe the activities of those vessels for nineteen days after the disappearance.[12] There are 1,000 pages of route slips and cables in the Records of Naval Districts and Shore Establishments about the Earhart flight and search,[13] and an eighty-one-page file in the Records of the Office of the Adjutant General in the War Department.[14] The State Department reentered the picture when it became necessary to secure permission to search in Japanese waters, at a period when relations with Japan required considerable finesse.

Speculation from private and official sources that Earhart and Noonan might have been prisoners of the Japanese ranges from a naval intelligence report[15] to letters in the records of the Military Intelligence Divison of the War Department General and Special Staffs[16], from civilians claiming to have received messages from Earhart. One curious episode concerned a sealed bottle washed up on the beach at Soulac-sur-Mer on the west coast of France on October 30, 1938. It contained a lock of light brown hair and a three-page note in longhand and shorthand purportedly from a sailor who was himself a Japanese prisoner, and who had seen Earhart and her male mechanic in Japanese custody in the Marshall Islands. The Department of State made some discreet inquiries and decided that the note was probably a hoax.[17]

12.   Extremely doubtful that Earhart ever sent signals after 0846,
2 July.

13.   Reports causing diversion of searching vessels should be, and
were, carefully investigated. Once the searching vessel receives such
a report it is required by public clamor to investigate.

14.   The San Francisco and Honolulu monitor systems did excellent
work and should be developed permanently.

15.   ITASCA's original estimate after three (3) weeks of search
problem still appears correct, that plane went down to northwest of
Howland.

16.   The release of all press details by Headquarters and the
Divisions from official despatches is a better solution to handle press
than to have searching vessel carrying correspondents whose despatches
load up air repeating information already officially given.

It is noted that reference (a) requested a written report of communications throughout the entire expedition with the Commanding Officer's
recommendations to be submitted for the information of the Division office.

The ITASCA has been at sea, out of touch with newspapers and commercial radio broadcasting programs. The foregoing report and these recommendations are, therefore, based entirely upon our discussion and study
of the matter within the ship. The ship's sole source of information is
in the radiograms contained in this report.

The ITASCA has been so close to the matter of the flight and search
that it may be this report lacks proper perspective and proportion.

The failure of Earhart to reach Howland and the failure of search
efforts to find her was felt by every officer and man on the ITASCA.
The ship's company fully appreciated the responsibility of the ship
to the Service and to the public.

In the course of time opinions on the Earhart flight and its
communications will definitely be formulated. Many of our opinions
would probably be changed if Miss Earhart were able to give her side
of the picture. It is with this in mind that the foregoing report has
been frankly written and it is considered that on this date (July 23)
it represents ITASCA thought.

There is a good deal of correspondence from private citizens in the records of many of the agencies noted. Some citizens offered helpful information about weather, radios, or planes while others deplored the expenditure of taxpayers' money and the risk of the lives of naval flyers in what one irate citizen described as an attempt "to find a couple of fools."[18]

Here, then, are at least two thousand pages of records, and further research might lead to others. The search began with the obvious hypothesis that whatever agency was handling aeronautical matters in 1932 and 1937 must have had contact with Earhart. The Records of the Federal Aviation Administration contain those of its predecessor agencies, including the Bureau of Aeronautics in the Department of Commerce. Once we had studied the thick file about Earhart in the records of that first agency, we were off and running. The problems discussed in correspondence, interoffice memorandums, and other clues in the records themselves sent us searching in other record groups, some of which yielded single documents while others provided large files that illuminated new segments of the story.

Applying the same principle on a broader scale, let us think of a few other agencies whose work has touched the lives of American women. The first one that comes to mind, of course, is the Women's Bureau in the Department of Labor.[19] If you can picture 885 feet of shelving, you have some idea of the volume of this group of records, all about women. The 1920 Act that established the bureau provides that the director must be a woman and stipulates that its mission is to "formulate standards and policies . . . [to] promote the welfare of wage-earning women, improve their working conditions, increase their efficiency, and advance their opportunities for profitable employment." To do this, the bureau investigates and reports its findings to the secretary of labor. The bureau accordingly has produced a formidable array of publications. Its nearly three hundred *bulletins* cover a broad range of topics. A major part of the records in the National Archives are tied to these publications and the investigations that supported them.

For example, Bulletin 88, a 210-page report published in 1931, describes *The Employment of Women in Slaughtering and Meat Packing*. The records consist of questionnaires filled in by hand by the bureau's field workers who visited thirty-four meat packing plants. They reported on cleanliness, ventilation, lighting, and other conditions affecting the comfort and safety of female employees. In one plant the investigator noted that girls and women were assigned to the Hog Kill and Offal Division, where they worked with their hands under a constant spray of warm water as they washed fat thrown down a trough to them from the killing room

The search for Amelia Earhart. The Coast Guard cutter *Itasca* was assigned to stand by to assist Amelia Earhart in her mid-Pacific landing on Howland Island on her 1937 round-the-world flight. *Itasca's* radio picked up the last transmission from Earhart and participated in the fruitless search after her plane disappeared on July 2. About three weeks later, the commanding officer of the *Itasca* sent to the commander of the San Francisco Division of the Coast Guard a 106-page memorandum, of which page 105 is reproduced here. (Item 65-601. ITASCA. Radio Transcripts Earhart Flight, July 19, 1937, File "601 Amelia Earhart," General Correspondence, Records of the United States Coast Guard, RG 26.)

above. Others trimmed livers, hearts, and kidneys, and pulled the brains out of skulls crushed by a machine usually operated by a man. The Women's Bureau investigator noted that there was proper lighting and that rubber aprons and boots were supplied by the company. Copies of payroll and personnel records of six thousand women were made, and home visits to about nine hundred of the workers completed the study.

Bulletin 88 summarizes the investigator's findings in statistical tables and narrative accounts, including some case studies resulting from interviews. Anyone reading the report may conclude that there is nothing further that could be learned about the employment of women in the meat packing industry, and this may be a correct conclusion. But fortunately the questionnaires and interview records were kept. Other researchers can approach this great mass of data with different questions and put it to excellent use in studies of aspects of the lives of the women who engaged in this kind of work other than those that were the focus of the Women's Bureau.

Another agency that obviously deals with matters that are very important to women is the Children's Bureau.[20] A recently published inventory, which is available free of charge from the Publications Sales Branch of the National Archives, contains in an appendix an outline of the filing system used by the bureau for its central correspondence files. This enables a researcher to call for records by subject. These records, however, may prove disappointing in some ways. Unlike the documentation of the Women's Bureau publications, the files of the Children's Bureau publications do not, as a rule, contain the manuscript survey questionnaires or other raw data. Rather, there are files which contain data on the structure of each study, a set of the forms used, and correspondence between the field workers and central office about the administration of investigations. Since many of the workers are women, these records may provide interesting insights into the history of the female government worker; the researcher will not learn a great deal more, however, about the subject of the study than appears in the published reports. In the correspondence files are many inquiries from citizens which were answered with a two-line letter transmitting a publication. The questions in these cases, of course, are much more interesting than the replies. One overwhelming impression the researcher gains from extended exposure to these records is an awareness of the isolation of some of the correspondents. Women whose nearest neighbor was miles away wrote to an impersonal government agency for help with the most intimate details of prenatal and child care.

On the military side there are obviously records of the women's military services, paramilitary auxiliaries, and nurses. The history of the Army Nurse Corps is particularly well documented.

In the Civil War, nurses were more likely to be male than female, but women were hired to work in hospitals as matrons, cooks, and laundresses, as well as nurses. Their signed contracts in the Records of the Adjutant General's Office give virtually no information about the women who served or the conditions of their service.[21] By the time of the Spanish American War, however, the nursing profession had come a long way, and the army benefitted from this progress.

A capable woman physician, Dr. Anita Newcomb McGee, proposed through the Daughters of the American Revolution that the armed services employ qualified female nurses. Dr. McGee was appointed acting assistant surgeon general and assumed responsibility for screening applications for nursing contracts and making assignments during the Spanish American War. In the Army Reorganization Act of 1901, the Army Nurse Corps was officially established. The records from this point on contain case files on individual nurses as well as registers, monthly returns, efficiency reports, and service records. In addition, the historical file includes articles, personal reminiscences, correspondence, clippings, uniform sketches, and a few photographs for the period through World War I. Dr. McGee's journal and correspondence file dealing with her service during the Spanish American War are also among the records.[22]

One source that yields information of a quite personal nature is the body of records relating to pension applications in the Records of the Veterans Administration.[23] After nearly every war, Congress has provided assistance for veterans and their widows or dependents with increasing liberality. Among widows' applications can be found some marvelous stories of ordinary women struggling to make ends meet in the harsh world of the nineteenth and early twentieth centuries.

Qualifications for pensions varied with each law passed by Congress, but in most cases a widow had to establish her husband's military service and her own legal widowhood. Widows who had the proper credentials on both these counts submitted them and received their pensions in due course; they created very small, dull files in our records. Especially is this true of the widows of famous husbands. Mrs. George Gordon Meade, widow of the hero of Gettysburg, had no trouble establishing her husband's military service or her legal relationship to him. Her application therefore contains little interesting information. Vivid pictures of feminine life emerge from the file of the woman whose assertions were questioned, whether she eventually got her pension or had her application rejected. Those cases were turned over to a special examiner who took depositions from the claimant and from friends, relatives, and acquaintances to determine her eligibility for an award.

One interesting application is that of Head Woman,[24] widow of Wakon Charging Cloud, who had served as an Indian scout in the Sioux campaign in South Dakota in 1890-91. In 1923 Mrs. Charging Cloud made an affidavit through an interpreter in which she described in detail the ceremony in which she married Charging Cloud in 1872 "according to Indian custom."

There are many applications where there was a "contesting widow," when it was not until after the death of the veteran that either wife learned of the existence of the other. The second wife was all too often a recent immigrant whose ignorance of the language and of local customs made her an easy victim. One woman thought her husband had been killed at Little Big Horn with Custer in 1876. Her first application in 1877 was rejected because her husband had served in the army under a different name from the one he had used when he married her. For the next forty years she applied and reapplied under each new law passed by Congress, while supporting her daughter by working as a nurse, laundrywoman, and cook. Before long she learned of a contesting widow, and was informed that her husband had not only survived the Indian Wars, but had remarried bigamously and raised a second family. Finally, in 1926, the last impediment to her eligibility was removed, and she received the handsome sum of $12 a month. The contesting widow's application was rejected.[25]

Then there is the story of the many women in the life of one black veteran named Edward Adams.[26] First there is the claimant, Malinda Adams, Edward Adams' third wife, who in 1913 entered a claim based on his Civil War service. Her life began in slavery on the Peck plantation in Catahoula Parish, Louisiana. Her deposition relates that the slaves were removed to Texas during the Civil War where they were kept for several years after the war because they did not know that they were free. Back in Louisiana she lived with a man on "Widow Knight's Place" until his death. Then she returned to the plantation of her former master. There she was a house servant and personal maid to the mistress, "Mrs. Bettie," and nurse to the Peck children, "Miss Hattie," "Miss Bettie," and "Miss Laura." After Mrs. Bettie's death, she continued as a maid to Peck's second wife, whom he married before his first wife "was cold in her grave." In 1872, Malinda, the claimant, was married in the plantation house parlor to Edward Adams, believing that she was his second wife. They lived together for twenty-eight years, in New Orleans where they had many residences, including "the yard of a white man." After her husband's death, she took a live-in job as a domestic servant but left her clothes and personal effects with a landlady in the old neighborhood.

Malinda had raised the two children of Edward and his first wife, Penny, who had married Edward immediately after the Civil War and had died in 1871. In the file there is the deposition of the forty-nine-year-old stepdaughter, Ada, describing her experience as a woman of the first black generation born free in the post-Civil War South.

Thus far the story is perfectly straight forward. The application went to a special examiner because there was a question about Edward's military service, not about the legality of Malinda's marriage. Once questions began to be asked, however, two other women entered the picture. It seems that Edward had been married in the early 1860s to a slave named Ann. Their daughter Ollie was interviewed in Montclair, New Jersey. She declared under oath that Edward Adams had married her mother in a Baptist church in Vicksburg, and that her father had bought her mother from her master for $1500. She had seen her mother's bill of sale. Edward and Ann had never been divorced. When Ann heard that Edward had supposedly married Malinda, she did nothing about it because she was what Ollie called "one of those easy going women." Ollie had married and moved to Chicago, taking her mother to live with her there. In 1913 Ollie was living with her second husband, a laborer, and working as a matron in the station of the Delaware, Lackawanna and Western Railroad. Ann had died a number of years before.

The investigation dragged on for more than four years. The last woman in this tangled story is Filicie Smith, herself the pensioned widow of a veteran of the 84th U.S. Colored Infantry, and owner of the house in which Malinda rented a room after Edward's death. Her only role in Malinda's application was to report on March 15, 1918: "Mrs. Malinda Adams is now dead and I went to her funeral and she was buried out at Holts Cemetery beside her husband. I stood by and saw her body put in the grave. . . . " Poor Malinda never qualified for a pension, but what a rich cast of characters her file provides! It reads like a novel, with characterizations that a brief account cannot reproduce. At the same time, the number of aspects of the life of black women represented make this a valuable source for the researcher in women's history or black history.

In any set of pension records, inevitably cases of fraud are found. T.A. Wood, a lawyer in Portland, Oregon, got himself elected grand commander of the Indian Wars Veterans of the North Pacific Coast and lobbied for a liberal pension law to benefit the membership. Meanwhile he secured muster rolls of all companies that fought in the appropriate wars and matched as many as possible of the names on the rolls with local veterans or widows with similar names. He filled out a pension application for each of them and sent it for signature to the prospective applicant with a covering letter which read, "In sending you the enclosed pension papers . . . I have . . . taken it for granted that you wanted me to act as your attorney." He mailed "about two cartloads" of declarations and fee contracts immediately after the pension law took effect.

Some of the widows were willing accomplices. Sarah Hill[27] based her claim on the service of her husband William who was a "horse trader by profession and a blacksmith by trade," and who was commonly known as "Buckskin Bill." He had been killed in a barroom brawl and was buried in the Lone Fir Cemetery. Sarah knew very well that the pension was only available to veterans' widows who had not remarried, so she neglected to mention that after William's death she had married a Mr. Thompson whose life was also a short one. At the time she was denied a pension, she was again a widow taking care of her daughter, "Drunken Annie."

Another widow caught in Lawyer Wood's snare was clearly a victim.[28] She refused to sign the first application sent her because the veterans' middle name was not that of her deceased husband, but when Wood sent her another application with only a middle initial in the veteran's name, she signed it without noting that there was a suspicious gap between the initial and the last name. Wood then filled in the name of a veteran whose widow he knew was remarried and would not file a conflicting claim. When Wood was caught and disbarred, many widows like this one were simply out of pocket for the costs of making a properly sworn deposition.

Finally, there was a lady forger living near Hopkinsville, Kentucky, who made a hobby of filing fraudulent pension applications based on Mexican War service.[29] She filed eight claims, several of which were successful. She was tripped up when the eighth one was submitted to a special examiner, and the widow named as applicant said she knew nothing about the claim and had no intention of filing. This criminal thought nothing of forging the signatures of the living or the dead or of composing declarations to be signed with purely fictitious names. She was finally indicted on thirty-seven counts of forgery and sentenced to eighteen months in prison. Although she pled guilty, she "disclaimed guilty intent," and she appears to have been trying to do a kindness to most of her clients, black and white. She must have derived some profit for herself, however, from the pension she secured for a widow who was already dead at the date of the application.

The records are rich with colloquial phrases that lend authenticity. A deponent describes one widow and her children as very poor and dirty, "the coal-picking-up-kind."[30] In St. Louis in 1920, a prostitute was a "sporting woman," and her place of business a "sporting house."[31]

Access to the pension application records is not difficult. There are name indexes on microfilm to most of them.[32] The amount and kind of information on the index cards varies, but it is always possible to tell whether or not the application was successful or rejected. In many cases the date of application is recorded as well as the date of the veteran's service on which the claim is based. Occasionally the date of the award of the pension is noted. The fullest files will be those with long periods between the date of application and either of the other two dates. Many of the cards also note the state in which the claimant was residing at time of application. For mid-nineteenth century western states where population was still relatively small, a researcher might wish to search the files for residents of a particular state to make studies of the paths followed by widows on their way to those states. Another kind of study might be made by searching the pension files of widows whose claims were based upon the service of men in a particular company, since companies were usually drawn from a small geographical area. For companies formed before 1860, this can be done by securing names from the company muster rolls and then using the name indexes. For pension claims based on service in the Civil War and later there is a name index on microfilm arranged by military organization.[33] Thus it would be very easy to discover what became of the women associated with the men who enlisted in Company A of the Second Regiment of Oregon U.S. Volunteer Infantry in Portland in the second week of May 1898.

Historians often complain that much is known about members of the upper echelons of society because they are rich and famous and about those at the bottom because someone is always studying them. Data are hard to come by for the great mass in the middle who go quietly through life minding their own business and leaving few traces. Yet there are two activities of the federal government that touch the lives of every one of us: income tax and the census. Individual income tax returns for the most part do not become archives. They are destroyed on a schedule prescribed by law. But the raw data from twelve federal censuses open to the researcher can answer a great many questions about how the average American lived.

Most of us are familiar with the published tabulations of the decennial censuses — the abstracts, the compendiums, the monographs. These are immensely valuable, and a great many of the statistics in these works are useful for the study of women's history. However, we would like to call your attention to the manuscript population schedules produced by the census enumerator as he went from door to door asking questions of his fellow citizens every ten years.

Until 1850 the population schedules are largely a head count, giving the name of the head of each family, and the number, sex, and age grouping of other members of the household. Beginning in 1850, the schedules list by name every person living in each household accompanied by a number of descriptors that increases with every census. National Archives Reference Information Paper No. 67, *Federal Census Schedules, 1850-1880* by Carmen R. Delle Donne is available free of charge. While it does not deal exclusively with women, its very careful description of the records makes it unnecessary for us to discuss these censuses here. Delle Donne's paper stops with the 1880 census because the census of 1890 was largely destroyed by fire and the 1900 census was not open for research when he wrote.

The 1900 census is now open. Note, if you will, the descriptors for every man, woman, and child: the location, by street address and by number of the house and of the family in the enumeration; name of each person whose place of abode on June 1, 1900, was in this family; relationship of each person to the head of the family; color or race; sex; date of birth by month and year; age at last birthday; marital status; number of years married; mother of how many children; number of these children living; place of birth; father's place of birth; mother's place of birth, if an immigrant, year of immigration to the United States, number of years in the United States, naturalization; occupation, months not employed; attended school; ability to read, write, and speak English; owner or renter of home; if owner, free of mortgage; farm or house; if farm, number of farm schedule (i.e., in census of agriculture for 1900). That is a great deal to know about a person and his or her housemates.

It is worth reemphasizing that, before a researcher plunges into this treasure, he or she should study carefully the publications of the Census Bureau based upon these schedules. The bureau put its statisticians to work with imagination and considerable appreciation for the data in hand, and no historian needs to repeat a study already accomplished by the bureau. Most of the tabulations are for large groups and major jurisdictions, however. In smaller geographical units such as the neighborhood, or special groups such as women in a particular occupation or age grouping, there is much that can be learned by working with these records.

To illustrate this, we took the 1900 schedules for a community within the city of Chicago called West Town (see table). It was predominantly a neighborhood of second-generation Americans, native born adults whose parents had been born in Europe. There were a few immigrant families and an even smaller number of black households. Almost without exception they were literate, and most of them rented single-family dwellings. We made a quick hand tabulation of the women in 150 families, retrieving by relationship to the head of the household and by the report of an occupation (without going the further step of counting specific different occupations).

Table 1
WOMEN IN WEST TOWN, ELEVENTH WARD, CHICAGO, 1900 CENSUS (Tabulations from 150 Households)

Relation to Head of Household	Occupation	No Occupation	Total
Wife	6	90	96
Mother or Mother-in-law	1	16	17
Adult sister or sister-in-law	7	12	19
Daughter-in-law	0	1	1
Niece	0	1	1
Unmarried daughters			
Age 10 to 20	11	32	43
21 to 30	19	11	30
31 and over	6	4	10
Roomers	15	13	28
Other	2	4	6
Women heads of household	5	5	10
Servants	2	0	2
Total	74	189	263

A few interesting facts did not lend themselves to further tabulation: of the six wives who reported an occupation, two were black. A third was a physician whose husband and grown son were also physicians, surely an unusual family for the period. The one mother-in-law who worked listed her occupation as "vocalist." Two of the nonworking daughters under twenty were "at college"; one was "in a convent."

Before beginning to generalize from data such as this, it is advisable to investigate the instructions given to enumerators about recording occupations. We should know whether a woman who did sewing or laundry in her home, or accepted piece work from a jobber, or worked in a family store was considered as having an occupation in the eyes of the census taker. It is also well to remind ourselves that the "facts" in the census are actually what the families wanted to go on record about themselves. They were not under oath when the enumerator interviewed them. With these caveats in mind, we can proceed to the very simplest of generalizations. For example, it is evident that it was not customary for wives, mothers, mothers-in-law, or adult sisters of the head of the family to have an occupation in this particular part of West Town in Chicago in 1900. It also seems clear that for this group it was not customary to house an extended family under one roof; there were few households with more than two generations living together, and there were few female relatives more distant than siblings and offspring, unless they were among the few classified as "other." There was little, if any, bringing of relatives from the family in the old country into these households. And finally, there were few roomers, so that method of extending the family budget was seldom used.

Since other information was not tabulated, we cannot go much further than these few conclusions. Perhaps this is enough to indicate, however, that much can be learned from the overwhelming mass of data in population schedules without resorting to computers, and even more if studies involve extensive quantification. By spreading our nets farther, making comparisons with similar neighborhoods in other cities, or in other parts of Chicago, other generalizations can be derived, old generalizations can be tested.

Archivists invited to write about topics like the one assigned to me, are often tempted to go through the holdings of their institution, record group by record group. I elected instead to provide more detailed descriptions of samples from the records of only a few agencies. Many of the papers that follow in this volume are based on records in the National Archives other than the ones that I have cited. In addition, the federal government has dealt with women as consumers, homemakers, inventors, farmers, landowners, businesswomen, professionals, artists, public servants, and in many other roles. It has heard their complaints and provided them with recipes. And records of much of this activity have been preserved in the National Archives.

NOTES

1. File 72A-E2, Records of the United States Senate, Record Group 46, National Archives Building. Hereafter records in the National Archives will be cited as RG__, NA.
2. Norman Armour, chargé d'affaires (Paris), to the Secretary of State, 14 June 1932, Decimal File 811.79640/5, General Records of the Department of State, RG 59, NA.
3. Daniel C. Roper, undated night letter, Central Files 835, "Earhart Flights, Amelia," Records of the Federal Aviation Administration, RG 237, NA. There is also material in Central Files 805.0, "History of Noted Fliers — Earhart, Amelia," RG 237, NA.
4. Decimal File 800.79611 Putnam, Amelia Earhart/1-/211, RG 59, NA.
5. Central Files 835, "Earhart Flights, Amelia," RG 237, NA.
6. File A4-3, General Correspondence, 1924-45, Records of the Hydrographic Office, RG 37, NA.
7. Memorandum, 5 February 1937, Decimal File 800.79611 Putnam, Amelia Earhart/47, RG 59, NA.
8. W.T. Miller, Airways Superintendent, Department of Commerce, to R.B. Black, Field Representative, Department of the Interior, Iolani Palace, Honolulu, 27 January 1937, Central Files 835, "Earhart Flights, Amelia," RG 237, NA.
9. Records of the Air Officer, Hawaiian Department, Records of United States Army Overseas Operations and Commands, 1898-1942, RG 395, NA.
10. Correspondence File 601, Amelia Earhart, Records of the United States Coast Guard, RG 26, NA.
11. File A4-5(5), General Records of the Department of the Navy, RG 80, NA. File A21-5 contains a file relating to Earhart's proposed flight. There are also ninety-five pages of

search reports by the U.S. Navy and Coast Guard during the period July 2-18, 1937, in Subject File (GV), Naval Records Collection of the Office of Naval Records and Library, RG 45, NA.

12. Logs, U.S.S. *Colorado,* U.S.S. *Ontario,* and U.S.S. *Swan,* Logs of United States Naval Ships and Stations, 1801-1946, Records of the Bureau of Naval Personnel, RG 24, NA.

13. Files of the Commandant of the Fourteenth Naval District, Records of Naval Districts and Shore Establishments, RG 181, NA.

14. File AG 580.81, Records of the Office of the Adjutant General, RG 94, NA.

15. Amelia Earhart File, General Correspondence, Office of Naval Intelligence, Records of the Office of the Chief of Naval Operations, RG 38, NA.

16. Letters dated 8 July 1937 and 1 November 1939, Military Intelligence Division, Records of the War Deparment General and Special Staffs, RG 165, NA. Also a ten-page summary of her flight and several reports concerning Earhart's 1935 goodwill flight to Mexico.

17. Decimal File, 800.79611 Putnam, Amelia Earhart/210 US/LW, RG 59, NA.

18. Letter dated 5 July 1937, Central Files 835, "Earhart Flights, Amelia," RG 237.

19. RG 86, NA.

20. RG 102, NA.

21. Service Records of Hospital Attendants, Matrons, and Nurses, Nurse Contracts (Female), and Hospital Papers, Records of the Record and Pension Office, Records of the Adjutant General's Office, RG 94, NA.

22. File "Journal of Dr. Anita Newcomb McGee, 1898-99" and File "Correspondence of Dr. Anita Newcomb McGee, 1898-1936," Records Relating to Military Personnel, 1775-1947, Regular Army Personnel Nurses, Records of the Office of the Surgeon General, RG 112, NA.

23. RG 15, NA.

24. Wakon Charging Cloud (Head Woman) File, Pension Application Files (hereafter referred to as P.A.F.) Indian Wars, Records of the Veterans Administration, RG 15, NA.

25. Charles Allen, alias Percy Walton (Lorenziar) File, P.A.F. Indian Wars, RG 15, NA.

26. File WO-1,008, 349 Edward Adams (Malinda), P.A.F. Civil War and Later, RG 15, NA.

27. William Hill (Sara E.) File, P.A.F. Indian Wars, RG 15, NA.

28. William Jackson Millholland (Elizabeth) File, P.A.F. Indian Wars, RG 15, NA.

29. File WO-11, 712, Frederick Burress (Sarah), P.A.F. Mexican War, RG 15, NA.

30. Philip Zwerlein (Martha) File, P.A.F. Indian Wars, RG 15, NA.

31. Charles Allen . . . File, cited above.

32. National Archives Microfilm Publications M313, T317, T316, T288, and T318.

33. National Archives Microfilm Publication T289.

DISCUSSION SUMMARY

In connection with the paper describing National Archives resources for women's history, Linda Maloney of the University of South Carolina noted with amusement that when she wrote to the Archivist, Dr. Rhoads, some eighteen months ago suggesting a National Archives Conference on Women's History, he had replied politely that he did not believe that the National Archives held enough records about women to justify a conference.

Gladys Kashdin of the University of South Florida inquired whether the Archives had material on artists, composers, dancers, and other creative women. Jane Smith, director of the Civil Archives Division at the National Archives, replied that there was material about federal art projects in which women were quite prominent, namely: the records of the Works Projects Administration, the Public Works Administration, and the Treasury Relief Art Project. Nancy Malan of the Audiovisual Archives Division answered another question from Kashdin about the National Archives' holdings in nontextual records by saying that these, like textual records, are arranged by record group and are not indexed by subjects, such as "women."

Judy Sealander of Duke University inquired about a preliminary inventory of the records of the Women's Bureau. She was told that there is an early one, but that an inventory covering all the records now accessioned is in preparation and will be published in the near future.

In response to a question from Laurie Crumpacker, a graduate student at Boston University, Andrea Hinding indicated that the Women's History Sources Survey (WHSS) would include hospital and patient records, collections in theological seminaries, employment records, and business and corporate archives on condition that such records were open on a reasonably regular basis to researchers. Women in religious orders, she added, have been "generous beyond belief" in contributing their records.

Jacquelyne Johnson Jackson of Duke University suggested that records about black women should not be categorized as either black history or women's history, but as black women's history. She then inquired about Justice Department records dealing with the Civil Rights movement of the 1960s. Jane Smith replied that the Archives has accessioned few records from the Justice Department and that none of the records of its Civil Rights Division were yet in the custody of the Archives. She advised interested researchers to confer with archivists in the Legislative, Judicial, and Fiscal Branch which holds Justice Department records. They could either direct the researcher to related records among the holdings or to the proper source in the Justice Department.

Virginia Purdy reminded the audience that records are transferred to the Archives only after the agency that created them is no longer using them on a day-to-day basis. Therefore the Archives often does not have the most recent records.

Debra Newman, an archivist in the Industrial and Social Branch of the Civil Archives Division, called attention to large amounts of material in the records with which she works that deal with black women in the early twentieth century. For example, when the Women's Bureau was established, Alpha Kappa Alpha (a black sorority), the Urban League, and the National Association for the Advancement of Colored People waged an unsuccessful campaign to employ one or two black women on the staff of the bureau to deal specifically with the problems of black women. Attempts were also made to call a conference on household employment because black women were heavily involved in that occupation. When domestic service was omitted from the provisions of National Recovery Administration codes and the Social Security Act, black women like Mary McLeod Bethune exerted political pressure. Programs for young black women are documented in the records of the National Youth Administration.

Eleanor Flexner of Northampton, Massachusetts, expressed concern about the records of institutions and organizations that no longer exist that may now be stored in the attics of persons who were active in them. Hinding and Chambers both emphasized that the WHSS staff and board were very aware of the importance of such records, realizing that much of the material that documents women's experience is not found in formal repositories. However, recording the material that is in repositories is a task so large that the WHSS can barely handle it, and cannot add other projects to that responsibility. The WHSS hopes that the survey may stimulate repositories to seek out hidden manuscripts and archives of women's history to be preserved and made available to scholars.

Vivian Wiser, a historian with the U.S. Department of Agriculture, called attention to the records of the Federal Extension Service on microfilm, including reports of home demonstration agents who worked with women. The National Archives Microfilm Publication is listed in the *Catalog of National Archives Microfilm Publications* and is available in many state extension service offices throughout the country. [National Archives Microfilm Publication No. T845-T897, Annual Reports of Extension Service Field Representatives, Records of the Federal Extension Service, (Record Group 33), can be purchased from the Publication Sales Branch, National Archives, Washington, D.C. 20408. Copies may be used in the Microfilm Research Room in the National Archives Building — ED.]

The guide resulting from the WHSS will be modeled after the National Union Catalog of Manuscript Collections (NUCMC) according to Hinding, replying to a question on the contents of the final product from Mary Lou Goodyear of the Reorganized Church of the Latter Day Saints in Independence, Missouri. It will be indexed by name and by subject, and possibly by geographic area if the publisher chosen has computer capability.

Nancy Malan closed the discussion with the advice that researchers should seek help from the reference archivist in charge of the records that interest them. These professionals have a vast knowledge of the records in their custody and are glad to share it.

II

WOMEN IN THE PRE-FEDERAL PERIOD

INTRODUCTION

Linda K. Kerber

In 1876 the National American Women's Suffrage Association demanded seats on the platform of the Centennial Commission's celebration of July 4th. The commission told them that they were elbowing in where they were not invited. Uninvited, Susan B. Anthony, Matilda Gage, and three other women appeared at the Centennial celebration at Independence Hall where they held a counter Centennial.

On one side of the building at the official ceremony, Richard Henry Lee of Virginia read the Declaration of Independence. On the other side, at the same time, Susan B. Anthony read an amended version of the Seneca Falls Declaration. Women were still taxed without representation, she said. They were still denied the right to be judged by juries of their peers. There were still in effect two codes of law, one for men and one for women. Anthony ended by suggesting that the proper way to celebrate the Centennial would be to impeach all officers of government on the grounds that they had been false to the promises of the Revolution. She said:

> *Now at the close of a hundred years we declare our faith in the principles of self government; our full equality with man in natural rights; that woman was made first for her own happiness, with the absolute right to herself . . . . We ask . . . no special favors . . . . We ask justice, we ask equality, we ask that all the civil and political rights that belong to the citizens of the United States, be guaranteed to us and to our daughters forever.[1]*

And here we are at the Bicentennial, and Anthony's manifesto still gives me goose pimples. Women like Anthony claimed that the Revolution meant something to them, that the meaning of the Revolution had been that all citizens have a responsible relationship to the political order. That claim, of course, could be attacked, and it was. It was an attack with which you are familiar, and one that Finley Peter Dunne would parody maliciously in 1910. Dunne's fictional Irish philosopher, Mr. Dooley, remarked of woman suffrage:

> *But why shud we give thim a vote, says I. What have they done to injiye this impeeryal suffrage that we fought an' bled f r? Whin me forefathers were followin' George Wash'n'ton an' sufferin' all th' hardships that men endure campin' out in vacation time, what were th' women doin'? They were back in*

51

Matsachoosetts milkin' th' cow, mendin' socks, followin' the plow, plantin' corn, keepin' store, shoein' horses, an' pursooin' th' other frivvlous follies iv th' fair but fickle sect. After th' war our brave fellows come back to Boston an' as a reward f'r their devotion got a vote apiece . . . . An' now, be hivens, they want to share with us what we won.[2]

The nature of the relationship of women to the revolutionary experience remains unexplained. There is an enormous amount we do not know, beginning with the difficulty of making a proper educated guess about the extent to which women supported the war at all. The common sense of the matter could be argued in either direction.

Perhaps the most substantial differences between the worlds in which colonial men and women lived is the sharp disparity in literacy, and to the extent that women lived in a nonliterate culture, they are harder to reconstruct. The papers prepared for this chapter by George C. Chalou and Chester W. Gregory are efforts to steer us on the road to reconstructing the lives and significance of many preliterate but very articulate women.

NOTES

1. Elizabeth Cady Stanton, Susan B. Anthony, and Matilda Joslyn Gage, *History of Woman Suffrage,* 3 vols. (Rochester, N.Y.: Charles Mann, 1887), 3:34.
2. [Peter Finley Dunn], "Woman Suffrage," *Mr. Dooley Says* (New York: Charles Scribner's Sons, 1910), pp. 27-28.

BLACK WOMEN IN PRE-FEDERAL AMERICA

Chester W. Gregory

The purpose of this paper is to make an honest effort to explore certain aspects of the position or the status of the black woman in pre-federal America relative to her work status, her responsibility for herself and family and, in the case of the slave, her master's family. The paper to some degree explores what it was like to be a free black woman or a slave black woman; to be sold on the block, to be listed as chattel or merchandise, to be forced to run away, to be head of a household, or to be a woman of revolutionary tendencies in search of freedom.

The paper may not be considered as a comprehensive, definitive, or complete study of black women in the pre-federal period, but one which will introduce us to a rather fertile area of exploration that can with further study deal with the black woman as a field hand, as a nurse — in terms of her daily activities on the plantations — as a slave and as a free woman.

Status of Female Slaves

Although neither judicial sanction of slavery nor statutory law had given any legal basis to slavery until 1662, at that time slavery was legalized in the colonies and all children born of slaves were to be slaves for life. One may therefore assume that after 1662 the majority of blacks in the colonies were slaves. One may also assume that since slavery was not legalized until 1660, blacks who were here perhaps had become either free or were being retained in some form of indentured servitude.

In 1652 the commissioners of the towns of Providence and Warwick in Rhode Island passed a resolution that neither "black mankind nor white should be forced by covenant bond or otherwise, to serve any man or his assignes longer than ten yeares." This was a reasonable and an enlightened approach to the prevention of lifelong enslavement, but it did not at that time have the force of a general law. A few years later Virginia, in 1662, established the principle that "all children born in this country shall be held bond or free only according to the condition of the mother.''[1]

In the colony of Maryland, in order to discourage free born English women who, ''forgetful of their free condition and to the disgrace of our nation, did intermarry with Negro slaves,'' the assembly enacted ''that whosoever free born woman shall intermarry with a slave . . . shall serve the master of such slave during the lifetime of her husband.'' Even though this enactment was to deter interracial marriages, it had serious repercussions as some unscrupulous masters or plantation owners forced their indentured female servants to marry slaves so as to extend the servant period.[2] Therefore, Maryland in 1681 followed Virginia in designating the status of the children by the condition of the mother.

As blacks who came to this country between 1619 and the 1660s were free or indentured, at which time in most colonies slavery became statutory, the question arises about taxation and whether there was discrimination between men and women. According to U.B. Phillips, until after the middle of the seventeenth century, ''the laws did not discriminate between the races. The tax laws were an index of the situation.''[3] It is noted that an act of 1649 designated the poll tax for males only above the age of sixteen years old. An act of 1658, however, included imported black females and Indian servants to be taxed the same as the males — a practice which was established on a permanent basis and even applied to the free black woman as well.

By 1668 a policy was developed for the use of taxes for racial distinction which seemed to settle the question as to whether black women who gained their freedom should pay taxes. The result was that black women, although given their freedom, were ''still liable to the payment of taxes.''[4]

Nevertheless, in certain instances a free black woman on request was given a chance of equality in certain kinds of work. In reference to the maritime slave trade, there was a notation that the government of Georgia in 1772, at the request of a slaver's captain, issued a certificate to a Fenda Lawrence ''a free black woman and heretofore a considerable trader in the river Gambia on the coast of Africa, hath voluntarily come to be in and remain for some time in this province.'' Fenda was to be given permission to ''pass and repass unmolested'' within Georgia ''on her lawful and necessary occasions.''[5] Such an arrangement for a free black woman was unusually irregular in that blacks who came to the New World, came largely by force and against their own approval or request.

Black women were listed in the appraisal lists and shipping records, as the following instance indicates, of the ship *Margarett* of London in which the Captain William Burnett in 1694 did not consider them as either commodities or goods. The list contained:

2 Negros, Sambo and Jack . . .
3 Negros, Judith Moll and Maria Girles . . .
2 Negro boyes, Rough . . . and Dick . . .

1 Mollato woman 7 years to serve
1 Negro Dick[6]

The list seems to show that even after 1662 at least not all of these were to be slaves but some were indentured. This group was to be delivered into Saint Mary's River in Saint Mary's County, Georgia.

In Virginia in 1682, William Fitzhugh made an arrangement with a Mr. Jackson of Piscataway in New England to have imported to him as many blacks as would amount to 50,000 pounds of tobacco. The amount of exchange was set into age categories as 3,000 pounds for every Negro boy or girl between the ages of seven and eleven, 4,000 pounds for every boy or girl between the ages of eleven and fifteen, and 5,000 pounds for every man or woman above the age of fifteen years. "The ages of the Negroes to be judg'd and determin'd by two or three such honest and reasonable men here as your self shall nominate and appoint."[7]

In another instance, an arrangement was made between Henry Laurens of South Carolina and John Knight of "Leverpoole" to make provisions for laborers in 1773. The cargo was to be an assorted one of "about 50 Men, 40 Women, and 20 Boys and Girls. . . . "[8]

It was no secret by any stretch of the imagination that women slaves were more desirable or as desirable in most instances as men. Women could not only do the day-to-day labor but could bear, nurse, and care for the children. The black woman nursed not only her babies, but those of the white mistress as well. She was the bearer of large families, as many as ten, twelve, and even twenty children.

On Coming to America

The year 1619 is the generally accepted date of blacks coming to the Eastern Shores of colonial America, at the time when a Dutch man-of-war ominously docked at the shore with its cargo of twenty blacks. By 1624 there were twenty-two blacks in the colony of Virginia, which is an indication that the increase was very slight in the first five years. By 1648, twenty-four years later, the black slave population numbered 300.[9] One of the first blacks, called Anthony, was sold to Captain William Tucker of Kecoughtan in Elizabeth City, North Carolina. Anthony married Isabella who was also one of the first blacks. The issue of this marriage was a son whom they named William Tucker. William Tucker, son of Anthony and Isabella, is believed to have been the first black born in the colonies and baptized in 1624 in the English settlement of Virginia.[10]

According to the *Reference Library*, in 1630 there were ten blacks in the North and fifty in the South. By 1780 the number had grown to 56,796 in the North and 518,624 in the South. Between 1780 and 1790, there was a growth to 697,624 slaves and 59,557 free, about 9 percent of the total black population. Note Table 1[11] which lists population growth of blacks from 1630-1780.

Table 1
GROWTH OF SLAVERY IN THE COLONIES (1630-1780)

	1630	1640	1650	1660	1670	1680	1690	1700
North	10	427	880	1,162	1,125	1,895	3,340	5,206
South	50	170	720	1,758	3,410	5,076	13,389	22,611
Total	60	597	1,600	2,920	4,535	6,971	16,729	27,817

	1710	1720	1730	1740	1750	1760	1770	1780
North	8,303	14,091	17,323	23,958	30,222	40,033	48,460	56,796
South	36,563	54,748	73,698	126,066	206,198	285,773	411,362	518,624
Total	44,866	68,839	91,021	150,024	236,420	325,806	459,822	575,420

Everyone may not be able to say as Professor De Pauw does that "in 1776 half the population was female."[12] Such may not have been true for the black population. One might reasonably assume, however, that the female population would be between 40 and 48 percent. If one, however, would take certain of the New England colonies as recorded by Lorenzo Greene, he or she would find that in the colonies of Massachusetts and Connecticut by counties, in fourteen counties in Massachusetts in 1764, the total black male population was 3,016, the female population was 2,219, thus showing a 797 male majority. In six counties in Connecticut of men and women over twenty years old in 1774, there were 1,572 men and 1,042 women, giving a difference or a surplus of 530 men.[13] It was noted that "only in a few towns were the two sexes equal in numbers," Derby, having twelve of each sex and Groton with forty-two of each sex. Several towns like Lebanon with a ratio of 22 men to 27 women and Windham with a 15 to 29 ratio showed an excess of women. The overall total difference between women and men was quite noticeable except in Rhode Island where the difference in numbers was listed in the census of 1782 as 1,463 Negro women as compared with 1,343 men, a difference of 120 females over males.[14]

The Indian population in the New England area indicates that there was a greater preponderance of the female than the male. In 1764 Massachusetts had 728 men and 953 women, showing a differential count of 225 women. It is interesting to recognize that "the scarcity of Negro women, on the one hand and of Indian men on the other, was undoubtedly a factor in the steady amalgamation of the two races."[15]

As there was a shortage of black women for black men it would seem that the growth of the black population in New England was somewhat less than it might have been, thus decreasing the overall numerical strength of the black woman for blacks in New England society but also dispersing that strength into the Indian life and that of the general society as well. What I am suggesting here is that the significance of the black women in colonial pre-federal America might not have been lessened by their scarcity, but that their contribution as individuals, wives, and mothers may have been equally as important and valuable.

Black Women Runaways

Both men and women slaves quite frequently ran away as attested by the following announcements. From Saturday, February 19 to Saturday, February 26, 1731-32, a forty shilling reward was offered by John Mortimer for the return of a pawpaw Negro woman named Jenny who had formerly belonged to the estate of Gills Cook. She was described as a lusty woman of about thirty years old.[16] In the same column there was an announcement for a runaway man, "Negro runaway about three weeks ago." A wench named Betty belonging to Mrs. Catherine Cattell on Ashley River had also run away. She was thought to be between twenty and thirty years old.

Another announcement read: "Run away about five weeks ago from Hugh Campbell, a Negro wench named Flora, she has a scar on her forehead and has been seen in Charlestown since. Likewise, stolen out of Mr. Vaughn's stable on the thirteen instance in the morning a horse marked Ep. on the mounting shoulder, has lost one eye, a star in his face, with white foam running from it to his nose. He is between black and chestnut. Whoever takes them up, them or either of them to Mr. Vaughn Bucklayer in Charlestown or to me shall have thirty shilling reward for the horse and thirty for the Negro wench."[17]

Between Saturday, August 7 and Saturday, August 14, 1736, the South Carolina Gazette announced for an Ann Dexter the loss of a Negro girl named Diana who had probably been stolen or led off for the purpose of selling her. It warned that any person of such an intent would be "persecuted [sic] to the utmost severity of the law."[18]

On Saturday, October 5, 1786, ten guineas reward was offered by William Clark because a number of slaves had run away on Sunday night September 10, 1786. Among them were Isaac, a tall black fellow, Juba, his wife, "a county born wench," Kate, "a stout well-made Mulatto wench," Batten, a short well-made fellow, his wife, Quahobe, "a short black wench," Ned, a stout well-made fellow, and Sue, his wife, "a small well-made wench." Since these blacks were previously from Florida, it was expected that they would return.[19]

In Rowan County, North Carolina, October 13, 1769, an announcement signed by a Francis Locke which appeared in the North Carolina Gazette stated that "on the third of September 1769, three 'outlandish' blacks had run away, Jack around 26 or 27 years old, 5 feet six, Arthur about 30 years, and a 'Negro wench' named Rachel about 30 years old." She was described as being "very well featured and not very black." There was also with them "a Negro wench named Phillis" who was the wife of Jack but belonged to a Mr. George Magoone.[20]

On January 10, 1778, Isaac Partridge offered a reward of $5 for a woman named Carolina who was the property of a minor, Robert Calf.[21]

If certain issues of the *North Carolina Gazette* may be considered as an index to runaway blacks, the men-women ratio would perhaps be 3 to 1 in Springfield, North Carolina.[22]

Anchors Aweigh to Nova Scotia

During the Revolutionary War, the British welcomed runaway slaves and gave them their freedom because this was an important means of weakening the southern patriots. At the end of the war, the British provided transportation to Nova Scotia for many of the former slaves who had joined them during the war. Because the Americans considered slaves property, they insisted at the peace negotiations that the British must make accurate lists of Negroes that were being evacuated to Canada to be used as a basis for claims against the British by their former masters. Some of these lists are in the National Archives, entitled "Inspection Rolls of Negroes, taken on board the undernamed vessels, on the 30th day of November 1783 at anchor near Statton Island previous to their sailing for Port Mattoon in the province of Nova Scotia."

Several ships were involved in this emigration. On board the ship *Peggy* whose master was a James Bagley, there were three listings of black females; the ship *Ranger* carried forty-seven; the Brig *Concord* with George Robinson, master, carried twenty-two; and His Majesty's ship *Abundance* with Master Phillips, carried twenty-nine women.

On board each ship, the former slaves were listed in the ship's inspection rolls indicating their names, ages, physical status, and former masters, and the year they left their masters.

The following sample listings of women are typical:

Sally Rivers 30 years, ordinary wench, . . . formerly slave to Molly Rivers, Charlestown, South Carolina, left her in 1776 . . . .

Jenny Frederick 32 years, ordinary wench . . . certified to be free by Jonah Frederick of Boston, New England.

Nelly Sawyer 12 years, likely wench . . . formerly Slave to James Hicherson, Norfolk County, Virginia left him in 1776 . . . .

Pinna Summer, 21 years, likely wench, formerly slave to Josiah Summer, Nancy Town, Virginia, left him in 1779 . . . .

Hannah Wallace, 22 years, ordinary wench . . . formerly Slave to William Arranstead, Gloucester, Virginia, left him in 1776 . . . .

Misey Henry, 25 years, ordinary wench . . . formerly slave to Joseph Convey, Philadelphia, left him in 1778 . . . . [23]

It is very noteworthy to see that the females who left their masters in search for freedom were very numerous in comparison with the number of males. Of a total count of 286 males and females listed in the inspection rolls of New York, there were 90 women, 142 men, and 54 children, all said to be in good health. The lowest age of the children was one year. This means that the females totaled 99 and ranged in ages from one year to seventy years. The total male listing was 187 with an age range from two years to sixty-eight years. As more than one-third of the inspection rolls were females, it seems quite evident that black women were very much interested in freedom from slavery and freedom of movement very similar in both intent and action in the pre-federal period of America.

Women Listed as Chattel

Both women and men slaves and servants were listed in the inventories of the estates of the deceased as goods and chattel. In 1773 in the listing of William Ottey of Baltimore County, Maryland, were two girls, Rosa McManns, five years and eight months valued at £8 and Catherine Winfiola, six months valued at four shillings.[24] Blacks were usually listed by first names (or only one name), age, and value in pound sterling. For example, blacks on the estate of William Cromwell were Nann, Dinah, Hannah, and Jack. Nann was twenty-five valued at £40, Hannah was twenty valued at £45, and Jack was thirty and was valued at £16.[25] In this listing each of the three women has a greater value than the man.

A record of goods and chattel of William Hamilton gives a relatively fair balance between women and men slaves as the following may indicate:

1 Negro girl called Pris	£30
1 Negro boy 9 yrs called Peter	£33
1 Negro girl 6 yrs old	£28
1 Negro boy 15 yrs called Harry	£37
1 Negro man 50 yrs called Adam	£30
1 Negro man 27 yrs called Tom	£55
1 Negro man 22 yrs called Stephen	£60
1 Negro girl 2 yrs called Nan	£10
1 Negro woman 26 yrs called Nel	£45
1 Negro woman 30 yrs called Laury	£40
1 Negro girl 7 yrs called Judy	£30
1 Negro boy 4 yrs called Abram	£18
1 Negro boy 2 yrs called Jacob	£10[26]

The above listing came as a part of a total listing of property valued at £555 and eighteen shillings. Of a thirteen-count listing, there were four girls and two women. The other seven included four boys and three men. In another example, on Monday, February 10, 1772, two announcements in the *Boston Gazette* read: "A Negro child to be given away, a likely Negro female child; a person in town would be most agreeable, Inquire of Edes and Gill."[27]

Black girls and women were passed on by wills from generation to generation. One example was the deed of a slave girl by Jonathan Bryan to Josiah the brother of William Bryan for his granddaughter Helen Neylly in 1786.

The will of Richard Cogdell of the town of Newbern, North Carolina, June 24, 1785, provided that if there should not be sufficient funds to pay his debts, then his "Negroes and chattel (Roxanna and her increase excepted) should be sold." Yet he leaves it to the discretion of his wife as to the future status of Roxanna. As he said, "It is my desire that my Negro girl Roxanna and her increase should she hereafter have any shall be disposed of as my wife Lydia shall think proper."[28]

In an account of a slave market in New Orleans, Fredrika Bremer relates that she watched the sale, on the block, of both women and men. She noted that in a certain sale women were fewer in numbers in comparison to men, some seventy or eighty of them. "A gentleman" she said, "took one of the prettiest of them by the chin and opened her mouth to see the state of her gums and teeth, with no more ceremony than if she had been a horse."[29] Thousands and even millions of Africans and Afro-Americans went through similar scrutiny on the slave blocks and the slave markets throughout the South.

Names of black female slaves, probable age, when born, to whom and how acquired, trades and qualifications, date of death, when sold, parentage, and character were recorded in the plantation records of the Pinckneys. Some names listed were:

Mira, 18-23, received from uncle, good field hand, died in the spring of 1853, daughter of Old Molly of a good character

Fabinia, 40-45, a tolerable field hand, died June 1823, parentage unknown, she was of a tolerable character

Betty, age 6-9, ½ hand daughter of Fabinia, she was of a tolerable character

Flora, acquired in 1812, 45-50 yrs old, was considered as ½ hand and as a midwife, daughter of Old Bets and of tolerable character

Bets, old, age 70-80, acquired in 1812, classified as midwife, died in 1817 of unknown parentage

Eliza, 5-8 yrs old, ½ hand 1819, daughter of old Flora and of an indifference character

(all acquired in 1812)

Patty, 18-23, good field hand, died in 1828 was of excellent character

Lydia and Betty, Betty was a full hand while Lydia was a ½ hand, Lydia died in 1826 and Betty in 1825

In the parentage column they were listed as the property of C.C. Pinckney.[30]

Free Black Heads of Families in the Pre-Federal Period

Through the years there has been much discussion and much emphasis has been placed on the matriarchal position of the black women. From that emphasis several pertinent questions have arisen. Is the matriarchal pattern an African practice or heritage which was retained by the colonial black woman, or is it mainly a modern makeup that has come from sociologists? Is the concept more imaginary than real? It is not the purpose of this research to answer these questions, but to make an attempt to observe the statistics of the family heads or heads of families among blacks during the pre-federal period — that is, according to a list of the original states in the 1790 census (Table 2).[31]

Table 2
BLACK HEADS OF HOUSEHOLD IN THE 1790 CENSUS

State	Male	Female
Connecticut	391	20
Delaware	126	
Maine	23	1
Maryland	658	160
Massachusetts	431	23
New Hampshire	77	7
New York	558	83
Pennsylvania	333	23
Rhode Island	352	23
North Carolina	546	92
South Carolina	198	60
Vermont	21	
Virginia	180	21
Total	3,894	513

It seems rather significantly questionable that neither Vermont nor Delaware in the 1790 census listed any women as heads of black families. The researcher wonders whether there were actually no women heads of families or whether the two states even listed women or just ignored them. If accurate, this evidence makes a telling mark against any thought of matriarchal family leadership in those states before 1790.

South Carolina seems to have had the largest ratio of men-women heads of families. There were 198 males and 60 females, or less than one-third were women. Compared with a total of approximately 3,894 black male heads of families of the thirteen new states of America, there was an approximate number of 513 women heads of families; that is, women made up about 12 percent. These figures may imply that there was not really a matriarchal society during the pre-federal period of America.

It may be noted also that with few exceptions, free heads of families had both first and last names such as "Ester Curtis" or "Kitty White" in all of the states. New York carried the largest number of listings without surnames while Delaware carried none; states like Virginia, South Carolina, and North Carolina carried very few. Virginia had only one.

The size of the family headed by women ranged from one to twenty. Penelope French of Virginia headed a family of twenty; only a few headed families of ten or more.[32]

Prominent Black Women of the Pre-Federal Period

A very interesting black woman was Elizabeth Freeman, who is better known as Mum Bett. She was born a slave and remained in that position until she was between thirty and forty years old. She had lived a portion of the youthful part of her life in Claverac, Columbia County, New York, with the Hogeboom family. Before she became an adult, she was taken over by Colonel Ashley of Sheffeld in Berkshire County in Massachusetts.[33]

Although slavery in Massachusetts did not operate on so broad a scale as in the state of South Carolina, slavery was slavery wherever it was practiced. Mum Bett found that the Ashley mistress could be rather brutal at times, as she learned when in defense of her sister, she took the brunt of a shovel blow that was meant for her sister. She was left with a lifelong scar on both her body and her mind. Because she so greatly opposed the treatment meted out to her, she left the Ashleys and refused to return, whereupon Colonel Ashley turned to the courts to regain possession of his slave. It so happens that even though the case was tried in Great Barrington, the 1780 Massachusetts Constitution with its Declaration of Rights asserting that "all men are born free and equal" had been written. Therefore, Mum Bett received her freedom.[34]

Mum Bett became a servant to the household of Judge Theodore Sedgwick and continued to have rather close connections with his family until her death in 1829. In the meantime Mum married and had one child but lost her husband in the Revolutionary War.

It may be interesting to note that during the servantship of Bett, Mr. Sedgwick's house was searched during the Shays's Rebellion. When Sedgwick was away in Boston, it is said that Bett accompanied the searchers through the house and into the cellar, carrying a large kitchen shovel which she indicated that she would use if necessary. When they broke a bottle of porter, she informed them that if they wanted porter she would bring a corkscrew so that they could drink as gentlemen. But if the neck of another bottle was broken, "she would lay the man that broke it flat with her shovel."[35]

The most famous and most often mentioned black woman of the colonial period is Phillis Wheatley (ca. 1753-1784). Fishel and Quarles find it unsurprising that in Puritan New England Phillis was the "only Negro who attracted wide attention."[36] John Henrik Clark refers to Phillis as "the Voice of Our First Woman Poet."[37] Prof. John Hope Franklin considers her as "perhaps the best-known Negro poet of the period."[38]

George Washington Williams indicates that Phillis Wheatley "readily mastered the art of writing; and within four years from the time she landed in the slave market in Boston, she was able to carry on an extensive correspondence on a variety of topics.''[39] He also suggested that ''her ripening intellectual faculties attracted the attention of the refined and educated people of Boston, many of whom sought her society at the home of the Wheatleys.''[40]

The cultural abilities and accomplishments of Phillis were relatively unusual at a time when education for the masses was far, far from a reality and for the blacks far, far from a semblance of reality.

In her famous poem "On Being Brought to America," she said, "It was mercy which brought me from my pagan land." Even so, those as black as Cain could be "refined and join the angelic train."[41] Phillis seemed to have been greatly influenced by the white man's definition of Christianity and paganism and the mythical concepts of Africa. In the work to Dartmouth, she seems, however, to be stepping into her own conceptualization of her real and true state. She had discovered that it was cruel fate that had taken her from Africa rather than Christian sympathy. She had been seized as a baby from her beloved father's arms. Now she spoke of freedom and hoped and prayed that no other would feel the "tyrannic sway."

Although Phillis Wheatley is the most famous and renowned black woman poet of the colonial period, she was not the first black woman poetess. Such an honor has been accorded to Lucy Terry, a slave of Ensign Ebenezer Wells of Deerfield, Massachusetts. Her poetry described the action of an Indian raid on Deerfield in 1746 during King George's War, 1744-1748. Lorenzo Greene states that "Lucy was not versed in syntax, but her poem gave a vivid picture of the massacre of the settlers by Indians on August 25, 1746." He further suggests that according to Sheldon, the historian of Deerfield, Lucy's description of the "Bars Fight" is the "fullest and best contemporary version of that struggle now extant."[42]

> August 'twas the twenty fifth
> Seventeen hundred forty-six
> The Indians did in ambus lay
> Some very valiant men to slay
> The names of whom I'll not leave out
> Samuel Allen like a hero fout
> And though he was so brave and bold
> His face no more shall we behold
> Eleazer Hawks was killed outright
> Before he had time to fight
> Before he did the Indians see
> Was shot and killed immediately.
> Oliver Amsden he was slain
> Which caused his friends much grief and pain.
> Samuel Amsden they found dead
> Not many rods off from his head.

> *Adonijah Gillet we do hear*
> *Did lose his life which was so dear.*
> *John Saddler fled across the water*
> *And so excaped the dreadful slaughter*
> *Eunice Allen see the Indians comeing*
> *And hoped to save herself by running*
> *And had not her petticoats stopt her*
> *The awful creatures had not cotched her*
> *And tommyhawked her on the head*
> *And left her on the ground for dead.*
> *Young Samuel Allen, Oh! lack a-day*
> *Was taken and carried to Canada*

Dorothy B. Porter points out that "because her record is the only historical evidence of the 'Bars Fight' she may be considered as a war historian."[44]

The Black Woman as Slave and Mother

As one views women in the pre-federal or colonial period, he or she sees the outstanding accomplishments of a Phillis Wheatley, a Lucy Terry, an Elizabeth Freeman, a Catherine Green, a Deborah Gannett or an Abigail Adams or a Betsy Ross. But what about the women who did the ordinary tasks from day to day?

The majority of black women were slaves subject to the long journey overseas, subject to the filth and the stench of the same. They were subject to the abuse of lustful and aggressive masters, subject to the anger, the rage and the lash of masters and mistresses, subject to the slave block from day to day. They were expected and encouraged to be prolific in conception and childbearing; prizes or sometimes promises of freedom or sometimes pittance rewards were offered to those who bore ten or more children. The bearing of children was only part of it, for there was work, always work from dawn until dusk. The ever-present work, however, and the long years of childbearing (although profitable and tiring tasks) were not to be compared with the ever-pending thought that her children might any day be taken away from her and sold one by one or in lots of several, or that she herself might be sold away from them or passed on by wills. This was an ominous agony which brought excruciating pain to her heart when such an instance occurred.

An example of such an experience has been recorded by Father Josiah Henson:

> My brothers and sisters were bid off first, and one by one, while my mother, paralyzed by grief, held me by the hand. Her turn came, and she was bought by Isaac Riley of Montgomery County. Then I was offered to the assembled purchasers. My mother, half distracted with the thought of parting forever from all her children, pushed through the crowd, while the bidding for me was going on, to the spot where Riley was standing. She fell at his feet, and clung to his knees, entreating him in tones that a mother only could command, to buy her *baby* as well as herself, and spare to her one, at least, of her

little ones. Will it, can it be believed that this man, thus appealed to, was capable not merely of turning a deaf ear to her supplication, but of disengaging himself from her with such violent blows and kicks as to reduce her to the necessity of creeping out of his reach, and mingling the groan of bodily suffering with the sob of a breaking heart? As she crawled away from the brutal man I heard her sob out, "Oh, Lord Jesus, how long, how long shall I suffer this way!" I must have been then between five and six years old. I seem to see and hear my poor weeping mother now.[45]

Frederick Douglass speaks affectionately in glowing terms of his mother in this way:

My knowledge of my mother is very scanty, but very distinct. Her personal appearance and bearing are ineffaceably stamped upon my memory. She was tall, and finely proportioned; of deep black, glossy complexion; had regular features, and, among the other slaves, was remarkably sedate in her manners. . . .

Yet I cannot say that I was very deeply attached to my mother; certainly not so deeply as I should have been had our relations in childhood been different. We were separated, according to the common custom, when I was but an infant, and, of course, before I knew my mother from any one else.[46]

The times and instances in which mothers or women across the Southland experienced the agony and the pain of being separated from the dearest and even the youngest of their issue could perhaps fill volumes. E. Franklin Frazier in the *Negro Family in the United States* points out in the context of the universal testimony of travelers and missionaries that the love of the African Mother for her children is unsurpassed in any part of the world, and in the words of Mingo Park, "maternal affection is everywhere conspicuous among them and creates a corresponding tenderness in the child."[47]

How much of this motherly devotion, care and concern that the mother had for her child and children is difficult to determine because of the long hours that she had to spend in the fields, and the short space of time allowed for maternal vocation. She also had to leave much of the care of the babies to the children of the ages of eight to twelve years with the lack of proper medical care and sanitation. Adding to the problem was the necessity, in many instances, of caring for the children of the master from the prenatal period to young adulthood. Sometimes the black woman served as a mother to her own children and as a foster mother or "mammy" to the master's. In such cases she became a highly devoted and dedicated mother. In a number of instances, she was the breast feeder of the master's babies. Frazier notes that:

Often the relations of the foster-mother or "mammy" to her white children offered greater hope for expression and impulses characteristic of maternal love than the contacts which she had with her own offspring, the attachment and devotion which the mammy showed for the white children began before the children were borne. The "mammy" who was always an important member of the household attended her mistress during pregnancy and took under her care the infant as soon as it was born. Often, she instead of the mother, suckled the child, and if the child was a girl, was never separated from her until she was grown.[48]

Another problem for the slave woman was that mixed marriages drew stiff penalties. The black woman had difficulty in having marriage legally solemnized. In July 1725 in North Carolina, a bill of indictment was brought against a John Cotton for marrying a mulatto man to a white woman. He appeared before the attorney general and was ordered to be dismissed "without day paying costs." Also in 1726 Rev. John Blacknall received a penalty of 50 pounds for having married a Thomas Spencer to Martha, a mulatto woman.[49]

The Urge for Freedom

During the revolutionary period, certain states-to-be like Rhode Island noted and resolved that "every abled-bodied Negro, mulatto, or Indian man slave in this state may enlist in any battalion of this state and upon his passing muster by Colonel Christopher Greene," he was to be "immediately discharged from the service of his master or mistress, and absolutely free, as though he had never been incumbered with any kind of servitude or slavery."[50]

The fact of freedom from all encumbrances from slavery because of revolutionary participation became a driving force among blacks, but was not always a reality.

William C. Nell recorded a report by a Hiram Williams that an aged woman who had been a slave girl during the French and Indian War was later employed as a bullet runner for the American revolutionists. In spite of her efforts in the Revolutionary War, "her patriotism was but miserably rewarded," because she remained in slavery until she was almost eighty years old, at which time she fled to Canada in order to gain her freedom. Such an instance would indicate that all blacks who took part in the independence movement were not rewarded with that freedom and independence.[51] Yet the following instance may show a special effort on the part of some to make freedom a reality.

Under a heading "Patriots of Olden Time" in Nell's *The Colored Patriots of the American Revolution,* there is a report of the reaction of Samuel Adams to the statement from his wife that someone had made her a present of a female slave which denotes an expression of his revolutionary philosophy. "She may come," he said, "but not as a slave, for a slave cannot breathe in my house. If she comes, she must come free."[52]

Freedom is such a wonderful thing. Some ask for it, some beg for it, some work for it, some give it, and some take it. Some fight and even die for it. Men, women, and even children of all faiths, creeds, and colors search and strive for it. The revolutionists and the founders of our nation made arrangements for it, upon the

Lockean concept of the equality of birth and the responsibility of government as outlined in the Declaration of Independence. Christianity and democracy are fundamentally and principally built upon freedom. But because freedom can be relative and can be taken or given, women through the years have sometimes been on the short end of freedom's balance, especially black women. This in 1782 was the feeling of the slave Belinda who presented a petition for her freedom to the legislature with the comment that in spite of the fact that she had been a servant to a colonel for forty years, "My labors have not procured me any comfort." Belinda in the observation of her state grows both philosophical and pessimistic but not completely without hope. "I have not yet enjoyed the benefits of creation. With my poor daughter, I fear I shall pass the remainder of my days in slavery and misery. For her and myself, I beg freedom."[53]

A Complex Network of Relationships

As we look at women in the pre-federal period, generally, and the black women, specifically, we may ask how or to what extent did women influence the attitudes of men either in the North or South? Did white women, slave women, or free black women have any real influence on the society, either for or against slavery? Did the black woman attempt to keep her male counterpart docile and obedient? Or did the network of relationships between white and black set the tone for docility, loyalty, and cooperation within the pre-federal period so as to give basis for both the activation of the revolutionary philosophy on one section of the country which moved toward freedom for all, and the other section of the country which moved toward entrenchment and institutionalization of slavery?

If one may look for words that may give some guide or a key to the influence of relationships, he or she might look at those recorded in the footnotes of School-craft's *The Black Gauntlet: A Tale of Plantation Life in South Carolina*. The words are as follows:

The Southern people never dream of any fear of the Negroes any more than the sheep on the plantations. Ladies are left alone when their husbands are away on a journey for several consecutive weeks, and though there may be a hundred or two hundred negroes belonging to the establishment, she has no feeling of fear, but that the slaves are a perfect protection.

A rabid Abolition historian of the North, with refreshing naiveté, describes a scene he lately witnessed in Cuba, never seeming to dream that what was such a novelty to his prejudiced mind was to be seen every day on a Southern plantation. He remarks, that on the steamer "The prominent figures are two African nurses — Cuban slaves of Ethiopia's darkest hue." . . . "They each have a beautiful white child in their arms." . . . "A young gentleman and lady are talking and laughing with them very pleasantly, without the slightest recognition of color. Indeed, it is by no means improbable that both of them have nestled in the bosom of these ebon nurses, drawing

from these breasts their nourishment.'' . . . ''The love of the nurses for the
children is manifestly hearty and sincere.'' . . . ''Such honest smiles and
caressings cannot be assumed.'' . . . ''One of these beautiful infant children
pats the cheek of her nurse, now one cheek, and now the other, and now
placing a hand on each cheek, she presses her little ruby lips to the thick dark
lips of her laughing attendant, and kisses her again and again, as lovingly as
ever child embraced its mother.''[54]

Such were the dichotomies of a complex network of relationships which brought
the white and the black into a close friendship of both blood and brawn. It tightly
institutionalized the South into a peculiar state that would lead to separation and
war at a time when the North was at least making tangible gestures toward a
fulfillment of the Declaration of Independence and the Constitution.

NOTES

1. Bradford Chambers, ed. and comp. *Chronicle of Black Protest* (New York: New American Library, 1968), p. 37.
2. Ibid.
3. Ulrich Bonnell Phillips, *American Negro Slavery* (New York and London: D. Appleton, 1918), p. 76.
4. Phillips, *American Negro Slavery*, p. 76.
5. Ibid., p. 20.
6. Elizabeth Donnan, *Documents Illustrative of the History of the Slave Trade,* Vol. 4, *The Border Colonies and the Southern Colonies* (New York: Octagon Books, 1965), p. 13.
7. Ibid., pp. 57, 58.
8. Ibid., pp. 465-66.
9. *Reference Library of Black America,* Vol. 5, Harry A. Ploski et al., eds. and comps. (New York: Bellwether Publishing Co., 1971), p. 2.
10. J.H. Brewer, ''The Twelve Epochs in the History of the Negro in America,'' *Negro Progress Calendar* (Durham, N.C.: Mutual Insurance Co. [no date]).
11. *Reference Library of Black America,* p. 2.
12. De Pauw, ''The Forgotten Spirit of '76: Women of the Revolutionary Era,'' *Ms. Magazine,* July 1974.
13. Lorenzo Johnston Green, *The Negro in Colonial New England, 1620-1776* (Port Washington, N.Y.: Kennikat Press, 1966), pp. 94, 347.
14. Ibid., p. 95.
15. Ibid., pp. 95-96.
16. *South Carolina Gazette,* 19 February-26 February, 1731-32.
17. Ibid., 9 March-16 March, 1734.
18. Ibid., 7 August-14 August 1736.
19. *Georgia Gazette,* 5 October 1786.

20. *North Carolina Gazette* (James Duris Printer, Newbern, N.C.), 20 November 1769.
21. Ibid., 10 January 1778.
22. Ibid., 16 January 1778.
23. "Inspection List of Negro Emigrants," 30 November 1783, Papers and Affidavits Relating to the Plunderings, Burnings, and Ravages Committed by the British, 1775-1784, Item 53, pp. 276-77, Papers of the Continental Congress, Records of the Continental and Confederation Congresses, Record Group 360, National Archives Building. National Archives Microfilm Publication M247, roll 66.
24. Inventories of Estates, Maryland Hall of Records, Book 117, p. 1, 1974.
25. Ibid., pp. 21-22.
26. Ibid., p. 87.
27. *Boston Gazette and Country Journal,* 10 February 1772, p. 3.
28. Bryan-Schreven Papers, 1779-1869, Folder 1-33, 349, University of North Carolina, and the Edward Ruffin Beckworth Papers, Southern Historical Collection, University of North Carolina Library, Chapel Hill, North Carolina.
29. Fredrika Bremer, *The Homes of the New World: Impressions of America,* translated by Mary Howett, 2 vols. (New York: Harper and Bros., 1853), 2: 202-9 as recorded in Willie L. Rose *History of Slavery in North America* (New York: Oxford University Press, 1976), pp. 168-69.
30. Pinckney Family Papers, Pinckney plantation records; book containing list of Negroes, births, deaths, sales, and purchases and probable ages, Southern Historical Collection, University of North Carolina Library, Chapel Hill, North Carolina.
31. U.S., National Archives, *List of Free Black Heads of Families in the First Census of the United States,* comp. by Debra L. Newman, Special List no. 34 (Washington, D.C., 1973). The figures may be taken as approximate figures rather than absolute.
32. Ibid.
33. William C. Nell, *The Colored Patriots of the American Revolution* (Boston: Robert F. Wallcut, 1855), p. 52.
34. Ibid., p. 55.
35. Ibid., p. 56.
36. Leslie H. Fishel and Benjamin Quarles, *The Black American: A Documentary History* (Glenview, Ill.: Scott, Foresman & Co., 1970), p. 37.
37. John Henrik Clark, "The Black Woman, A Figure in World History," Part III, *Essence,* July 1971, p. 43.
38. John Hope Franklin, *From Slavery to Freedom* (New York: Alfred A. Knopf, 1974), p. 111.
39. George Washington Williams, *History of the Negro Race in America, 1619-1800* (New York: Bergman Publishers, 1968), p. 197.
40. Ibid., p. 199.
41. *Memoirs and Poems of Phillis Wheatley* (Boston: Menemosynemana, 1969), p. 48.
42. Greene, *The Negro in Colonial New England, 1620-1776,* pp. 242-43.
43. Ibid.
44. Porter, "Negro Women in Our Wars," *Negro History Bulletin,* June 1944, p. 195.
45. Josiah Henson, *Father Henson's Story of His Own Life.* Introduction by Mrs. H.B. Stowe (Northbrook, Ill.: Reprint Metro Books, 1972), pp. 12, 13.
46. Frederick Douglass, *My Bondage and My Freedom* (New York: Orton & Mulligan, 1855), p. 52.
47. E. Franklin Frazier, *The Negro Family in the United States* (Chicago: The University of

Chicago Press, 1966).

48. Ibid., p. 39.
49. N.C. Cases 591 and 662, in Helen T. Catterall, ed., *Judicial Cases Concerning American Slavery and the Negro* (New York: Octagon Books, 1968), 1: 11.
50. Nell, *Colored Patriots,* p. 50.
51. Ibid., p. 215.
52. Ibid., p. 96.
53. Ibid., p. 52.
54. Mary Howard Schoolcraft, *The Black Gauntlet: A Tale of Plantation Life in South Carolina* (New York: Negro University Press, 1969), p. 375.

United States –.

Massachusetts District –

Deborah Gannett, of Sharon, in the county of Norfolk, and District of Massachusetts, a resident and native of the United States, and applicant for a pension from the United States, under an Act of Congress entitled an Act to provide for certain persons engaged in the land and naval service of the United States, in the revolutionary war, maketh oath, That she served as a private soldier, under the name of Robert Shurtleff – in the war of the revolution, upwards of two years in manner following, viz – Enlisted in April 1781. in the company commanded by Captain George Webb – in the Massachusetts Regiment commanded then by Colonel Shepherd – and afterwards by Colonel Henry Jackson – and served in said corps, in Massachusetts, and New York – until November 1783 – when she was honorably discharged in writing, which discharge is lost. During the time of her service, she was at the capture of Lord Cornwallis – was wounded at Tarrytown – and now receives a pension from the United States, which pension she hereby relinquishes – She is in such reduced circumstances, as to require the aid of her country – for her support ————

Deborah Gannett

Mass. Dist. Ss. Sept. 14. 1818

Sworn to before me

Wᵐ Davis
Distᵗ Judge
Mass. Dist

WOMEN IN THE AMERICAN REVOLUTION: VIGNETTES OR PROFILES?

George C. Chalou

In 1804 that master artisan and midnight rider, Paul Revere, wrote to Massachusetts Congressman William Eustis on behalf of Deborah Sampson Gannett.[1] She was the second enlisted woman soldier of the War for Independence, and Revere urged that she be granted a veteran's pension by the federal government. The story of Gannett's disguising herself as a man and serving in the army is well known to most of us. Therefore, I wish to explore for a moment Revere's attitude toward Gannett. The silversmith admitted in his letter to Eustis that until recently he had never seen Gannett. When Revere heard her spoken of as a soldier, he "formed the idea of a tall masculine female who had a small share of understanding, without education, and one of the meanest of her Sex." Revere carried around this stereotype of an American Amazon until he met her. "When I saw and discoursed with [her]" wrote Revere, "I was agreeably surprised to find a small effeminate, and conversable woman, whose education entitled her to a better situation in life." Revere informed Congressman Eustis that he had enquired about Gannett's situation since "she quitted the male habit and soldier's uniform for the more decent apparel of her own sex." To many persons and Revere, Gannett was of "handsome talents, good morals, a dutiful wife and an affectionate parent."

Deborah Sampson Gannett's account of her Revolutionary War service. In her declaration, Deborah Gannett "maketh oath that she served as a private soldier, under the name of Robert Shurtleff in the war of the revolution upwards of two years . . . ." Much related documentation in the National Archives and in the Massachusetts Historical Society corroborates her claim.
(File S32722, Deborah Gannett alias Robert Shurtleff, Revolutionary War Pension and Bounty-Land-Warrant Application Files, Records of the Veterans Administration, RG 15.)

Revere had, in his best tradition, galloped from one stereotype to another.

Paul Revere is still riding today. In many respects, he is no different from nineteenth- and twentieth-century Americans. Stereotypes fill our minds, stories become inflated, and incidents articulated by pen obtain better treatment when we write of the past. Women's history is, in my view, overloaded with stereotypes supported by impressionistic data and sometimes hardly more than a long succession of anecdotes or vignettes.

It is not so much that this information is false but rather that it is also incomplete. It does not relate to us a true slice of the past. This does not mean that the thoughts and actions of Abigail Adams, Mercy Warren, or Deborah Sampson Gannett should be ignored or discarded. It does mean, however, that women's history must be enriched by the use of a much wider base of documentation and a greater analysis of this documentation. Consequently, we jump from the seventeenth- and eighteenth-century-town studies of New England to the women's rights struggles of the 1840s. There are, of course, exceptions such as Julia Cherry Spruill's *Women's Life and Work in the Southern Colonies* and, to a lesser extent, Eugenie A. Leonard's *The Dear-Bought Heritage*.[2] The former perused a great deal of unpublished documentation but failed to give analysis to her narrative. The recent work by Leonard moves toward a more conceptual framework.

In examining the roles of women during the American Revolution, I prefer to call these roles collective profiles because they are constructed on the basis of the activities and articulations of several or many women rather than one or few. These profiles or composites of activity patterns are tentative and may be incorrect, but at least we need to begin such a process. Such collective outlines are not easily constructed, but the documentation exists if we are willing to dig for it. These composite roles of women utilize principally pre-federal documentary resources of the National Archives. Many of these profiles are somewhat occupational in nature, but there are major political and social implications within them. I will return to this point later.

The first profile relates to a process that is fundamental and part of the heritage of the English-speaking world, the right of petition. Any person who appeals to his or her government for redress is participating in the political process. We sometimes overlook political participation because we equate it with suffrage. Anne F. Scott, in commenting on papers presented at a session of the 1975 Southern Historical Association Convention, made this point, which too many historians overlook. Suffrage is only one part of an essential feature — woman and her relationship with the state.

In the spring of 1776, the lioness of Quincy, Massachusetts, Abigail Adams, exasperated after a turbulent exchange with John Adams, wrote to Mercy Otis Warren. She was provoked by her husband's attitude toward women's rights, and she complained to Mercy that he was "very saucy to me in return for a list of female grievances which I transmitted to him. I think I will get you to join me in a petition to Congress."[3] To my knowledge the two women never petitioned the Continental Congress. Other women did.

Of some two thousand petitions or memorials submitted to Continental and Confederation Congresses between 1776 and 1789, forty-three were from women. These were either signed or marked by one woman or by both husband and wife.[4] Other memorials or petitions containing multiple signatures can also be found among the Papers of the Continental Congress.

Let us focus on these forty-three petitions since they represent the actions of individual women taking part in government. Would these women have written if they felt that government would not respond? They hoped for a response and they hoped for redress or assistance. Despite their political participation in the redress process, not one of the forty-three petitions dealt with a strictly political issue. Nor did one carry out Abigail's threat concerning women's rights.

The right of petition and even quick and favorable action by Congress are only aspects of full political participation. Women, for the most part, were excluded from standing in the political arena. In our twentieth-century vernacular, she could only phone in her appeal. But knowing this has hampered some students of women's history from exploring other aspects of political activity. My profile of these women is something like this. Their ages ranged from the early twenties to the late sixties with most of them probably twenty to forty-five years of age. Some ages were given, and this deduction was based upon related information that the petitioner supplied. Additional data were gathered from other documentary sources such as Revolutionary War Pension and Bounty-Land-Warrant Application Files. Few petitions came from women residing in southern states, although the distribution was spread throughout the Middle Atlantic and New England regions. Many resided in the larger cities, and petitions from Philadelphia outnumbered those from any other urban area. This must be discounted because the war forced more to relocate than we care to admit while others traveled there to seek help from the Congress.

The petitions of patriot women tend to revolve around those who were separated from their husbands or those who were widows. In most of these instances their "distressed condition," as they put it, was a combination of loss of the husband's income, loss of property, and the psychological pressures of attempting to fulfill two parental roles. The loss of husband combined with the loss of economic security reduced some widows to extreme want. Of the forty-three petitions twenty-six were from widows, and most of them lost their husbands as a direct result of the war. Of this number about half were wives of officers. Many widows delayed sending memorials or petitions despite their knowledge of the acts of the Continental and Confederation Congresses making them eligible for pensions. Pride and independence, I suspect, were very strong during the hectic war years and the early 1780s. It may be incidental but the severe economic dislocations of 1785 through 1788 might have forced many widows to ask for help. This may have contributed to the long delays in appeals to Congress.

Widow Mary Giddens declared in her petition of 1777 that her husband, John Giddens, was killed on board the Continental ship *Alfred* in action against the *Glasgow*. She enclosed a certificate of her husband's death on May 7, 1776, and sought the $200 bounty from the Navy Board. "Ware [sic] it in my power," wrote the widow, "to support myself and family, I should not have troubled this honorable House so often as I have." On July 30, 1777, Congress resolved that Mary Giddens be paid the $200 due her and that it be taken out of the prize money of the *Alfred*.[5] In another case Congress informed widow Lydia Wallingford that she was entitled to $300 out of the prize money but that she would have to obtain it from the agents for the crew of the ship *Ranger*. In other words she was left to her own devices in dealing with the agent. Wallingford had waited until 1787 before petitioning Congress, although her husband had died over six years previous while serving as a lieutenant in the marines.[6]

Hannah Morris and Mary McMyers petitioned Congress on August 25 and 27 of 1778. The former's husband had fallen at Whitemarsh while the latter's husband was killed at the Battle of Germantown. McMyers declared that she was without means of supporting five small children. Not until March 20, 1779, did Congress act and then it ordered both appeals to lie on the table.[7] I could find no subsequent action on the petitions. In our experiences in the Center for the Documentary Study of the American Revolution this most likely means that their memorials were buried without action. There is some chance, however, that they were turned down and never recorded by Secretary of the Congress Charles Thomson.

In March 1787 Elizabeth Gaudins of Boston wrote Congress seeking "something to keep me from starving." She recounted that her departed husband had died in the Continental navy and she was therefore eligible for his prize money and wages. One might ask what prompted her to wait so long to apply. In her petition Gaudins indicated that she had taught school during the war and was "never assisted by the Publick [sic]." She was an independent, proud woman. After a long delay Congress denied her appeal.[8]

Cornelia Anderson wrote that American troops moving to New York City "took my house and converted it to a prison in which time it received great damage." She then moved to the country for the duration of the war where she was "plundered and suffered many hardships — being blind." During that time her son was killed in the army and her husband passed away. The widow returned alone to New York City in 1783 and found her "houses burnt, so all my hope was gone." In desperation she leased her lot and rented a room for £5 per year. The landlord later claimed that the £5 was rent for one quarter, not per annum. The woman refused to pay it, and he took the case to court. She lost.

To add to her worries, the local authorities presented her a bill for digging and paving the street in front of her lot. This cost her £4 15s, and widening the street took five feet off the lot. "This expense will reduce me to great distress," lamented Cornelia Anderson, "which is the only cause that induces me to desire satisfaction for the damage done to my house while the army had it in possession." The widow admitted that the damage to her house — "now burnt" — could not be determined. "So it is left to your generosity which if you take in conciteration [sic], your petitioner will be in duty bound to pray for you. Signed Cornelia Anderson." She had paid the price many times over — forced from her home, the loss of her husband and son, many additional hardships because of her blindness, and great economic anxiety. Her words, "so all my hope was gone," need no comment. When reduced to "great distress" the woman sought compensation for damages caused nearly a decade before. Congress read the petition the same day it was presented. The use of finding aids to the various pre-federal records has not produced any evidence that Congress acted to assist the discouraged widow.[9]

Sarah Kennedy was the widow of Dr. Samuel Kennedy and executrix of his estate. The major piece of property, called Yellow Springs, was about sixty miles from Philadelphia and in 1777 became the site of a general military hospital. Sarah Kennedy, in letters and petitions written during 1779, desired compensation, buildings repaired, and a tenant evicted. Congress read the petition on February 11, 1779, and referred it to the Board of Treasury for study. The case was complicated by a civil case in Pennsylvania and the demands of the tenant. On June 29, 1779, Congress awarded the heirs of Samuel Kennedy $5,000 for the rent of the farm and buildings. It refused to award damages at that time "until Congress has worked" and fixed a policy of war damages.[10]

Two widows hoped that Congress would grant them pensions in order to provide for the education of their children. Both had suffered considerable property losses during the war and had little means at their disposal. No record of Hannah Thomas' petition could be located. Ann Ledyard was denied assistance on the ground that her husband was an "appointed and commissioned" officer of Connecticut and acted "without the order of requisition of any officer in the service of the U.S." Congress declared that it could not grant the petition "without establishing a precedent which will be productive of great inconvenience."[11]

Philadelphian Hannah Sweers was in a most perplexing situation between 1778 and 1782. Her husband Cornelius was a deputy commissary general of military stores and handled large sums of money in order to procure military stores. Because of suspected fraud by forgery, Sweers was thrown in jail and all his personal property was seized and moved. Because his trial was delayed almost a year, Hannah Sweers was without her "goods and chattels" and this was "to the no small distress" of the memorialist. Mrs. Sweers "and her tender little ones" were plunged "into the deepest calamities and afflictions." Congress continued to hold the impounded goods. Not until May 21, 1782, did Congress resolve that the seized goods be sold and the income be used to satisfy U.S. claims. If funds were left, they were to be paid to Cornelius Sweers.[12]

Rachel Wells of Bordentown, New Jersey, petitioned Congress in 1786 and claimed that she was robbed by both American and British soldiers during the war. Congress read the petition but refused to grant her compensation. Margaret Yorke of Philadelphia complained that Colonel Barber, an American officer stationed at Elizabeth Town, New Jersey, had promised to safeguard her trunk. Later when she returned for it, he claimed that the trunk was confiscated because some articles inside were prohibited. She desired restitution. Congress referred the complaint to military authorities in New Jersey.[13]

Madam Bentley of the Illinois region wrote to Congress in 1783 complaining about insults and property losses she and others suffered from the petty despot, John Dodge of Kaskaskia. By 1782 this frontier freebooter was acting as the law and attempted to intimidate those opposing him. Marguerite Bentley refused to bow to Dodge and sought congressional action. She reminded the readers of her petition that Dodge had seized her land, houses, slaves, furniture, and paper money. She wanted this corrected. Congress received few individual petitions from frontier women.[14]

The Continental army encamped near Whitemarsh in November 1777 and proceeded to tear down fences, cut woods for firewood, and take forage. Elizabeth Loeser, one of eight petitioners from Whitemarsh, informed Congress that she lost 8,352 rails, eighty posts, and four acres of woodland. The matter was eventually referred to Q.M. Gen. Nathanael Greene for settlement.[15]

One record in the Papers of the Continental Congress lists 135 claimants of Westchester County, New York, who in 1780 supplied Washington's forces with forage for their animals. Although this is not a formal petition, the 135 proprietors of farms, including nine women, sought fair compensation. This record indicates the name of the proprietor of the farm, the location of the farm by district within the county, the claimant's name, and the amount of hay and oats provided the army. Of the nine women claimants, eight were widows. These 135 persons had provided the troops 1,864 tons of hay and 8,234 bushels of oats. Of this total the women supplied 43¼ tons of hay and 401½ bushels of oats.[16]

To make certain the claims were valid and payment fair, Gen. William Heath established a three-person board of arbitrators who acted as an investigative board. In 1782 this group toured the country and held sessions at various taverns where persons could produce vouchers and certificates or give testimony. There is a ninety-page-manuscript journal in the Miscellaneous Numbered Records — sometimes called the Manuscript File — which provides a great deal of additional information. In this journal we find that many other articles were furnished, but everything was converted to oats and hay by the board. This record indicates that women gave testimony and that other women submitted the claims that were rejected.[17]

In February 1778 Lt. William Preston was on his way to Valley Forge when he was captured by the British and sent to a prison on Long Island. His wife, Elizabeth, decided in December 1778 to go to Philadelphia and seek assistance from Congress. The petition seeking her husband's back pay and rations was read and decided the same day. Congress ordered on February 9 that the wife be paid $160, his pay and rations for the time between his capture and the last pay period. In August of the same year, Elizabeth appealed again and expressed her great relief for the rations furnished by order of Congress to her and her four small children but that they were now cut off from this support. To her knowledge, her husband still remained a prisoner. The endorsement on her petition reads that she is empowered to receive her husband's pay — "nothing more can be done for her."[18]

One petition relates to the assistance of American prisoners of war. Elizabeth Burgin and her three children were living in New York City where "she possessed everything comfortable about her." In the summer of 1779 that changed when she began helping American POWs to escape. Before long she was forced into hiding because the British put out a £2,000 reward for her capture. She hid in the city for two weeks and then fled in a manner "unsuitable to her sex and age." Burgin had to leave her children for at least six weeks while she moved from Long Island to Connecticut to Philadelphia in the autumn of 1779. General Washington provided her and her children rations and wrote Congress on her behalf. The commander provided the rations because she had "risked so much" helping American soldiers. "She has been," added Washington, "indefatigable for the relief of the prisoners." In 1781 Congress awarded the widow $53.50 per annum because of her outstanding service to American soldiers.[19]

Accounts of women aiding prisoners can be found in the primary and secondary documentation of the American Revolution. American officers felt so strongly about the assistance given them by Martha Gray while they were prisoners in Philadelphia that they drew up and signed a certificate commending her.[20] I have located the names of at least fifteen women who aided prisoners of both sides. More research needs to be done in substantiating these accounts in order that some generalizations can be made.

To my knowledge there are no petitions or memorials from black women and only one from an Indian. The petition on Nonhelema, alias Catherine the Grenadier, deserves some background. In 1778 Shawnee warriors crossed the Ohio River and attacked Fort Randolph, which was located where the Great Kanawha River joins the Ohio. The 400 Shawnees drew a siege around the stockaded post and attempted to starve the Americans. At a critical time Catherine, a woman of huge stature — she was reported to be six-and-a-half-feet-tall — somehow drove "48 horned cattle" into the stockade. This saved the inhabitants from starving and broke the siege. This remarkable warrior had fought the whites since the 1750s. Her martial skills were respected by both races. In her petition of 1785, she mentioned that her relations included white people taken and adopted during the French and Indian War. Since her deed at Fort Randolph, Catherine lived near the whites. The Indian woman petitioned Congress for 2,000 acres of land for herself and her relatives. Although Catherine did not sign her petition, several whites

(pages 80-81) George Washington's support for the relief of Elizabeth Burgin. Although Washington's letter to Samuel Huntington, president of the Continental Congress, is in the hand of a clerk or secretary, his signature attests to his appreciation for Burgin's sacrifices in the cause of America. He described her as "indefatigable for the relief of the prisoners, and in measures for facilitating their escape, in consequence of this conduct she incurred the suspicions of the enemy and was finally compelled to make her escape under . . . distressed circumstances. . . . " He could "not forbear recommending to consideration a person who has risqued so much and been so friendly to our officers and privates, especially as to this we must attribute her present situation."
Washington, Commander in Chief of the Army, 1775-84," 8, no. 312, PCC, RG 36 (M247, roll 170).

Head Quarters Morristown
25th Decr 1779.

Sir

I have the honor to lay
before your Excellency the represent-
tion of a certain Elizabeth Burgin
late an inhabitant of New-York.
From the testimony of different persons, and particularly many of
our own officers who have returned
from captivity, it would appear,
that she has been indefatigable
for the relief of the prisoners, and
in measures for facilitating their
escape. in consequence of this con-
:duct she incurred the suspicions
of the enemy, and was finally
compelled to make her escape,
under the distressed circumstances
which she describes. I could not
forbear recommending to consi-
:deration a person who has risqued

so

so much and been so friendly to our officers and privates, especially as to this we must attribute her present situation.

From the sense I entertain of her services and sufferings I have ventured to take the liberty of directing the commissary at Philadelphia to furnish her also her children with rations till the pleasure of Congress could be known. Congress will judge of its justice and propriety, and how much she may be entitled to further notice.

I have the honor to be with the greatest respect
your Excellency's
most obdt servt
G. Washington

His Excellency
Saml Huntington Esqr

signed attesting to its truthfulness. George Rogers Clark and Richard Butler also had written President of Congress Richard Henry Lee urging favorable consideration of the petition. Congress ordered her compensated for the cattle and granted her 1,000 acres on the west side of the Scioto River in southern Ohio. Finally in 1788 Congress set the compensation for the cattle. Catherine was awarded "one suit or dress of clothing" including a blanket every year and one ration of provisions each day during her life. She could receive this at any U.S. post in the western territory.[21]

Of the five Loyalist women petitioners, Susanna Connolly, wife of John Connolly, who assisted Lord Dunmore in 1775-76, was in the most extreme straits. Both husband and wife ended up in a Philadelphia jail in 1776. Having a low regard for her cell, Susanna petitioned for her return to Pittsburgh. Congress finally granted the request in 1778 but refused the appeals of her husband.[22] The four remaining Loyalist women asked permission to go to New York City — the stronghold of British power on the continent. Mrs. Antil wrote Congress on October 22, 1776, asking that she, her sister, and children be permitted to go to New York City. Congress assented but added that the party take "especial care" to "carry no intelligence to the enemy." Three women, acting in concert, asked permission to travel to Philadephia in mid-August 1778. One of the three, Mrs. Wilson, gave her honor that she would not carry letters or newspapers to New York. Congress refused them permission.[23]

In order to gain some perspective on the appeals made by women, I studied about fifty petitions from men. I would estimate that about three-fourths of these petitions were from military personnel. Economic issues still appeared uppermost with these petitioners. The major difference in the treatment of female and that of male petitioners was detected in how Congress responded to male military participants who lost limbs or were otherwise incapacitated and how it responded to widows. In 1776 Congress resolved that officers and men disabled in the service of the United States were eligible for half pay during the disability. Sometimes orphans were provided for by the passing of private acts. The sons of fallen Generals Warren and Mercer were to be educated at the expense of the Congress.[24]

The central element of this legislation appeared to be that if the man lost his means of support, aid was needed. If the wife lost her soldier husband, she might receive a pension if she were fortunate enough to be married to an officer who qualified. The inadequacy of the pension legislation was indicated in the April 1787 report of the Board of Treasury concerning the memorial of a widow whose late husband was a marine officer. The board reported to Congress that the August 26, 1776, congressional resolve made provision "for such Officers and seamen, as may lose a limb, or be otherwise disabled; but that it does not appear that it has ever been extended to the widows of such as were killed in the service of the United States." A small part of the injustice was removed on August 24, 1780, when a resolve offered half-pay-for-life to widows and orphans of officers in the Line of the Army of the United States.[25] The same widow was refused a pension under this act because her husband was a marine officer on board the *Ranger*. This act excluded most naval service claims. It must be stressed that the widows of all enlisted men were excluded from federal pension benefits until 1832, when some were included.

The study of various resolves and acts of Congress relating to federal pensions and the study of Revolutionary War Pension and Bounty-Land-Warrant Application Files in the National Archives may become a significant means of learning more about the early nineteenth-century woman and her society. Thousands of widows applied for pensions under acts passed in 1836, 1838, 1848, 1853, and 1855. Sometimes these widows' files are windows that provide us a view of one aspect of the century.

Earlier in my paper I mentioned crimes against property. Women were also subjected to crimes against themselves. In their affidavits and depositions, girls and women called themselves ravished. We, today, would say they were raped. All thirteen states were, at one time or another, the hosts of armies and could not escape from the realities of war. Uniformed male visitors often invaded the privacy of home and person. Most of these rape cases were documented in Item 53 of the Papers of the Continental Congress and stem from British activity in three locations: Hunterdon County, New Jersey; Fairfield, Connecticut; and New Haven, Connecticut.

The sworn depositions taken in Hunterdon County in March 1777 pertain to acts committed by British soldiers against Abigail Palmer, age thirteen, Elizabeth Cain, age fifteen, her sister Sarah, eighteen, two married women, and a widow. The accounts are graphic and brutal. One day in December 1776 two British soldiers came to the house where fifteen-year-old Elizabeth Cain, her sister, and Abigail Palmer were staying. The soldiers insisted that the three go to their camp, about a mile away. Elizabeth Cain pleaded not to go when one soldier "swore he would blow her brains out if she did not go," and "this terrorized her." Elizabeth related that he seized her and the other soldier grabbed Abigail Palmer "and pulled them both into a room together" while the girls "screamed and begged of them not to use them in that manner." Both Cain and Palmer interceded but in vain. Finally the soldiers "ravished them both and took them away to their camp where they was [sic] both treated by some others of the soldiers in the same cruel manner." Later a British officer came and took the two girls to the house of Cornelius Hoof where they stayed until Elizabeth's father arrived and took them home.[26]

Abigail Palmer's deposition is similar except we find that the raping had been going on for three days. Earlier a group of soldiers had appeared at the house and demanded entrance. Once inside, one soldier told the thirteen-year-old girl he wanted to talk to her in the next room. She refused. He then "took hold of her and dragged her into a back room." She "screamed and begged" but to no avail. Three of the soldiers "ravished her" and likewise for three days "successively divers soldiers treated her in the same manner." There is no need to go to the other depositions.[27] The crimes in Fairfield were on the same order. In New Haven, Christiana Gatter, of lawful age and married, swore that on July 5, 1779, British soldiers broke into their house at two o'clock in the morning where she, her husband, and two children were sleeping. Two soldiers "laid hold of me and threw me on the bed and swore if I made any noise or resistance they would kill me in a moment." One, then the other, had their "will of me." There are at least twelve sworn statements in these records, and they were forwarded to the Congress.[28]

Another example of possible harassment of women took place at Long Cane Creek in the Abbeville District of South Carolina. Isabella Reid recounted that while her husband was out soldiering, a group of Tories, as she recollected at age eighty, broke into her uncle's house. The women "were stripped by the Tories of all their clothing except their undergarments." It is quite possible that the women were made to undress because they might have carried hidden weapons. Accounts of frontier Loyalist and patriot women ending the lives of soldiers with concealed weapons are true enough that this may not have been a case of sexual harassment.[29]

The author has made no survey of crime against Loyalist women. The manuscript sources, if searched, would no doubt provide documentation. One student of the Loyalists has written that Ebenezer Slocum's Loyalist mother was pilloried, her ears cut off, and both cheeks branded because of her steadfast political views.[30]

The occupational roles of women within military organizations need a great deal of study. One profile worth sketching is that of the military nurse. During the establishment of the Continental Hospital Department in July 1775, Congress set the pay of nurses at $2 per month and limited nurses to one for every ten sick soldiers. Their duties were simply stated: to attend the sick and obey the matron's orders. The matron had a great deal of authority in the hospital; consequently her pay was higher. Some wives of officers and soldiers functioned in these two capacities in the general hospitals. More desired, instead, to join the staffs of the regimental hospitals because these moved with the troops. The work was demanding and notices for nurses were found in newspapers. Their pay in the Continental Service increased from $2 a month to $1 per week between 1775 and 1777. This was during a time when inflation was moderate. Women also worked as clerks, commissaries, servants, washerwomen, and cooks in the hospitals. The resident surgeons or surgeons general appointed women to these positions.[31]

In many instances, it is difficult to identify nurses or matrons because names are not provided. The hospital return of March 20, 1780, for the general hospital of the Northern Department at Albany furnishes us a view that is probably representative. There were seven nurses identified and three had children with them. Nurses with one child were not given an extra food ration, but those with two children received one extra food ration. The matron, Sarah Ray, was accompanied by a son and given two rations.[32] In the peace establishment army regulations, no regiment was allowed to draw rations and pay for more than four nurses. Each was to receive $4 per month and a ration per day. Privates received $2 per month and a ration per day. Military nursing was demanding day and night work and the Continental Services, the states, and private parties competed for nurses' services.[33]

In some instances women who ran taverns and boarding houses also provided nursing care. The state of Virginia paid Rachael Warrington for nursing sick soldiers in 1775, and the Pennsylvania Board of War directed that Margaret Clay be paid £10 for nursing two deserters from the British army. The Continental Congress employed Elizabeth Slaydon and Rachel Hewen in nursing and boarding soldiers during the summer of 1776.[34]

Matrons, nurses, washerwomen, servants, and cooks accompanied the armies in an official capacity during the war. They were not part of that aggregate known as campfollowers. Before we can begin to understand the nature and composition of campfollowers, we must isolate those who were part of the army. Campfollowers, if we must continue using the term, probably should include the wives, children, private servants, sweethearts, women of loose and easy virtue, and refugees from enemy-held areas who had no place to go. More than once Washington complained of the multitude of women and children who marched in his troops' wake. But he well knew the valuable services they performed. Linda Grant De Pauw overstates the case when she writes that these women "have been totally blacked out of the historical record or else dismissed as women of 'vicious character.' "[35] My thoughts are that we do not know enough.

Another source of information on women with the army would be army returns and related statistical data. In the Revolutionary War Rolls series of records in the National Archives, there is a weekly return of January 24, 1783, for several regiments and corps stationed at and in the vicinity of West Point and New Windsor. This was the main Continental army waiting for peace to be settled by the diplomats. The return lists 10,380 officers and rank-and-file in twenty-one regiments. The return also includes 405 women and 302 children drawing 556 rations. A woman received a ration and a child half a ration. Each regiment has separate figures and the variations are extreme. The 1st New York Regiment accounted for fifty-two women and fifty-eight children while the regiment had 524 rank-and-file. This high number probably is because the Continental army was encamped along the Hudson River in New York. The 2nd New Hampshire Regiment had 416 rank-and-file and only four women and three children. This was the lowest total in the army. The variations at this time cannot be accounted for, but because this was virtually a peacetime army, the policies or determinations of regimental commanders probably were decisive.[36]

Women and children marched with British troops as well. In 1777 there were 75 women and 121 children in prison near Lancaster, Pennsylvania. These people were captured with the British forces in Canada during 1775 and 1776. Fifteen of the women had no children with them, and twelve had one. Some had as many as five children with them.[37] Manuscript orderly books in the National Archives contain occasional references to women and children being with the troops.

The last profile involves women that were employed in civilian capacities behind the scenes. This documentation is widely scattered and hard to locate because so much was a volunteer effort. These women's products were of considerable benefit and were highly prized by soldiers. Eugenie Leonard's *The Dear-Bought Heritage* and the work *The American Woman in Colonial and Revolutionary Times, 1565-1800* provide names of some of these women. Leonard claims in the former study that about five hundred women were employed in Philadelphia to make cloth. This work was done in their homes.[38] During the war women were employed by the Commissary General of Military Stores in making musket cartridges. There is a list of "hired men" at the top of one of the original ledger books, but the names Jane Kinnecut, Edith Stuart, Sarah Cribs, and so on tell us otherwise. In another record I located orders for pay by the Commissary General of Military Stores Department. In the orders the women signed their names or made their marks for their pay. Sarah Cribs, for example, made 22,000 musket cartridges between March 13 and May 3, 1780, for which she received £120. Edith Steward made 37,000 cartridges between February 11 and May 25, 1780, and earned £138. They were paid at the standard rate of 75 shillings per 1,000 musket cartridges. Hannah Thomas cooked for a company of twelve artificers and earned $5 a day or £54 for twenty-nine days of cooking. Rebecca Young made 500 linings for Light Horsemen's caps and earned £187. Later she cut and sewed 293 shirts at $3 apiece. Mary Dennison was paid £18 on May 25, 1780, for spinning six pounds of shoe thread.[39] Mary Hurrie was the janitor and firekeeper in the Office of the Secretary of the Continental Congress and received $86 back pay in February 1779. The delegates of Congress in 1785 granted a pension to Elizabeth Thompson, "late a domestic in the family of the Commander-in-Chief during the war." At the age of eighty-one she was "reduced to proverty [sic] and distress." If the journals state her age correctly, she was between seventy-three to seventy-seven when she served the general between Valley Forge and the Battle of Yorktown.[40]

I have examined the records of women petitioning their government and the government's response. The main current of this stream of appeals carried economic issues — not political issues. These women's hardships revealed, however, that in some instances underlying political commitment generated their behavior which caused them economic difficulties. In other instances the loss of spouse created major problems. The profiles of women as military nurses, campfollowers, workers in civilian capacities, wives and mothers, and as objects of men's sexual desires provide us insights into society as well as women's history.

Vignettes are available which bill the American woman as heroine. Are they representative? Have we thus far constructed an elitist view of women's history? The examination of new data and fresh insights hopefully will force us to discard some stereotypes. Let us reduce the number of Paul Reveres riding around.

The October 1975 issue of the *Quarterly Journal of the Library of Congress* was devoted to women's history. One contributor James H. Hutson, in his article, "Women in the Era of the American Revolution" maintained that women's suffrage is "still dictating the shape and character of today's writing about women during the American Revolution."[41] In the development of his thesis, Hutson remarked that Elizabeth F. Ellet's three-volume publication, *The Women of the American Revolution*, and another work by her were the "data banks" from which subsequent writers have retrieved their information about revolutionary women and events. That author continues to press his case by adding: "It is safe to say that Mrs. Ellet's work mentions virtually every individual and episode which appear in present-day accounts of women during the Revolution and many more which do not."[42] I grant that too many authors have relied on the *History of Woman Suffrage*[43] and Ellet's work when writing on women during the Revolution. But much has been written that goes far beyond Ellet from a data standpoint. Ellet provided about 142 vignettes in her work on the Revolution. Of the over 150 women documented in my paper, only one is found in Ellet's work. Other serious students could do the same.

The role of the early American family demands a great deal of study. We need to start evaluating the demographic data available. I have not seen a women's history work that mentions that the average free family size was 5.7 persons in 1790. This statistic was based upon the 1790 federal census. Between 1774 and 1789, there were eleven colonial or state censuses and some provide valuable data on women. This information and additional census data through 1900 have been available since 1909 when the U.S. Census Bureau published *A Century of Population Growth*.[44] Over thirty-five years ago, Spruill, in her classic study of colonial women in the South, comprehended the value of using family records in order to study marriage patterns, childbearing, infant and child mortality, and adult mortality rates. This type of research must continue. About 125 illustrated family records in the National Archives provide a glimpse into the nature of the family. These records are scattered among the Revolutionary War Pension and Bounty-Land-Warrant Application Files that are available on Microfilm Publication 804.

Some authors of women's history are now trying to go beyond straight narrative by developing some conceptual framework. This has led some of the best writers into difficulties because they know that a history of the women of the American Revolution cannot be cut off from women in the colonial and early national eras of American history. Women's history today is debating whether women between 1750 and 1850 were making progress toward equality in the political, economic, and social marketplace. In order to begin answering this question we need to delineate women in the years prior to the Revolution.

There is no satisfactory history of women in the American Revolution. The way to build toward this larger picture is to examine particular aspects of women's history during this time. An excellent example is found in an article by Sophie H. Drinker, "Women Attorneys of Colonial Times," in the *Maryland Historical Magazine*.[45] Other possibilities have been mentioned in this paper. In my three years of assisting persons doing research on pre-federal subjects, I have found few who were willing to spend the time needed to do women's history research. What will the next decade bring? In the long term you will answer my initial question — "Vignettes or Profiles?"

NOTES

1. Letters reproduced in Julia Ward Stickley, "The Records of Deborah Sampson Gannett, Woman Soldier of the Revolution," *Prologue: The Journal of the National Archives* 4 (Winter 1972): 236.

2. Julia Cherry Spruill, *Women's Life and Work in the Southern Colonies* (Chapel Hill, N.C.: University of North Carolina Press, 1938); Eugenie Andrus Leonard, *The Dear-Bought Heritage* (Philadelphia: University of Pennsylvania Press, 1965).

3. Abigail Adams to Mercy Otis Warren, 27 April 1776, "Warren-Adams Letters," *Massachusetts Historical Society Collections* 72 (1917): 235.

4. Most of these memorials or petitions are from Item 41, "Memorials Addressed to Congress, 1775-88," and Item 42, "Petitions Addressed to Congress, 1775-89," Papers of the Continental Congress, 1774-89, Records of the Continental and Confederation Congresses and the Constitutional Convention, Record Group 360, National Archives (National Archives Microfilm Publication M247, rolls 48-56). (Hereafter cited as Item ___, PCC, RG 360, NA (M247, rolls(s) ___.))

5. Item 42, 3: 178, PCC, RG 360, NA (M247, roll 54); Worthington C. Ford et al, eds., *Journals of the Continental Congress,* 34 vols. (Washington, D.C.: Government Printing Office, 1904-37), 8: 588. (Hereafter cited as *JCC*.)

6. Item 42, 8: 381-83, PCC, RG 360, NA (M247, roll 56); *JCC,* 32:212.

7. Item 42, 5: 118-22, PCC, RG 360, NA (M247, roll 55); *JCC* 13: 342.

8. Item 42, 3, 301-4, PCC, RG 360, NA (M247, roll 54); *JCC,* 34: 621.

9. Item 42, 1: 71-74, PCC, RG 360, NA (M247, roll 53); *JCC,* 29: 714n.

10. Item 41, 5: 15-18, PCC, RG 360, NA (M247, roll 50); *JCC*, 163, 192-94, 208, 782. See also Item 78, "Miscellaneous Letters Addressed to Congress, 1775-89," 18: 497, 501, PCC, RG 360, NA (M247, roll 100).

11. Item 42, 7: 422-25, PCC, RG 360, NA (M247, roll 56); Item 42, 4: 430-34, ibid. (M247, roll 54); *JCC*, 34: 468-69.

12. Item 41, 9: 48-49, PCC, RG 360, NA (M247, roll 52); *JCC*, 11: 628, 737 and 22: 277, 280.

13. Item 42, 8: 354-56, PCC, RG 360, NA (M247, roll 56); Item 41, 10: 707, ibid. (M247, roll 52).

14. Item 48, "Memorials of the Inhabitants of Illinois, Kaskaskia, and Kentucky, 1780-89," pp. 15-16, ibid. (M247, roll 62), PCC.

15. Item 41, 9: 62-69, ibid. (M247, roll 52).

16. Item 157, "Letters from General Officers, 1775-89," pp. 151-66, ibid. (M247, roll 177).

17. "Proceedings of Arbitrators Relative to the Forage Taken in Westchester County in 1780," MS. no. 29580F, Miscellaneous Numbered Records (The Manuscript File), War Department Collection of Revolutionary War Records, RG 93, NA (M859, roll 11) (Hereafter cited by manuscript file number and microfilm location).

18. Item 41, 8: 66, PCC, RG 360, NA (M247, roll 51); Item 42, 6: 222-25, ibid. (M247, roll 55); *JCC* 13: 157.

19. Item 42, 1: 254-55, PCC, RG 360, NA (M247, roll 53); Washington to Samuel Huntington, 25 December 1779, Item 152, "Letters from General George Washington, Commander in Chief of the Army, 1775-84," 8, no. 312 (M247, roll 170); *JCC,* 21: 850-51, 908.

20. Photostat of Certificate in Benjamin Harrison Papers, Manuscript Division, Library of Congress, Washington. See also Henry S. Commager and Richard B. Morris, eds., *The Spirit of 'Seventy-Six,* 2 vols. (Indianapolis and New York: Bobbs-Merrill, 1958), 2: 853-54, for the efforts of widow Sarah Smith.

21. Item 56, "Records Relating to Indian Affairs, 1765-89," pp. 165-72, PCC, RG 360, NA (M 247, roll 69); *JCC,* 28: 488, 34: 536. For a biographical sketch of Catherine the Grenadier, see Reuben G. Thwaites and Louise P. Kellogg, eds., *Frontier Defense on the Upper Ohio, 1777-1778* (Madison: Wisconsin Historical Society, 1912), p. 26, and Allan W. Eckert, *The Frontiersmen* (New York: Bantam, 1970), p. 95.

22. Item 78, 5: 67-70, PCC, RG 360, NA (M247, roll 93); John Hancock to John Connolly, 23 May 1776, Item 12A, "Letter Books of the Presidents of Congress, 1775-87," p. 138, ibid. (M247, roll 23); *JCC,* 6: 748.

23. Item 78, 3: 107-10, ibid. (M247, roll 91); 19: 265-72, ibid. (M247, roll 101); 23: 541-42, ibid. (M247, roll 104); *JCC,* 6: 896 and 11:825.

24. *JCC,* 3: 702-5.

25. Ibid., 32: 212-13, 5: 702-5, 17:773.

26. Item 53, "Papers and Affidavits Relating to the Plunderings, Burnings, and Ravages Committed by the British, 1775-84," pp. 28-30, PCC, RG 360, NA (M247, roll 66).

27. Ibid., pp. 31-40.

28. Ibid., pp. 238-46.

29. Revolutionary War Pension Application File of Joseph Reid, W9249, Revolutionary War Pension and Bounty-Land-Warrant Application Files, Records of the Veterans Administration, RG 15, NA (M804, roll 2021).

30. Wallace Brown, *The King's Friends: The Composition of the American Loyalist Claimants* (Providence: Brown University Press, 1965), p. 48.

31. *JCC,* 2: 209-10, 858 and 8: 162, 245; *Virginia Gazette,* 26 July 1777, in Spruill, *Women's Life,* p. 271; Maryland Historical Society, *Archives of Maryland* 2 (1893): 257, 298; Broadside, Hospital Department, Item 78, 22: 567, PCC, RG 360, NA (M247, roll 103).

32. Return of General Hospital, Northern Department, 30 March 1780, Miscellaneous Jacket no. 3-58, Revolutionary War Rolls, 1775-1783, RG 93, NA (M246, roll 135).

33. *JCC,* 25: 735.

34. Virginia Accounts, 1775, no. 37777, Photographic Copies of State Records, ca. 1775-83, RG 93, NA; Pennsylvania Board of War, 8 April 1777, *Pennsylvania Archives,* 2d ser., 1: 27; *JCC,* 5: 547, 610.

35. Linda Grant De Pauw, "The Forgotten Spirit of '76: Women of the Revolutionary Era," *Ms. Magazine,* July 1974, p. 55.

36. "Return of women and children who drew provisions in the Army," extracted from return of 24 January 1781, Miscellaneous Jacket no. 10-3-259, Rev. War Rolls RG 93, NA (M246, roll 136).

37. In *Pennsylvania Archives,* 2d ser., 1 (1884): 418-19.

38. Leonard, *Dear-Bought Heritage,* pp. 190-196; Eugenie Andrus Leonard, Sophie Hutchinson Drinker, and Miriam Young Holden, *The American Woman in Colonial and Revolutionary Times, 1565-1800* (Philadelphia: University of Pennsylvania Press, 1962).

39. "List of Hired Men," MS. no. 21816, p. 15, Miscellaneous Numbered Records, RG 93, NA (M859, roll 73); "Orders for Pay, Commissary General of Military Stores Department," 128 (2 March-2 October, 1780): 69-159, RG 93 NA (M853, roll 40).

40. *JCC,* 14: 310, 28: 84.

41. James H. Hutson, "Women in the Era of the American Revolution, the Historian as Suffragist," *Quarterly Journal of the Library of Congress* 32 (October 1975): 290.

42. Ibid., p. 291. Ellet's two influential works were *The Women of the American Revolution,* 3 vols. (New York: Baker and Scribner, 1848-50) and *Domestic History of the American Revolution* (New York: Baker and Scribner, 1850).

43. Elizabeth Cady Stanton et al, eds., *History of Woman Suffrage,* 3 vols. (New York: Fowler and Wells, 1881).

44. U.S., Bureau of the Census, *A Century of Population Growth* (Washington: Government Printing Office, 1909), pp. 3-15.

45. Sophie H. Drinker, "Women Attorneys of Colonial Times," *Maryland Historical Magazine* 56 (December 1961): 335-51.

DISCUSSION SUMMARY

Linda K. Kerber offered the following comment on the papers presented:

I think that the two papers illustrate better perhaps than Bill Chafe could have expected some of the difficulties involved in moving from individuals' perceptions and experiences to aggregates to collective arguments. What I think we have just heard are examples of minds of historians struggling first to uncover the building blocks of women's history and struggling even harder to put them together. The shape has not yet taken form, but we are beginning, I hope, to see a little more clearly what it will ultimately be made of.

I want to say that one of the difficulties in writing papers of this sort is the recalcitrance of archival material as it is currently organized. George Chalou, particularly, made it sound very simple as he outlined his fifty-three memorials and his forty-three petitions and his thirty-odd women who were paid for service to the military. But just as the thirty-odd women come under the heading of hired *men,* it is almost impossible for a nonarchivist to find this material in this building, as I can testify from a sad experience.

In part, I think this is due to the original purpose of the building, which Virginia Purdy mentioned. That is, the archives are organized by way of the agency that generated them. If the Continental Army generated the records of the Continental Army, then those of us who look for materials dealing with the women who came in contact with the Army will have first to go through all the battle records of all the men who fought in it.

And I think it is fair to say that most of the archives are most easily used by those of us trying to write histories of the agency which provided the materials in the first place. The challenge that we face is forcing these materials to answer historians' questions that are not the questions that they were organized to answer. As a historian, I am here to plead with the archivists to help us reorganize the material in the record groups so that we can use them more readily to answer the analytical questions that we bring to them.

Virginia Purdy expressed sympathy with Kerber's plea, but said that archives cannot be reorganized. Arrangement in the order that the records were created is a basic principle of archival management for the very good reason that it is the only one that works for everyone using them. One of the problems with the Papers of the Continental Congress is that a nineteenth-century government clerk, trying to be helpful, rearranged them into what, according to his lights, was a good subject order. The trouble is that one individual's subject order is another individual's total confusion. Arranging by subject, and even indexing, tends to limit access to the subjects chosen by the cataloger or indexer. The researcher tends to think that if a subject is not listed, it is not covered.

"Even though archivists cannot oblige researchers by rearranging the records," Purdy said, "what they *can* do is to provide good finding aids so that researchers can approach the records logically and decide for themselves where to look for the materials that they need." For example, she hoped that the guide to records in the National Archives relating to women's history that she was working on would be helpful to women's historians.

Kerber said that the guide should be issued in informal installments as parts were completed so that historians would not have to wait several years for the information.

Margaret Masson of the University of Maryland asked Chalou if he knew of any programs to facilitate the study of American women before 1750, to obviate the necessity of going to the records of each of the thirteen original colonies for source materials. "Many major libraries," Chalou replied, "have sets of published colonial records, such as the *Pennsylvania Archives* series, but often poor indexes, or none at all, make these difficult to use." "Researchers must be flexible," he said, "not giving up if they do not find the word 'women' in an index." Also available are early state records that were microfilmed by the Library of Congress and the University of North Carolina in the 1940s under the direction of William Sumner Jenkins. The finding aid is *A Guide to the Microfilm Collection of Early State Records* published by the Photoduplication Service of the Library of Congress in 1950. The microfilm publication also includes many records from the British Public Record Office.

In response to a question from Phyllis Woodworth of East Los Angeles College, Chalou said he thought that women gained very little from the Revolution despite their contribution. When the loss of family, of property, of psychological unity in families that were divided, and the relocations often occasioned by the war are taken into account, women were little better off than before the Revolution. Moreover, they were expected to return to domesticity when the war was over, regardless of the roles played during the conflict.

Ena Farley of the State University of New York College at Brockport was disturbed by Chalou's statement that he had found no petitions that could be unquestionably identified as having been filed by black women. Were there any from black males? Chalou said that he had sampled only about 50 of the 2000 petitions in the federal records and suggested that state records might be a good source of petitions from black women.

Chester Gregory was questioned by Beverly Smaby of the University of Pennsylvania about his reference to black heads of household in the 1790 federal census. She wondered whether the nuclear families recorded in the census reflected the state of society or what the census taker was looking for. Did census takers list males as heads of household, even where there may have been some communal living, just because society considered males to be the proper heads of household?

Gregory said that his remarks had been based on the National Archives Special List No. 34, *List of Free Black Heads of Families in the First Census of the United States, 1790* (1973) compiled by Debra Newman. Newman commented that her work in the census records had convinced her that census takers cared very little about their work. For example, in the 1790 population schedules for Philadelphia, a listing may read, ''Blacks, 12,'' or ''Blacks, 10,'' with no indication of sex. Virtually no information was supplied about black families other than the name of the head of the household until 1820. She had found very few women's names listed as heads of black household, but she thought that this was partly due to the custom of listing as head of household any male over sixteen years of age in the family. Sometimes no race is given, but Newman reasoned that most entries under ''All Other Free Persons'' were black. Indians, the only other nonwhite free persons in 1790, were listed only if they were taxed, and few of them were.

Kerber closed the session on that note of the difficulty of dealing with recalcitrant materials.

III

EMERGENCE OF THE NEW NATION

INTRODUCTION

Mary Lynn McCree

As white men set about creating on the North American continent a nation where they and their families could live and develop in freedom, two groups of nonwhite residents were not invited to participate in the great enterprise – the Indians and the blacks. The Indians, in the judgment of the whites, required measures directed toward "civilizing" them. Mary Young has addressed herself to the role of Indian women in this process. At the same time, the plight of the black slaves weighed heavily on the consciences of many thoughtful Americans. Judith Wellman has made a study of the part women played in forcing this problem to national attention.

WOMEN, CIVILIZATION, AND THE INDIAN QUESTION

Mary E. Young

Americans have achieved historical notoriety for their energetic efforts at self-reformation and their equally vigorous attempts to convert other societies to a (rather statically defined) "American Way." While nineteenth-century citizens strove by exhortation and organization to reform the home, the church, the school, and the community in the name of liberty, order, industry, and Christian principle, they also labored to convert native American Indians to the emulation of an idealized model of "Christian civilization."

Part of America's mission to itself entailed the elaboration of a "cult of true womanhood," or female domesticity. The cult confined middle-class, or ideal, woman to the household or the school. In her separate sphere, she was enjoined to subordinate her will — to her father, her husband, or the nearest appropriate male surrogate — and to direct her energies to the efficient management of resources her men might bring from the marketplace, to the transmission of approved cultural disciplines and values to children, and to the exercise of selfless, gentle, benign, and humane moral influence over all.[1] Positively, the constriction of women's activity to the private sphere while men went public in work and politics implied an increasingly critical role for women in transmitting "civilization" to the rising generation.

One might therefore suppose that efforts to civilize the allegedly childlike savages would entail a similar emphasis on the role of women as transmitters of culture. For both practical and ideological reasons, however, the overwhelming emphasis of official prescriptions for "civilizing" the savage fell on the role of men in relation to work, property, and law. Such emphasis reveals, I believe, a general assumption that woman's place could be defined properly only in the context of a market society in which property-owning males dominated production and politics.[2] In addition, of course, federal officials believed that if Indian families could be confined to small farms and induced by private possession to work the land intensively, they could and would turn over millions of acres of "surplus" hunting ground for white farmers to use. Federal policy aimed at *that* conversion above all others.[3]

As early as 1789, Secretary of War Henry Knox suggested to President Washington that introducing the love of exclusive property was the best way to civilize Indians. Knox proposed to begin by presenting domestic animals to chiefs, or their wives, and by appointing missionaries to live among the tribes with tools and stock.[4] Subsequent secretaries elaborated the plan: Indians should receive plows and hoes to encourage them to farm; both academic and vocational education would make them better farmers; and their adoption of regular laws would protect their property. Eventually each family should be allotted a farm it could own exclusively. Various officials differed as to whether education, tools, and stock, or laws took precedence in the process. They nearly all agreed, however, on the centrality of private property as an inducement to laborious and cultivated living. T. Hartley Crawford, Van Buren's commissioner of Indian Affairs, argued that "at the foundation of the whole social system lies individual property. It is, perhaps nine times in ten, the stimulus that manhood first feels. It has produced the energy, industry, and enterprise that distinguish the civilized world. . . . With it come all the delights that the word home expresses. . . ."[5]

Ironically, the man who proposed so abrupt a transition from property to domestic delight proved the first and indeed the only commissioner of his era to give more than passing attention to the civilizing role of women. By contrast, Lewis Cass and William Clark in their comprehensive proposal of 1829 for the reformation of Indian policy dismissed the distaff contribution in a sentence: "The females will learn sewing, spinning, and weaving, and the making of useful garments."[6]

Crawford, a Pennsylvania politician who had taken an active part in the legislative establishment of his state's school system, expatiated at length in two annual reports on the importance of educating at least as many Indian girls as Indian boys: "Unless the Indian female character is raised, and her relative position changed, such education as you can give the males will be a rope of sand. . . . Necessity may force the culture of a little ground, or the keeping of a few cattle, but the savage nature will break out at every temptation. If the women are made good industrious housewives, and taught what befits their condition, their husbands and sons will find comfortable homes and social enjoyments, which, in any state of society, are essential to morality and thrift. . . . [Educated women] will acquire influence and weight, and must form, in good degree, there as elsewhere, the characters of their children. . . ."[7]

Crawford's brief tenure of the Indian Office offers the sole example, in the antebellum period, of official adoption of the ideology of domestic feminism. But agents in the field, and especially Christian missionaries, paid closer attention to the education of females and to inducing change in family structure, family life, and the division of labor between the sexes. An outstanding illustration of their concern for modifying sex role definitions can be found in the work of U.S. agents and Presbyterian-Congregationalist missionaries among that exemplary "civilized tribe," the Cherokee.

Like most eastern tribes, the Cherokee of the southern Appalachian region had been so far drawn into the international trade in skins and furs that they had become dependent on that trade for weapons, tools, clothing, and cosmetics.[8] As the supply of game diminished, they sought other means to get the kettles, guns, cloth, and vermilion their deerskins had brought them. Cloth proved an especially significant item, for many Cherokee were fond of elegant dress. Moreover, their yearly "conciliation" ceremony entailed — among other activities — going into the river, letting their old clothes float downstream, and emerging to put on new clothes and a fresh outlook.[9] Consequently, when President Washington proposed to give them spinning wheels and looms, they welcomed the gift. Benjamin Hawkins, the first U.S. agent to the southern tribes, and his assistant Silas Dinsmoor, found many women eager to receive implements and instruction.[10] Although some hunters initially opposed gifts that might make their wives oppressively independent, the agents found Cherokee men easy to convert. One, Bold Hunter by name, returned from a disappointing winter in the woods to find that his wife and daughter had produced several dozen yards of cloth. According to legend, he remarked that "they had become better hunters than he — and took up the plow."[11]

Bold Hunter's was not the universal reaction. Rather, women generally took to cultivating cotton themselves, and they sent their town chiefs to the U.S. agency to demand increasing quantities of wheels, cards, and looms. By February 1805, Cherokee agent Return J. Meigs reported to Hawkins that raising cotton, spinning, and weaving were indeed carried on widely in Cherokee Nation, "but this is totally done by the females, who are not held in any degree of respectable estimation by the real Indian & therefore have no charms to tame the savage." The male savages had informed their agent that "they are favorites of the great Spirit & that he never intended they should live the laborious lives of whites."[12]

So impressed was Meigs by the "industriousness" of the female Cherokee that he actively encouraged their marriages to neighboring white men. He hoped such men in turn might set good examples for the "indolent" Indian males.[13] If we may judge from the Cherokee census of 1835, such men at least found imitators among their mix-blood sons, hundreds of whom became managers of extensive farms and plantations.[14] The wealthiest also acquired over twelve hundred slaves as early as 1825. By the indirect but highly effective route of intermarriage, Cherokee women contributed substantially to the growing agricultural wealth of the tribe and to the production of an elite whose activity on behalf of modernizing tribal institutions gave the Cherokee Nation its preeminence among the "civilized tribes."[16]

Yet throughout Meigs's tenure as Cherokee agent (1801-1823), he continued to complain of Cherokee "indolence." Of course, he defined dancing all night as dissipation rather than effort. Moreover, he shared with all the officials of his generation the tacit assumption that societies in which males hunted and females farmed were "hunting" societies; and towns where women hoed corn during the day while men smoked, conferred, and slept, were "abodes of indolence." In truth, Meigs did not need to promote agriculture as such among the Cherokee, whose women had cultivated corn, beans, squash, and pumpkins for centuries. But Meigs required a man behind a plow to define his tribe as a "nation of farmers." So he gave away plows. By 1811 he estimated that approximately five hundred of these critical implements had found their way among the tribe's farmers. This would amount to approximately one plow for every four or five (nuclear) families.[18]

In many parts of the world, the introduction of the plow has fostered a transition from female to male agriculture.[19] In the long run, the Cherokee proved no exception. No tradition proscribed male participation in agricultural work. William Bartram, writing in the 1770s, insists that men did most of the "hard labor" on Cherokee fields. Certainly they normally participated in preparing the ground and harvesting the crop; neither of these activities occurred during the principal hunting season. One may reasonably suppose a period of transition in which men prepared the fields by plowing that eliminated weeds and thus made subsequent cultivation less time-consuming for whoever happened to wield the hoe.[20]

Many material and technical innovations that whites introduced lightened the burden of female labor without greatly augmenting the amount of agricultural labor required of males. Cloth was easier to work into garments than skins; iron pots and kettles relieved the potter; gristmills saved women the labor of grinding corn into meal. At the same time, men came at least partially to substitute stock-raising for hunting as a source of meat. Their search for grazing land led them to disperse their settlements, and in the nineteenth century the Cherokee found no need to work in groups to protect themselves against military attack. By the mid-1820s, a town field worked collectively "at the mother's side" was a rarity.[21] Thus a variety of influences molded the Cherokee pattern of farming on the model of the white. Variations in individual taste for "leisure" time activity meant that some expanded their fields and improved the elegance of their households, while those who preferred playing ball, watching ball-games, gossiping, and all-night dancing combined with daytime rest maintained their reputations for "indolence."

Intermarriage, the rise to social prominence and political power of a mix-blood elite of planters, merchants, millers, and ferry-keepers, and the shift to male agriculture changed the status as well as the work of Cherokee women. Tradition-

(pages 102-105) Petition to preserve Hopi matriarchal landholding. Efforts to "civilize" the Indian continued throughout the nineteenth and early twentieth centuries. In 1887 the Dawes Act sought to accelerate the process of changing him from a hunter to a farmer by breaking up tribal lands into individual allotments. The Hopi of Arizona, who were already engaged in agriculture, feared that their laws of inheritance were about to be set aside. There is no record of a direct response to this petition, but the lands of the Southwest Indians were not allotted.

(Hopi Indian Petition, March 27-28, 1894, No. 14830, Letters Received, 1881-1907, Records of the Bureau of Indian Affairs, RG 75.)

Moqui Villages 2728
Arizona March 1894

To the Washington Chiefs:

During the last two years strangers have looked over our land with spy-glasses and made marks upon it, and we know but little of what this means. As we believe that you have no wish to disturb our possessions, we want to tell you something about this Hopi land.

None of us were asked that it should be measured into separate lots, and given to individuals for this would cause confusion.

The family, the dwelling house and the field are inseparable, because the woman is the heart of these, and they rest with her. Among us the family traces its kin from the mother, hence all its possessions are hers. The man builds the house but the woman is the owner, because she repairs and preserves it; the man cultivates the field, but he renders its harvest into the woman's keeping, because upon her it rests to prepare the food, and the surplus of stores for barter depends upon her thrift.

A man plants the fields of his wife, and the fields assigned to the children she bears, and informally he calls them his, although in fact they are not. Even of the field which he inherits from his mother, its harvest he may dispose of at will, but the field itself he may not.

He may permit his son to occupy it and gather its produce, but at the father's death the son may

—1—

not own it, for then it passes to the father's sister's son, or nearest mother's kin, and thus our fields and houses always remain with our mother's family.

According to the number of children a woman has, fields for them are assigned to her, from some of the lands of her family group, and her husband takes care of them. Hence our fields are numerous but small, and several belonging to the same family may be close together, or they may be miles apart, because arable localities are not continuous. There are other reasons for the irreg-ularity in size and situation of our family lands, as interrupted sequence of inheritance caused by extinction of families, but chiefly owing to the following condition, and to which we especially invite your attention.

In the Spring and early Summer there usually comes from the Southwest a succession of gales, oftentimes strong enough to blow away the sandy soil from the face of some of our fields, and to expose the underlying clay, which is hard, and sour, and barren; as the sand is the only fertile land, when it moves, the planters must follow it, and other fields must be provided in place of those which have been devastated. Sometimes generations pass away and these barren spots remain, while in other instances, after a few years, the winds have again restored the desirable sand upon them. In such event its fertility is disclosed by the nature of the grass and shrubs that grow upon it. If these are promising, a number of us unite to

clear off the land and make it again fit for
planting, when it may be given back to its former
owner, or if a long time has elapsed, to other heirs,
or it may be given to some person of the same
family group, more in need of a planting place.

These limited changes in land holding are
effected by mutual discussion and concession
among the elders, and among all the thinking
men and women of the family groups interested.

In effect, the same system of holding, and the
same method of planting, obtain among the Tewa,
and all the Hopi villages, and under them we
provide ourselves with food in abundance.

The American is our elder brother, and in
everything he can teach us, except in the method
of growing corn in these waterless sandy valleys,
and in that we are sure we can teach him.

We believe that you have no desire to change our
system of small holdings, nor do we think
that you wish to remove any of our ancient
landmarks, and it seems to us that the
conditions we have mentioned afford sufficient
grounds for this requesting to be left undisturbed.

Further it has been told to us, as coming
from Washington, that neither measuring nor
individual papers are necessary for us to keep
possession of our villages, our peach orchards
and our springs. If this be so, we should like
to ask what need there is to bring confusion into
our accustomed system of holding corn fields.

We are aware that some ten years ago

a certain area around our lands was proclaimed
to be for our use, but the extent of this area is
unknown to us, nor has any Agent ever been able
to found it out, for its boundaries have never
been measured. We most earnestly desire to have
one continuous boundary ring enclosing all the
Tewa and all the Hopi lands, and that it shall
be large enough to afford sustenance for our
increasing flocks and herds. If such a scope can
be conformed to us by a paper from your hands,
securing us forever against intrusion, all our
people will be satisfied:

1. Há-nyi of A-la. (Walpi)
2. Ho-ni of Icüa (Walpi)
3. Wü-nü-tca of Pá-kab (Walpi)
4. Na-syün-we-ve of Ka-Kop (Walpi)
5. Ona-wi-ta of Pat-Ki (Sitcomovi)
6. Intiwa of Ka-tci-na (Walpi)
7. Tü-wás-mi of Pa-Kab (Walpi)
8. Ha-ni of Pi-ba (Walpi)
9. Syün-o-i-tü-wa of Ica-Kwai-na (Walpi)
10. Supela of Pat-Ki (Walpi)
11. Kwa-tca-Kwa of Pat-Ki (Walpi)
12. Tü-ni-ma of Ho-ná-ni (Sitcomovi)
13. Po-la-Ka-Ka of Ku-lon-to-wa

14. Kwa-la-Kwai of O-Kü-wa tc-wa (Té-wa)
15. Ka-nü of Pa-Kab-nyá-mü (Walpi)
16.
17. Lo-ma-nak-cü of Tü-wa (Mü-con-inovi)
18. Pa-lün-au-üh of Ká-la (Cipaulovi)
19. Si-Kyá-hon-ava of Katcina (Mü-con-in-ovi)
20. Kwa-vi-o-ma of Cya-zro (Mü-con-in-ovi)
21. Ta-las-yau-ma of Pa-tüña (Mü-con-in-ovi)
22. of Kwá-hü (Mü-con-in-ovi)

ally, they attended village council meetings and exercised at least indirect influence upon their deliberations. Women held two important councils of their own during a critical controversy over the proposed removal of the tribe in 1817 and 1818. The first such council firmly admonished the males against selling land that belonged to women and children; it precipitated the formation of a constitutional law that for the first time carefully defined and restricted the agencies of tribal government who might negotiate for the sale of the tribe's land. Yet the more famous and more comprehensive Cherokee constitution of 1827 disfranchised women.[23]

Since Cherokee law awarded land to those who cultivated it, women who did not farm no longer "owned" the family homestead. The first recorded law of the tribe (1808) provided for the possibility of inheritance through the male line. Long-term shifts from matrilineal to patrilineal inheritance patterns and from lineal to generational definitions of "kin" are reflected in gradual changes in kinship terminology. As early as 1829, the Cherokee *Phoenix* reported that prohibitions against marrying members of the parents' clans could be disregarded with impunity.[24]

Despite far-reaching changes in women's political and economic status, and shifts in the direction of patrilineal and patriarchal family structures, Cherokee legislation continued to protect the economic status of women who farmed or directed slaves in farming. A woman's husband could not control her property; no one could levy on her property to pay his debts. Widowers, or widows, and children each enjoyed an equal claim on the property of an intestate parent.

While U.S. agents and male Cherokee legislators focused their attention on matters of property and contract, missionaries who managed educational institutions in the Nation concerned themselves with the subtler nuances of the female role.[26] Their main object was to convert the heathen, but they believed that a common school English education and vocational training would reinforce Christian professions with the practical values of the Puritan ethic. Missionaries of the American Board of Commissioners of Foreign Missions proved especially active in establishing schools where both boys and girls boarded with missionary families. The girls learned to read, write, cypher, and reproduce Bible verses and responses to the catechism. They spun, wove, quilted, made clothing, and did household chores. Several young Cherokee women who studied grammar, geography, and fancy sewing became teachers. All the young women learned to set a proper table, and to display neatness, reserve, and modesty — or so their teachers hoped. Yet as Presbyterians viewed Cherokee culture, neatness, reserve, and modesty ran counter to the grain of common practice.

The responsible and independent economic position of the traditional Cherokee woman, together with the importance the society accorded to avoiding direct interpersonal conflict, produced marital and family relations different from those the missionaries found respectable. The Cherokee accorded little importance to premarital chastity. Their custom prescribed "joking" relationships among persons of similar age whose paternal or maternal grandfathers belonged to the same clan. Frequent social and ceremonial dances — which might last all night —

provided appropriate occasions on which young people were expected to tease, tickle, and exchange clothing with members of the opposite sex and appropriate clan. Through such acquaintance the young man could place himself in a situation to obey his father's jokingly serious injunction: "You must marry my aunt."[27]

The young peoples' carefully prescribed behavior appeared to missionaries as merely promiscuous, and in truth obscene. They expelled students and suspended church communicants for sexual experimentation, and even for attendance at ball-plays and all-night dances.[28] They explained to young women that only decorous behavior would attract cultivated young men — and bemoaned the attractiveness of their cultivated and well-dressed young women who left the mission's watchful supervision without having internalized the code of respectability.[29] They encouraged Christian marriage and deplored the traditional custom of divorce at the will of either partner. By keeping the young people unremittingly at work and beating them when they misbehaved, they set an example of the "family government" they hoped to substitute for the subtler disciplinary methods of the Cherokee. Though missionary correspondence reflects much heart-burning and discouragement, they frequently hoped to succeed.[30] The Cherokee National Council offered an appreciation of their efforts by outlawing polygamy, though the law carried no penalty. More seriously, the council provided severe penalties for abortion, a practice traditional society had left to the mother's discretion.[32]

Although they accepted children of the poor, and proved especially hospitable to orphans, the American Board schools self-consciously focused their efforts on training children of the tribal elite. As the board's corresponding secretary, Jeremiah Evarts, informed a member of the Cherokee mission in 1827, "It is of great consequence to have the females of the principal families well instructed. In this way only will education become popular & fashionable." Certainly education became "popular and fashionable" among the Cherokee, who established their own public school system at a time when other states in the South had none. A law of 1851 also established seminaries — one for males, another for females. Just how much this concern for learning and female education attests to female domestication and influence remains conjectural. Certainly both female education and the values it sought to inculcate both reflected and reinforced the social class divisions that burgeoning wealth had created within the tribe.

One can no more judge behavior by propaganda among the Cherokee than one can read the lives of children in antebellum New York and Philadelphia from the manuals directed to their parents. Nor can one derive much direct information about role changes from objective data that seems to suggest them. Hence, the changes in female roles we can identify through archival sources perhaps raise as many questions as they resolve. Censuses and records of claims for lost property give an impressive measure of the diffusion of plows, spinning wheels, delft pottery, and teaspoons throughout the Cherokee Nation by the fourth decade of the nineteenth century.[34] They cannot tell us definitively the proportions of male and female participation in agriculture, or whether most families ate from delft or merely exhibited it. Agency and missionary archives, Cherokee legal records, and the field reports of modern anthropologists indicate the directions of cultural changes in female roles we can identify through archival sources perhaps raise as establishing patrilineal and patriarchal norms.[35] They do not tell us to what extent and with what results fathers replaced mothers' brothers as disciplinary authorities — though a change in kinship terminology to designate "mother's brothers" as "step-fathers" is suggestive.[36] Nor do the records indicate how far "family government" among the Cherokee approached the rigor of the missionary model. Did industrious and enlightened mothers commend "industry" to their sons? How? With what results? We cannot be sure.

Nor do I seek to leave the impression that the Cherokee experience was "typical" rather than "exemplary." Instead, I intend to suggest some questions that agency records, in combination with other sources may answer; what further questions they raise; and perhaps what further explorations in archival materials may contribute to the comparative study of both the expected and the actual roles of women in the modernization of Native American societies.

NOTES

1. Barbara Welter, "The Cult of True Womanhood, 1820-1860," *American Quarterly* 18 (1966): 151-74; Gerda Lerner, "The Lady and the Mill Girl: Changes in the Status of Women in the Age of Jackson," *Midcontinent American Studies Journal* 10 (1969); Glenda L. Riley, "The Subtle Subversion: Changes in the Traditionalist Image of American Woman," *Historian* 32 (1970): 210-27; William R. Taylor, *Cavalier and Yankee: The Old South and American National Character* (New York: George Braziller, 1961); Kathryn Kish Sklar, *Catherine Beecher: A Study in American Domesticity* (New Haven: Yale University Press, 1973).
2. Elizabeth Fox-Genovese, "The Paradoxical Paradigm: The Domestic Origins of Bourgeois Ideology," delivered before the Union of Radical Political Economists, New Brunswick, New Jersey, 22 March 1976.
3. Mary Elizabeth Young, *Redskins, Ruffleshirts, and Rednecks: Indian Allotments in Alabama and Mississippi, 1830-1860* (Norman: University of Oklahoma Press, 1961).
4. Knox to Washington, 17 July 1789, *American State Papers: Indian Affairs* 1: 53-54.
5. Crawford to Poinsett, 25 November 1838, *New American State Papers: Indian Affairs* 1: 512 (hereafter cited as *NASPIA*).
6. Cass and Clark to Porter, 2 February 1829, *NASPIA*, 1: 151.
7. Crawford to Poinsett, 5 November 1839, *NASPIA*, p. 594. For Crawford's background, see Ronald N. Satz, *American Indian Policy in the Jacksonian Era* (Lincoln: University of Nebraska Press, 1975), p. 259.
8. David H. Corkran, *The Cherokee Frontier: Conflict and Survival, 1740-62* (Norman: University of Oklahoma Press, 1962).
9. Fred O. Gearing, *Priests and Warriors: Social Structure for Cherokee Politics in the 18th Century, Memoirs of the American Anthropological Association* 64, no. 5, pt. 2 (October 1962): 3-4.

10. Benjamin Hawkins, *A Sketch of the Creek Country in the Years 1798 and 1799* (New York: Kraus Reprint Corp., 1971); Hawkins, "A Sketch of the Present State of the Objects under the Charge of the Principal Agent for Indian Affairs South of Ohio," 8 December 1801, *NASPIA,* 5: 176.

11. John Ridge to Albert Gallatin, 27 February 1826, John Howard Payne Transcripts, 8: 103, Newberry Library, Chicago, Illinois.

12. Meigs to Hawkins, 15 February 1805, Records of the Cherokee Indian Agency in Tennessee, vol. 3, Records of the Bureau of Indian Affairs, Record Group 75, National Archives Building, National Archives Microfilm Publication M208 (hereafter cited as RG __, NA __, M __). Compare Meigs, Journal of Occurrences in the Cherokee Nation, 1802, ibid., vol. 1, M208.

13. Meigs to Chulio, draft, 14 March 1808, vol. 4, RG 75, NA, M208.

14. Census Roll, 1835, of the Cherokee Indians East of the Mississippi and Index to the Roll, RG 75, NA, T496.

15. McKenney to Barbour, 13 December 1825, Letters Sent by the Office of Indian Affairs, 1824-1881, vol. 2, p. 298, RG 75, NA, M21.

16. The most recent of many fine works on the subject is Thurman Wilkins, *Cherokee Tragedy: The Story of the Ridge Family and the Decimation of a People* (New York: Macmillan, 1970).

17. For example, Meigs to Dearborn, 3 June 1808, Records of the Cherokee Indian Agency in Tennessee, 1801-35, vol. 4, M208; Meigs to Eustis, 5 April 1811, ibid., vol. 5, M208.

18. Meigs to Eustis, 10 May 1811, ibid. I have computed the rough proportions by dividing the census figures for 1809 (Meigs to Lee, 11 March 1820, ibid., vol. 8) by the average family size reported in the census for 1835.

19. Esther Boserup, *Woman's Role in Economic Development* (New York: St. Martins Press, 1970), pp. 15-25.

20. Compare William Bartram, "Observations on the Creek and Cherokee Indians, 1789," *American Ethnological Society* 3, pt. 1 (1858): 30-33; Gearing, *Priests and Warriors,* pp. 2, 3; Boserup, *Woman's Role in Economic Development.* Obviously the pace, extent, and manner by which the introduction of the plow leads to change in sex roles in agriculture will vary according to the social situation of the groups involved. On this point in general, see Claude Meillassoux, *Femmes, Greniers, & Capitaux* (Paris: Maspero, 1975), p. 64.

21. Ridge to Gallatin, John Howard Payne Transcripts; Ridge's observation is borne out by the various records of Cherokee claims for farm improvement in RG 75, NA. On the impact of stockraising, see Hawkins, *A Sketch of the Creek Country.*

22. On household matters, see Chamberlain to Greene, 21 February 1832, Records of the American Board of Commissioners for Foreign Missions, ABC 18.3.1, vol. 7, Houghton Library, Harvard University, Cambridge, Massachusetts.

23. On the women's councils, see "Address of Women at Amoiah Council," 2 May 1817, Andrew Jackson Papers, Library of Congress Microfilm, reel 22; and Journal of the Cherokee Mission, 30 June 1818, ABC 18.3.1. On changes in women's political role and legal status, see Rennard Strickland, *Fire and the Spirits: Cherokee Law from Clan to Court* (Norman: University of Oklahoma Press, 1975).

24. *Laws of the Cherokee Nation, Adopted by the Council at Various Periods* (Tahlequah: Cherokee Nation Press, 1852), pp. 3-4; Fred Eggan, *The American Indian: Perspectives for Study of Social Change* (Chicago: Aldine Publishing Co., 1966), pp. 31-39;

Cherokee *Phoenix* 1 (February 1829): 49. (Microfilm edition, Western Historical Collections, University of Oklahoma).

25. See, in general, Strickland, *Fire and the Spirits: Laws of the Cherokee Nation,* 6 May 1817, pp. 3-4; 2 November 1819, p. 10; 9 November 1826, p. 82; 2 November 1829, pp. 142-43.

26. On the missionary subculture and its special sensitivities, see Robert F. Berkhofer, Jr., *Salvation and the Savage: An Analysis of Protestant Missions and American Indian Response, 1789-1862* (Lexington: University of Kentucky Press, 1965).

27. W.H. Gilbert, Jr., "Eastern Cherokee Social Organization," in Fred Eggan, ed., *Social Anthropology of the North American Tribes* (Chicago: University of Chicago Press, 1955), pp. 285-340.

28. Mary Young, "Indian Removal and the Attack on Tribal Autonomy: The Cherokee Case," in John K. Mahon, ed., *Indians of the Lower South: Past and Present* (Gainesville: University of Florida Press, 1975), pp. 129-30.

29. Sawyer to Evarts, 21 August 1824, ABC 18.3.1, vol. 5; Sawyer to Greene, 6 July 1833, ibid., vol. 8.

30. Kingsbury, Hall, and Williams to Worcester, 25 November 1817, ibid., vol. 2; Journal of the Cherokee Mission, 21 January 1819, ibid., vol. 8; Chamberlain to Evarts, 30 July 1824, ibid., vol. 4; Chamberlain to Wisner, 4 June 1833, ibid., vol. 9.

31. *Laws of the Cherokee Nation,* 11 November 1825, p. 58; ibid., 16 October 1826, p. 79.

32. Evarts to Proctor, 3 January 1827, ABC 1.01. vol. 6: 21.

33. Grace Steele Woodward, *The Cherokee* (Norman: University of Oklahoma Press, 1963); Althea Bass, *Cherokee Messenger* (Norman: University of Oklahoma Press, 1936).

34. For claims, see the records of the Board of Cherokee Commissioners, RG 75, NA; Cherokee Collection, Tennessee Department of Archives and History, Nashville; John Ross Papers, Gilcrease Institute, Tulsa, Oklahoma.

35. In addition to the works of Eggan and Gilbert, cited above, see Leonard Bloom, "The Cherokee Clan: A Study in Acculturation," *American Anthropologist* 41 (1939): 266-68; and John Gulick, "Language and Passive Resistance among the Eastern Cherokees," *Ethnohistory* 5 (1958): 64.

36. Eggan, *The American Indian,* p. 21.

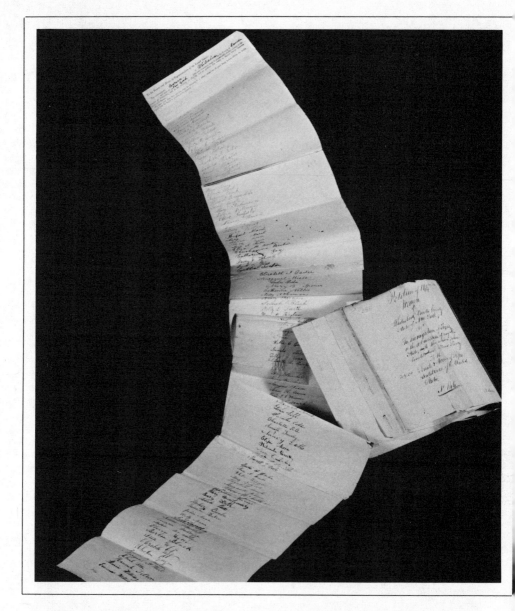

Women's antislavery petitions. The twenty-fifth Congress, elected in 1838, received two petitions from the women of Whitesboro expressing their opinions on two different aspects of the slavery question. The petitions were folded for filing, and a label or "endorsement" on the outside of the folded document allowed easy reference.
(Petition of 144 Women of Whitesboro, Oneida County, State of New York agt. the Annexation of Texas, and Petition of 147 Women of Whitesboro, Oneida County, State of New York For the Abolition of Slavery in the District of Columbia, File HR 25A-H1.8, Records of the U.S. House of Representatives, RG 233.)

WOMEN AND RADICAL REFORM IN ANTEBELLUM UPSTATE NEW YORK: A PROFILE OF GRASSROOTS FEMALE ABOLITIONISTS

Judith Wellman

Angelina Grimké, ex-southerner, ex-slaveholder, ex-Quaker, woman, and thoroughgoing abolitionist, believed with her sister, Sarah, that "whatever is *right* for man to do, is *right* for woman."[1] Accordingly, in the late winter of 1837 she spoke to a "mixed" audience of men and women at a public antislavery rally in Poughkeepsie, New York.

Though the actions of Angelina and Sarah Grimké roused a storm of hostility from conservative opponents, the American Antislavery Society itself, for the first time recognizing women abolitionists, gave warm support. In its *Fourth Annual Report*, published in 1837, the society gave "heartfelt thanks to God" for the work of the Grimkés. "Let them hold on their course till universal womanhood is rallied in behalf of the bleeding victims of wrong," the society urged.[2] Little did the

This paper is part of a larger study being conducted with support from the University Awards Committee of the State University of New York and the Family and Social History Program of the Newberry Library. Special thanks to the staff of the Family and Social History Program, and to Carol Kaulfuss, Patricia Ruppert, David Rowe, and Michael Haines for their assistance and advice.

society realize, perhaps, how seriously women would respond to this invitation. Nor did they realize how important the implications would be within a few short years for the organized abolitionist movement itself.

Even as the American Antislavery Society was meeting, several dozen women abolitionists in New York City were attending the first of three national women's antislavery conventions. There, it was clear that the Grimkés were not the only women active in the cause of abolition. Seventy-one women registered as delegates, almost half of them from New York City or Philadelphia, and 103 women listed themselves as corresponding members.[3]

But these women did not intend that abolitionist activities should be confined to themselves. The goal of the convention, as Sarah Grimké stated it, was much, much broader. It was, said Grimké, "to interest women in the subject of antislavery, and establish a system of operations throughout every town and village in the free states, that would exert a powerful influence in the abolition of American slavery."[4]

To accomplish this, the convention decided in part to publish an *Appeal to the Women of the Nominally Free States*. Released in 1838, this appeal asserted that:

the women of the North have high and holy duties to perform in the work of emancipation — duties to themselves, to the suffering slave, to the slaveholder, to the church, to their country, and to the world at large: and, above all, to their God. Duties which if not performed now, may never be performed at all.[5]

Others argued that women had quite different responsibilities. Woman's place was not in the world, some said, but in the home. And her basic allegiance was quite decidedly not to herself, the slave, the world, or to God but to her husband and her children. Anything less than total devotion to her family was an abrogation of the very definition of womanhood.

The appeal, however, was based on quite a different assumption. Uncompromisingly it addressed itself to women "on the broad ground of *human rights and human responsibilities*" and argued that "*all moral beings have essentially the same rights and the same duties,* whether they be male or female." Explicitly it denied that women's responsibilities lay first of all in maintaining family ties. Penetratingly it asked:

Are we aliens because we are women? Are we bereft of citizenship because we are the *mothers, wives,* and *daughters* of a mighty people? Have women no country — no interest staked in public weal — no liabilities in common-peril — no partnership in a nation's guilt and shame?[6]

For the authors of the appeal, these questions were obviously rhetorical. The real query was directed toward action. As mothers, wives, and daughters — who were, above all, moral and responsible citizens — what could they do for the slave? The question, no sooner asked, was answered. First, suggested the appeal, women could organize themselves into antislavery societies. They could then read about slavery, informing themselves and sharing their information with others. They could refuse to use slave-grown products. They could work to eradicate within themselves the terrible sin of race prejudice, reaching out to and identifying with "our oppressed colored sisters." And last, a point that was to be emphasized over and over again, they could send antislavery petitions to Congress.[7]

As petitioners women would join with men in what was one of the largest reform campaigns of the nineteenth century. Beginning in 1835, abolitionists sent petitions to Congress literally by the thousands. Deluged with an avalanche of paper about a topic so sensitive, the House responded with a series of "gag" rules, which they passed annually from 1836 to 1844. These gag rules automatically tabled all petitions relating to abolition and so provided the abolitionists with a far more appealing argument than they themselves could ever have devised alone. Abolition became identified in the public mind with the right of free speech, with freedom therefore for northern whites as well as southern blacks. And far from discouraging the petitioners, the gag rule provided added incentive. By 1838 so many petitions had arrived in Washington that they entirely filled a room 20 by 30 feet, packed to the ceiling.[8]

Today these petitions are in the National Archives. Almost all of them were folded to a size of 3 by 8½ inches and gathered in bundles for filing. Most of them bear an endorsement indicating the type of petition, often the number of signers, the date, the name of the person who presented it, and the action taken upon it.[9] These petitions are obviously a primary source — perhaps the primary source — for understanding not what abolitionist leaders on a national or state level wanted people to do, but what they actually did do. In particular, they allow us to explore, as no other source does, the extent to which women were actively involved in the abolitionist movement.[10]

One could, of course, treat these petitions as literary evidence, looking specifically at the content of their requests. I would like to treat them here, however, rather as nonliterary artifacts, and — borrowing some general techniques from geographers and anthropologists — to trace the geographic origins of these petitions in one small, but perhaps for our purposes a particularly significant, area of the country, upstate New York, in 1838-39 and 1850-51.

I chose to focus on the years 1838-39 for several reasons.[11] First, while most of the petitions sent to Congress before 1840 apparently were kept, many of those sent afterwards were destroyed.[12] So 1838-39 may be one of the few years for which a relatively complete set of petitions exists.

Second, the period was crucial for defining the position of women within the abolitionist movement itself. Female abolitionists, particularly in Philadelphia and Boston, had begun to organize and to exhort other women to action. The women's antislavery conventions of 1837, 1838, and 1839 are only one example of their work. Presumably, by 1838-39 women abolitionists on a local level were in part responding to, and were almost certainly encouraged by, this call for action from national leaders. And while women's activity, particularly women's public speaking, met almost immediate resistance, the official stand of the American Antislavery Society remained mildly positive until the annual meeting of May 1839. The petition movement of 1838-39 would therefore perhaps be less affected by adverse reaction from within the abolitionist movement itself than it would be after the official split in 1840.

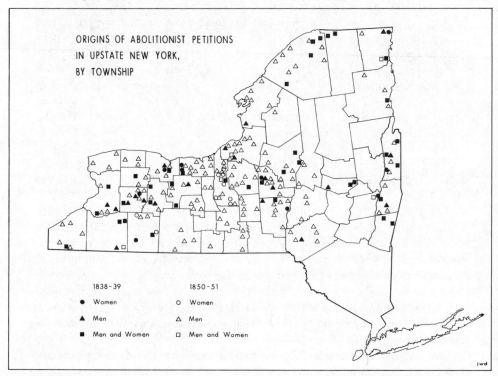

ORIGINS OF ABOLITIONIST PETITIONS
IN UPSTATE NEW YORK,
BY TOWNSHIP

1838-39	1850-51
● Women	○ Women
▲ Men	△ Men
■ Men and Women	□ Men and Women

Third, in 1838-39 prime responsibility for maintaining the forward thrust of the movement shifted from a national to a local level. As a result of the panic of 1837, the American Antislavery Society had withdrawn most of its paid agents from the field. But unlike many reform organizations (the American Sunday School Union, for example), which severely curtailed their activities after 1837, the abolitionist movement continued to exert a powerful influence in public affairs. And it did so because state and local antislavery societies assumed the burden of financial support and decision-making which the national society could no longer sustain.

In New York State, the Executive Committee of the New York State Antislavery Society clearly emphasized and reemphasized that the real strength of the abolitionist movement lay in individual action on a local level. National societies are not ''self-moved and self-moving machines,'' the committee stressed in 1838. Indeed,

there seems abundant cause to fear that *individual responsibility, and personal effort,* and local operation, and patient, *persevering industry* and attention to *minute detail,* are becoming too little appreciated in these days of extensive associated effort.[13]

They reminded town antislavery societies that "abolitionists have relied upon agents and lecturers to do the great work of the antislavery reformation, seeming to forget how much they, as individuals, can and must perform in their own towns, if they ever expect to see the slave enjoy his liberty."[14] "Local work cannot be done by the great central committees," the society reiterated in 1839, "whether State or National, whether located at Utica or New York. Yet the nation is made up of localities; and *local* effort everywhere existing, is the whole work we wish and need to have accomplished."[15]

In this shift to local action, the petitions proved an ideal vehicle for implementing local activity. Not only did petitions force congressional attention on abolition; they also forced abolitionists to confront their own neighbors with carefully constructed antislavery arguments. Collecting names for petitions thus became a perennial duty for local antislavery societies.

In 1839 the women attending the Third Antislavery Convention of American Women, held in Philadelphia in May, echoed this emphasis on local petition activity, highlighting the importance of *women's* activity. In a circular published by the convention, the women argued that the circulation of petitions was "peculiarly incumbent" upon women. "It is," they declared,

> our only means of direct political action. It is not ours to fill the offices of government, or to assist in the election of those who shall fill them. We do not enact or enforce the laws of the land. The only direct influence which we can exert upon our Legislatures, is by protests and petitions. Shall we not, then be greatly delinquent if we neglect *these?*
>
> We shall not be suspected of party motives . . . . They will believe in our *sincerity,* and this belief will be greatly advantageous to the success of our memorials.[16]

"We know, dear sisters, that this is a weary work," they admitted. "We have deeply felt the difficulties and trials that attend it. We know how painful it is to endure the scornful gaze, or rude repulses of strangers. . . ." Yet such was the importance of the task that they asked each woman, if it were at all in her power, not only to sign antislavery petitions but to circulate them. "It may be that from the heavy pressure of domestic duties, or from other causes, you are not able to spend even an occasional hour in pleading the cause of the slave among your friends and neighbors," they acknowledged. But,

> we would only suggest that before making such a decision, you will, as nearly as possible, place your soul "in his soul's stead." Let the mother gather her children about her, and see them seized, sold, and driven away to southern markets and plantations, there to spend their lives in mental and moral degradation, that they may minister to the avarice and ambition of taskmasters, whose "tender mercies are cruel!" Let the daughter and the

sister imagine to themselves a home made desolate by slavery's polluting touch, — let us all endeavor, for a few hours at least, to "remember those in bonds as *bound with them,"* and then answer the question, Shall I circulate an antislavery petition?[17]

For many women, the answer was an obvious "yes."[18] Their diligence was rewarded by the number of names they collected on a variety of petitions. Titus Gilbert, writing to Gerrit Smith from Siloam, New York, in 1845, half apologized for his own efforts, compared to those of his daughter. "I think I might have obtained the names of men enough to equal those of the women," he explained, "had I taken as much pains to seek for them as my daughter Caroline did for women's names."[19]

So successful were the efforts of women that in 1838-39, of the 304 petitions sent to Congress from upstate New York that were identifiable by sex, 14.5 percent (44) were signed by women alone and 54.9 percent (167) were signed by men and women together. Thus, women, either alone or with men, signed almost 70 percent (69.4 percent) of the petitions received by Congress in those years (Table 1).[20]

From what kinds of places did these petitions originate in 1838-39? In particular, what, if anything, distinguished those townships that sent petitions signed by women either alone or with men from those townships that sent petitions signed by men only? And in turn, how were those townships different from those that sent petitions only in 1850-51 and from those that sent no petitions at all?

Table 1
DISTRIBUTION OF EXTANT PETITIONS IDENTIFIABLE BY SEX OF SIGNERS

Year	Men	Women	Men and Women	Total Signed by Women	Total
1838-39	93 (30.6%)	44 (14.5%)	167 (54.9%)	211 (69.4%)	304
1850-51	511 (97.7%)	0	0	12 (2.3%)	12 (2.3%)	523

Implicit in these questions is the assumption that, to some extent at least, the abolitionist movement was a community affair, and that community institutions were one of the main avenues by which abolitionist activity was sustained. A study of the presence or absence of certain kinds of institutions or certain large aggregates of people should therefore provide some clue as to why abolitionism flourished in some areas and not in others. The intent here is not to perpetuate an ecological fallacy but to help define the question more clearly and to suggest some potentially productive middle-level hypotheses for further exploration.

To begin to generate debate, I chose a sample of 115 townships from upstate New York, north of Dutchess County.[21] This sample included 79 townships that sent no petitions, 19 that sent them only in 1850-51, and 34 that sent petitions in 1838-39.[22]

Obviously, many variables may be important in explaining why certain communities generated abolitionist petitions and others did not. Place of birth, race, voting patterns, type of agricultural activity, location in relationship to major transportation routes, and so forth all suggest themselves for future research.

Much of the previous debate over the nature of Jacksonian reform, however (as well as over the nature of Jacksonian politics), has centered on the relative influence of economic vs. ethnocultural factors. I therefore chose for preliminary analysis two variables to act as broad indices of these two factors on the local level. One variable was the percentage of the work force in each township that in 1840 was employed in each sector of the economy. The other was the kind of churches each township contained in the early 1840s. For a third variable, I considered population size in 1840.

In terms of mean population, those townships that sent no abolitionist petitions were considerably lower in mean population in 1840 than either the 1838-39 townships or the 1850-51 townships — 1,992 for the nonabolitionist townships compared to 2,790 for the 1838-39 townships and 2,641 for the 1850-51 sample (Table 2). Abolitionist townships were thus comparatively well established and substantial rural areas.

Table 2

POPULATION AND OCCUPATIONAL TYPE, 1840 (Data from U.S. Census, 1840)

| | Number of Townships | Mean Population | Mean Population in Work Force | Percent of Work Force in | | | | |
				Agri-culture	Com-merce	Manu-facturing and Trade	Navi-gation	Professional
Sample Nonabolitionist Townships								
Total	79	1992.1	117	76.7	2.0	16.6	1.3	1.3
Sample Abolitionist Townships, 1838-39								
Men	9	2884	948	67.4	3.4	25.0	1.3	2.9
Men & Women	18	2461	741	77.4	1.3	18.7	.8	1.9
*Others	7	3514	967	59.3	1.5	29.9	1.7	1.9
Total	34	2790	842	70.2	1.9	23.2	1.1	2.2
Sample Abolitionist Townships, 1850-51								
Total	19	2641	693	77.2	2.8	17.1	1.0	1.9

*Includes those townships that sent petitions signed only by women, or those that sent more than one type of petition.

Agriculture was the main economic pursuit of citizens in all the townships. But, while more than three-quarters of the workers in both the nonabolitionist sample and the sample of 1850-51 were farmers, only 70.2 percent of those in the 1838-39 townships worked in agriculture. Correspondingly, a larger percentage of people in the abolitionist townships of 1838-39 worked in manufacturing and trade in 1840 than did those in either the 1850-51 abolitionist townships or the nonabolitionist townships.

The larger proportion of workers in manufacturing and trade in the 1838-39 townships may be simply a factor of township size. It also suggests, however, potentially more interesting correlations. Were abolitionists themselves, for example, closely associated with the manufacturing sector? And did "manufacturing" refer to preindustrial or industrial production? Neither of these questions can of course be answered completely with available township level data. Yet both of them appear to be important areas for further investigation.

To consider the patterns of religious organization within the townships, I enlarged the sample of 1838-39 abolitionist townships to include more than half the total number of abolitionist townships in those years (59 of 109), in order to provide a broader base for comparison of less common denominations (Table 3).[23] While conclusions must remain tentative at this point because of low sample size for some of the variables, preliminary analysis suggests some interesting but not altogether unexpected correlations. The number of Methodist churches per thousand population, for example, was relatively stable, whether townships did or did not generate petitions. But the number of Baptist, Congregational, Presbyterian, Episcopal, and Quaker organizations varied considerably.

In those townships that sent petitions signed by men only in 1838-39, there were fewer Baptist churches than in those townships that sent petitions signed by men and women together. The same pattern held true for the Quakers and the Presbyterians. This suggests, of course, that among these groups, women may have found greater acceptance for their own activism than they did where other denominations were strong. It also suggests that the Baptists may deserve more historiographical attention for their antislavery activism than they have generally received.

The pattern among Congregationalists was somewhat different. Townships that generated petitions in 1838-39, with both male signers alone and male and female signers together, had about twice as many Congregationalist churches per thousand people as did either the nonabolitionist townships or the townships that sent petitions in 1850-51. Congregationalist support for the petition campaign quite clearly waned in the 1840s, perhaps as a result of the changing nature of the abolitionist movement itself.

Among those townships with Episcopal churches, there was yet a third pattern. While townships that contained Episcopal churches often generated abolitionist petitions, they tended to produce petitions signed by men rather than by men and women together, raising questions about the position of women with the Episcopal church structure.

Table 3

NUMBER OF CHURCHES PER THOUSAND POPULATION BY DENOMINATION

Baptist	Methodist	Congre-gational	Presby-terian	Episcopal	Catholic	Quaker	Dutch	Universal-Unitarian
Sample Nonabolitionist Townships (N=79)								
.37	.50	.13	.30	.08	.05	.06	.10	.06
Sample Abolitionist Townships, 1838-39 *Men and Women signers (N=27)*								
.40	.49	.24	.34	.05	.07	.11	.07	.08
Sample Abolitionist Townships, 1838-39 *Men signers only (N=14)*								
.24	.48	.26	.19	.15	.02	.02	.11	.04
Sample Abolitionist Townships, 1850-51 (N=19)								
.39	.48	.10	.36	.12	.00	.02	.04	.10

Data on number of churches in each township is compiled from the New York State Census, 1845, and from [John Disturnell], *Gazetteer of the State of New York* (Albany, 1842).

Although the differences between abolitionist communities in 1838-39 and 1850-51 and the nonabolitionist townships are suggestive, perhaps the most dramatic results appear from a comparison of abolitionist activity, particularly women's abolitionist activity, over time. While the total number of petitions extant from 1850-51 is more than one and one-half times the number for 1838-39 (488 compared to 310), the percentage sent by women is astonishingly smaller. Women signed only 2.3 percent of the petitions extant for 1850-51, compared to the 69.4 percent they had signed in 1838-39. It is clear that by 1850 the petition campaign had shifted from a combined female-male effort to virtually an all-male effort.

The far broader participation in the petition movement by 1850-51 was primarily a response to the threatened passage of the Fugitive Slave Law. But what had happened between 1839 and 1850 that might explain the almost total lack of women's participation in the vast mass protest surrounding the Compromise of 1850?

I would suggest that women dropped out of the petition campaign primarily in response to changes that were taking place within the abolitionist movement itself in the late 1830s and early 1840s. So disruptive was the discord of this period that it split the American Antislavery Society itself apart in 1840. Chief among the crises were two — the question of the relationship of abolitionism to other reform causes, principally the cause of women's rights, and the question of political action.

The two issues were not unrelated. As large numbers of abolitionists moved away from moral suasion and toward political action, the opportunities for women to participate in the movement were drastically reduced. And as a corollary to this, there occurred a third and a parallel shift, one in which many abolitionists began to deemphasize moral absolutes, fostered and supported in particular local environments, and began instead to respond to secular political values, articulated at a state or national level.

In support of this argument, it is clear, first of all, that the abolitionists of the 1830s were motivated basically by moral considerations. Second, it is clear that the abolitionist movement of this period attracted earnest and highly committed women — and these in large numbers — as well as men. And third, it is clear that, at least in upstate New York, abolitionists strongly emphasized personal local action as their main source of sustenance.

Yet abolitionists of the 1830s, like other Americans, had become highly aware of themselves as members not only of local communities but of a national community. Influenced by the virtual revolutions in transportation and communication, these abolitionists viewed themselves not only as members of a moral Christian community, centered in a local church body, and not only as members of specific local political communities like Brighton, Salem, or Java, New York, but as citizens truly of a national America. As Christians, they owed their allegiance, as the delegates to the national women's antislavery convention in 1837 had reminded their sisters, not only to themselves but to God and the larger community. And as Americans of the 1830s, they defined that community in national terms. To that American national community they brought the same sense of moral and personal responsibility that they had nurtured in church and community on a local level.

In the late 1830s, it was this quality of the abolitionist movement, its definition of the nature of community as both moral and political, both local and national, which the petition campaign expressed so well. And it was precisely this quality that attracted women to it in such large numbers. As a moral campaign it could not deny women the right to participate. Yet to sign a petition to be sent to Congress itself meant unavoidably that women also participated in a political act, as citizens of a secular political unit. It was, thus, one of the few ways, perhaps the only way, that women could assert themselves as citizens of the United States of America.

Such political activism by women, however, inevitably caused repercussions. Some of these came from within the abolitionist movement itself. Charles Stuart, for example, British abolitionist, mentor of Theodore Weld, and in 1841 an abolitionist agent touring central New York, presented his own conservative views (presumably ones which he had also discussed with other abolitionists in New York State) in a private memorandum to Gerrit Smith, wealthy abolitionist of Peterboro, New York. Stuart, obviously in mental anguish over the question, carefully marshalled his arguments against women activists. "The consciences of abolitionists differ on the woman question," he wrote:

> Admitted — How do they differ? I suppose you have fairly expressed it. "The one part, thinks it *not right,* for women to mingle with men in public debate." I am of this part. The other party, "believe that women can properly participate with men in public debate." With this party, you agree.
>
> Now between the two modes of conscience, is there not this obvious difference — that the one party believes the matter to be more fundamental to morality, than the other does, that the one party could not abandon its ground, without transgressing *right,* in its view — while the other party, would only transgress *propriety* in its view, by quitting its ground? . . .
>
> Now, I do fully believe, that I should transgress God's clearly revealed will, and should be at war with God's structure of human nature, could I admit, in *general* terms, as you affirm it "the propriety of women's participating, with me, in public debate;" and I therefore could not assent to this proposition without trampling my conscience in the dust.[24]

Such were the arguments that women, and men who supported their public activity, faced.

There is other scattered evidence that at least some upstate male abolitionists were disturbed by the enthusiasm of their female compatriots. William I. Savage, for example, then an abolitionist agent in northern New York, reported his own views to the *Friend of Man*, the New York State abolitionist newspaper, in 1839. Enclosing a donation of $28 from the Champlain Female Antislavery Society (which the women had earned through the sale of articles they had sewn), Savage took the opportunity to discuss the "right or wrong" of public female antislavery activity:

> Much, you are aware, has been said against females forming societies, meeting together in public assemblies, and addressing them on this or any other subject. Now with regard to the right or wrong of this practice, I for one am perfectly willing to leave it to the conscience of each individual. But here is a practice (the one alluded to at the head of this article) against which no *reasonable* objection can be raised. We have had the decision of public opinion on this practice long since. Who ever objected to the practice of females meeting together to sew and raise funds for indigent pious students, in our theological and other seminaries? Who ever thought of raising the cry of "out of your sphere" when females exerted themselves in this way for the relief of the oppressed Poles? And who I ask, will dare to raise the almost sacrilegious cry of, out of your sphere, against females, or lay their polluted hands upon them, for endeavouring in this way to assist in abolishing slavery in our very midst? Not a *man* surely! Nothing is more in accordance with the strictest propriety, than this practice. My only wonder and astonishment is that it is not more universally adopted.[25]

Women abolitionists faced not only hostile or ambiguous responses from many males within the abolitionist movement; they also discovered that opponents of abolitionism used female petition activity to demean not only women petitioners but the cause of abolition as well. Congressman Roane of Virginia, for example, suggested that women petitioners were simply tools of "fanatical, vile, and designing men." Roane argued with great flourish that:

> it is utterly denied [by northern abolitionist sympathizers] that fanaticism constitutes any part of the spirit which actuates our Northern brethren, in thus eternally stirring a question which they must know is *vital* to us of the *South*. Oh, no — it is not fanaticism, it is not humanity, it is not philanthropy, but it is *patriotism!* It is only to assert and maintain inviolate the great right of petition! I perceive, sir, that one of the petitions presented this morning is signed by, I think, 111 women. Allow me to ask when before, on what other occasion, on what other great question, have the females thought it their imperious duty to step forth as the asserters and champions of the great right of petition? Allow me to believe, sir, that such a motive constituted no part of their feelings, never for one moment entered into their brain; no, sir, it is the *false* fire of philanthropy, so easily kindled in their warm and tender hearts, and too easily fanned into flame by fanatical, vile, and designing men.[26]

Such hostility both from within the abolitionist movement and from outside of it, led women in upstate New York virtually to withdraw from the petition campaign. By 1850 abolitionist petitions had clearly become primarily an avenue for the expression of male, not female, sentiment.

It was no coincidence that this shift away from active female participation in the petition campaign — and presumably from other areas of abolitionist activity as well — paralleled that other major readjustment within the abolitionist movement, the shift by many abolitionists away from moral suasion and toward political action. For with the emergence of political abolitionism, the responsibilities of citizenship were no longer defined as moral imperatives. And no longer was the national community conceptualized primarily in religious terms.

By 1850 the very definition of citizenship itself originated no longer in the religious and cultural network of family and community life on a local level but in the newly dominant realities of life in a national state. This concept of citizenship, excluding as it did a religious definition of community, also excluded women. For in a legal sense, women were not only nonvoters but nonentities. Thus, as important elements within the abolitionist movement itself shifted their perspective from a moral to a political emphasis, they also closed to women one of the few ways in which women had been able to express their sense of themselves as moral and responsible beings, as members in good standing of a community both religious and political.

NOTES

1. *Letters on the Equality of the Sexes and the Condition of Woman,* reprinted in Miriam Schneir, ed., *Feminism: The Essential Historical Writings* (New York: Random House, 1972), p. 40. And, Catherine H. Birney, *The Grimké Sisters* (1885; reprint ed., Westport, Conn.: Greenwood Press, 1969), pp. 170-71. Birney does not give a specific date for the Poughkeepsie meeting, but based on the dates of their other meetings, this one was probably held in March 1837.

2. *Fourth Annual Report of the American Antislavery Society* (New York: William S. Dorr, 1837), p. 36.

3. *Proceedings of the Antislavery Convention of American Women* (New York: William S. Dorr, 1837), pp. 4-6.

4. Ibid., pp. 3-4.

5. *An Appeal to the Women of the Nominally Free States* (Boston: Isaac Knapp, 1838), p. 3.

6. Ibid., pp. 6, 19.

7. Ibid., pp. 58-64.

8. *Friend of Man,* 11 April 1838. Quoted in Gilbert Barnes, *Antislavery Impulse* (1933; reprint ed., New York: Harcourt, Brace, and World, 1964), p. 266. The story of this petition campaign has been told many times, most thoroughly by Gilbert Barnes in *The Antislavery Impulse.* Unfortunately, Barnes footnoted his work by reference to the location of the petitions in the Library of Congress. Since the petitions have since been moved to the National Archives and most of them removed from the Library of Congress boxes in which Barnes found them, his notes referring to the petitions are virtually impossible to trace. Other secondary works including references to the petition campaign include Dwight L. Dumond, *Antislavery: The Crusade for Freedom in America* (Ann Arbor: The University of Michigan Press, 1961), especially chapter 29, "Petitions"; Louis Filler, *The Crusade Against Slavery, 1830-1860* (New York: Harper and Bros., 1960); Alice Hatcher Henderson, "The History of the New York State Antislavery Society" (Ph.D. diss. University of Michigan, 1963); James H. McPherson, "The Fight Against the Gag Rule: Joshua Leavitt and Antislavery Insurgency in the Whig Party, 1839-42," *Journal of Negro History* 48 (July 1963); 177-95; and Russel B. Nye, *Fettered Freedom, Civil Liberties and the Slavery Controversy, 1830-60* (Urbana, Ill.: University of Illinois Press, 1963). In addition, much information is scattered through abolitionist newspapers, the *Congressional Globe,* and published speeches of congressmen involved.

9. Endorsements would read, for example, like the following: "New York, Petition of Archibald Green & 73 citizens of Cayuga, New York, for the repeal of the act of 1793 authorizing the capture of fugitive slaves. February 24, 1843. Laid on table by W. Morgan." (File HR27A-H1.7, Records of the United States House of Representatives, Record Group 233, National Archives). Reference to many of these petitions appear in general form in the *Congressional Globe,* but the *Globe* does not give details and, of course, does not list the names of the signers themselves.

10. Other evidence for women is either nonexistent or very unsystematic. In New York State, for example, the *Friend of Man,* the newspaper of the New York State Antislavery Society, makes only sporadic references to women's activities.

11. The petitions sent to Congress in 1838-39 were all sent to the Twenty-fifth Congress in either its second or third session, which met beginning 11 September 1837 and 3 December 1838, respectively.

12. *Antislavery Impulse,* p. 266. While it is not clear how many of the total number of petitions collected were really sent, and, of those sent, how many were really presented to Congress (and of those presented how many are still extant), I am assuming for the purposes of this paper that, for the years 1838-39 and 1850-51, the number of petitions from upstate New York now on file in the Archives is either the total number sent or a reasonably representative sample of the total. Gilbert Barnes suggested that after 1840, "antislavery petitions were not received by the House, and only a chance few thousand were filed." Barnes went on to indicate that,

> twenty years ago there were several truckloads of abolition petitions stored here and there about the Capitol. The late Dr. C.H. Van Tyne used to tell his classes at the University of Michigan how, when he was making his *Guide to the Archives,* he found a caretaker in the Capitol keeping his stove hot with bundles of antislavery petitions. There were so many of them, the caretaker said, that those he used would never be missed.

13. "Second Annual Report of the New York State Antislavery Society," in *Friend of Man,* 27 September 1837.

14. *Friend of Man,* 25 April 1858.

15. "Fourth Annual Report of the New York State Antislavery Society," *Friend of Man,* 2 October 1839.

16. "Circular of the Antislavery Convention of American Women," *Proceedings of the Third Antislavery Convention of American Women* (Philadelphia: Merrihew and Thompson, 1839), p. 26.

17. Ibid., p. 28.

18. Those who circulated petitions, however, met with constant rebukes, some overt, some more subtle, like the one in the following imaginary conversation, printed in the *Friend of Man,* 1 February 1837. Here, the abolitionist is designated as "A" and the potential signer, "B":

> A: Here is a petition to Congress for the abolition of slavery in the District of Columbia, which is circulating for signature among the ladies of this village. I wish you would take it home and let your wife sign it, if she wishes to do so. You see there are 30-40 names already.
>
> B: With all my heart! My wife is a *thorough-going abolitionist,* and will sign it with great pleasure.
>
> B: Here is the petition you gave me. My wife says she is rather a stranger here, and does not like to put her name so near the top; when the paper is filled up or nearly so, she will be glad to sign it.
>
> A *(to himself):* Thorough-going abolitionist! — Hope there are not many such — Won't acknowledge those as abolitionists who are afraid to put their names at the TOP. They can't be depended upon — would perhaps sign a contrary petition if it had a long list of respectable names.

19. 24 November 1845, Gerrit Smith Papers, George Arendts Research Library, Syracuse University.

20. There are about 310 extant petitions, but six of these were sent from church bodies or were otherwise unidentifiable by sex.

21. These included every sixth township listed in the 1855 census, minus those townships (15) that had not yet been formed in 1845. I made no attempt to adjust for possible changes in township size during the intervening period, assuming that change in size would probably be randomly distributed. I also dropped Utica, Albany, and Rochester, the three cities that appeared in the sample, as well as Salina township. Salina formed the core of the future city of Syracuse and, while not yet incorporated in 1840, it did have a population of 11,013, comparable to Utica's 12, 782 and substantially above that of any other township.

The geographic focus of this paper is somewhat broader than the one that Whitney Cross used in *The Burned-Over District* (Ithaca: Cornell University Press, 1950). The territory I have chosen to consider covers eastern New York as well as central and western New York. It extends from the Massachusetts border in the east to the Niagara River in the west and from Delaware, Green, and Columbia counties and the Pennsylvania border in the south to the Canadian border in the north. This is not the place to debate whether or not upstate New York was peculiarly a "burned-over" district. All I wish to suggest here is that the area was a major area of abolitionist activity, particularly women's abolitionist activity, without arguing that it was *the* major area.

22. Of this latter group, eighteen also sent petitions in 1850-51. Any of these townships may, of course, also have generated petitions in years other than 1838-39 or 1850-51. I made no attempt to weed out of these samples townships which may have sent petitions in other years.

23. Sources for the data on denominational distribution were [John Disturnell], *Gazetteer of the State of New York* (Albany, 1842), and the *New York State Census for 1845*. For many townships, the census listed more churches than did Disturnell. Where there was a conflict, I used the larger number, assuming that churches would be more likely to be underrepresented than overrepresented. Even so, the data may not be very accurate. In some cases, for example, Disturnell and the census gave widely varying figures. To cite the most extreme case, Disturnell listed only one Methodist church for Owego, in Tioga County, while the census listed six.

24. 15 August 1841, Gerrit Smith Papers.

25. *Friend of Man,* 20 November 1839.

26. *Congressional Globe,* 11 December 1837, p. 34.

DISCUSSION SUMMARY

Because she felt that there was increasing evidence in papers and discussions that historians do not understand the reasons for archival arrangement, Lindsay Nauen of the Philadelphia Jewish Archives Center opened the discussion by reemphasizing the "rule of provenance" for the organization of archives. "Organizing the materials according to the way they are created," she said, "enabled the researcher to learn something about the agency, which in turn explains how the agency dealt with the problems it had to confront." Even personal letters in manuscript collections cannot be arranged by subject because one letter may deal with more than one subject.

Mary Young commented that she had no complaints about the organization of archives. Her comment about the difficulty of using nineteenth-century records was directed toward the quality of documentation available. The documents, for example, were not written by Indian women, but by officials with certain systematic biases. "There is no way," she said, "to get answers from available documents for many of the questions we would like to ask."

Pointing out that both black and white women participated in the female antislavery conventions that Judith Wellman had mentioned, Jean Yellin of Pace University noted that black women abolitionists were a neglected group, even by such an eminent historian as Benjamin Quarles in his book *Black Abolitionists* [Benjamin Quarles, *Black Abolitionists* (New York: Oxford University Press, 1969)]. Had Wellman encountered any black women abolitionists in her study of upstate New York?

Wellman replied that upstate New York was essentially a white culture, with no black population whatever in some of the townships she studied. For this reason, she found it interesting that the women who signed the petitions were often aware of black women in slavery as sisters, with whom they could be sympathetic and empathetic as women, even though they had no firsthand acquaintance with blacks, either female or male. Cooperation between black and white women for a common objective was difficult because there were so few blacks in the rural areas that Wellman studied.

Jo Ann Robinson of Morgan State University commented that historians should be careful not to oversimplify their accounts of black and white women struggling together toward abolition in the nineteenth century. Many whites who signed petitions avoided social contacts with blacks and were reluctant to give them jobs. We should remember that there were all kinds of ambivalences and tensions in the nineteenth century just as there are today.

Jacquelyne Johnson Jackson applauded Wellman's reticence about cooperation between black and white women and suggested that there may have been some conflict as well. She further commented that attributions of psychological motivation to the signers of petitions was quite conjectural. Wellman agreed and reiterated her statement that she had encountered almost no black persons in her studies because the black population of New York state was concentrated in the cities and the lower Hudson Valley, both of which were outside the geographical scope of her study.

Comparing the women abolitionists with contemporary politically active women, Helena Halperin of Rutgers University expressed the opinion that it must have been much more difficult for the women of the 1830s than for modern women to brave ridicule and perhaps husbands' disapproval. She asked Wellman to comment on the possible personal factors that precipitated the action of the women in the 1830s and why not even those same women participated in the movement in the 1850s.

Wellman answered that this was an important question, one that is very difficult to answer. The earliest census containing the names of individual women is the census of 1850, a poor source of information for women who signed petitions in the 1830s. In the ten to twenty intervening years many had moved or died or changed their names by marrying. Church records are scattered and often poorly documented. Local historical societies have few diaries. Although she has concluded that the women's antislavery movement was basically a middle-class movement, that meant little in rural upstate New York where it was hard to find people who were not basically middle class. The two key variables in her search for motivation seem to be the churches and the presence of manufacturing in the township.

She reported that she began her examination of church influence expecting to find a high correlation between abolitionist townships and those containing active Quaker or nonhierarchical churches like the Congregational. Somewhat to her surprise, she has found this to be only partially true. Townships with Congregational churches sent many women's petitions, but they sent even more men's petitions, and one cannot be sure that the petitioners were Congregationalists. She believes that Baptist and Methodist churches generated more reform sentiment than has previously been suspected, and that probably the key variable here is the degree of pietism present, that is, whether or not communicants are instilled with a sense of the individual's personal responsibility for moral action.

In regard to the presence of manufacturing, Wellman's current research in Paris, New York, leads her to suspect that highly abolitionist townships were often factory townships. Some abolitionist sentiment in Paris came from the Congregational Church, directly out of New England, traceable to Guilford, Connecticut, where there seem to have been some feminist leanings. It may also have come from the factory, though one does not know whether the women petitioners worked in the factory.

Carole Srole of the University of California at Los Angeles noticed that Wellman's presentation dealt with changes in the number of women participating in petition activity and in the type of geographic area represented by the petitions. She asked what bearing these two changes might have had on each other.

"In the huge outpouring of petitions related to the passage of the Fugitive Slave Act in 1851, one reason for the change in the type of townships in the movement was the increase in the number of townships that sent petitions," said Wellman. They are not confined to any particular area but spread all over the map. She did not expect to learn why townships that sent petitions in 1839 rejected the later petition movement until she was able to compare particular townships.

Women's activity in the 1850s movement may have been rejected because of real sexism like that of Charles Stuart mentioned earlier, but it may also have been a pragmatic response to congressional reaction to women's petitions. Congressmen's comments recorded in the *Congressional Globe* reflect the legislators' ridicule, in effect saying, "These are women's petitions. We don't have to think about them." Since the real goal of the antislavery movement was the abolition of slavery, women's petitions may have been dropped as being poor strategy. If Congress defined citizenship as male, white, and over twenty-one, abolitionists sent petitions signed by persons who could meet those qualifications.

In response to a further question from Halperin whether there were not new groups of people supporting the petition campaign in 1850, Wellman said that the cause was more popular and easier to support in 1850 than in 1839.

Keith Melder of Washington, D.C., was interested to have more specific information about the New England component in the petition movement among women. Did the petitioners originate in New England and have family backgrounds in that area?

Yes, they did, according to Wellman, but this turned out to be a less significant variable than she had expected. There were many geographical connections, and this fact is "one thing that makes the 'burned-over district' burned over." The Susquehanna River was also a main corridor for the transmission of Pennsylvania culture and Quaker sentiment, providing a dual thrust with ideas from New England.

Wilda Smith of Fort Hays Kansas State College in Hays, Kansas, suggested that one possible reason why there were fewer women circulating abolitionist petitions in 1850-51 was that women were circulating women's rights petitions instead. Wellman agreed. Her searches in the journals of the New York state legislature in the 1840s revealed an astonishing number of petitions about married women's property rights and abortion. A tremendous female moral reform network mounted a campaign against what it called "licentiousness and seduction."

The conference was reminded by Gladys Kashdin of the University of South Florida that the timing of the Seneca Falls Women's Rights Convention in 1848 would indicate that women were attending to their own rights after their consciousness had been raised by rebuffs suffered in the abolition movement. She was also interested in the educational level of the signers of women's petitions.

"An examination of the petitions themselves," said Wellman, "gives one some clues about the literacy level of the petitioners." Sometimes an entire petition is signed in one hand with a little note saying it had been copied because the original was too messy, or another might have five signatures in one hand followed by several in another. In some cases where signatures were barely legible, a check of the census showed that the column "Cannot read" had been checked, even though they could sign their names.

Wellman is at work on a collective biography of the women in the 1848 convention. Judging from printed sources about them, there were not only women with egalitarian ideological perspectives but also some prominent women who were quite aware of property.

She agreed with Kashdin's further suggestion that the decreased number of female petitioners might represent a reaction like the one currently taking place against the Equal Rights Amendment in some places.

Someone raised the question of whether, in view of the fact that women seemed to have no political role at all in the later abolition movement, women were permitted to "knit socks or make tea or something" for the cause. Wellman said she had sought records of organized women's abolition societies as one source for her study and had found evidence of only seventeen in upstate New York. Of these, one society in Champlain sewed things for sale in the local store. This was not considered to be stepping out of woman's sphere. In another case, a minister's wife who was opposed to women's rights debated a man who was in favor of women's speaking in public and being active in public affairs. The minister's wife argued her case so well that the audience decided that her opponent was right. She had proved herself wrong!

IV

WORLD WAR I AND THE GREAT DEPRESSION

INTRODUCTION

Harold T. Pinkett

The papers in this chapter deal with some aspects of the experiences of women during two critical periods of our national history. Although Penny Martelet has done research on the recruitment and employment of women in agriculture in both world wars, she has confined her attention here to a novel effort made by women to increase agricultural production during World War I. Mary W.M. Hargreaves has given us a broad picture of women at work during the depression of the 1930s, and Elaine M. Smith has offered a portrait of an especially dynamic woman during these years.

THE WOMAN'S LAND ARMY, WORLD WAR I

Penny Martelet

The participation of women in the American work force broadened considerably during World War I, as women became involved in many nontraditional occupations outside the home while contributing to the war effort.[1] The major impetus for this participation was twofold: the desire for patriotic service and the seeking of better paying jobs. The war effort justified these radical changes in life style as the American woman met the challenges of a wartime economy. The Woman's Land Army (WLA) was one of the unique ways in which this womanpower was applied to wartime production. The Land Army also demonstrated one of the ways that the cooperative efforts of the private sector and government agencies were utilized in solving home-front problems. The Land Army was part of a woman's movement, for it helped to open a door for the partial acceptance of hard physical labor for women, and class barriers were overcome as women from various walks of life lived and worked together in cooperative communities.

The WLA was organized by private women's organizations because of the manpower shortages in agricultural areas during the war. It was not until peacetime that the government became convinced to accept direction of the program. The reasons for this skepticism were apparent. Women were not considered suited for the rigors of farm work, and the government officials doubted that the farmers would accept women as laborers. Though women had traditionally participated in agriculture as migratory laborers and as farm wives and daughters, the physical labor of farm work was still considered inappropriate for women. The press of wartime production requirements and the successes of women farm workers in the WLA, however, assured the eventual acceptance of women as farm laborers.

This study is concerned with the initial organization of the WLA during World War I and how it set the groundwork for the women's movement that would be used in peacetime and revived during World War II.

The idea of mobilizing women as agricultural workers originated in Great Britain. In 1918 there were 40,000 women serving in the British Women's Land

136

Army, which was directed by the government. It consisted of shop girls, domestics, secretaries, and similar working women. France, Italy, and Canada had similar units, and they were responsible for a greater part of the agricultural production in these areas during wartime.[2]

As the imperfect distribution of labor across the nation during the war particularly affected agriculture, and the drain of manpower into the armed services and essential industry created a labor scarcity in rural America, the idea of adapting the European solution to American circumstances took shape.[3]

Ida H. Olgivie and Delia W. Marble, both geology professors at Barnard College, jointly owned a 680 acre dairy farm in New York. In 1917 as an experiment in interesting women in agricultural pursuits, they turned their farm work over to a dozen young women students. Their work was so successful that Olgivie spent the rest of the year "barnstorming" the country promoting the idea of a Woman's Land Army in the United States. Olgivie's work aroused the interest of women's colleges and students in training and volunteering for farm work as patriotic duty during wartime. These institutions continued to develop and encourage the program as one of great importance to the war effort.

Other civic and private organizations began sponsoring the training and placement of women as farm laborers. In 1917 the New York Woman's Suffrage Party organized the Bedford Training Camp in upstate New York where city recruits learned basic farm skills while being paid a regular laborers wage (25¢ per hour). They organized a statewide campaign to recruit city women for rural service assisted by various other women's clubs. These trainees worked the berry fields in the upper part of the state and were credited with saving the crop in 1917.

Another group was organized by the New York City mayor's Committee of Women on National Defense. Their purpose was to convince skeptical farmers that women were capable of performing farm work. Farmers were also concerned with providing proper housing and board for the women workers. The committee utilized a unit system camp that relieved the farmer of responsibility for housing and feeding the workers. The unit plan was developed at the Bedford Training Camp by the Farm and Garden Club of America.[6] During the summer of 1917, two experimental units were established by the committee. The Mount Kisco Unit consisted of sixty-five trade school girls and Barnard students. These recruits lived in old farm houses or slept in tents. The unit was totally self-supporting with a geology professor acting as camp director, an agricultural expert available to direct training, and dieticians hired as cooks. The farmers paid the unit $2 per day for each worker and the unit then paid each recruit a $15 per month wage. The remainder was used for the camp expenses. Before enlistment, the recruit was required to pass a basic physical examination. The first two weeks at the camp were spent in training on the house garden before the recruit was assigned to a work squad. Squads were bussed to neighboring farms needing workers on a day-to-day basis. Hoeing, gardening, and haying were the most frequently assigned tasks. Local farmers were so pleased with the women that the demand for recruits was soon greater than the unit could provide.[7]

The second unit was comprised of trades union women and situated in the fruit farm area along the Hudson River. Less professional and more democratic, this unit elected a captain as director and hired a cook and housekeeper. Each recruit contributed 50¢ per week from her wages to meet the common expenses of the camp. The fruit farmers paid these workers piece rates for berry picking and peach thinning. This unit made it possible for working women from the seasonal trades to find gainful employment for the summer. These recruits sought out farm jobs in order to make a living during their slack months in contrast to the college recruit who enlisted out of a purely patriotic response.

An important aspect of the mayor's committee program was that the assistance of the Employment Bureau of New York was enlisted to help direct recruitment. Farm Bureau agents were also consulted about where manpower shortages existed and asked to help with communication between the committee and the farmers.[8]

The committee's work demonstrated that women were capable of doing many types of farm work with a minimal amount of training. It also established that the unit plan was by far the most acceptable way to organize camps, at least in the eastern agricultural areas. The success of these units proved that women from varied backgrounds could work together effectively and happily. Members of these experimental units hoped to demonstrate that a national plan under the direction of a federal agency was feasible and desirable.

The Department of Agriculture (USDA) officials anticipated that the farm labor shortage would not require the use of women laborers and that adequate help could be obtained by mobilizing men from the towns and cities during emergencies. USDA officials were convinced that women could only perform light tasks and would probably be more useful doing household chores, thus freeing the farm wife for field work or helping her care for additional farm hands. The mayor's committee had discovered, however, that women were reluctant to volunteer for rural domestic duty.[9]

The Department of Labor began registering women for possible farm work in February 1918. The facilities of the United States Employment Service (USES) were closer to the labor supply than any USDA department, since most of the recruits came from towns and cities.[10] The registration of women for farm work was still viewed as purely an emergency measure. The USDA was consulted by women's groups to assist in determining where labor needs existed, but the agency continued to have no interest in directing a national program for enlisting women as farm workers.[11]

(pages 139-140) A World War I farmer describes her day. The excitement of a new experience and the satisfaction of service to her country in wartime come through clearly in this letter written by a recently placed Woman's Land Army recruit to the Superintendent of the Women's Division of the U.S. Employment Service in Nebraska. USES was responsible for finding WLA volunteers for farmers who were suffering from the shortage of farm labor.
(Hazel Nicholson to Kathleen O'Brien, July 10, 1919, Correspondence, 1917-1919, Women's Division, Office of the Federal State Director, Omaha, Nebraska, U.S. Employment Service, Records of the Bureau of Employment Security, RG 183.)

Stanton Nebr.
July 10-19

Dear Miss O'Brien:-

Have arrived at my des-
tination & like the place
& people very much. They
have a little girl with
the housework so they
asked me to inform you
that they will not need
another girl now.

Just think I helped
to pick raspberries & also
I milked two cows, while
tomorrow I am to shock
wheat & next week cultivate
corn. Some life! Its great

don't think I shall come
back to Omaha until
after corn-picking is
over. Think I shall too.
The people are very con-
genial and pleasant.
If you have any other
girls to go out I certainly
hope that they are as
fortunate as I.
'Tis now 9:30 & the bed
looks very good to me
so will drop you a
note later on.

Sincerely
Hazel Nicholson.

In anticipation of the eventual general call for additional farm laborers, the Women's National Farm and Garden Association, the Garden Clubs of America, the Women's Committee of the Council of National Defense, and several women's colleges organized the American Woman's Land Army in Febuary 1918. The purpose of this organization was to supply trained women workers to the farms to aid in meeting the need for increased food production during wartime. Emphasis was placed on the patriotic response of the recruit to the wartime needs of her country. The WLA was organized on a committee structure. A general executive committee of nationwide representatives was established in New York, with auxiliary committees organized in states and counties. These grassroot groups directed the local units and regulated the labor supply to meet the demand. The advice of local Farm Bureau agents and specialists from the USDA assisted the committees in determining camp locations and work sites. The Women's Division of the USES assumed direction of the recruitment program nationwide, and the WLA executive committee directed the training, placement, and camp organization.[12]

Recruits were required to pass a physical exam and had to agree to at least two months of duty. These women were enlisted from among college students, professionals, and women laborers in the seasonal trades. Using the unit plan, these self-supporting communities or camps were directed by a captain or supervisor appointed by the local committee.

Before enlistment the prospective recruit was guaranteed to receive minimum wage for the appropriate work. This was to assure male workers that they would not be undercut by a female labor force. Methods of pay varied depending on the work situation. The farmers paid the recruits an hourly, daily, or piece rate; or the camp units paid recruits a straight rate of $15 dollars per month and collected directly from the farmer for the entire unit's work. The local WLA committees were responsible for the initial financing of the camps, but the expense was to be repaid by the camp over a period of several years.

The recruits went to the farms in work squads on a daily basis, and while they were in the field the farmer acted as supervisor. During the 1918 season, the work included dairying, livestock care, poultry raising, fruit picking, market gardening, canning, and lighter field tasks such as planting, transplanting, thinning, weeding, hoeing, and mowing. Some women became involved in more technical work and also operated farm machinery, but the majority performed work assignments that required a minimal amount of training. Training was available through the state agricultural colleges, especially in more skilled specialties such as dairying. Several women's colleges also began a training program, preparing students for farm work during their summer vacations. Most training was still done in the field, however, and often skilled male laborers helped prepare recruits to replace them when they left for military service.

Farmers were full of praise for the work of these first WLA units. As the word spread about their successes, the demand for women laborers increased. The quality of the WLA work steadily overcame the farmers' skepticism. What the recruit may have lacked in physical strength, she more than equaled in enthusiasm and conscientiousness.[13] The farmerette soon became one of the symbols of the homefront effort by women. Newspapers and magazines featured articles extolling and promoting the Land Army's work. An editorial in the *New York Times*, August 28, 1918, commented that "the farmerette is not a joke: she is a factor in the fight." In April 1918 President Wilson personally commended the national direc-tor of the Land Army, Mrs. Henry Wade Rogers, and expressed the hope that the farmers of America would utilize the women's help in meeting the agricultural labor crisis.[14]

By the end of the summer of 1918, 15,000 women in 127 units had been formally placed by the WLA in twenty states. Thirty-four women's colleges were recruiting and training women for farm service. This accounted for the fact that the greater number of recruits tended to be students.[15] There is no account of the number of women who were involved in rural work through private organizations and on a purely local basis. Many local unorganized groups of housewives worked on nearby farms while their children were in school and then returned home in the evening. Near large cities, office workers would contribute a few hours after work.

The problems faced by the WLA during the early organizational period were numerous. Convincing farmers to accept women workers was the greatest problem at first. This was overcome partly by the reputation the recruits earned for the quality of their work and also by an extensive promotional campaign to advertise the WLA program. Camp organization and living conditions became a large problem. The lack of funds made it difficult to establish and maintain adequate facilities. Recruits sometimes complained bitterly about the food and living conditions, but few dropped out of the service because of these problems.[16] The WLA Executive Committee appointed a Camp Standards Committee to investi-gate and improve the camp situation. Their recommendations, published in April 1919, were used as the model for the WLA organization of units during the peacetime program. The WLA Executive Committee sought funds from the public through a WLA membership or sponsorship drive. Farmers were reluctant to provide financial assistance beyond the role of employer, and urban dwellers were too remote from the agricultural situation to have any interest. American soldiers saw the WLA work as vital to their effort and many contributed support by purchasing memberships while they were serving overseas.[17] Most financial aid came from the thirty-two women's organizations who assisted the WLA.

Promotional ideas were often unique. The New York State WLA Committee sponsored the filming of a movie using professional actors on a New York farm showing the success of the land workers during 1918. The story concerned a farmer who was persuaded by his wife to hire WLA recruits who successfully harvested his crops. The film, which was released in Feburary 1919, emphasized the effective on-the-job training and the hard work and dedication of the women.[18]

The WLA National Committee also developed ideas to help bring the recruits in touch with each other and provide a means for the sharing of ideas and experiences.

The Camp Standards Committee published a monthly newsletter, the *Farmerette*, which contained words from the WLA leaders, news about work progress throughout the country, plans for the next season, and suggestions and letters from the recruits.[19] A certain amount of clubbishness developed around WLA membership which stemmed from the deep sense of pride a recruit felt toward the work of the movement. A special uniform bearing a red WLA insignia was worn for field duty, and a green arm band was worn when the recruit was at home. The uniform, however, had to be purchased by the woman, and some complained that it was shoddy and did not wear well.[20] Women's garden clubs offered scholarships to recruits who wished to further their agricultural expertise by improving their technical abilities. These women's groups were interested in preparing women for a more permanent involvement in agricultural occupations.

The shortages of farm labor did not subside immediately with the end of the war. The attraction of better paying industrial jobs meant that many men would not return to the farms, and the emergency need for farm laborers continued into 1919. In December 1918 the secretary of labor signed an agreement that established the Land Army as a division of the USES for peacetime work. The WLA organization remained private on the state level, but the national policies were implemented by the National Board of Directors elected by the state committees. With the headquarters moved to Washington, D.C., the old New York office was converted into a data collection center for the tabulation of information from the various state units. It also served as a publications center and speakers bureau, and issued the uniforms.[21] The peacetime organization also had the new dimension of establishing a foothold in agricultural occupations for women. During the 1918 season, the women had shown particular interest and skill in truck gardening, dairying, and poultry raising.[22] These were potential areas for the permanent employment of women agriculturists.

The Land Army camps were now seen as established business units rather than temporary housing facilities. A professional approach was taken with organizational problems. The National Board assigned field surveyors to travel to each region to study and evaluate the possibilities for permanent WLA units in the area. The individual state committees assisted by sending summary reports on the 1918 season to the New York office. These results were tabulated and published in a state by state account by the *Farmerette* and the Department of Labor. This report outlined the various types of work in which the women were engaged, wage differentials, hour regulations, and camp locations. Though not a qualitative report, it was the only collective account of WLA work in its first year.[23] The Land Army also conducted internal surveys such as the Wellesley Training Camp's scientific analysis of the work structure of a WLA unit, which included a determination of the recruits' efficiency and fatigue.[24] All these studies were geared to the professionalization of agricultural work for women. This new emphasis was especially evident in the extensive training programs for both recruits and camp supervisors. Added to the training centers already developed at state agricultural schools and at women's colleges were special WLA training camps established in each state where units existed. These training units were made self-sufficient often by marketing their own produce in nearby towns and cities.

The *Handbook of Standards* for the WLA camps compiled by the Camp Standards Committee also emphasized the professional spirit of the movement. The purpose of the committee report was to make recommendations on how the welfare of the women workers would be assured through the establishment of minimal work and camp standards. Their recommendations included the use of a contractual agreement between the farmer and each laborer, and also the encouragement of specializing those work areas in which women had proven to be most suited. The contract agreement was to establish the security of a minimum wage, maximum hours, rest periods, sanitation provisions, job descriptions, and a guaranteed term of employment.[25] The 1918 season had shown that most units had problems with getting the farmer to fulfill the initial oral arrangement. The farmers had a tendency to often take advantage of the informal work arrangement and the patriotic spirit of the recruits. Another widely mentioned problem was the lack of funds. When the emergency work was completed in an area, recruits were sometimes stranded with no means of support, or needed equipment and supplies that they could not purchase to maintain the camp. The standardization of the program under a government agency provided more efficient channels to communicate and correct these problems, but funding remained the greatest obstacle for the peacetime program. Government appropriations were only temporary and the end of the war stopped many organizations from continuing their patriotic support. The WLA was unable to solicit sufficient funds and congressional support ended in October 1919. The USES was obliged to close down all of its placement offices.[26] Without the continued support of a government agency and the financial support of the private sector, the WLA was unable to provide camp facilities for its workers, and the organization was forced to demobilize by January 1920.

The organization of the WLA for war emergency work and the peacetime federal program were two distinct movements. During the war, most recruits were motivated by patriotic spirit, as were the supportive organizations. The peacetime organization was primarily concerned with developing opportunities for permanent professional acceptance of women in agriculture, and it attracted recruits who were looking for a more varied and better paying occupation than the job market offered. This movement proved to be short-lived because the WLA could not convince a tradition-bound society to accept women in agriculture. This does not mean that the work that the Land Army women performed was inadequate, but that without the war emergency their work was considered unnecessary and inappropriate. The importance of the peacetime federal program was in the model it developed that would be utilized when the WLA was revived during World War II.

The work of the Land Army was one of the many ways American women applied their time and skills to war work. Besides giving evidence of the deep sense of patriotic spirit among American women and their dynamic organizational ability, the Land Army also signaled the growing desire on the part of a number of women to seek out new avenues of employment. Their adaptibility to farm work demonstrated that women had an immense and untapped capacity for hard physical labor. The work of the Land Army involved a number of women in a special environment. Not only was the nature of the work considered inappropriate, but the clothing and living arrangements were radically removed from accepted standards of feminine behavior. The World War I farmerette represented a unique example of the potential of the American woman to adapt to new and challenging social and economic roles. The Land Army thus proved to be a small part of a larger movement that would involve millions of women during World War II.

NOTES

1. See discussion in William H. Chafe, *The American Woman: Her Changing Social, Economic, and Political Roles, 1920-1970* (New York: Oxford University Press, 1972), pp. 22, 48, 51-54.
2. U.S., Department of Labor, *Reports of the Department of Labor 1918* (Washington, D.C.: Government Printing Office, 1919), pp. 201-21.
3. *New York Times,* 3 February 1918, p. 10.
4. Esther M. Colvin, "Another Women's Land Army," *Independent Woman,* April 1942, p. 126.
5. *New York Times,* 25 June 1917, p. 17.
6. *Farmerette,* January 1918, p. 7.
7. "Women Farm Workers," *New Republic,* September 1917, p. 132.
8. Ibid., p. 133.
9. Dr. R.A. Pearson, "Memorandum for Professor Spillman," 7 February 1918, Subject File: Labor (Women) 1918, Records of the Office of the Secretary of Agriculture, Record Group 16, National Archives Building; Memorandum for Dr. R.A. Pearson (unsigned), ibid.; Woodrow Wilson to David F. Houston, 18 September 1918, ibid.; and "Women Farm Workers," p. 132.
10. For a discussion of the USES organization, see *Reports of the Department of Labor, 1918,* pp. 201-21; Houston to George Creel, 25 March 1918, Subject File: Labor (Women) 1918, RG 16, NA; and Wilson to Houston, 18 September 1918, ibid.
11. Houston to Creel, 25 March 1918, ibid.
12. For a description of the complete organization, see *New York Times,* 3 February 1918; U.S., Department of Labor, *Reports of the Department of Labor, 1919* (Washington, D.C.: Government Printing Office, 1920), p. 297; Ethel Puffer Howes, "The Woman's Land Army of America Prospectus," 27 February 1918, File 16/634, Chief Clerk's File, General Records of the Department of Labor, RG 174, NA; Dorothy H. Hubert to State Land Army Directors, 29 April 1919, Women's Division, Office of the Federal State Director, Omaha, Nebraska, 1917-19, U.S. Employment Service, Records of the Bureau of Employment Security, RG 183, NA; and Director General to Federal Directors of the Woman's Land Army, 10 May 1919, ibid.

13. Woman's Land Army of America, Inc., "What the Farmers Say About the Work of the Woman's Land Army of America in 1918," Woman's Land Army Unit, Marcus J. Cain Employer, ibid.
14. *New York Times,* 11 April 1918, p. 15.
15. *New York Times,* 12 August 1918, p. 8.
16. Evelyn J. Murphy to Anita Voorhees, November 1975, personal experiences in the Woman's Land Army, Personal Files of the author, Chicago, Illinois.
17. *New York Times,* 27 October 1918, p. 6.
18. *New York Times,* 27 October 1918, p. 6; 2 February, 28 August 1919, p. 11.
19. *Farmerette,* December 1918; January 1919.
20. Evelyn J. Murphy to Anita Voorhees, November 1975, Personal Files of the author, Chicago, Illinois.
21. For description, see *Farmerette,* January 1919.
22. Ibid.
23. *Farmerette,* December 1918; January 1919; Reports of the Department of Labor 1919, pp. 941-1051.
24. "Training Camp for Women Land Workers," *Survey,* 28 June 1919, p. 490.
25. Woman's Land Army of America, "Handbook of Standards," April 1919, Women's Division Records, Office of the Federal State Director, Omaha, Nebraska, 1917-19, Records of the U.S. Employment Service, Records of the Bureau of Employment Security, RG 183, NA.
26. U.S., Department of Labor, *Reports of the Department of Labor, 1920* (Washington, D.C.: Government Printing Office, 1921), p. 933.

April 28, 1941

Mr. Orren H. Lull
Regional Director, Region IV
Colorado

Mary McLeod Bethune
Director, Division of Negro Affairs
National Office

Negro Adviser in Omaha, Nebraska

I have read your letter and the report of Miss Risher concerning Bennie Brown.

There is only one thing to say. If Bennie Brown does not measure
up to the needs of the position, please, by all means, let us get
someone else. If you cannot find a good man, then get a good,
strong woman. Do not keep anyone in the position if he cannot
deliver.

MMB:THUXE?ADEXXISTON

Memo from Mary McLeod Bethune. The force of Bethune's personality as well as her administrative methods can be seen in the few lines of this memorandum. She pressed for the appointment of blacks to NYA staff positions and to the agency's advisory councils at the local, state, regional, and national level, but her ultimate goal was an effective program for Negro youth.
(Bethune to Orren H. Lull, April 28, 1941, Miscellaneous Alphabetic-Name Correspondence, 1935-41, Records of the Deputy Executive Director, Records of the National Youth Administration, RG 119.)

MARY MCLEOD BETHUNE AND THE NATIONAL YOUTH ADMINISTRATION

Elaine M. Smith

"If I were a young woman," declared a short, stout black woman in 1937, "I would go to Congress." This was about three decades before a black female went to the United States Congress and two years before such a person sat in a legislative assembly at even the state level. Nevertheless, when the sixty-two-year-old Mary McLeod Bethune flung out this idea to the New York City Association of Women's Clubs, she electrified the Negro women with the "mightiness of her enthusiasm."[1] As the president of the National Council of Negro Women and a former president of the National Association of Colored Women, she characteristically promoted the cause of black women in this way. She once commented, "Next to God, we are indebted to women, first for life itself, and then for making it worth having."[2] She was well aware that the "work of men is heralded and adored while that of women is given last place or entirely overlooked." But regardless of society's attitude she told women, "We must go to the front and take our rightful place; fight our battles and claim our victories!"[3]

Throughout her life Mary McLeod Bethune symbolized what she preached. Born in 1875 near Mayesville, South Carolina, to Samuel and Patsy McLeod, ex-slaves who ran a small farm, Bethune became educated through a local school, a girls' seminary, and a Bible institute. She married a fellow teacher, Albertus Bethune, and became the mother of a son. She could not conform to the restricted role of most women in American life, however, because she chose to pattern

This article is based in part on research supported by a Graduate Fellowship for Black Americans administered by the National Fellowships Fund. I wish, also, to acknowledge the assistance of Beauford J. Moore, former director of the Bethune Foundation and Richard V. Moore, former president of Bethune-Cookman College, for facilitating my use of the Mary McLeod Bethune Papers, Bethune Foundation at Bethune-Cookman College, Daytona Beach, Florida.

herself after two of the most outstanding black women in the South, Emma Wilson, her first teacher, and Lucy Laney, principal of the first school in which she worked as a young adult. Both of these women had established their own boarding schools; and in 1904 in Daytona Beach, Florida, she followed suit with an institution which developed into Bethune-Cookman College.

When the eminent sociologist and journalist, W.E.B. Du Bois, visited this college in 1929, he noted it had been created by "the indomitable energy of one black woman and her enthusiastic spirit inspires it and makes it live."[4] Agreeing with this evaluation and recognizing that despite insuperable difficulties, Bethune made the school into a standard junior college, and in 1935 the National Association of Colored People presented her its Spingarn Medal, an annual award signifying meritorious service to the Negro race. Within six weeks after receiving this round, gold medallion on a black, red, and gold sash, Bethune started down a different road toward a career in the National Youth Administration (NYA).

The National Youth Administration existed from 1935 to 1944 primarily to assist young people aged sixteen to twenty-four in getting work. During the middle of the Great Depression with its unprecedented and staggering unemployment in America, this age group justified a special agency in constituting about one-third of all the unemployed and in lacking work experience and work habits vis-a-vis other workers. Even when defense spending began to turn the economy around, many youths still needed the NYA services to get a job.

The NYA's major objective was to find employment for jobless youths in private industry. In line with this, all youth in the out-of-school work program maintained active registration with their State Employment Services. The NYA placed some young people in private employment during the late thirties but even more in the early forties. In the war projects of 1942-43, it virtually guaranteed jobs through its inter-state transfer plans.[5]

Besides placement, two other objectives of the agency were to provide employment through work-relief projects and vocational training projects. In the 1930s, the NYA required all youth who participated in these programs to come from families certified as eligible for relief services. It paid them approximately $15 or $16 per month for about forty-four hours of work. Most early projects centered around public-service activities, but after the first year the agency placed increasing emphasis upon vocational training. In 1937 it initiated a resident training center program through which youth were trained for employment near to or in cooperation with educational institutions. The first centers were oriented toward agriculture, but beginning in 1938 with the resident center in Quoddy, Maine, the NYA emphasized industrial training. Later, it created standardized workshops throughout the country to prepare young people for jobs in areas such as aviation mechanics, sheet metal welding, pattern making, electrical work, radio, forge, foundry, and industrial sewing.

The NYA training projects in 1942 concentrated solely upon enabling persons to develop a single skill necessary for a war production job such as operating a lathe, drill press, or a welder. In addition to placement and developing projects, the

Youth Administration was directed to provide part-time employment for needy high-school and college students. The rationale for this was to keep youth usefully occupied and off the saturated labor market. At the secondary level, the agency supplied school authorities with funds to pay some students from relief families between $3 and $6 per month for educationally valuable work. Without any relief strings, it allotted college and university officials funds to enable them to pay from $10 to $25 to undergraduates and $30 to graduate students for hours in the NYA student work program.[6]

The number of youths the NYA assisted through placement services, work-relief, and vocational training projects, and the school program fluctuated. For example, in 1936-37, with $51,156,505, it helped 450,000 persons; in 1940-41, with $157,159,000, it reached 758,000.[7] The agency was created through Executive Order Number 7086 on June 16, 1935, under the Emergency Relief Appropriation Act of that year and resided within different larger organizations beginning with the Works Progress Administration, then the Federal Security Administration, and finally the War Manpower Commission. Throughout it all, however, the NYA administrator maintained much autonomy while he directed the program through a state system and then a regional one.

Both blacks and whites dubbed the NYA one of the more liberal New Deal agencies in its relationship to Negro people. Its most influential policy-makers cast it in this mold. Among these were Eleanor Roosevelt, wife of the United States president, and Aubrey Williams, the NYA's sole administrator. Along with the U.S. Office of Education and the Children's Bureau, Mrs. Roosevelt was among the chief sponsors of the NYA. During the early years, she provided critical support and continued thereafter to identify actively with the program.[8] Williams, an outstanding social worker, had come to head the NYA via his position as assistant administrator to Harry Hopkins in the Federal Emergency Relief Administration and later in the Works Progress Administration. His attitude toward minorities was akin to the well-known liberal attitude of Mrs. Roosevelt. Although as a native of Alabama he may have occasionally used the word "nigger," nevertheless, he wanted the NYA to make at least a small beginning toward alleviating Negro problems. This type of sentiment and the hope that eventually the NYA would become a permanent program reflecting the idealism of American democracy led to the agency's recognition of blacks.[9]

Initially, this recognition was manifested by having two blacks on the National Advisory Committee, a group consisting of thirty-five persons representing business, agriculture, education, and youth. The NYA formulators probably selected Mordecai Johnson and Mary McLeod Bethune because of their status as educators and their high visibility. As president of Howard University, a distinguished black institution in Washington, D.C., relying heavily upon federal funding, Johnson was known to the NYA inner circle and had been among the select informal advisers on the youth program immediately after its creation.[10] Bethune came to the inner circle's attention through Josephine Roche, assistant secretary of the treasury and chairman of the NYA's six-member executive committee. A few weeks before advisory members were selected, Mrs. Roche had been caught up in Bethune's oratory, personality, and achievement as Bethune received the Spingarn Award in St. Louis, Missouri. No doubt, Eleanor Roosevelt, who had met Bethune about eight years earlier, endorsed Roche's proposal to have Bethune on the committee, for she personally asked her to represent Negro youth.[11]

Of all youth reeling from the depression, Negro youth suffered most because of the earlier marginal existence of their families. Bewildered, frustrated, and defeated, they had reason to lose hope for a better life. They constituted roughly 13 percent of all youth in America but about 15 percent of youth on relief. Most had received grossly inferior education in the segregated schools of the South. With southern states denying them a proportionate share of federal funds for vocational education in addition to other injustices, their vocational training was "scarcely more than crude instruction in obsolete crafts and skills."[12] Regardless of education, black youth were hampered on the job market by the general conditions of Negro occupational life. When they could find work, it was usually in agriculture or domestic and personal service which employed nearly two-thirds of all Negro workers. But their chances of finding work even in traditionally Negro jobs were somewhat diminished because white workers were taking employment in these.[13]

Sensitive to this distressed status of Negro youth and oriented toward public service, Mary McLeod Bethune jumped at the opportunity to serve on the NYA's National Advisory Committee. Although the position demanded primarily attendance at committee meetings scheduled once or twice a year, the aggressive Bethune immediately transcended this limited role. Seeing in the NYA the best potential aid for Negro youth, she publicized the program among blacks all over the country. Concentrating on Florida, however, her home base, she worked closely with state officials to ensure black youth a proportionate share of benefits and helped to get two Negroes appointed to the NYA Florida advisory committee at a time when all other states except Alabama had appointed either one or none. By working with farmers, Bethune assisted in developing an extensive rural recreation project. She also obtained NYA programs at her own Bethune-Cookman College.[14]

At the national level, Bethune endeavored to have the NYA adopt policies that would extend its benefits to more blacks. Thus, she advocated that the agency drop the requirement of relief certification before allowing out-of-school youth to receive aid. She and other blacks emphasized that in many areas, especially the South, the Works Progress Administration, which determined whether youth were qualified for relief, would not declare some Negroes eligible regardless of the evidence. Nevertheless, Aubrey Williams believed that the southern states were doing a good job with certification, and throughout the depression-oriented program Bethune went unheeded.[15] She was persuasive, however, on the point of a special fund for Negro college and university students. Negro students who could not receive part-time aid from their institutions' regular NYA funds — even after the institution had given Negroes a fair share of this aid — could apply through the school for special fund assistance. Black students needed the extra help because most came from families that lacked sufficient incomes for higher education. And, too, they needed it for the increased costs of going to school in states other than their own because southern and border states generally denied them training opportunities at the graduate and professional levels and in some areas of undergraduate work.[16]

For Mary McLeod Bethune, however, the burning issue for extending NYA benefits to more blacks focused on neither certification nor the special fund. It was Negro leadership within all components of the program. She believed as she once said, "The white man has been thinking for us too long; we want him to think with us now instead of for us."[17] Arguing that blacks needed opportunities for leadership if they were to become effective citizens and if democratic values were to be realized in race relations, she urged the National Advisory Committee and NYA officials to permit black leadership over the youth program as it affected blacks. In doing this, her primary concern was not the segregation-integration issue but a greater measure of equality for Negroes within the existing contours of American society. She explained that where there was no need for dual programs she "heartily recommended" a single integrated program; but where racism made this impossible, she recommended two, provided proper leadership existed. This meant Negro leaders, she said, for they had greater understanding and sympathy for the problems of Negro youth than whites.[18]

Bethune proposed a permanent national advisory committee on Negro affairs and later, she advocated simply adding another Negro to the existing National Advisory Committee. She also suggested that the NYA administrator and his deputy should each employ a Negro assistant. At the state level, Bethune campaigned for hiring black assistants to state directors to interpret their own needs. Locally, she wanted the leaders to determine the nature of black projects and black supervisors employed who would receive compensation equal to that of their white counterparts.[19]

The NYA responded positively to two aspects of Bethune's agenda for black leadership. With the prodding of the black press, it employed in the Washington office one Negro specialist. Also, in states with concentrated numbers of blacks, it advised the state director to employ a black assistant. In 1936 this was about as far as the agency would go in the interest of in-house black advancement, for when Aubrey Williams proposed to his Executive Committee that the NYA place three or four Negroes in regular staff positions, the committee refused to take it seriously.[20]

Mary Bethune's status as a mere NYA adviser changed primarily as a result of her encounter with President Franklin Roosevelt on April 28, 1936. As a climax for the second meeting of the National Advisory Committee, she and other advisory members went to the White House to present resolutions adopted on major issues in the youth program. They had made no specific reference to Negro participation but permitted Bethune to compensate for this through an oral report.[21] In meeting the president for the first time, Bethune hoped to reinforce his support for the agency. As was her custom, she spoke positively and optimistically.

Basically, she said, "We are bringing light and spirit to these many thousands who for so long have been in darkness." When she finished, Roosevelt grasped her hands as he pledged his best efforts to improve the status of the Negro people.[22] Within two months after this initial meeting, Roosevelt had her back at the White House offering her the top position in the NYA Office for Negro Affairs. Like thousands of other educated whites who had heard Bethune, the president probably had been struck by her sincerity, fearlessness, and zeal for social justice.[23] He believed that she was a leader possessing the tact, common sense, and courage to obtain more benefits for blacks through the NYA than anybody else. Roosevelt said of Bethune, "I believe in her because she has her feet on the ground; not only on the ground, but deep down in the ploughed soil."[24] No doubt, the chief NYA officials influenced the president's attitude. They were pleased with Bethune's work and wanted to give her latitude in continuing it. Both Charles Taussig, the chairman of the Advisory Committee, and Richard Brown, the NYA assistant administrator, had commended Bethune for her contributions. She had been one of the most active advisory members, and Brown declared that she could not have done more for the NYA had she been on the payroll in Washington. Perhaps they respected her most for establishing clear goals, then working persistently but patiently for their realization.[25]

Believing that it was important to have talented black women such as herself working in responsible federal jobs just as white women did, Bethune started work in June 1936. In doing so, she displaced the competent Juanita Saddler, the NYA's "Administrative Assistant in charge of Negro Affairs" who had been previously the student field secretary for the Young Women's Christian Association in New York City. With Bethune's laudatory recommendation, the NYA had employed her in December 1935 because of the keen interest she had shown in the agency from its inception and more importantly, because she had been the best qualified candidate for the Negro job.[26] Initially, however, it had failed to define her role and was slow in providing a secretary and suitable office space. Saddler had seen her major responsibility as fostering Negro leadership in every phase of the program affecting Negroes. She believed that as long as society sanctioned a dual system, the provisions for whites and blacks had to be equalized regardless of the inherent duplication, economic waste, and division.[27] Thus, Saddler and Bethune shared a basic philosophical outlook on how to promote adequate Negro participation in the NYA. And too, they worked closely when Bethune was only an advisory person. Nevertheless, within three weeks after Bethune's arrival in Washington, Saddler submitted a curt resignation. She was uncomfortable in seeing Bethune in her former position as the chief Negro specialist.[28]

Bethune began work in Washington ostensibly as the director of the Division of Minority Affairs, which the agency soon changed to Division of Negro Affairs. She later recalled that she occupied the first federal position in the history of the country created for a black woman. Yet the news media did not immediately publicize her new status. For example, the *Pittsburgh Courier,* a leading black weekly, omitted mentioning it for about six weeks and the Democratic party failed to list her among "Roosevelt's Negro Appointees" advertised in the *Courier* to win black votes in the 1936 presidential election.[29] The most reasonable explanation for this curious development was that Bethune's appointment could not bear close scrutiny. The Civil Service Commission did not recognize a Negro division within the NYA nor Bethune as a division director. Instead, Bethune's official title was the same as Saddler's had been "Administrative Assistant in Charge of Negro Affairs." Characteristically, however, Bethune lived her hopes. After acting for two and a half years, the commission made her official director on January 16, 1939.[30] With this new reality, Bethune observed that her division paralleled the six others in the NYA regarding salary schedules, grade levels, and other matters.[31] Regardless of title, the black lady administrator was typical of directors who firmly controlled their divisions. For example, when her assistant director once submitted a site visit report directly to one of their administrative superiors while she was out of the office, she wrote him: "Our procedure is that all field reports be made to my desk and together we will study them and send such part of them we deem wise to Mr. Lasseter over my signature."[32]

Mary Bethune was able to employ in her office several individuals. In the first year she employed three. When sixty-seven persons constituted the entire NYA national office force in the next year, she still had three workers. By 1941, however, when the agency had shifted from a depression orientation to national defense, the number had increased to seven and included an assistant director, an administrative assistant, a section chief for Negro Relations, two stenographers, and two secretaries. In the course of her seven years with the Youth Administration, she had four capable assistant directors. The first two, Frank Horne and R. O'Hara Lanier, came from academic backgrounds; the next, T. Arnold Hill, from the National Urban League in New York City; and the last, Charles P. Browning, from the NYA staff based in Chicago.[33] Bethune's right hand, however, was another competent and out-going black woman, Arabella Denniston. She had graduated from Bethune-Cookman College and had worked in the Urban League and such organizations in New York before joining the NYA as a secretary. In the Office of Negro Affairs, she became involved in all phases of Bethune's professional activities. She consistently offered her basic support as both an employee and friend. In one Denniston-to-Bethune letter, for example, she expressed concern for Bethune's well-being; reminded her to send a card of sympathy to her friend Bishop Reverdy C. Ransom, whose wife had just died; delivered messages that had come to the office during her absence; indicated Bethune's pending travel arrangements; passed on news of the NYA operations; and reported on the Washington visit of the Liberian President Barclay whom Roosevelt had entertained at dinner with two black Americans present, Dr. Mordecai Johnson and Gen. Benjamin O. Davis.[34]

As a recognized black leader, Mary McLeod Bethune's importance to the administration transcended her activities in the NYA. She was an administration representative to blacks. As Gunnar Myrdal noted in *An American Dilemma*, politically, blacks and whites dealt with each other through the medium of

plenipotentiaries. Only their leaders normally interacted across racial lines. Therefore, the white power structure needed black leaders, for through them it could
indirectly influence the Negro people.[35] As a sagacious leader, Bethune was
mindful of this aspect of her position. She ardently worked to build support for the
administration and judging from her popularity among blacks in the late thirties
and early forties, she did this job well. Bethune was careful in what she said about
President Roosevelt so as not to cause embarrassment. When the Associated Negro
Press, for example, pressured her for a formal statement on how the president
received recommendations from the 1937 NYA-sponsored Conference on the
Negro, she high-lighted his sympathetic attitude: "The President was most interested and cooperative in his consideration of the problems confronting us. He
was deeply interested in the forward steps that Negroes were taking toward a more
definite integration into the American program. The Negroes of America may
depend upon the interest and the sincerity of our President in his efforts to justify
their confidence in him and his program." Despite this innocuous tone, Bethune
waited for approval from Stephen Early, the assistant secretary to the president,
before releasing her comment.[36]

As an administration official, Mary Bethune publicly cast the New Deal program in the most favorable light possible. Her article, "I'll Never Turn Back No
More" in a 1938 issue of *Opportunity* magazine summarized the points she made
time and time again. She emphasized that blacks could not afford to turn back to
the times before the New Deal. In every respect they were "the real sick people of
America in need of every liberal program to benefit the masses." The programs
she referred to included the NYA, the large-scale relief efforts, adult education,
social security, the Housing Authority, resettlement projects, farm loans, credit
unions, cooperatives, soil reclamation, rural electrification, and long time purchase plans. She claimed that although the doors of opportunity were not open
wide enough, it was still the dawn of a new day for Negroes.[37]

As national defense became the primary political concern, Bethune promoted
ideas favorable to the war effort. In February 1941 she spoke briefly on the
Columbia Broadcasting System radio network for the Committee to Defend
America by Aiding the Allies to generate support for Lend-Lease. In June 1942 she
went to the War Department for about five days to help select candidates for the
Woman's Army Auxiliary Corps officers training school in Fort Des Moines,
Iowa, and from that beginning she continued to identify publicly with this new
camp.[38] More importantly, she preached a "Close Ranks" message: "These are
not the days to consider from whence one came, nor the traditional customs of
social standing, caste and privilege. These are the days for a united front with a
united purpose to fight for that victory which we must have, or regardless of caste,
creed or position, we will all sink together."[39] In addition, she attributed transcen-
dent moral purposes to the war in statements such as: "We are fighting for a
baptism in that spiritual understanding that all mankind has been created in the
image of God" and "We are fighting for the perfection of the democracy of our

own beloved America, and the extension of that perfected democracy to the ends of the world.''[40]

In whipping up Negro support for the war effort, she observed that the Roosevelt administration had recognized Negroes as an integral part of American life. She recited the New Deal programs that offered benefits to blacks and pointed out the Negroes who were in responsible positions in the federal government such as Robert Weaver, William Pickens, Hobart Taylor, William Hastie, and Crystal Byrd Faucett. She hailed Roosevelt's Executive Order 8802 that banned racial discrimination in government and defense industries as a big step forward, yet she warned that it would not immediately solve the problems for which it was designed. Blacks, themselves, had to be the constant aggressors: ''We must not be content to sit and wait for someone to bring the opportunities of today to us. . . . [You must] organize into groups and ask to be heard and insist that you be considered.''[41]

Bethune's activities for the administration were rooted in personal loyalty and respect for Franklin and Eleanor Roosevelt. Mentally, she separated Roosevelt from his Democratic party, especially its flagrantly racist southern wing and clung fervently to his idealism. In the midst of escalating black criticism of the administration, she emphasized that ''FDR is fair at heart in his attitude toward the Negro, and regularly inquires of the New Deal agencies as to what is being done for the Negro.''[42] She saw his greatest contribution to blacks as bringing hope through sponsorship of such programs as the NYA.[43] Bethune was especially devoted to the president's wife and proclaimed her a ''great humanitarian,'' ''a grand and charming personality,'' ''a symbol of true unadulterated democracy,'' and a friend.[44] She had good reasons for these attitudes. Eleanor Roosevelt publicly identified with all of Bethune's interests. In the 1940s she visited Bethune's school and participated in a series of its fund-raising activities that included a small meeting of potential donors at the White House. She regularly appeared at conferences of the National Council of Negro Women, arranged for the organization to use government facilities for its meetings, and entertained council women at teas in the White House. She assisted Bethune in her NYA work most visibly by supporting and addressing the two Negro conferences over which Bethune presided. In addition, Mrs. Roosevelt solicited Mrs. Bethune's opinions and advice, invited her to social functions at the White House, contacted the president and government officials on her behalf, and arranged for her to see the president.[45]

In an era of plenipotentiaries for racial blocs, blacks potentially gained from the black-white leadership contact just as whites did. Their leaders not only represented the white establishment to blacks but also expressed to it the concerns they had as black people. More specifically, Negro leaders influenced the establishment to act favorably on Negro-related issues.[46] Bethune conceived of herself primarily in this role as a Negro leader. She frequently declared that this was her purpose for being in Washington. For example, after one White House affair she remarked, ''It is for me a sacred trust so to touch these fine people as to interpret to them the dreams and the hopes and the problems of my long-suffering people.''[47]

Understandably, confrontation with government officials was not her style and she was pleased that President Roosevelt partially acquiesced to the demands of the black March on Washington movement in June 1941 without the march having taken place.[48] In attempting to influence whites, she usually dealt with them on an individual basis. She appealed to a person's noble instinct and usually expressed confidence in her or him regardless of what she actually thought. This was the case with Paul V. McNutt, chairman of the Fair Employment Practices Committee and governor of the War Manpower Commission. In January 1943 she told him: "I want you to understand that I have the utmost confidence in you and your relationship to my people and the deepest appreciation for what you have done in the past and what you will do in the future."[49] Yet in a cautiously worded letter to a black editor she revealed a different attitude: "The President has placed the entire Fair Employment Practice Committee under the directing hand of Mr. McNutt. I think political pressure has brought this about. In my mind, it seems that the whole thing will not be as active, yet we cannot tell how things will work out."[50] Though unquestionably championing Negro causes, Mary Bethune's success in influencing the administration outside of the NYA was centered upon getting particular exceptions to generally discriminatory policies and procedures.

Bethune had the support of the black masses, for they perceived her as a "symbol of greatness without ostentation; of action without subservience, and of thorough sympathy and understanding" of their problems.[51] In order to further enhance her capabilities and credibility as a black spokesperson, she organized several groups of Negro leaders in the center of the political spectrum, most notably the National Council of Negro Women, the Federal Council on Negro Affairs, and the National Conferences on the Problems of the Negro and Negro Youth. She listened carefully to the participants in each and then tried to harmonize divergent viewpoints within a group because she believed ardently in a black united front.

The National Council of Negro Women grew out of Bethune's yearning for an organization to represent black women forcefully in public affairs. On December 5, 1935, at the 137th Street Branch of the Young Women's Christian Association in New York City, Bethune had thirty representatives of national women's organizations listen to her reiterate her philosophy and goals:

> I am interested in women and believe in their possibilities. . . . We need vision for larger things, for the unfolding and reviewing of worthwhile things . . . through necessity we have been forced into organization. . . . We need a united organization to open doors for our young women so that when it speaks, its power will be felt.[52]

Responding to the Bethune charisma and a motion made by Addie Hunton of Alpha Kappa Alpha Sorority and seconded by Mabel Staupers of the National Association of Colored Graduate Nurses, the women voted to create the National Council of Negro Women. When Mary Church Terrell of the National Association of Colored Women moved that Bethune become president, the women then unanimously voted approval.[53] A few months later President Bethune stood before the NYA National Advisory Committee explaining the nature of the National Council and the assistance it would give to the NYA programs throughout the country.[54] Though individual council women may have backed the NYA locally, the council itself lacked the resources to do it. In the early forties, however, it was becoming established and demanding recognition. In October 1941, for example, when the Public Relations Bureau of the War Department failed to invite any black women to participate in a conference to organize the women behind the national defense effort, Mary Bethune, in the name of the council, protested to Secretary of War Stimson; Brigadier General Surles, chief of the Public Relations Bureau; William Hastie, civilian aide to the secretary of war; Mrs. William Hobby, president of the women's group which the Public Relations Bureau organized; and Eleanor Roosevelt. In a widely publicized letter she wrote:

> We cannot accept any excuse that the exclusion of Negro representation was an oversight. We are anxious for you to know that we want to be, and insist upon being considered a part of our American democracy, not something apart from it. We know from experience that our interests are too often neglected, ignored, or scuttled unless we have effective representation in the formative stages of these projects and proposals. We are not blind to what is happening. We are not humiliated. We are incensed. We believe what we have asked is what we all desire — unity of action, thought and spirit.[55]

The same belief in the efficacy of black cooperation which inspired Mary McLeod Bethune to establish the National Council of Negro Women also led her to organize the Federal Council on Negro Affairs, an informal group which was popularly dubbed the "Black Cabinet." Though the term cabinet was inaccurate because the group was not the president's council, nevertheless, it did influence some patterns of thinking within the government. Its primary concerns included nondiscrimination in government-sponsored facilities such as cafeterias, expansion of opportunities especially in government jobs, prevention of government actions potentially harmful to Negroes, and promotion of Negro support for the New Deal.[56]

In August 1936 less than two months after Bethune arrived in Washington to work for the NYA, she assembled in her home at 316 T Street Northwest seven other prominent blacks in government who were all male and college-trained. At that time, she set the tone for the group she was organizing with: "Let us forget the particular office each one of us holds and think how we might, in a cooperative way, get over to the masses the things that are being done and the things that need to be done. We must think in terms as a 'whole' for the greatest service of our people."[57] Throughout her NYA tenure, she tended to hold this informal and somewhat elusive council together and was critical to its operations because of her access to the White House. The council's membership fluctuated over this period, but in September 1939, thirty individuals belonged to it.[58] Jane R. Motz, who studied this Black Cabinet, identified its inner circle as including William Hastie of the Department of the Interior and the War Department; Robert Weaver of Interior, Housing, and several manpower agencies; Henry Lee Moon and Booker T. McGraw, two of Weaver's assistants; Frank Horne of the NYA and Housing; William Trent, Jr., of Interior and the Federal Works Agency; Ted Poston of the Office of War Information; Campbell Johnson of the Selective Service System; Alfred E. Smith of the Federal Emergency Relief Administration and the Works Project Administration; and Lawrence Oxley of the Labor Department.[59]

The federal council helped Bethune in planning and arranging for the National Conference on the Problems of the Negro and Negro Youth which also strengthened her position as a black spokesperson to the administration. The striking virtues of the conferences were that they focused the government's attention on the inferior status of blacks in American life, and they constituted a forum through which Negroes spoke for themselves about the problems they wanted the government to address. Bethune personally presented the conference reports to the president and had her office distribute thousands of copies to government officials and interested citizens. The first meeting was held at the Labor Department January 6-8, 1937. Though Aubrey Williams was reluctant to have the NYA sponsor this gathering because a comprehensive consideration of Negro problems was beyond the scope of his agency, nevertheless, Bethune prevailed upon him.[60]

The conference was not national in terms of the geographical homes of the participants, for very few of the eighty-three conferees and twenty consultants resided west of the Mississippi. However, it was national in terms of the interests it represented. The federal government, six major newspapers, eighteen civic, fraternal, and professional organizations, five religious denominations, and numerous educational institutions and organizations sent participants. The delegates categorized the basic problems of the Negro into four areas: unemployment and lack of economic security, inadequate educational and recreational facilities, poor health and housing conditions, and fear of mob violence and lack of protection under the law. They gave overwhelming attention to the economic problem with fourteen specific recommendations. In terms of general policy, they urged the government to offer leadership in abolishing de facto segregation but where legally mandated, they wanted it to provide more opportunities and facilities.[61] The second conference held two years later was convened to evaluate the status of the Negro since the last meeting, highlight problems which the government could help alleviate, and consider the possible effect of more recent legislation. It was on a grander scale in that two hundred and twenty-five delegates, approximately fifty visitors, and thirty-five consultants participated. Yet, the conference organization, the problems, and the solutions were similar to the first.[62]

Though very proud of the conference proceedings, Bethune was disappointed that they had not noticeably stimulated the government to act in behalf of the Negro. For this reason, she privately turned thumbs down on another such gathering. In relation to the conference recommendations, she cataloged the most obvious government failures in this way: insufficient Negro personnel in policy-making positions in key federal agencies affecting Negro life, the absence of Negroes on important emergency committees, neglect in integrating Negroes into army and navy active combat units and providing equal opportunities for advancement in the military, and a steady decline in Negro employment in the permanent government agencies.[63]

Backed by the National Council of Negro Women, the Federal Council on Negro Affairs, and the National Conferences on the Problems of the Negro and Negro Youth, Mary Bethune urged President Roosevelt to lead the civil rights struggle on several fronts such as antilynching and voting, but most frequently, she seemingly called on him to appoint blacks to top-level jobs. Though Bethune was more interested in programs and policies designed to reach millions of blacks than in the "token" employment of a Negro here and there, she viewed getting blacks in major positions as an essential step toward elevating the Negro people.[64] Sometimes she requested that a specific individual be given a certain office: for example, that Charles Houston, the NAACP attorney who in 1938 successfully argued the Lloyd Gaines case before the Supreme Court, be appointed to that Court.[65] Usually, however, she did not recommend specific individuals but concentrated only on the positions. She asked the president to appoint a Negro to either a federal district court or a circuit court noting that while it was encouraging to have a Negro federal judge in the Virgin Islands, he did not have indefinite tenure as federal judges do in the continental United States. She requested that in the military establishment he name a Negro to the Office of War Information, a Negro special assistant to the secretary of war, and twenty Negroes to the Military Academy at West Point and the Naval Academy at Annapolis. She petitioned for more blacks in the New Deal agencies, especially the Civilian Conservation Corps, the Social Security Board, the Federal Housing Authority, and the Home Owners Loan Corporation. In addition, she called for blacks on various other staffs: the Board of Appeals of the Civil Service Commission, the Labor and Agriculture Departments, the Office of Education, and the White House. Though pushing primarily for new jobs, Bethune also requested that positions blacks had previously occupied be restored to them such as the register of the treasury, minister to Haiti, auditor of the navy, and collector of customs at several ports.[66] Roosevelt made a few black appointments but Bethune's role in these cannot be assessed. Although the president listened to her, he did not act upon most requests. In January 1942 she was really concerned about this and probably pressed the issue by asking that he appoint blacks to positions other than those related exclusively to race problems.[67]

The emphasis on appointments did not preclude Mary Bethune from making other requests in behalf of blacks. Noting that Negroes North and South were irked by the president's periodic visits to the segregated Warm Springs, Georgia, when no comparable black rehabilitation center existed, at least twice she tried to interest the NYA in rectifying the situation. She suggested that it create a special fund to train unemployed, physically incapacitated Negro youth for work careers, but the agency vetoed it.[68] Going outside of the NYA framework, Bethune turned to Eleanor Roosevelt to help improve the status of blacks by facilitating the approval of certain projects. Usually, Mrs. Roosevelt obliged. Frequently, her intervention did not mean immediate approval, but Bethune always gained from it a better understanding of a given situation. This was the case with the Community Colored Hospital in Wilmington, North Carolina. In September 1941 Bethune pointed out that the expansion of this hospital was essential because Negroes were flocking to Wilmington. They were lured by the two recently established army camps and defense jobs in the shipyard that was constructing thirty-seven steel freighters weighing ten thousand tons each. Bethune asked Mrs. Roosevelt to "take a moment and see to it that this one project is brought to the attention of the proper persons with your personal emphasis." She complied and reported that the Federal Works Agency was making every effort to expedite the project.[69] Sometimes when Bethune turned to Eleanor Roosevelt the results were immediate. This happened in 1939 when Bethune asked her by telephone to facilitate the approval of a 167-unit Negro housing project in Daytona Beach, which had been stalled for some time. After Mrs. Roosevelt contacted Nathan Strauss, head of the Federal Housing Authority, things moved smoothly for the $500,000 project.[70]

Though frequently working outside of the NYA framework, Mary McLeod Bethune was always mindful of her NYA responsibilities. As the top Negro specialist, she continued to strive for greater Negro leadership within the agency. This involved getting blacks named to all the advisory committees in southern states, and she accomplished this in 1941. Also, it meant having blacks hired in the NYA professional jobs outside of her division. By 1941 the Youth Administration had employed six blacks in such positions, four of whom were women.[71] Bethune concentrated, however, on placing black administrative assistants in the offices of the state youth directors. She had first proposed this on August 8, 1935, before the NYA had crystallized. She quickly won an endorsement for the idea from the National Advisory Committee and her persistence in pursuing it led to its realization. When she became the agency's chief Negro specialist, there were about fourteen states with assistants. The number employing them gradually increased to twenty-seven and in 1941 included all southern states except Mississippi. In addition, New York City and the District of Columbia each had a black administrative assistant.[72] The assistants' monthly pay varied from state to state. In 1939, Robert J. Elsy, the assistant for New York City received $333.34, the highest salary among them, and Venice Spraggs of Alabama received $140.00, the lowest.[73] William H. Shell of Georgia, who in 1940 headed a state Negro staff of eleven, was the outstanding assistant in the South as Charles Browning of Illinois was in the North. Their success stemmed from their own capabilities and the leeway and support they obtained from their state directors. Most state directors, however, denied black assistants such substantive opportunities for leadership. Some were plainly prejudiced, insensitive to Negro needs, or unwilling to improve black-white relations. They prohibited black assistants from attending meetings with the regular staff, failed to make needed materials available for their work, provided inferior office arrangements and paid them lower salaries than they did whites.[74]

Early, Bethune advised assistants to convert unsympathetic directors, be patient, use common sense, and glorify their work and not themselves.[75] Behind the scenes, she endeavored to eliminate black-white salary differentials and to improve working conditions. In addition, she tried to bring the assistants together for periodic national or regional conferences as one method of keeping them informed of the changing policies and programs of the agency and to better prepare them to promote the interest of Negro youth. Seeing the assistants as agents of her division, she also attempted to strengthen their ties with her office. It was always an uphill battle because the Youth Administration frowned upon any administrative framework wherein Bethune could develop a closely knit relationship with the assistants. Williams promoted state autonomy and emphasized to the black personnel that their purpose was to assist the state directors in allotting a proper share of the NYA program to Negroes.[76] Consequently, Negro assistants made reports to the national office usually through the state directors, and comprehensive and accurate data on Negro activities were difficult for Bethune to obtain. Some state directors even intimidated assistants for communicating with Bethune's division because they interpreted it as disloyalty to their own offices. Despite these obstacles, Bethune persevered in her efforts until 1942 when the NYA completely ended the state programs in favor of a regional one. Within the new structure, the program employed nine regional Negro Affairs Representatives, and Bethune tried to help them cope with problems similar to those experienced by the former state assistants.[77]

As director of the Negro Division, Bethune sometimes got caught in the middle of disputes involving blacks who expected her support and whites who did likewise. On the one hand, she had to champion Negro rights to be a creditable leader; on the other, she had to maintain white support to be an effective employee. In one such case, Bethune attempted to fudge the issues but nevertheless veered toward the white establishment. This was in the summer of 1940 after George R. Vaughns, president of the Dumas League in Oakland, California, protested the abolishment of the Office of Negro Affairs and dismissal of the Negro administrative assistant, Vivian Osborne Marsh by the California NYA. Believing that the state office was insensitive to Negro needs, Vaughns contacted Eleanor Roosevelt to facilitate a satisfactory adjustment of the problem. In doing so, he referred her to Mary McLeod Bethune for "all the facts in the case." In response to Roosevelt's inquiry, Bethune, who personally knew Mrs. Marsh, noted that Marsh had done an excellent job in California. Then her facts became: "The policies, activities, and records of the NYA show definitely that discrimination because of race will not be, and has not been tolerated. . . . There would be evidence of discrimination if the State Administration refused to employ Negroes in any capacity." She understood, however, that the state administrator was willing to hire blacks in clerical and supervisory positions and Marsh could apply. Stating that the administrator was doing all he could to adjust the matter satisfactorily, Bethune also endorsed his right to abolish the Negro office. He should know whether such a scattered California youth population could justify a state office. Furthermore, she claimed, even some of the state's black leaders were opposed to the Negro office because "they felt that it would bring about a form of segregation." The records failed to reveal why Bethune emphasized the general integrity of the NYA when she knew so well its shortcomings at the state and local levels. Maybe this was only a public stance, for Mrs. Roosevelt had asked for a statement that she could give to Mr. Vaughns, and Bethune exerted constructive pressure within the agency. Maybe she believed that black visibility in California was a losing battle and she needed to conserve her moral weight for more promising ones. Whatever the truth, the situation illustrated the dilemma of a black leader in government.[78]

Bethune spent much time interpreting the NYA to Negro groups so as to encourage them to become involved in the program either as youth participants or project sponsors. In doing this, she naturally publicized notable projects. One was Camp John Hope in Macon, Georgia, a rural recreational center consisting of twenty-four cabins, a dining room and assembly hall, and other buildings which NYA Negro youth had constructed. Another, involving the Civilian Conservation Corps and the Works Progress Administration as well as the NYA, was the National Park Service project in San Francisco, California, which employed youths under competent supervision for work in photography, blueprinting, woodworking, and art.[79] Even more than substantive projects, however, Bethune publicized the psychological impact and the potential of the NYA. During the depression, she stressed this in order to buoy the spirit of black youth. She never claimed that the NYA was meeting their needs adequately but more modestly that it was "indicating the path along which lies increased opportunity" for education, job training, employment, and recreation. The NYA was a priority agency for blacks, Bethune broadcast, because its administration was characterized by a spirit of justice and fair play. She repeated this message from the beginning to the end of her association with the agency. After President Roosevelt's Executive Order 8802, she specifically publicized Aubrey Williams's immediate affirmation of the antidiscrimination order to the NYA staff.[80] Bethune got this message across in several ways. She used letters, the NYA booklets, magazines, and newspapers. In 1937 and 1938, she even wrote a column, "From Day to Day," for the *Pittsburgh Courier*. Her most effective means of publicizing the NYA, however, was personal contact with groups of people, of which she had a great deal. During her first year as a specialist, she traveled forty thousand miles through twenty-one states. She generally kept up this pace until 1940 when Negro regional representatives were employed. Her most extensive single tour was a swing through the central and western part of the United States from April 5 to May 18, 1938.[81]

In addition to publicizing the NYA, Mary McLeod Bethune's primary responsibility as specialist was to insure equitable black participation in each of the major program components. Although this was an ideal that was not generally realized, especially in terms of proportionate expenditures for black youth vis-a-vis white, nevertheless, Bethune enjoyed considerable success in the student aid program. From the very beginning of the NYA until 1942 when the student program was curtailed, it was the most satisfactory component of the program for blacks. In July

1939 the NYA even acquiesced to longstanding requests from Negroes for an official statement banning discrimination in student aid. It adopted a policy regarding the distribution of school aid funds to a minority racial group which specified that it could "not represent a smaller proportion of the total school aid fund quota than the ratio which this racial group bears to the total population of the school, district or state."[82]

Probably, Bethune's most striking contribution toward an equitable program at the secondary level related to the training of teachers for rural Mississippi. Though she characteristically saw something positive in every situation, when she visited Mississippi in 1937 she reported that the problems were so grave she could not publicly discuss them but she would continue to work toward their alleviation.[83] In doing this, she helped to influence the agency to approve a plan whereby some funds allocated for Negro high school youth in Mississippi were diverted into the employment and training of teachers for Negro rural schools in that state. Prior to this, rural Negro youth had received few NYA school funds because with so few high schools available to them, they simply were not in school. Under the new plan, the NYA made available a yearly average of one hundred and twenty-five teachers for rural schools in an intensive nine-month training program that the State Department of Education approved. The training was conducted in five high school centers located at Brookhaven, Clarksdale, Edwards, Greenwood, and West Point. Such a program was in line with Bethune's suggestions for rural areas when she initially joined the NYA staff.[84]

Bethune did even more toward assuring blacks equitable participation in the college and graduate programs even though relatively few blacks benefited from them. She worked, for example, to include Negro institutions in the Civilian Pilot Training Program that the NYA administered from 1939 to 1941. As a result, it became the major avenue through which blacks entered aviation and paved the way for black pilots in the military. Six black colleges participated: Howard University, Washington, D.C.; Tuskegee Institute, Tuskegee Institute, Alabama; Delaware State College, Dover, Delaware; Hampton Institute, Hampton, Virginia; North Carolina Agricultural and Technical State University, Greensboro, North Carolina; and West Virginia State College, Institute, West Virginia. West Virginia State was the first black institution to win approval for the aviation program and in addition to training black male pilots, it also trained black female pilots and white male pilots. Tuskegee Institute operated the largest program among the black schools in that it offered advanced as well as primary training.[85]

Bethune's greatest contribution in promoting more equitable benefits in the higher education program, however, revolved around administering the special fund for Negroes. It began as a fund for Negro graduate students but was expanded in 1938 to include Negro colleges as well. Since black students also benefited from regular NYA higher education work-relief, this fund was justifiable in terms of the greater needs of Negroes and as a means through which the NYA could somewhat approximate the aid it gave to white students. In its first year, the fund accounted for black students receiving 7.4 percent of higher education aid as compared to 2.5

percent in the previous year.[86] During the seven years of the fund, four thousand one hundred eighteen students participated in a total of $609,930. From a beginning of $75,060 in 1936-37, the fund reached its highest level in 1940-41 with $111,105. This was below the $200,000 annual allotment which Bethune wanted, but she was still encouraged.[87] With the fund, she supported two notable programs. The first was graduate training to make available one hundred librarians for high schools that needed them in order to become accredited. Participating institutions were Atlanta University, Atlanta, Georgia; Fisk University, Nashville, Tennessee; Prairie View College, Prairie View, Texas; and Hampton Institute, Hampton, Virginia. The other was commercial dietetics training to prepare students for positions as dieticians, chefs, and waiters. Tuskegee Institute offered this program.[88]

Mary McLeod Bethune was unable to influence the out-of-work work-relief and training program for Negroes as she did the student-aid program. Her division did not administer any funds for these projects, and it had neither an approval role nor a regular feedback regarding Negro participation in them. Nevertheless, through various actions and recommendations, Bethune had some success in broadening the base of Negro participation in this component, as in the others.

Initially, her concern was getting projects into immediate operation. The easiest projects to start for Negroes were those relating to their unskilled occupational status. This was especially true since projects required organizational sponsorship and Negro communities possessed relatively few financial resources for advanced training. Cognizant of this reality and a believer in industrial education somewhat in the Booker T. Washington mold, Bethune promoted training in domestic service, cooking, sewing, beauty culture, laundering, truck gardening, chicken raising, and other such areas.[89] In 1937 she saw the establishment of resident training projects in twenty-five southern communities as a major step forward in the Negro program. These centers were located on or near black college campuses and recruited trainees from nearby rural areas. They continued to train youth in agriculture and domestic and personal service occupations.

After a year's experience with the resident projects, Bethune reported to Aubrey Williams that this type of training was entirely too narrow, and black youth needed opportunities in other areas. In addition, she sharply criticized black projects across the board. They were poorly organized, they were not the equivalent of projects for whites, and they did not begin to approach needs. With uncharacteristic bluntness, Bethune told Williams, "There is no really outstanding NYA project for Negroes in the country."[90] At a time when the NYA was beginning to invest in showcase projects for whites, Bethune requested that it do the same for blacks. She believed that it was not enough to have some black youth participate in these projects in places such as Charleston, West Virginia, and Quoddy, Maine. If, despite Negro protests, whites could conduct a segregated regional project in metal arts and crafts, auto mechanics, and aeronautical mechanics in Algiers, Louisiana, blacks needed something superior also. In June 1938 one among her several ideas for a superior Negro project was a permanent and imposing building in

Washington, D.C., to house a Little Theater and Arts Center. It would provide for stage productions, choral concerts, exhibits of African art, and other such activities. In making the recommendation, she noted the limited platforms blacks possessed for such artistic expressions despite their talents in these areas. In the next year she proposed expanding the existing aviation-oriented black project in Chicago into a Negro-supervised national resident program for machine shop practice, aviation ground mechanics, metal crafts, and specialized woodwork.[91]

Bethune's hopes for a truly superior Negro project along these lines were unfulfilled in the NYA's depression-oriented program but realized in its War Production Training Project at Wilberforce, Ohio. This project was so outstanding that it became the symbol for expanding Negro youth participation in the war training phase of the NYA. Several agencies sponsored it: the Army Ordnance, Fairfield Air Depot, Wilberforce University, Cedarville High School, and the NYA programs in both Wilberforce and Columbus, Ohio. From relatively small beginnings in September 1938, by 1942 the project had developed into one employing 350 youth in residence and twenty-three staff persons and containing twelve modern prefabricated buildings for living, working, recreation, and health. It offered training in machine shop, sheet metal, radio, arc welding, and auto mechanics.[92]

In addition to Bethune's emphasis upon a few superior projects, around 1938 she placed even greater priority upon getting NYA black youth out of the service-oriented projects into those offering construction and mechanical and metal working activities. In that year, the NYA decided as a matter of policy to train youth in such skills because shortages were apparent or expected. The agency, at that time had neglected to hire black youth because industry in general had refused to hire them in construction and mechanical jobs, and there were few immediately available jobs for blacks in 1940 and 1941 when it undertook the training program in earnest. In light of this, Bethune worked hard to see that black youths were not ignored in manpower training for vital war industries. She exhorted Negro young people to "Prepare Today for Tomorrow's Jobs" and successfully pressured the agency to expand Negro opportunities.[93] In February 1941 the number of black youth in out-of-school projects reached 63,622 which represented 13.2 percent of all such youth employed.[94] In April 1943 though the number had decreased to 10,742, they constituted roughly 20 percent of all youth in work projects. Certainly, not all of these Negro youth were given advanced training but a large proportion were.[95]

During the depression, Mary McLeod Bethune was least successful in facilitating equitable Negro participation in the placement component of the NYA, but her persistent efforts toward this end led to some achievements during World War II. In the 1930s there was a continuing scarcity of youth jobs, and many of the existing few were closed to blacks. The State Employment Services that were associated with the NYA program made no systematic effort to place blacks. The NYA employed few Negro junior placement counselors — for example, in 1937, it had only four in the whole country — and its white counselors generally found their hands full trying to get white youth employed without addressing the more difficult problems of black youth unemployment. Bethune believed that the crux and the culmination of the NYA was the placement of blacks into viable employment and that the agency would aggravate an already serious problem by supporting education and training without conscientiously assisting blacks in finding jobs. She argued further that this was so important that, if necessary, it should be promoted at the expense of school-aid and work-projects. In 1937 she recommended the employment of a national field representative to promote guidance and placement among Negroes, the publication and dissemination of materials on vocational opportunities, and the employment of more junior placement counselors.[96]

Over the next few years, the agency moved toward implementing these recommendations, but major changes did not occur until its defense and war-training phases. Then the NYA provided "the crack in the door" which led to the employment of Negroes on assembly lines in plants such as Bell Aircraft, Buffalo, New York; Sun Shipbuilding in Chester, Pennsylvania; Radio Corporation of America in Camden, New Jersey; and Kane Manufacturing Company in Louisville, Kentucky. One of its guiding principles was that "Negro youth should, if feasible, be introduced along with other NYA workers when a plant is just being opened or is expanding, and like in NYA both white and colored employees should be permitted to progress in their jobs together."[97] In 1942-43 the agency placed more than three thousand Negro youth in jobs through its interstate transfer plan. After training individuals, the plan involved transferring them to labor-shortage areas and introducing them to jobs through the medium of the NYA resident induction projects to industrial sites. Between May 1, 1942, and January 30, 1943, in Rocky Mount, North Carolina, 963 males participated in the largest induction project for blacks. From there they received jobs in the Norfolk Navy Yard.[98]

In July 1943 when Congress terminated the services of the National Youth Administration, black people, in particular, had reason to mourn its passing. Black newspapers had consistently given the agency a good press.[99] In the early program, blacks seemed to have appreciated most its school-aid component as indicated in an editorial comment from the *Pittsburgh Courier:* "Perhaps one reason why nothing but good is said of the NYA is because it has been doing a so obviously necessary work in aiding young people to complete their schooling and to adjust themselves to the developing social order."[100] In the later program, they valued most the training component. In December 1941 Walter White, executive director of the National Association for the Advancement of Colored People made this point clearly: "The N.Y.A. has offered the best opportunity for shop training and work experience according to modern industrial procedures which Negro youth could obtain."[101] Blacks knew that Mary Bethune was a significant force within the NYA and regretted seeing her lose her job with the agency's demise. Whether in Durant, Mississippi, or Detroit, Michigan, they had hailed her as a great leader.[102] Such leadership involved "will power, sensitivity to the age, clear thinking rather than profound thinking, the ability to experience the emotions of a group and to voice their aspirations, joined with control over those emotions in oneself [and] a sense of the dramatic.''[103] When Consuelo Young-Megahy of the *Chicago Defender* met her in 1937, she publicized that Bethune was "the angel" in the black NYA.[104] Most people were more restrained and there was reason to be because Bethune tended to monopolize situations unduly, dominate others, and exaggerate the truth.[105]

Mary McLeod Bethune managed to build a record of substantive achievement within the NYA despite great obstacles within the agency, an extended workload (for she was still president of Bethune-Cookman College until late 1942), recurring illnesses, and harassment from the House Committee on Un-American Activities.[106] She was able to use a relatively minor advisory position as a springboard to power on the NYA staff. She persuaded the agency to recognize Negro leadership through an expanded Office of Negro Affairs and the employment of black administrative assistants in more than twenty-five states. She guided it toward addressing the special needs of black people notably through the Special Graduate and Negro College Fund. She also promoted a somewhat "color-blind" approach to blacks by assuring them the same defense training and placement opportunities as whites. Records, publications, and correspondence fail to provide evidence of the same substantive achievement for Bethune as a black leader or a representative to the Roosevelt administration. In this capacity, which was intricately meshed with her NYA activities, instead of obtaining general policies geared toward antidiscrimination and a recognition of special black needs, Bethune got specific exceptions to unfavorable policies or procedures. This reflected no lack of zeal on her part in advocating black equality within government but rather the administration's unwillingness to give civil rights any priority. Bethune knew that the deeply rooted racism in American life dwarfed her best efforts toward improving the status of the race. She said that faith alone sustained her as it did oppressed peoples everywhere. She looked to the future noting that "It may take a long time, but because enough of us are willing to work for a better world, we will finally attain it."[107] A division directorship in the NYA was a low echelon position for an individual of Bethune's leadership capability. But then, she was both black and female and encountered the difficulties of belonging to both minorities. In the 1930s and 40s, a little niche in a temporary agency was the best that the government could offer a luminous black woman.

NOTES

1. *Chicago Defender,* 27 November 1937, in scrapbook, Mary McLeod Bethune Papers, Bethune Foundation, Daytona Beach, Florida. Since only the Mary McLeod Bethune Collection at Bethune Foundation and the Amistad Research Center were used, papers from these repositories will be referred to by repository name only after the first citation. All references to "Williams" are to Aubrey Williams except where otherwise indicated.
2. *National Notes,* July 1928, p. 3. This was the periodical of the National Association of Colored Women.
3. *California Eagle* (Los Angeles), 20 August 1926, p. 1.
4. Du Bois's statement found in Sadie Iola Daniel, *Women Builders* (Washington, D.C.: Associated Publishers, 1931), p. 79. Bethune's recollections are contained in "Interview with Dr. Johnson," typescript, undated, Bethune Foundation. Book-length biographies are Catherine Owen Peare, *Mary McLeod Bethune* (New York: Vanguard Press, 1951); Emma Gelders Sterne, *Mary McLeod Bethune* (New York: Alfred A. Knopf, 1957); and Rackham Holt, *Mary McLeod Bethune* (Garden City: Doubleday, 1964).
5. Published accounts of the NYA from a national perspective are found in Betty Lindley and Ernest K. Lindley, *A New Deal for Youth* (New York: The Viking Press, 1938); Palmer O. Johnson and Oswald L. Harvey, *The National Youth Administration* (Washington, D.C.: Government Printing Office, 1938); and National Youth Administration, *Final Report* (Washington, D.C.: Government Printing Office, 1943).
6. The defense orientation of the NYA was highlighted in the following: Aubrey Williams, *The Role of the NYA in the Nation's War Training Program,* undated; and *Youth, Jobs and Defense,* a NYA booklet, July 1941, both located at the Bethune Foundation. The rationale for the school-aid program was offered in Lindley, *A New Deal for Youth,* pp. 33-34.
7. NYA, *Youth, Jobs, and Defense,* p. 23.
8. Minutes, Conference of the National Youth Administration, 10 July 1935, File "Conferences, Aubrey Williams," File of Agenda, Stenographic Transcripts, and Proceedings of Conferences Called by the Executive Director and the Administrator, 1935-39, Records of the Executive Director and Administrator, Records of the Office of the Administrator (hereafter referred to as Proceedings of Conferences, Records of the Administrator), Records of the National Youth Administration, Record Group 119, National Archives (the Record Group will hereafter be referred to as RG 119, NA); Proceedings, Conference of State Youth Director, 19-21 May 1936, p. 13, Publications Issued by the Central Office, NYA File of Processed and Printed Materials, 1935-42, NYA Publications File (hereafter referred to as NYA Publications File), ibid. Mrs. Roosevelt's interest in the NYA is most apparent in the Charles Taussig Papers and the Aubrey Williams Papers, Franklin D. Roosevelt Library, Hyde Park, New York (hereafter referred to as FDRL).
9. Proceedings, National Advisory Committee Meeting, 28-29 April 1936, and Proceedings, Conference of State Youth Directors, 19-21 May 1936, NYA Publications File, RG 119, NA. In the report of another State Directors' Meeting, 26 October 1937, Williams used the word "niggers" (p. 8). On a transmittal slip, Bethune called this to the attention of Richard R. Brown, the assistant director, and asked that it be deleted on 24 November 1937. (Quasi-official Correspondence and Data File of the Deputy

Executive Director, 1935-38. Records of the Deputy Executive Director and Deputy Administrator, Records of the Office of the Administrator, RG 119, NA.)

10. Minutes, Conference of the National Youth Administration, 10 July 1935, File "Conferences, Aubrey Williams," Proceedings of Conferences, Records of the Administrator, RG 119, NA.

11. Rackham Holt, *Mary McLeod Bethune,* pp. 191-92; Mary McLeod Bethune, "My Secret Talks with FDR," in *The Negro in Depression and War,* ed. Bernard Sternsher (Chicago: Quadrangle Books, 1969), p. 57, reprinted from *Ebony,* April 1949, pp. 42-51. Florence Roane was with Mrs. Bethune when Mrs. Roosevelt called her in Daytona Beach to ask her to serve on the Advisory Committee in 1935. Interview, Florence Roane, 9 June 1972. Mrs. Bethune first met Mrs. Roosevelt in December 1927 when she attended the buffet luncheon for presidents that Mrs. Roosevelt gave as a part of the biennial meeting of the National Council of Women of the United States in New York City.

12. In 1935, Negro youth constituted 12.8 percent of the youth population but 15.3 percent of youth on relief. Marian T. Wright, "Negro Youth and the Federal Emergency Programs: CCC and NYA," *Journal of Negro Education* (July 1940), p. 405; and Final Report of the Division of Negro Affairs, 31 December 1943, pp. 12 and 22, Bethune Foundation.

13. Final Report of Negro Division, 31 December 1943, pp. 2-3 and 7-8.

14. Bethune to John J. Corson, 24 August 1935, and Corson to Bethune, 27 August 1935, File "Executive Committee," Correspondence and Reference File of Thelma McKelvey, Secretary to the Chairman, Records of the Chairman, Records of the National Advisory Committee (hereafter referred to as File of Thelma McKelvey); National Advisory Committee Meeting, 28-29 April 1936, pp. 143 and 153, NYA Publications File; and Report of the NYA State Advisory Committees, 14 April 1936, Inactive Correspondence, Negro Affairs, RG 119, NA.

15. Report of Conference on Negro Activities, 8 August 1935, File of Early "Inactive" Correspondence, 1935-38, Records of the Director, Records of the Office of Negro Affairs (hereafter referred to as Inactive Correspondence, Negro Affairs); and Conference of State Youth Directors, 19-21 May 1936, p. 4, NYA Publications File, RG 119, NA.

16. National Advisory Committee Meeting, 28-29 April 1936, pp. 167-71, ibid.

17. *Pittsburgh Courier,* 30 November 1940, p. 3.

18. National Advisory Committee Meeting, 28-29 April 1936, pp. 167-71, NYA Publications File, RG 119, NA.

19. Conference on Negro Activities, 8 August 1935; Juanita Saddler to Brown, 17 June 1936, Inactive Correspondence, Negro Affairs; National Advisory Committee Meeting, 28-29 April 1936, pp. 167-71, NYA Publications File; Bethune to Corson, 24 August 1935, File "Executive Committee," File of Thelma McKelvey, ibid.

20. Unofficial Minutes of Executive Committee Meeting, 2 December 1936, File "Meetings of the Executive Committee, August 1935 to the present," File of Thelma McKelvey, ibid.

21. National Advisory Committee Meeting, 28-29 April 1936, pp. 219, NYA Publications File, RG 119, NA.

22. Mary Bethune, "Secret Talks," pp. 57-58. Here, Bethune placed the meeting in 1934. Since it was the first committee meeting to report on the accomplishments of the agency, it took place in April 1936.

23. *Boston Chronicle,* 10 December 1938, scrapbook, Bethune Foundation; *New York Times,* 18 February 1931, Mary McLeod Bethune Papers, Amistad Research Center, Dillard University, New Orleans, Louisiana.

24. Bethune, "Secret Talks," p. 59.

25. National Advisory Committee Meeting, 28-29 April 1936, pp. 153, NYA Publications File, RG 119, NA.

26. Brown to Williams, 21 November 1935; Saddler to Carl A. Jessen [*sic* for Karl E. Jensen], 12 July 1935, File "Juanita Saddler," File of Copies of Letters Sent by Officials in the NYA Central Office and Accumulated in the Office of the Deputy Executive Director and the Deputy Administrator, 1935-40, Records of the Deputy Executive Director and Deputy Administrator, Records of the Office of the Administrator (hereafter referred to as Correspondence, Office of the Deputy Administrator), ibid.

27. Report Covering First Six Months, 15 July 1936, Inactive Correspondence, Negro Affairs, RG 119, NA.

28. During the Conference of Negro Administrative Assistants, 2-3 June 1936, Bethune even urged the assistants to cooperate with Saddler. (Report of the Conference, File "Negro Administrative Assistants, June 1936," Inactive Correspondence, Negro Affairs, RG 119, NA). Saddler submitted her resignation on 11 July 1936, and it became effective July 15. (Brown to Saddler, 18 July 1936, ibid.) Saddler's uneasiness with having Bethune in the NYA Office was confirmed to me in interviews with Lawrence Oxley, 3 November 1972, and Edward Rodriquez, 9 June 1972, both of whom were familiar with this situation.

Historian B. Joyce Ross presented a warped view of Saddler, Bethune, and the Office of Negro Affairs during the early period of the NYA in "Mary McLeod Bethune and the National Youth Administration: A case Study of Power Relationships in the Black Cabinet of Franklin D. Roosevelt," *Journal of Negro History* 60 (January 1975): 1-28. Her misunderstanding of the early Negro Affairs Office damages the credibility of a major segment of her article. In attempting to delineate Saddler's and Bethune's racial philosophies and to analyze Bethune's actions and problems during the agency's formative period, she misconstrued the relationship of Saddler and Bethune to the NYA. She saw Bethune as director of the Negro Office from 1935 to 1943 and Saddler as Bethune's assistant who "served for less than two years." Bethune, however, did not become an NYA employee until 24 June 1936. See copy of Bethune's record from the Civil Service Commission, Bethune Foundation. Saddler was employed only for about six and a half months. She was offered the job on 25 November 1935, reported to work on 2 December 1935, and left on 15 July 1936. See telegram, Brown to Saddler, 25 November 1935, ibid., and Report Covering First Six Months [July 1936], Inactive Correspondence, Negro Affairs, RG 119, NA. She was not Bethune's assistant except for twenty-two days. When Saddler began work, Brown notified twenty Negro leaders that she was the NYA "Negro Liaison Officer," a title early discarded in favor of "Administrative Assistant in Charge of Negro Affairs." Letters announcing her appointment were dated either 2 December 1935 or 3 December 1935. Regarding Saddler's title, see memo, Elizabeth S. Sanders to Mrs. Holmes, 24 February 1936, File "Juanita Saddler," Correspondence, Office of the Deputy Administrator, RG 119, NA. Therefore, for about six months Juanita Saddler was the only staff member in the Office of Negro Affairs.

Yet, during this period, Joyce Ross attributed to Bethune ideas, actions, and problems that belonged to Saddler. In this respect she ascribed authorship of the "Report Covering First Six Months of the Work of the Office of Negro Affairs" to Bethune instead of Saddler. Using this source she wrote: "According to Mrs. Bethune's account, her division began operation in December 1935, with no clearly designated functions or procedures. After remaining in her office for two weeks without having any contacts with national executives, she unilaterally formulated a tentative outline of the division's potential work. . . . " (Ross, "Mary McLeod Bethune," p. 21). This key report consisting of four pages was both undated and unsigned. Nevertheless, Saddler's authorship can be determined by an analysis of the document. The report included the following: the Negro Office began on 2 December 1935; the author submitted an outline to Brown two weeks later regarding the Negro program; very soon after the author arrived she visited Pennsylvania, New Jersey, and New York; and the author had been interested in evaluating projects. Saddler started work at the NYA the day the Negro Office began. She wrote the outline (Saddler to Brown, 16 December 1935, File "Juanita Saddler," Correspondence, Office of the Deputy Administrator, RG 119, NA). She made the visits and wrote reports about them. See for example, Report of Visits to Ithaca, Albany, Dutchess Junction, and Buffalo, 2-4 January 1936, Inactive Correspondence, Negro Affairs, RG 119, NA. And Saddler, not Bethune, characteristically made critical written evaluations of projects. In the report just noted, she observed that in some projects exclusively for Negroes, paternalistic whites had pre-empted all the staff positions.

29. Bethune, "Secret Talks," p. 58; *Pittsburgh Courier,* 1 August 1936, p. 9, and 17 October 1936, p. 9.

30. Copy of Civil Service Commission Record of Mary McLeod Bethune, Bethune Foundation.

31. Statement undated [1940], Bethune Foundation. R. O'Hara Lanier is listed as the assistant director in the statement.

32. Bethune to T. Arnold Hill, December 1940, Bethune Foundation.

33. Lindley, *A New Deal for Youth;* Annual Report of the Division of Negro Affairs, 1 July 1936-30 June 1937, File "Administration, Miscellaneous," General Subject File of the Director, Records of the Division of Negro Affairs, RG 119, NA (hereafter referred to as Annual Report, 1936-37, File "Administration, Miscellaneous," General Subject File of the Director, Negro Affairs, RG 119, NA); Annual Reports, 1936-38 and 1940-41, Negro Division Bethune Foundation.

34. Arabella Denniston to Bethune, 27 May 1943. Denniston's background was related to me in an interview with James C. Evans, 10 November 1972.

35. Gunnar Myrdal, *An American Dilemma* (New York: Harper, 1944), pp. 721-26.

36. Bethune to Stephen Early, 16 February 1937, President's Personal File, Number 4266, FDRL. Handwritten O.K. on letter, 17 February 1937.

37. Bethune, "I'll Never Turn Back No More," *Opportunity,* November 1938, pp. 324-26.

38. *Pittsburgh Courier,* 15 February 1941, p. 9; Aubrey Williams to Henry L. Stimson, 13 June 1942, Aubrey Williams Papers, FDRL.

39. Bethune, "What Are We Fighting For?" speech, The Southern Conference on Human Welfare, undated, Amistad Research Center, Dillard University, New Orleans, Louisiana.

40. Ibid.

41. Bethune, "The Negro and the National Defense," speech, patriotic demonstration, Detroit, Michigan, 3 August 1941, Bethune Foundation.
42. *Pittsburgh Courier,* 22 June 1939, p. 4; *Tampa Bulletin,* undated, scrapbook, Bethune Foundation.
43. Statement on the Blue Radio Network after the death of FDR, 13 April 1945, Bethune Foundation; *Pittsburgh Courier,* 2 October 1937, p. 14.
44. Introduction of Eleanor Roosevelt, Conference on the Problems of the Negro and Negro Youth, 12 January 1939, NYA News Release; radio script on Kathryn Craven's Program, Station WNEW, New York City, 30 April 1943, Bethune Foundation; and *Pittsburgh Courier,* 1 January 1938, p. 2.
45. Evidence of these activities is found in the Bethune Papers, Bethune Foundation, and Eleanor Roosevelt Papers, FDRL.
46. Myrdal, *An American Dilemma,* pp. 721-26.
47. *Pittsburgh Courier,* 5 June 1937, p. 8.
48. Bethune to Eleanor Roosevelt, 10 July 1941, Eleanor Roosevelt Papers, FDRL.
49. Bethune to McNutt, 22 January 1943, Bethune Foundation.
50. Bethune to Robert Durr, 5 August 1942, Bethune Foundation.
51. *Boston Chronicle,* 10 December 1938, scrapbook, Bethune Foundation.
52. Ruth Caston Mueller, ed., *Women United: Souvenir Year Book* (Washington, D.C.: National Council of Negro Women, 1951), p. 16.
53. Ibid.
54. National Advisory Committee Meeting, 28-29 April 1936, p. 171, NYA Publications File, RG 119, NA.
55. *Pittsburgh Courier,* 25 October 1941, p. 1.
56. Jane R. Motz, "The Black Cabinet: Negroes in the Administration of Franklin D. Roosevelt," (M.A. Thesis, University of Delaware, June 1964). My thanks to Mr. DeWitt Dykes for bringing this thesis to my attention.
57. Federal Council on Negro Affairs, 7 August 1936, Bethune Foundation.
58. Dutton Ferguson to Bethune, 23 September 1939, Bethune Foundation.
59. Motz, "The Black Cabinet," pp. 23-24.
60. Minutes, Executive Committee, 30 November 1936, File "Executive Committee," File of Thelma McKelvey, RG 119, NA.
61. Report of the National Conference on the Problems of the Negro and Negro Youth, 6-8 January 1937, NYA Publications File, ibid.
62. Proceedings of the Second National Conference on the Problems of the Negro and Negro Youth, 12-14 January 1939, Bethune Foundation.
63. Bethune to Williams, 17 October 1939, Bethune Foundation.
64. Bethune to James L. Fieser, 16 October 1943, Bethune Foundation.
65. Bethune made the suggestion in this manner: "It is interesting to notice that the press generally and Negro newspapers particularly are featuring the recent suggestion that Charles H. Houston of Washington be appointed to the United States Supreme Court bench." Bethune to Franklin D. Roosevelt, 27 November 1939, Bethune Foundation.
66. Ibid.; Bethune to Franklin D. Roosevelt, undated, Bethune Foundation; Bethune to Eleanor Roosevelt, 8 April 1941, Eleanor Roosevelt Papers, FDRL; Bethune to Eleanor Roosevelt, 4 February 1943, Bethune Foundation. Correspondence relating to the Federal Council on Negro Affairs also reveals an emphasis on appointments.

67. T. Arnold Hill to Bethune, 6 January 1942, and "Motions Passed at Conference" to reflect the wishes of the Negro people, statement, 7 January 1941, Bethune Foundation.

68. "Project on Crippled Youth," Bethune to Brown, 17 September 1936, File "Negro Administrative Assistants, June 1936," Inactive Correspondence, Negro Affairs, and "Negro Participation in NYA," Bethune to Williams, 6 June 1938, General Subject File of the Director, 1936-41, Negro Affairs, RG 119, NA.

69. Bethune to Eleanor Roosevelt, 26 September 1941, and John M. Carmody to Secretary to Mrs. Roosevelt, 8 October 1941, Eleanor Roosevelt Papers, FDRL.

70. Bethune to Eleanor Roosevelt, 25 May 1939, Eleanor Roosevelt Papers, FDRL; and *Sentinel Star* (Orlando, Florida), 25 June 1939, scrapbook, Bethune Foundation.

71. Annual Report, 1940-41, Negro Division; Karl Borders to Bethune, 20 October 1939, Bethune Foundation.

72. Conference on Negro Activities, 8 August 1935, Report of Conference of Negro Administrative Assistants, 2-3 June 1936, and Report of Activities with Special Reference to Negro Youth, undated [April 1936], File "Negro Administrative Assistants, June 1936," Inactive Correspondence; Negro Affairs, RG 119, NA; Annual Report, Negro Division, 1940-41, Bethune Foundation.

73. List of Negro Personnel on State Staffs, statement, 31 July 1939, Bethune Foundation.

74. Confidential Report on the Negro Program, undated [1938], Inactive Correspondence, Negro Affairs, RG 119, NA; Annual Report of the Negro Divison, 1936-37, File "Administration, Miscellaneous," General Subject File of the Director, Negro Affairs, RG 119, NA; Annual Report, 1938-39, Negro Division, Bethune Foundation.

75. Conference of the Negro Administrative Assistants, 2-3 June 1936, File "Negro Administrative Assistants, June 1936," Inactive Correspondence, Negro Affairs, RG 119, NA.

76. Ibid. See for examples, letter, J.P. Bond to Bethune, 28 July 1939, Bethune Foundation; notes of a telephone conversation, Brown to Garth Akridge, 14 October 1936, File "Field Reports General, Garth Akridge, July '36 thru July '37," Reports Received from Field Representatives and Regional Directors, 1935-1938, Records of the Office of the Deputy Administrator, RG 119, NA.

77. Annual Report, 1936-37, File "Administration, Miscellaneous," General Subject File of the Director, Negro Affairs, RG 119, NA, and Bob Brown to Bethune, 27 February 1943, Bethune Foundation.

78. George R. Vaughns to Eleanor Roosevelt, 11 July 1940; Secretary to Mrs. Roosevelt to Bethune, 22 July 1940; Bethune to Eleanor Roosevelt, 1 August 1940; and Secretary to Mrs. Roosevelt to Vaughns, 9 August 1940, Eleanor Roosevelt Papers, FDRL.

79. Annual Report, 1938-39, Negro Division, Bethune Foundation; *Pittsburgh Courier,* 2 April 1938, p. 14 and 7 May 1938, p. 15; and Final Report of Negro Division, 31 December 1943, pp. 187-88, Bethune Foundation.

80. "The Contribution of the National Youth Administration to the Development of Youth," speech, Kentucky Negro Education Association, Louisville, Kentucky, 15 April 1937, and "The Negro and the National Defense," speech, Patriotic Demonstration, Detroit, Michigan, 3 August 1941, Bethune Foundation; *Pittsburgh Courier,* 21 August 1937, p. 14 and 29 January 1938, p. 14.

81. Annual Report, 1936-37; File "Administration, Miscellaneous," General Subject File of the Director, Negro Affairs, RG 119, NA, and Annual Report, 1938-39, Negro Division, Bethune Foundation. Bethune's column which began on 23 January 1937, was originally labeled "Weekly Chats" but was changed on 20 March 1937 to "From Day to Day."

82. Report of Activities with Special Reference to Negro Youth, undated [April 1936], Inactive Correspondence Negro Affairs, RG 119, NA; and Policy prohibiting discrimination, adopted 25 July 1939, NYA letter, Bethune Foundation.

83. *Pittsburgh Courier,* 4 December 1937, p. 14.

84. Final Report of Negro Division, 31 December 1943, pp. 109-10, Bethune Foundation.

85. The Negro and the National Youth Administration, statement, undated [1944], p. 10; Patricia Strickland, *The Putt-Putt Air Force: The Story of the Civilian Pilot Training Program and the War Training Service* (Washington, D.C.: Department of Transportation, n.d.), pp. 39-47. My thanks to Mr. James C. Evans for giving me this book and emphasizing the role of the NYA in the development of Negro aviation.

86. Annual Report, 1936-37, File, "Administration, Miscellaneous," General Subject File of the Director, Negro Affairs, RG 119, NA.

87. Final Report of Negro Divison, 31 December 1943, p. 102; Bethune Foundation; and Annual Report, 1940-41.

88. Final Report of Negro Division, 31 December 1943, pp. 107-8, Bethune Foundation.

89. Bethune to Arthur Williams, 20 August 1936, Inactive Correspondence, Negro Affairs, RG 119, NA.

90. Confidential Report, undated [1938], and "Negro Participation in NYA," 6 June 1938, General Subject File of the Director, Records of the Division of Negro Affairs, RG 119, NA.

91. Ibid.; and Annual Report, 1938-39, Negro Division, Bethune Foundation.

92. Final Report of Negro Division, 31 December 1943, pp. 165-68, Bethune Foundation.

93. Ibid., pp. 116-20; *Pittsburgh Courier,* 14 May 1938, p. 14.

94. Final Report of Negro Division, 31 December 1943, p. 125, Bethune Foundation.

95. Aubrey Williams, Participation of Negroes in the War Program of the NYA, statement, undated [June 1943], Bethune Foundation.

96. Annual Report, 1936-37, Negro Affairs File "Administration, Miscellaneous," General Subject File of the Director, RG 119 NA; *Pittsburgh Courier,* 7 March 1937, p. 8.

97. The Negro and the National Youth Administration, statement, undated [1944], pp. 16-17, Bethune Foundation.

98. Final Report of Negro Division, 31 December 1943, pp. 149-50, Bethune Foundation.

99. See, for example, Annual Report, 1938-39, Negro Division, Bethune Foundation.

100. Ibid.

101. Circular letter, Walter White to members of Congress, 29 December 1941, Bethune Foundation.

102. *Pittsburgh Courier,* 8 May 1937, p. 8 and 4 December 1937, p. 14.

103. This description of leadership qualities given in "In Quest of Leadership," *Time,* 17 July 1974, pp. 21-34.

104. *Chicago Defender,* 25 September 1937, scrapbook, Bethune Foundation.

105. An example of Bethune monopolizing a situation was her keeping her presidential position at Bethune-Cookman while she also served as NYA Negro specialist; an example of stretching the truth was her saying that she was a division director before it became a fact. Several writers mention her domineering trait. See, for example, Motz, *The Black Cabinet*, p. 22.

106. Bethune was also investigated by the Federal Bureau of Investigation. Benjamin Davis, Jr., to Bethune, 27 September 1942, and Bethune to Benjamin Davis, Jr., 6 October 1942, Bethune Foundation. Bethune was named under H.R. 105, 78th Cong., 1st sess., as one of the government employees to be investigated on charges of subversive activities by the Dies Committee. Bethune was also investigated by the Federal Bureau of Investigation acting under the authority of Public Law No. 135, 77th Cong. See R.M. Barnett to Bethune, 31 August 1942, Aubrey Williams Papers, FDRL.

107. Radio script on Kathryn Craven's Program, Station WNEW, New York City, 30 April 1943, Bethune Foundation.

DARKNESS BEFORE THE DAWN: THE STATUS OF WORKING WOMEN IN THE DEPRESSION YEARS

Mary W.M. Hargreaves

Two excellent monographs of recent years, focusing upon the roles of women in the period between the world wars, have reached the conclusion that this was, indeed, a time of darkness for the cause of "equal rights." J. Stanley Lemons's account of *The Woman Citizen: Social Feminism in the 1920s* ranges well into the depression decade to recount the collapse of women's leadership in social reform as their movement splintered on the issue of protective legislation. The so-called "hard core" feminists' demand for an Equal Rights Amendment, when supported by the National Association of Manufacturers and opposed by the National Women's Trade Union League, carried overtones of a callous elitism that alienated laboring women from those engaged in professions and checkmated women's advance on all fronts.[1] The business and professional women's organizations generally opposed protective legislation until well into the thirties, when accessions from the growing ranks of clerical and mercantile workers began to leaven their membership.[2] The National Woman's Party, unsuccessful in its efforts to win congressional action on ERA, turned in the thirties to lobbying for international agreement on the rights of women; but such resolutions of endorsement, when adopted, were merely advisory.[3] And the Women's Bureau of the Department of Labor, after surveying the effects of protective legislation, presented in 1928 a report in the nature of a compromise, emphasizing the service of such standards in bettering conditions for men and women alike.[4]

William H. Chafe's *The American Woman: Her Changing Social, Economic, and Political Roles, 1920-1970* — a study which points up the wealth of data in the working papers of the Women's Bureau deposited in the National Archives — questions whether women as workers had made significant advances during the decade from 1910 to 1920 and views the intervening period to 1940 as a stalemate which culminated in the nadir of women's rights under the impact of depression.[5] During the 1920s, as he notes, the percentage of women who held jobs increased by only 1 percent.[6] The proportion of women in the professions rose in that decade from 11.9 percent to 14.2 percent, but over three-fourths were employed in school teaching and nursing, work traditionally identified as feminine. Less than 3 percent of the working women were classified in each of the categories of architects and lawyers, and those proportions remained stationary from 1910 to 1930. The number of women doctors declined by over 24 percent. And even in the domain of education, women lost ground as the percentage of teachers who were women declined from 85 in 1920 to 78 in 1940. During the thirties the proportion of women employed in the professions, generally, declined from 14.2 to 12.3 percent.[7]

A variety of contemporary surveys support and amplify Professor Chafe's account. Chase Going Woodhouse, reporting on the occupations of members of the American Association of University Women, showed no real change in the occupational distribution in 1927 from that in 1915. Over three-fourths were engaged in teaching or educational administration, and those not so identified were mostly in library and social work or, next most commonly, in secretarial and clerical jobs.[8] A 1938 survey of the occupational experience of members of the Business and Professional Women's Club showed that the numbers in the professions had increased most rapidly during the decade of the twenties but, as evidenced in other accounts, the chief gains had come in teaching and nursing.[9] Sophonisba P. Breckinridge, writing on "The Activities of Women Outside the Home," for President Hoover's Research Committee on Recent Social Trends, noted the same preponderance of professional women in the fields of education and nursing and the strides made in the professional advancement of women during the twenties, but she found a sharp decline in the percentage of women in medicine and surgery (to 4.6 percent by 1940) and a 1 percent decline in the already low proportion of women in the legal profession (to 2.4 percent by 1940).[10] Her more glowing report of the progress made by women on college faculties, from 19 percent in 1910 to 33 percent in 1930, stands as a measure of the decline during the thirties, when the proportion dropped to 25.5 percent by 1940. Even the Breckinridge account showed women comprising but 68.5 percent of the faculty in women's colleges, 16 percent in the coeducational schools, and 1 percent in male institutions, with the proportions of women in inverse ratio to the levels of rank. While women by 1930 held about one-third of the graduate degrees, they constituted but 4 percent of the full professors and 23.5 percent of the instructors.[11] The National Education Association in 1936 reported that although four-fifths of the public school teachers were women, they were greatly outnumbered by men in the

ranks of high school teaching, supervisors, principals, and school superinten-
dents.[12]

The role of women in the professions has been the most frequently discussed
aspect of women's status, but of over eleven million women employed in the
United States in 1940, less than one and a half million were classified as professional or semiprofessional. The largest group, nearly three and one-quarter million, were in service or domestic service categories; next were over three million
clerical and sales workers; and third, over two million factory operatives and
kindred workers.[13] Stenographers and typists, bookkeepers and accountants, telephone and telegraph operators, salespeople and store clerks had been rapidly
developing categories of women workers since 1880. The occupations of hairdres-
ser or manicurist and that of insurance or real-estate agent had come to the fore
around the turn of the century.

Whether professional, semiskilled, or unskilled, women workers were low paid
and received little more than half as much as men in the same job categories.
Breckinridge reported that in a study of Land-Grant Colleges in 1930-1931,
women were paid below the median salary at every academic rank, notably so
above the level of instructors. She noted, too, that in 1925 women workers in
cotton manufacturing averaged $793 annually — men, $1,015; women in tobacco
factories, $543 — men, $978; women in glass factories, $540 — men, $1,650.[14]
About one-fourth of the NRA codes of 1933-34 authorized a lower minimum wage
for women than men, as much as ten cents an hour lower in a day when a minimum
wage of 25 cents an hour was a standard yet to be attained. Labor contracts of the
International Ladies Garment Workers Union did not provide for equal pay or
nondiscriminatory seniority lists.[15]

During the first years of the depression, as factory workers experienced the
principal impact of declining business, a higher proportion of men than women lost
their jobs. By 1932 the trend had alleviated: service industries, in which women
predominated, were then reflecting the business decline but generally somewhat
less severely. A study by the National Industrial Conference Board, published in
1936, after surveying the differences in job classifications between men and
women in relation to the employment ratios over the period 1890 to 1930, found
evidence "almost entirely lacking" that the lower paid women workers had been
substituted for men or that women had "encroached" on so-called "male occupations." It reiterated the conclusion after reviewing the data for the period 1930 to
1935, but the evidence was less conclusive. In Ohio recovery in hiring of men for
clerical employment exceeded that of women by 5 percent and for the transportation and public utilities fields, by 30 percent; in general, however, the decline in
female employment had been less and the recovery level higher. For other States
— Illinois, New York, Tennessee, and Virginia — the latter trends were also
evidenced.[16] Nationally the percentage of employed women rose from 24.3 to 25.4
during the depression decade, the same rate of increase which had characterized
the decade of the twenties.[17]

Under the code of prevailing social mores the disparities of women's salaries were appropriate and the role of women as employees in an economy where jobs were scarce was reprehensible. Men were charged with a responsibility as family breadwinners, which was presumably not shared by women. Girls, it was argued, worked for only a few years, until they married, and, since they had only themselves to support, for wages which represented little more to them than "pin money." Frances Perkins, who was to become secretary of labor under the New Deal, in 1930 condemned the "pin-money worker" as "a menace to society, a selfish short-sighted creature, who ought to be ashamed of herself."[18]

Public censure during the early years of the depression quickly focused upon working wives. A survey of the members of Business and Professional Women Clubs, even before the depression, had shown that single women earned most, widows and divorced or separated women next most, and married women least.[19] Both the BPW and the Women's Bureau of the Department of Labor emphasized that women were working to support themselves or dependents.[20] But critics were not prepared to analyze the needs and, still less, to consider the relevance of payment according to the quality of service performed. When a public opinion poll in June 1937, asked whether a married woman should earn money "in business or industry if she . . . [had] a husband capable of supporting her," 82 percent of those interviewed replied, "No"; 18 percent, "Yes." In October, 1936, 34.6 percent of those surveyed conceded that a wife might hold a full-time job outside the home if the family needed her earnings; but even with such a consideration, 47.7 percent of those questioned replied, "No."[21]

The executive council of the American Federation of Labor in 1932 recommended that, when the husband was working, a married woman should not be hired.[22] Congress, by law enacted in that year and continued until 1937, required personnel reductions in the federal government under guidelines that released those whose spouses were also in the public service.[23] Repeated surveys by the National Education Association over the period showed a steady deterioration in the willingness of school boards to hire married teachers, from 61 percent who rejected such applicants in 1928, to 76.6 percent in 1930-1931, to 87 percent in 1940-41, although in the last year 29 percent were willing to make exceptions where there were dependents.[24] Bills were introduced in over half the states during the decade against the hiring of married women as public employees. Only Louisiana passed such a measure, and it was shortly repealed; but the policy widely prevailed.[25] A National Industrial Conference Board study, published in 1939, reported that 84 percent of the insurance companies, 65 percent of the banks, and 63 percent of the public utilities applied restrictions against employment of married women.[26]

Professor Chafe has seen World War II as "a watershed in the history of women at work. . . . " "In 1940," he notes, "the percentage of females at work was almost exactly what it had been in 1910, and there seemed little reason to expect any change in the future."[27] But this "bleak" picture ignores some significant changes which had emerged in the decade of the thirties.

Professor Chafe has himself noted the impetus given to activity of women in political affairs through the influence of Eleanor Roosevelt. "As the Depression deepened," he adds, "women reformers flocked to Washington to help manage the nation's emergency relief and social-welfare programs. Most of the women who came took professional positions in the WPA and other agencies. . . ."[28] Study of the planning activities of such programs as the Farm Security Administration shows the role of these women in the Civil Service, not only in Washington but also in the field, in agricultural regions where women's sphere as paid employees was generally limited to extension work.[29] Lucille Foster McMillan, herself United States Civil Service Commissioner in the late thirties, has presented a graph of the percentage of appointments of women in the Washington departments from 1883 to 1940 which strikingly reflects the surge of this movement in 1934 and again at the end of the decade.[30] By 1940 the proportion of women in the federal government, apart from the postal service and defense, amounted to 33.5 percent of all federal employees, and the ratio of women in Washington agencies was 40 percent.[31]

More important changes in the role of women in employment were evidenced by several fundamental shifts in the composition of this segment of workers. John D. Durand, who published in 1948 a projection of the labor force from 1890 to 1960, argued that young women who had begun work in their twenties would be less deterred by social pressures against continuing work as they grew older, that "each successive generation of women seems to have retained the greater propensity to be in the labor force which it developed in early adulthood. . . ."[32] Whether or not for that reason, the proportion of working women who were thirty-five years old and over increased from 33.1 percent in 1920 to 36.2 percent in 1930, to 40.4 percent in 1940, and to 43 percent by 1950, when it began to level off.[33] And despite the disapprobation of their employment, the proportion of working women who were married rose dramatically from 28.9 percent to 35.5 percent during the decade of the thirties.[34] Principally because of the decline in immigration, still a third difference delineated the working women of this period — Sophonisba Breckinridge noted that only 58 percent of the employed women in 1900 were native-born whites; by 1930 the proportion had risen to 71 percent; and by 1940 the distinction was no longer recorded.[35]

The pressure for added family income was certainly a factor in the accession of such women to the labor force in the depression years. Several studies have shown a negative correlation between average income and the proportion of the population in employment, and the coefficients of correlation are largest for women and for persons at either end of the age groups.[36] Robert W. Smuts, who has described the attitude toward working women at the turn of the century, noted that even then those who held extreme views of "women's place in life" were principally of the middle and upper classes: "a family had to have the means to support its women in sheltered idleness before it could come to believe that this was their natural state."[37] The South, which traditionally placed its women on a pedestal, was the poorest region of the nation in 1940 and had the highest percentage of married women working, a proportion of nearly seven out of eight with husbands present in the household. Census data in 1940 placed the national proportion at about six out of seven.[38] Mary Anderson reported to Eleanor Roosevelt in 1938 that 56 percent of the married women were employed in domestic and personal service or factories, low-paying occupations, "so it is correct to deduce," she concluded, "that the married woman must be at work because her husband's wages are not enough."[39]

Another aspect of the changing character of women's movement into the labor force at this time was manifest in the influx of girls from rural areas. Nora Miller, discussing *The Girl in the Rural Family* in 1935, saw the situation as one requiring readjustment programs for those who returned to the farm home when city jobs were lost during the business decline.[40] The Southern Woman's Educational Alliance published in 1930 the results of an extensive survey of *Rural Girls in the City for Work*. Of 255 girls interviewed, 84 were employed in mills or factories, 59 in stores, 67 in offices or as business students, 12 as waitresses, and the remainder in nurses' training. Well over half of them (142) were under twenty-one years of age. They tended to be the older children of large families. Most of them came from farms that their parents owned, but their families were of "comparatively low economic status" and two-fifths of the girls were contributing to their family's support. Eighty-nine cited financial reasons for moving to town.[41]

These were, however, only part of the explanation offered and, the report noted, "by no means always the strongest."[42] For some, this desire "to get work" was found to be an urge "to express" themselves by working outside the home. The proportion who had worked as farm laborers was small, but many had found that home duties in rural areas were drudgery — "the excessive amount of such work under especially difficult conditions and the many kinds of work not required of city girls evidently depressed and discouraged many of them," the report commented.[43] The loneliness of rural life was cited as another significant factor, "as large . . . as any single motive in bringing them to the city. . . . "[44] A desire for adventure, lack of adequate recreation facilities in rural communities, and a hope for more social contacts, especially male, were also reported as major incentives for the move. The investigators found that the girls worked long hours, a median of nine and a half hours a day, for low wages, but concluded that three-fourths of them had improved their general situation. Eighty-six percent of the girls themselves considered their condition bettered.[45]

Surveys of emigration from the Plains states, a movement heightened by the drought experience of the thirties, report the same picture of an exodus of women from rural regions at this time. Professor Kraenzel of the Montana Agricultural Experiment Station viewed it as "to be expected" that in the rural and agricultural part of the state "women migrated in larger numbers and at earlier ages than men. They were pushed out by the lack of occupational opportunities as well as attracted elsewhere by relatively better economic opportunities."[46] In North Dakota, too, more women departed than men, especially in the age group eighteen to twenty-five.[47] A South Dakota study in 1935 showed that more than twice as many girls as boys left home before reaching age eighteen, although the median age for women at the time of leaving was 20.48 years. Women moving from the state greatly outnumbered male migrants, and 29.1 percent of the women who left were employed, as contrasted with but 16.2 percent of the women who remained in the state. Three out of ten of the South Dakota women who left the state were professionals, principally school teachers; but the remainder were predominantly domestic and clerical workers.[48] Valerie Oppenheimer, who has studied *The Female Labor Force in the United States,* recognizes this urban shift of rural women workers in the period and explains it on other grounds than the hardships and loneliness of rural life. She finds that the employment of women in farm occupations, which had begun to decline in 1920, dropped sharply in the decade of the thirties, while for men the decline was gradual until 1940.[49]

Of particular concern to analysts of this rural migration was the fact that those who moved were a group who had attained more schooling than the average educational level in the state, and the women migrants were notably better educated than the men. Of thirty-nine male college graduates among the South Dakota migrants, twenty-four were still in the state in 1935; but of forty-three women college graduates, only seventeen remained. Over half of these women who stayed near home were teaching or had husbands who taught, but none of them had married farmers.[50] Mirra Komarovsky, who has surveyed the problems for educated women in their sociological roles, has pointed to another aspect of the educational distinctions, a tendency for power in the marriage relationship to reflect the difference in educational level of the woman, particularly in "blue-collar" society, where the high school diploma constituted a status symbol.[51] In 1940 only 12 percent of the men in the United States had finished high school, as compared with 16.2 percent of the women; 5 percent of the men had completed three years of college, but 6 percent of the women.[52] The upward climb of women from the grassroots in the thirties was challenging mores, not only in the labor market but in the broader range of sexual relationships. Historians have been slow to note the impact of the rising levels of education in the twentieth century on social mobility.

Glimmerings of daybreak in the position of working women were showing even before the "watershed" of Pearl Harbor. The depression years had been a period of particular difficulty for professional women, but developments in the status of other categories of women in employment were more promising. The family which depended on a woman's income or even on the ability of a young girl to support herself developed a concern about pay inequities. It benefited as the National War Labor Board contracts and those of the Congress of Industrial Organizations set an equality of standards to which the American Federation of Labor had long been hostile. Working women, at the same time, were becoming a more stable and mature force, increasingly identifiable as native-born, often representing the traditionally wholesome virtues of rural background, and standing in the vanguard of the rising general educational level. The public scorn which had been affixed to feminism of the twenties as elitist or even "socialistic" had lost the semblance of relevance.[53] While public opinion polls of the 1940s generally continued to show heavy majorities in opposition to employment of married women, some of them — notably in reference to hiring of women who lacked responsibility for child rearing — reflected a considerable softening of attitude. Dr. Oppenheimer concludes that the "attitudinal flexibility" demonstrated in growing approval of women working·in the first few years of married life "has probably been an important factor in making possible the great increases in female labor force participation in the 1940s and later."[54] The acceptance that was to be accorded the new feminism of the postwar period owes much to the democratization and stabilization of the movement in the depression years.

The women who contributed so largely to a climate for acceptance of the later movement have not, however, afforded it leadership. The philosophy of need on which they rested their demands was a very different concern from the professional woman's plea for "equal rights." Those who won a place in the labor market of the thirties learned that, like ethnic minorities, they survived because they did a job better, often cheaper, and because they exploited those attributes; those who hung on, to advance notably during the expansion of the war and postwar years, knew thay they held their position only because they were needed. Such women have found their social and cultural ethic far apart from the modern movement for "women's liberation." But like the union member who reluctantly pays his dues, they know that they gain as all women achieve recognition. Theirs is the muffled "Amen" in the corner for today's evangelistic crusade. If the current campaign to win acceptance of ERA is to be successful, it must recognize and cultivate the base provided by the upward mobility of those who advanced the· cause of women's rights through the darkness before the dawn.

NOTES

1. J. Stanley Lemons, *The Woman Citizen: Social Feminism in the 1920s* (Urbana: University of Illinois Press, [ca. 1973]), pp. 190, 191, et passim ch. 7.
2. Ibid., pp. 182, 204.
3. Ibid., pp. 196-99.
4. U.S., Department of Labor, Women's Bureau, *The Effects of Labor Legislation on the Employment Opportunities of Women*, Bulletin no. 65 (Washington: Government Printing Office, 1928), p. 19. The investigators emphasized that generalization was difficult. They noted that in some cases, where labor laws were applied to occupations differing from those for which they were drafted, they had proved a handicap. "But," their report concluded, "the findings seem to show that the instances of handicap, which have been diligently sought by the investigators, are only instances and should be dealt with as such, without allowing them to interfere with the development of the main body of legislation."

5. William Henry Chafe, *The American Woman: Her Changing Social, Economic, and Political Roles, 1920-1970* (New York: Oxford University Press, 1972), pp. 51-55, 58, et passim.

6. Ibid., p. 54; U.S., Department of Commerce, Bureau of the Census, *Sixteenth Census of the United States: 1940, Population,* vol. 3, *The Labor Force . . . ,* Pt. 1: *United States Summary . . .* (Washington: Government Printing Office, 1943), Table 37, p. 54. Cf. John D. Durand, *The Labor Force in the United States, 1890-1960* (New York: Social Science Research·Council, 1948), Appendix A, pp. 195-97. Durand argues that the Census data for 1910, particularly in reference to the employment of women and children, may have been inflated.

7. Chafe, *American Woman,* pp. 58, 59, 89, 92.

8. Chase Going Woodhouse, "The Occupations of the American Association of University Women," National Association of Deans of Women, *Fifteenth Yearbook, 1928,* p. 206.

9. National Federation of Business and Professional Women's Clubs, Inc., *Why Women Work . . .* (New York: Public Affairs Committee, 1938), p. 8.

10. S.P. Breckinridge, "The Activities of Women Outside the Home," in President's Research Committee on Social Trends, *Recent Social Trends in the United States* (New York: McGraw-Hill, 1933), pp. 722-26. The 1940 comparisons are derived from *Sixteenth Census: 1940, Population,* vol. 3, *The Labor Force,* Pt. 1, Table 58, p. 75.

11. Chafe, *American Woman,* pp. 91, 278 n.

12. National Federation of Business and Professional Women's Clubs, Inc., *Why Women Work,* pp. 8-9.

13. *Sixteenth Census: 1940, Population,* vol. 3, *The Labor Force,* Pt. 1, Table 58, pp. 75-80.

14. Breckinridge, "The Activities of Women . . . ," pp. 735-36. Cf. also *Sixteenth Census: 1940, Population,* vol. 3, *The Labor Force,* Pt. 1, Table 73, pp. 150, 154; Chafe, *American Woman,* p. 61; Beulah Amidon, "Women Breadwinners, They Don't Work for Pin Money," *Survey Graphic* 27 (March 1938): 151.

15. Chafe, *American Woman,* pp. 85, 86.

16. *Women Workers and Labor Supply* (New York: National Industrial Conference Board, 1936), pp. 2, 28, 37, 40, 42.

17. *Sixteenth Census: 1940, Population,* vol. 3, *The Labor Force,* Pt. 1, Table 37, p. 54.

18. "The Woman 'Pin-Money Worker'," *Literary Digest* 104 (1 March 1930): 12. She did concede that these "rich women" might enter "Politics and charitable work, law, medicine, and teaching," "artistic endeavor," or "agriculture," which needs workers.

19. Margaret Elliott and Grace E. Manson, "Earnings of Women in Business and the Professions," *Michigan Business Studies* 3, no. 1 (September 1930): 2.

20. National Federation of Business and Professional Women's Clubs, *Why Women Work . . . ,* pp. 16, 30; Agnes L. Peterson, *What the Wage-Earning Woman Contributes to Family Support,* Woman's Bureau Bulletin no. 75 (Washington: Government Printing Office, 1929).

21. Hadley Cantril, ed., *Public Opinion, 1935-1946* (Princeton: Princeton University Press, 1951), p. 1044.

22. Chafe, *American Woman,* p. 108.

23. Economy Act of 30 June 1932, sec. 213 (47 *U.S. Stat.,* 406), repealed 26 July 1937 (50 *U.S. Stat.,* 534). For a review of the effect of this legislation, see Lucille Foster

McMillin, *Women in the Federal Service,* 3d ed. (Washington: U.S. Civil Service Commission, 1941), pp. 30-32.

24. "Employment of Married Women as Teachers," National Education Association Research Bulletin no. 10 (January 1932): 19-20; "Teacher Personnel Procedures . . . ," ibid., 20 (March, May, 1942): 60-61, 107. Cf. also, David Wilbur Peters, *The Status of the Married Woman Teacher* (New York: Teachers College, Columbia University, 1934).

25. Six other states in 1940 operated under joint resolutions or executive orders restricting married women in employment, and three others "made a general practice" of such prohibition. Ruth Shallcross, *Should Married Women Work?* National Federation of Business and Professional Women's Clubs, Public Affairs Pamphlet no. 49 (New York: Public Affairs Committee, 1940), pp. 5-6.

26. Ibid., p. 9. Only 14 percent of the manufacturing and 11 percent of the mercantile concerns applied such limitations.

27. Chafe, *American Woman,* pp. 135-36.

28. Ibid., p. 39.

29. Despite the fact that women were in the majority of those abandoning the rural regions during this period, most state planning committees included no women. South Dakota finally provided in 1940 for designation of three women, one-fourth the farmer representation, as members of the state committee. They took their seats in 1941. South Dakota Land Use Program Committee, Minutes . . . , 12 July 1940, p. 3; 30 September 1940, pp. 13-15; and 2 January 1941, p. 2. State and Local Planning, South Dakota, Records of the Bureau of Agricultural Economics, Record Group 83, National Archives Building, hereafter cited as RG__, NA). In North Dakota there was specific criticism of the limited roles accorded women in planning activities. N.D. Agricultural Advisory Council, Minutes . . . , 13 March 1940, p. 3, RG 83, NA.

30. McMillin, *Women in the Federal Service,* p. 13.

31. *Sixteenth Census: 1940, Character of the Population,* vol. 2, Pt. 1, Table 22a, p. 975; *Population,* vol. 3, *The Labor Force . . . ,* Pt. 1, Table 74, p. 181. Frances Cahn, *Federal Employees in War and Peace, Selection, Placement, and Removal* (Washington, D.C.: The Brookings Institution, 1949), p. 61, places the percentage of women among all federal employees in June, 1938, at only 19.5. The McMillin graph, showing a percentage of 60 percent in the hiring of women for the Washington agencies in 1940, may explain the discrepancy.

32. Durand, *Labor Force,* p. 124.

33. Compiled from *Eighteenth Decennial Census of the United States, Census of Population: 1960,* I, Pt. 1, Table 160, p. 362. A 42.3 percentage was given in *Sixteenth Census: 1940, Population,* vol. 3, *The Labor Force . . . ,* Pt. 1, Table 66, p. 106.

34. *Sixteenth Census: 1940, Population,* vol. 3, *The Labor Force . . . ,* Pt. 1, Table 40, p. 57.

35. Breckinridge, "Activities of Women . . . ," p. 714. The proportion of foreign born women who worked remained constant at 19 percent from 1900 to 1930, and that of Negro women in employment declined slightly, from 41 percent in 1900 to 39 percent in 1930. Ibid.

36. Durand, *Labor Force,* p. 91.

37. Robert W. Smuts, *Women and Work in America* (New York: Columbia University Press, 1959), p. 137.

38. *Sixteenth Census: 1940, Population,* vol. 3, *The Labor Force* . . . , Pt. 1, Table 40, p. 57.
39. Anderson to Roosevelt, 22 January 1938, quoted in Chafe, *American Woman,* p. 57.
40. Nora Miller, *The Girl in the Rural Family* (Chapel Hill: The University of North Carolina Press, 1935), pp. 4-5 et passim. This volume reveals with remarkable clarity the traditional roles of women in rural society.
41. O. Latham Hatcher, *Rural Girls in the City for Work: A Study Made for the Southern Woman's Educational Alliance* (Richmond: Garrett and Massie, [ca. 1930]), pp. 1-2, 29-30, 40-51, 133.
42. Ibid., p. 41.
43. Ibid., p. 45. Cf. also, Mary W.M. Hargreaves, "Women in the Agricultural Settlement of the Northern Plains," *Agricultural History* 50 (January 1976) 79-89.
44. Hatcher, *Rural Girls,* p. 46. For other motives, see pp. 46-53 et passim.
45. Ibid., pp. 62, 84.
46. Carl F. Kraenzel, *Montana's Population Changes, 1920 to 1950, Especially as to Numbers and Composition,* Montana Agricultural Experiment Station Bulletin no. 520 (Bozeman, 1956), p. 27.
47. Stanley W. Voelker and Thomas K. Ostenson, *North Dakota's Human Resources: A Study of Population Change in a Great Plains Environment,* North Dakota Agricultural Experiment Station Bulletin no. 476 (Fargo, 1968), p. 20.
48. Walter L. Slocum, *Migrants from Rural South Dakota Families: Their Geographical and Occupational Distribution,* South Dakota Agricultural Experiment Station Bulletin no. 359 (Washington, D.C.: Brookings, 1942), pp. 8, 9; John P. Johansen, *The Influence of Migration upon South Dakota's Population, 1930-50,* ibid., Bulletin no. 431 (Washington D.C.: Brookings, 1953), pp. 20, 30-31, 35.
49. Oppenheimer, *Female Labor Force,* p. 150. Dr. Oppenheimer notes, too, that the movement of women in employment generally presages the shifting trends in the labor market (pp. 143, 151, 153).
50. Slocum, *Migrants from Rural South Dakota,* pp. 9, 14-15. Only 25 percent of the male, as compared with 42 percent of the female, migrants had completed high school.
51. Mirra Komarovsky, with Jane H. Philips, collab., *Blue-Collar Marriage* . . . (New York: Random House, [ca. 1964]), pp. 225-26.
52. *Sixteenth Census: 1940, Characteristics of the Population,* vol. 2, Pt. 1, Table VI, p. 11.
53. Lemons, *Woman Citizen,* pp. 33, 46, 58, 121-24, 202-3, and ch. 8.
54. Cantril, ed., *Public Opinion,* pp. 1046-47; Oppenheimer, *Female Labor Force,* p. 49. Dr. Oppenheimer does not view attitudinal change as the "decisive factor." Her analysis emphasizes the importance of labor demand in leading to the employment of married and older women. *Female Labor Force,* pp. 187-89. Her conclusion makes evident the responsiveness of the female labor supply to demand, and it indicates that social mores will react positively to such pressures.

DISCUSSION SUMMARY

Addressing Penny Martelet, Martin Claussen of Historiconsultants inquired about the attitude of rural women toward women from the city who wished to become farm laborers. Martelet said that the matter was not discussed in the sources she had used for World War I, but by extrapolating from records of World War II, she would say that rural women did oppose the farmerettes because they thought that urban women were not suited for farm life and could not stand its rigors. They also objected to having women undertake work that conjured up the image of the European peasant woman, working in the fields, lugging bales of hay. The proper responsibilities of American farm women lay primarily inside the farmhouse. Martelet had found no indication that rural women viewed the Woman's Land Army as competition in the rural labor market in the World War I period.

Miriam Crawford of Temple University asked Hargreaves to comment on how historians can give more attention to the role of black women and their activities in all of the questions that are being researched. "I think," she said, "this is the only way we're going to increase understanding, and advance the cause of women generally."

Hargreaves said that she would prefer not to discuss this issue because she is against discrimination in any form. She dislikes programs to hire women as women, or blacks as blacks. "I would much rather," she said, "that we were all hired on the basis of our abilities." In research, she added, "when we hone in on whether they are black women, or whether they are women, we in a sense establish a kind of segregation ourselves."

Smith agreed with Crawford that more research is needed on black women, but said that the sources for this work are very limited. She cited a recent experience at the Library of Congress where she was looking for material on the National Association of Colored Women, which has been in continuous existence since 1896. She found nothing. Yet there are quantities of publications about the General Federation of Women's Clubs. She has found significant material about black women, but it has taken a great deal of digging to do so.

THE IMPACT OF WORLD WAR II ON SEX ROLES

INTRODUCTION

Stanley L. Falk

With the following two papers we are moving into the World War II period. Susan Hartmann, who has written a very good book about the Truman administration, has made a study of women in the military service, and Eleanor Straub has described women in the labor force, a subject about which she has published elsewhere.

WAAC recruiting poster, World War II. (No. 44-PA-231, Records of the Office of Government Reports, RG 44.)

WOMEN IN THE MILITARY SERVICE

Susan M. Hartmann

The entrance of women into the military, one of the last bastions of male exclusivity, was among the most noted expansions in sex roles accompanying World War II. To be sure, women constituted only about 2 percent of total personnel, and the 275,000 women who served represented just a tiny portion of American women. Nonetheless, the incorporation of women into the military presents a fruitful field of investigation for students of social change. As one example of the expansion of women's traditional spheres, such a study can illuminate the ideological and social factors which both facilitated and inhibited change. In examining the legislative history of the women's corps, the policies and procedures regarding female personnel, and the roles assigned to women in the armed services, this paper attempts to assess the relative significance of military expediency, public attitudes, and women's own ambitions in promoting attitudinal and material alterations in women's status. In focusing on considerations which governed the men and women leaders who determined military policy, I do not deny the importance of examining the meaning of military service for those thousands of women who enlisted; such an approach is equally necessary for understanding how war influences sex roles, but lies beyond the scope of this paper.[1]

Women's entrance into the armed services reflected, in part, the changing nature of warfare and the military establishment. The global scope of American involvement, the increasing complexity of modern war, and the development of military technology resulted in a decreasing proportion of military personnel directly engaged in combat. During World War II, 50 percent of military personnel never left the United States, and only about one-eighth actually saw front-line duty. While during the Civil War 93.2 percent of army personnel engaged in purely military occupations, by World War II only 34.1 percent fell in this category. Thus, the increasingly "civilian" nature of many military duties — and by World War II, 14.6 percent of these were administrative and clerical — made possible the employment of women in the defense establishment.[2]

Most military leaders, however, were not quick to grasp this possibility, despite the precedent of World War I when more than 10,000 women had served in the

U.S. Navy and Marine Corps and several thousand civilian women had performed clerical and communications duties for the army. As the situation in Europe deteriorated during 1939 and 1940, both army and navy staffs considered the utilization of women, but neither branch would make a commitment to the establishment of women's corps until prodded by women themselves. In the spring of 1941, Republican Congresswoman Edith Nourse Rogers of Massachusetts gave political voice and focus to the demands of women's organizations and individual citizens when she informed Chief of Staff Gen. George C. Marshall that she planned to introduce legislation creating a women's corps. Fearing the establish- ment of a corps not to its liking, and specifically opposed to full military status for women, the War Department then began to prepare a bill that it could comfortably sponsor. Acceding to the army's insistence that the women's corps not be part of the army, Rogers introduced the War Department's bill to establish the Women's Army Auxiliary Corps (WAAC) in May 1941.[3]

Navy officials likewise responded to Rogers' initiative. When asked if the navy was interested in similar legislation, Rear Adm. Chester W. Nimitz, chief of the Bureau of Navigation, hedged but subsequently requested views from the various bureaus and offices. The only enthusiastic replies came from the Bureau of Aeronautics, the newest and least tradition-bound branch of the navy, and from the chief of naval operations who perceived the potential of women in communica- tions work. Despite the negative responses from seven other offices and bureaus, the navy decided to submit a bill. The momentum generated by the army's legislation suggested that further hesitation might result in legislative imposition of a corps that the navy could not effectively administer. For reasons of discipline, security and convenience, Secretary of the Navy Frank Knox wanted the women's corps in the navy, and such a bill was introduced in March 1942.[4]

In justifying their requests for the establishment of women's corps, both army and navy officials stressed manpower considerations. Arguing that the employ- ment of women could release men from noncombatant duties, they also insisted that women were better suited for certain jobs. By the summer of 1941, Marshall had recognized the inexpediency of using men for the kinds of military duties that women were regularly performing in the civilian sector. Citing the importance of the Army Aircraft Warning Service, Assistant Chief of Staff John H. Hildring testified that such work was very tedious, "and we have found difficulty in getting enlisted men to perform tedious duties anywhere nearly as well as women will do it." In presenting examples of other duties that women might perform, military officers routinely indicated that they would be used as switchboard operators, typists, clerks, dieticians, and laundry operators. Finally, they argued that for reasons of security, permanence, and flexibility in assignment it was necessary to have support personnel under military control. Civil service employees, unlike military personnel, could resign at will, were not subject to transfer, and had limitations on their hours of work. In rationalizing its request for women's corps, the military's emphasis on expediency and control over personnel was not unique, for such considerations also dictated its approach to male personnel. Where it did treat women differently was in its assumptions that all women were by nature better fitted for a specific and limited set of duties.[5]

The arguments that women themselves used in favor of women's corps had a different focus. Individual women, as well as organizations like the General Federation of Women's Clubs and the American Association of University Women, asserted, above all, women's right to full participation in all the responsibilities of citizenship. In addition, women advocates were sensitive to the plight of those earlier women who had served with the army during World War I and had been denied hospitalization and other benefits after the war. The Women's Overseas Service League had cared for these women and as early as 1940 had called for the creation of a women's corps, believing that military status was essential to protect those who would inevitably serve in World War II. The woman most active in the establishment of the corps, Edith Nourse Rogers, combined appeals to expediency and justice. Along with the military officials she promoted a women's corps as a solution to military labor problems, and she too maintained that women were better qualified than men for certain kinds of work. Referring to women's demonstrated capabilities as clerks, cooks, librarians, telephone and telegraph operators, dieticians and health workers, she also suggested that women might be used in technical and mechanical occupations. Moreover, Rogers had observed the inadequate care provided for women serving in France during World War I and had campaigned without success to obtain veterans' compensation for them. "I was resolved," she said, "that our women would not again serve with the Army without the protection that men got." Finally, Rogers urged passage of her bill on the grounds that women both wanted and deserved equal opportunity to serve their country.[6]

Open opposition to the women's corps legislation was relatively weak due largely to the reluctance of legislators to hinder the military in a time of national crisis. Those who did speak and vote against the bills expressed anxiety about disturbing the traditional sexual order and the "sanctity of the home." These opponents did not question women's capabilities, with the exception of one congressman who maintained that women were not trained to the unquestioning obedience necessary for military order. But they did argue that women should not be distracted from their domestic duties: "Who will do the cooking, the washing, the mending, the humble homey tasks to which every woman has devoted herself; who will rear and nurture the children?" And they suggested that women in the military would reflect unfavorably on American men: "What has become of the manhood of America, that we have to call on our women to do what has ever been the duty of men?"[7]

With the United States committed to a global war, congressional opposition scarcely prolonged the debate. The House passed the WAAC bill, 249-86, in March 1942, and the Senate followed in May by a vote of 38-27. (Only after experiencing the legal and practical difficulties in administering an auxiliary corps did the War Department move to support full army status for women, and in June 1943, Congress passed legislation converting the WAAC to the WAC). With the ground broken by the army legislation, both houses approved the navy bill establishing the Women's Reserve after little debate and without roll call votes. Reassured that the numbers of women would be limited, that women would not command men, and that they would be excluded from dangerous situations, legislators were most impressed by the expediency arguments regarding manpower problems and women's proven capabilities in traditionally feminine areas of work. In addition, they also responded to the expressed desire of women for equal opportunity to serve their country. Along with military officials, legislators believed that such opportunity would symbolize the varying but important roles that all women must play in the war effort and would promote morale among civilian women.[8]

Given the rationale for incorporating women into the military, it is not surprising that women's service in the army and navy reflected the gender-based division of labor in the civilian economy. Of the 55,000 WAVES who took advanced training, 32.4 percent were in yeoman ratings, the clerical category; 30.1 percent were trained in hospital corps work; and another 14.6 percent were trained as storekeepers. While their work in aviation attracted the most publicity, only 13.7 percent were trained for such jobs as aviation machinist (4.7 percent) and aviation instructor (3.2 percent). Like its naval counterpart, the U.S. Army Air Force was most innovative in utilizing women, yet even in that branch about 50 percent of the WACS did administrative and office work. Because the primary military interest was in maximum procurement and utilization of personnel, women were most often assigned to work normally done by women in civilian life, and relatively few were trained in traditionally masculine skills. As the war progressed military officials modified their assumptions about female capabilities, and the variety of duties performed by women expanded; nonetheless, the great majority of WACS and WAVES served in the traditional female areas of office work, communications, and health care.[9]

The military policies and procedures which treated women differently from men also reflected the expediency rationale and a persistent concern to preserve the existing sexual order. While male officers focused primarily on the most expeditious use of personnel, they occasionally sacrificed this consideration to congressional and public opinion. Women leaders were more sensitive to the issue of equality and were reluctant to accept special privileges for women. WAVES commander Mildred McAfee objected to the proscription against female supervision of male personnel, and such a ban created inefficiency in both the army and the navy, but male officers were unwilling to ruffle "too many feathers in Congress." To McAfee, the limitation of WAVES to stateside service hindered recruitment, prevented women from feeling full-fledged members of the navy, and insulted women with the implication that they could not be trusted abroad. Because of strong opposition in the Senate and House Naval Affairs Committees, the Navy Department refused to press for overseas duty until 1944 when WAVES were permitted to serve in the American Theater. Although the traditional military ban on social relations between officers and enlisted personnel applied to WACS, and although McAfee urged that women be granted no special consideration, the Navy Department relaxed the proscription for WAVES on the grounds that the public expected a greater degree of social democracy for women.[10]

On the other issues concerning the differential treatment of men and women, Captain McAfee and her counterpart in the WAC, Col. Oveta Culp Hobby, were in accord with their male superiors. Both women accepted the prevailing public opinion that women's family roles were paramount. Thus, mothers with children under fourteen were ineligible for the WAC, and the navy excluded those with children under eighteen. While the enlisted man's wife and children were automatically eligible for a family allowance, dependency allowances were granted to a woman's relatives only if she in fact provided their main support. WAVES were rarely allowed to resign to be with sick parents, but such permission was granted more often to women than to men, in McAfee's words, "not as a favor to the women but in response to social pressures, which gave family obligations for a woman volunteer priority over military demands." The army and navy recognized the primacy of women's domestic relationships in demobilization regulations which gave priority in discharges to women whose husbands had been discharged.[11]

Policies regarding conduct, discipline, and sexual behavior reflected the need to convince the public that prevailing social norms would not be violated in the military. This was a matter of special concern to the Women's Army Corps when in 1943 vicious rumors about WAC immorality swept the country and required a specific defense of enlisted women by President and Mrs. Roosevelt and by Secretary of War Stimson. Concurring with Director Hobby's belief that contraceptives should not be issued to women "for social as well as public relations reasons," Stimson made clear to army personnel that regulations concerning prophylaxis applied to men only. The WAC slanders caused navy officials to delay distribution of pamphlets and movies on sex hygiene for WAVES and to drop completely a movie on contraception. WAVES regulations on the one hand held women to more stringent standards regarding their public conduct, but at the same time recommended that women not normally be put in the brig.[12]

Motivated by their determination to see the corps succeed as well as by their own conceptions of women's appropriate behavior, female officers concurred in much of the differential treatment of women in the services. They were acutely aware that military service represented a test of women's capabilities and believed that public opinion would not tolerate substantial deviations from the prevailing social order. Though different in backgrounds, McAfee and Hobby shared similar beliefs about the desirable roles for women. Captain McAfee came from a female dominated work environment, having served as president of Wellesley before installation as director of the WAVES; while Colonel Hobby's experience had been that of radio and newspaper executive, lawyer, and parliamentarian of the Texas legislature. Because both McAfee and Hobby viewed military service for women as a temporary phenomenon necessitated by a national emergency, they were only lukewarm to the establishment of permanent corps at the end of the war.

While both women recognized women's limited opportunities within and without the military, they seemed determined to avoid any appearance of feminism. They stressed the vital importance of women's service, but they were quick to add that women's contributions could not approach the sacrifices demanded of men. Finally, both women sought to convince the public that military service did not threaten traditional female characteristics and attitudes. McAfee attributed to servicewomen relatively unambitious postwar plans: while those who sought civilian jobs would want equal opportunity, they would be "as likely as other women to make marriage their profession." Publicly and privately, Hobby averred that WACS retained "their charms as women," and that military service only increased their attachment to domestic responsibility and feminine behavior. Woman's place was still in the home, she believed, but "to keep those homes happy and free," women must leave them.[13]

Such considerations also guided the women directors in determining recruitment and publicity policy, where they frequently had to struggle against the efforts of men both to trivialize women and to glamorize women's military service. WAC leaders had to specify that WACS be referred to as "women" or "soldiers," not as "girls," while women in both services tried to restrain the use of "cheesecake" publicity with its emphasis on romantic appeal. At the same time they sought to limit material which emphasized excitement and adventure, believing that such publicity raised false expectations and belied the routine, often dull and drab reality of most women's military service. Where private enterprise dictated the images of servicewomen, these guidelines often did not prevail. Newsreels frequently referred to women as "girls" or "gals" and stressed the most dramatic activities as well as the more frivolous aspects of servicewomen's experience, such as their uniforms and their patronage of beauty shops.[14]

In official military publicity women's corps leaders were generally successful in dignifying servicewomen and highlighting the seriousness of their contributions. Yet they challenged little of the conventional wisdom about women's natural attributes and their appropriate roles. Reflecting studies which suggested that a primary deterrent to recruitment was women's fear of losing their femininity or of being considered unfeminine, WAC publicity policy sought to impress the public that WACS were "just as feminine as before they enlisted," that, in fact, they developed "new poise and charm." Army policy prohibited pictures of women soldiers smoking or drinking and urged avoidance of references to military activities requiring strenuous physical exertion. Colonel Hobby sought to portray women's service in terms of their traditional feminine relationships and responsibilities, and she recommended advertising copy that pointed out that servicewomen would be hastening the return of their sweethearts and husbands and that demonstrated that WACS were "only performing the duties that women would ordinarily do in civilian life."[15]

A product both of the need to appeal to prevailing public attitudes and of the views of the women officers, military propaganda encouraged a larger, yet still limited, vision of women's capabilities and responsibilities. Films, posters, and advertisements asserted the equivalency of women's duties and contributions — they were doing a "man-sized" job, marching "shoulder to shoulder with men," for it was "a woman's war, too," and they were getting equal pay. Moreover, women were pictured in nontraditional activities, training pilots and working on motor vehicles. But this media image also emphasized women as relatives of men, portraying the admiration of men for their wives, daughters, sweethearts, and sisters who enlisted, encouraging women to sign up in order to bring their men safely home and to ensure a secure future for their children. Finally, the propaganda called attention to those skills traditionally associated with the female nature. The army needed women's "delicate hands" for "precision work at which women are so adept," and it required female personnel in hospital work because "there is a need in a man for comfort and attention that only a woman can fill."[16]

Assumptions about innate feminine characteristics also played a significant role in postwar deliberations about the future of women in the armed services. By 1945 military leaders were convinced that any future emergency would require the utilization of women and accordingly wanted to retain a nucleus of trained women who could provide the base for rapid expansion. However, many male officers sought to meet this requirement by offering women only Reserve status, and they continued to resist a permanent corps in the Regular Army and Navy. Unlike their predecessors, WAC Director Mary A. Hallaren and WAVES Comdr. Jean T. Palmer argued for permanent Regular status both to promote military efficiency and to provide women opportunities and benefits equal to those of men. While the military proposed legislation providing for Regular status early in 1947, it was not until May 1948 that Congress approved the Women's Armed Services Integration Act. Congressional action accorded with polls which indicated that 53 percent of the public favored women's units in the peacetime military (35 percent were opposed, and 12 percent had no opinion). While women registered approval slightly more frequently than did men (54 to 52 percent), women under thirty expressed significantly more enthusiasm than did older women.[17]

The military's rationale for placing the WAC and WAVES on a permanent peacetime basis focused primarily on the necessity of maintaining a trained nucleus for rapid expansion in the next emergency, and secondarily, on the current shortage of personnel. In both instances male officers again and again listed the superior ability and willingness of women to perform specific duties. Women's manual dexterity, patience, attention to detail, and enthusiasm for repetitious, monotonous work made them superior to men in clerical work, communications, cryptography, aerial photography interpretation, and hospital work. As their arguments reinforced the gender-based division of labor, they also supported the conventional view that women's primary interests were domestic. Eisenhower predicted that "after an enlistment or two enlistments women will ordinarily — and thank God — they will get married."[18]

Again, women's own arguments evinced a different perspective. Former WAC Director Westray Battle Boyce and Mrs. Oswald B. Lord, chairperson of the National Civilian Advisory Committee for the WAC, emphasized women's opportunities for personal and occupational development in the military. Lord viewed women's military service as a "step further in a collective advancement of women in a new career field," and noted the widespread support of women's organizations for the legislation. Although women employed expediency arguments and did not completely shun the special attributes rationale, they did present women's military service in the light of women's interest in more equal opportunities for career development and participation in all aspects of public life.[19]

Surveys of enlisted women's expressed motivations indicate that the permanent establishments met different female needs and interests than did the original wartime corps. In World War II women most frequently enlisted out of patriotism and a desire to promote the war effort, while during the Korean War almost one-half joined for educational and vocational opportunities, 20 percent for adventure and travel, and only 9 percent for patriotic reasons. For women, then, what was originally an opportunity for selfless service became a means to individual development and self-fulfillment.[20]

As expediency promoted the expansion of women's traditional sphere, it also defined the parameters within which the expansion would occur. In the twentieth century, transformations in warfare had produced a military establishment capable of utilizing women, and the feminization of areas in the civilian economy had produced an occupational structure which provided women with the skills required by the military. The national emergency of 1941 promoted the intersection of these developments, and the cold war crisis made that integration permanent. But military expediency also operated to sustain gender distinctions. Reflecting the importance of placating public and legislative opinion, military policies and propaganda supported the conventional wisdom that women needed special protection, that they had natural feminine characteristics, and that their familial and domestic roles were paramount. Governed by its need for the maximum use of personnel, the military employed women for the most part in traditionally female jobs and did little to effect any permanent alterations in the sex-based division of labor.

Within the dictates of expediency there were differences between the men and the women who had the power to influence military policy. While male officers were willing to tolerate only that amount of deviation from tradition necessary to alleviate the labor supply crisis, women combined purely tactical considerations with attention to the needs and interests of their sex. Limited by the exigencies of war and by their inferior power within the military establishment, their own perceptions of what was appropriate to and desirable for women also minimized the degree of change they attempted to promote. Along with the mainstream of organized women in the inter-war generation, they placed more emphasis on women's responsibilities than on their rights. Reluctant to make specific demands for women as women in a time of national crisis, they used that emergency less as an opportunity for assaulting the ideological and institutional structures which subordinated women than as a means of demonstrating women's capabilities and patriotism. Those women leaders who promoted the integration of women into the military did so on a pragmatic basis, possessing neither a feminist critique of the military nor a form of feminist ideology which would have called for integration on the basis of complete equality. They contributed to the expansion of opportunities for some women, but that expansion did not challenge substantially either the material or the attitudinal barriers to the emancipation of women in general.

NOTES

1. This study focuses on the army and navy, the two branches in which the vast majority of women served. During World War II, women were distributed among the services as follows: WAC — 140,000; WAVES — 100,000; SPARS (Coast Guard) — 13,000; Women Marines — 23,000. An additional 74,000 women served with the U.S. Army and Navy Nurses Corps.

2. Morris Janowitz and Roger W. Little, *Sociology and the Military Establishment,* 3d ed. (Beverly Hills, Calif.: Sage Publications, 1974), p. 47.

3. Mattie E. Treadwell, *The United States Army in World War II* (Washington, D.C.: Government Printing Office, 1954), vol. 8, *The Women's Army Corps,* pp. 6-10, 15-18.

4. "United States Naval Administration in World War II, Bureau of Naval Personnel, Women's Reserve" (unpublished manuscript, 1945), pp. 1-13, Navy Department Library; Chief of the Bureau of Aeronautics to Chief of the Bureau of Navigation, 1 January 1942 (attachment to memo, Chief of Naval Personnel to Chief of Bureau of Aeronautics, 7 July 1942), File QR8, General Correspondence, 1925-42, Records of the Bureau of Aeronautics, Record Group 72, National Archives (hereafter referred to as RG ___, NA); Frank Knox to Sen. David I. Walsh, 18 June 1942, File QR8(64), General Correspondence, 1925-45, Letters Received and Copies of Letters Sent Interfiled, 1885-1945, Correspondence 1798-1950 (hereafter referred to as General Correspondence, 1925-45), Records of the Bureau of Naval Personnel, RG 24, NA; James Forrestal to Eleanor Roosevelt, 10 June 1942, File QR8(63), ibid. (In May 1942 the Bureau of Navigation became the Bureau of Naval Personnel.)

5. Treadwell, *The Women's Army Corps,* p. 20; U.S., Congress, Senate, Committee on Military Affairs, *Hearings on H.R. 6293,* 1 and 4 May 1942, pp. 6-7; U.S., Congress, Senate, *Congressional Record,* 77th Cong., 2d sess., 17 March 1942, pp. 2583, 2588; Rear Adm. Randall Jacobs to Sen. David T. Walsh, 11 May 1942, File QR8(15), General Correspondence, 1925-45, RG 24, NA; Jacqueline Van Voris, "Quiet Victory: The Waves in World War II" (unpublished manuscript, n.d.), p. 7, Operational Archives, Naval History Division, Washington, D.C. (hereafter referred to as OANHD).

6. Resolutions of the General Federation of Women's Clubs, January 1942, U.S. Congress, Senate, *Congressional Record,* 77th Cong., 2d sess., 5 February 1942, p. A394; Statement by Kathryn McHale, General Director, 7 May 1942, American Association of University Women (AAUW) Papers, Folder 58, Schlesinger Library, Radcliffe College, Cambridge, Massachusetts; ibid., *Hearings on H.R. 6293,* pp. 40-43; ibid., *Congressional Record,* 77th Cong., 1st sess., 28 May 1941, p. 4531, 12 December

1941, p. 9747; ibid., *Congressional Record,* 77th Cong., 2d Sess., 17 March 1942, p. 2584; Treadwell, *The Women's Army Corps,* p. 17.

7. U.S., Congress, Senate, *Congressional Record,* 77th Cong., 2d sess., 17 March 1942, pp. 2592-93, 2606; 12 May 1942, p. 4090.

8. Chief of Staff George C. Marshall to Representative Andrew J. May, February 1943, File "WAAC, Legislation," Historical and Background Material Relating to the Legislation and Administration of the Women's Auxiliary Army Corps and its Successor, the Women's Army Corps, 1942-49 (hereafter referred to as WAC Historical File), G-1, Records of the War Department General and Special Staffs, RG 165, NA; U.S., Congress, Senate, *Congressional Record,* 77th Cong., 2d sess., 17 March 1942, pp. 2586, 2589, 2591-93; 12 May 1942, pp. 4090-93; 16 April 1942, p. 3515; 2 July 1942, p. 5922.

9. Chief of Naval Personnel to Deputy Chief of Naval Operations (Air), 2 January 1948, File QR8/16-3, 1 June 1945-, General Correspondence, 1925-45, RG 24, NA; Officer in Charge to Chief of Naval Personnel, 2 February 1943, File QR8/P17, ibid; Treadwell, *The Women's Army Corps,* pp. 282-89; Dorothy Schaffter, "Educational Implications of Women's Military Training," *Annals of the American Association of Political and Social Science* 251 (May 1947): 160; Dorothy Schaffter, *What Comes of Training Women for War* (Washington, D.C.: American Council on Education, 1948), pp. 7, 38-39.

10. "United States Naval Administration in World War II, Women's Reserve," pp. 18-19, 20-21, 74; Transcript of interview with Lt. Comdr. Mary Jo Shelly, 9 February 1970, p. 44, OANHD; Transcript of interview with Mildred McAfee Horton, August 1969, pp. 10-13, OANHD.

11. War Department, Bureau of Public Relations, Press Release, "The Women's Army Corps," 1 February 1945, AAUW Papers, Folder 58; "United States Naval Administration in World War II, Women's Reserve," pp. 28, 54, 78; Mildred McAfee Horton, "Women in the United States Navy," *American Journal of Sociology* 51, no. 5 (March 1946): 449; William M. Fechteler, Assistant Chief of Naval Personnel, to Chief of Naval Air Technical Training, 25 May 1945, File QR8, General Correspondence, 1925-45, RG 24, NA.

12. Daily Journal, 31 May 1943, 10 June 1943, Office of the Director, WAC Historical File, G-1, RG 165, NA; War Department Circular No. 172, 2 May 1944, File "WAC Policy File, Vol. II, Medical," ibid; "United States Naval Administration in World War II, Women's Reserve," p. 75; Circular letter, Randall Jacobs, Chief of Naval Personnel to all shore stations, 30 April 1943, Bureau of Naval Personnel Records, Series I, Historical (1943-1946), OANHD.

13. Treadwell, *The Women's Army Corps,* pp. 723, 748; Mildred McAfee Horton to Chief of Naval Personnel, n.d., Bureau of Naval Personnel Records, Series I, Historical Data OANHD; Horton, "Women in the United States Navy," p. 450; *New York Times,* 3 February 1943; *Hail and Farewell,* Film No. 111-M-801 (1943), Records of the Office of the Chief Signal Officer, RG 111, NA; Daily Journal, 14 July 1943, Office of the Director, WAC Historical File, G-1, RG 165, NA; Col. Oveta Culp Hobby, Address to the Women's National Press Club; U.S., Congress, Senate, *Congressional Record,* 77th Cong., 2d sess., 14 September 1942, pp. 7150-51.

14. Transcript of interview with Mildred McAfee Horton, p. 25; "United States Naval Administration in World War II, Women's Reserve," pp. 70-73; "WAC Public Relations Policies," 24 June 1944, File "Field Memos," WAC Historical File, G-1, RG 165, NA; "Policies Affecting Women's Army Corps Recruitment for the Army Air

Forces," 9 December 1943, File "Recruiting Organization," ibid.; Paramount News Films, 1943, 1944, National Archives Gift Collection, RG 200, NA.

15. "The WAAC — The Girl Who Wouldn't Be Left Behind," *The Aframerican Women* 3, nos. 1-2 (Summer-Fall 1942): 7; "WAC Public Relations Policies," 24 June 1944, File "Field Memos," WAC Historical File, RG 165, NA; "Handbook for Procurement Personnel," File "Posters and Newspaper Clippings (1940-45)," Records of the Recruiting and Advertising Section Relating to the Navy Recruiting Program, 1940-45, RG 24, NA; Office of War Information, *Women in the War for the Final Push to Victory* (printed for interoffice distribution only, 1944), File "Women, Miscel.," WAC Issuances, 1942-45, Records of the Women's Advisory Commission, Records of the War Manpower Commission, RG 211, NA.

16. Posters, File "Posters and Newspaper Clippings (1940-45)," Records of the Recruiting and Advertising Section Relating to the Navy Recruiting Program, 1940-45, RG 24, NA; File "Advertisements," WAC Historical File, G-1, RG 165, NA; *The Servicewoman* 1 (July 1943): 8; *Chief Neely Reports to the Nation*, (1943), Film No. 208-160, Records of the Office of War Information, RG 208, NA; *Battle Stations* (1943), Film No. 208-42, ibid.; *Calling All Dieticians* (1943), Film No. 111-M-933, RG 111, NA; *We're in the Army Now* (1943), Film No. 111-M-1000, ibid.; *It's Your War Too* (1944), Film No. 111-M-958, ibid.; *To the Ladies* (1944), Film No. 111-M-1030, ibid.; recruiting booklets, Elizabeth Reynaud Papers, Schlesinger Library.

17. Louis Denfield, Chief of Naval Personnel, to Sen. Millard Tydings, 7 December 1945, File QR8, General Correspondence, 1925-45, RG 24, NA; Denfield to Secretary of the Navy James Forrestal, 11 December 1945, File 70-2-15, Records of Secretary of the Navy James Forrestal, 1940-47, General Records of the Department of the Navy, RG 80, NA; Memo, unsigned, to Chief of Naval Personnel, 12 March 1946, Naval Personnel Records, Series I, Historical File, OANHD; Earl E. Stone, Chief of Naval Communications, to Chief of Naval Personnel, 26 March 1946, ibid.; Notes from meeting of bureaus, boards and offices, "Waves in the Postwar Navy," 14 May 1946, ibid.; Jacob L. Devers to Chief of Staff, U.S. Army, 5 September 1945, File "WAC in the Army Ground Forces," Director's Desk File, WAC Historical File, G-1, RG 165, NA; Mary A. Hallaran to General Haislip and Chief of Staff's Advisory Group, Women's Army Corps Report, 10 March 1947, WAC Historical File, ibid.; Jean T. Palmer to Chief of Naval Personnel, 25 March 1946, Naval Personnel Records, Series I, Historical Data, OANHD; Jean T. Palmer to Captain J.H. Nevins, 8 March 1946, ibid.; George H. Gallup, *The Gallup Poll: Public Opinion, 1935-1971*, 3 vols. (New York: Random House, 1972), 1 (1935-48): 667.

18. U.S., Congress, Senate, Committee on Armed Services, *Hearings on S. 1103, S. 1527, S. 1641, Women's Armed Services Integration Act of 1947*, July 1947, pp. 10, 12, 14, 22-25; U.S., Congress, House, Committee on Armed Services, Subcommittee on Organization and Mobilization, *Hearings on S. 1641*, 18 February-3 March 1948, pp. 5564, 5569-70, 5572-76, 5580-99.

19. U.S., Congress, Senate, *Hearings on S. 1103, S. 1527, S. 1641*, pp. 21-22; U.S., Congress, House, *Hearings on S. 1641*, pp. 5611-13.

20. Daily Journal, 13 July 1943, Office of the Director, WAC Historical File, G-1, RG 165, NA; Department of Defense Armed Forces Information and Education Division, Attitudes Research Branch, "Women in the Air Force: A Study of Recent Enlistees," January 1952, Defense Advisory Committee on Women in the Services, Box 8, Schlesinger Library.

WOMEN IN THE CIVILIAN LABOR FORCE

Eleanor F. Straub

"The ultimate solution of the manpower question," ran a popular wartime cliché, "is women."[1] During World War II, women were regarded as the largest and most easily tapped reserve of civilian labor. The rapid mobilization of six million additional women into the civilian labor force presented government planners and publicists with a number of challenges: persuading women to accept jobs, convincing employers and unions to admit women, adapting plant and community facilities to women's needs, and convincing women to remain on the job until the war's end. Each of these tasks was important and at times troublesome, but the first problem — recruitment — received top priority throughout the war.

An examination of the national effort to bring women into the civilian labor force during World War II provides an interesting vantage point from which to examine the administration of wartime policy toward women and the impact of the war mobilization on the definition of sex roles. Such an analysis also reveals some of the assumptions about women workers which underlay the government's entire program for women during World War II.

The establishment of the War Manpower Commission (WMC) in April 1942 allowed, at least in theory, the development of a unified approach to the problems of civilian labor supply.[2] The mobilization of women workers became and remained one of the agency's most pressing chores, and one of the WMC's earliest policy statements sought to provide guidelines for the recruitment of women.[3] Yet, official policy statements provide little insight into the actual recruitment effort. The United States never adopted compulsory measures or sanctions to force women to work, and the mobilization of American women remained entirely dependent upon the effectiveness of publicity, special promotions, and public relations techniques. A survey of the direction, objective, and content of this effort lends substantiation to the Office of War Information's (OWI) prediction in 1942 that "bringing enough women into the labor force to meet the demands of the war effort will be a formidable task."[4]

206

Immediately after American entry into the war, the idea of a national registration of women aroused public interest.[5] Employment Service officials, however, quickly concluded that such a course was unwise since no nationwide demand for women workers existed. In May 1942 War Manpower Commissioner Paul V. McNutt relayed this advice to President Roosevelt who in turn announced that national registration was, for the moment, unnecessary.[6] The appeal of a registration campaign, which would allow women to do something concrete in support of the war effort and would supply the government with a quick source of facts and figures, remained powerful. Consequently, the proposal was not totally discarded, and small, localized versions, called "enrollment drives," were very popular during the first months of the war. Enrollment campaigns varied greatly as to sponsorship, methods and goals, yet all relied on some sort of a census, conducted either by mail or by house-to-house canvas, which was used to determine the availability of women for work in a given area. The usual practice involved having women complete a questionnaire that described their work experience, willingness to accept paid employment and child care responsibilities. The survey was expected to provide the Employment Service with a thorough roster of women to interview and refer to jobs. First tested in Oregon in February 1942, this statewide enrollment drive discovered that 302,000 women were ready and willing to work.[7] After such impressive results, similar programs were initiated in Connecticut, Michigan, Akron, and Seattle during the spring and summer of 1942.[8]

The August 1942 enrollment drive in Detroit, the nation's most important war production center, was often cited as the most successful use of the technique.[9] Planned by local manufacturers, the Employment Service, and the War Production Board, the drive used air raid wardens to distribute cards to 300,000 local women who returned the cards to the Employment Service for tabulation.[10] Preliminary results revealed that 180,000 women were willing to enter factory work.[11] While an Employment Service official warned that the registration "does not prove that employers are agreeable, or will be agreeable to hiring this number of women, and certainly does not prove that they will be agreeable to hiring those who are colored, Jewish, of foreign birth, middle-aged, etc.," such hesitation was rare.[12] For most persons the dramatic increase in the number of women in manufacturing in Detroit from 44,000 in August 1942 to 107,000 in February 1943 seemed ample proof of success. Following Detroit's experiment, Rochester, Dayton, Evansville, San Diego, and several Massachusetts towns held similar drives during the fall of 1942.[13]

Despite such initial signs of success, the WMC began to recommend the use of the technique only when it proved "the best solution to the problem."[14] In mid-November the agency further cautioned that enrollment must be only one ingredient in "an over-all program for the most effective utilization of local labor."[15] The WMC now recommended that efforts to halt in-migration, to improve the utilization of available labor and to hire persons still unemployed should precede any enrollment drive. Enrollment programs, under WMC direction, should be used only if these steps proved insufficient, and only after obtaining commitments from employers to hire women thus recruited.[16]

The manpower agency soon became convinced that enrollment should be a last resort. Analysis of long-term results of the drives had proved discouraging. For example, in New Bedford, Massachusetts, 50,000 forms were sent out, 7,000 were returned, 2,000 women indicated availability. In Akron, 87,500 housewives were personally interviewed, 18,700 indicated willingness, while only 630 women actually accepted work when offers were tendered. Even in Detroit the preliminary indications of success had not revealed the entire picture. Of the 180,000 women who had expressed a desire to work, only 11,000 were ever registered and referred to jobs by the Employment Service.[17] The statistics suggested that the increase in women's employment in these cities was only loosely linked to the enrollment drives. The expense and the loss of public confidence in the Employment Service that resulted from these poor showings demonstrated that enrollment was not the "sound and proven formula" needed to recruit women for war work.[18]

During the fall of 1942, however, the WMC was testing in Baltimore an alternate kind of recruitment program that proved more promising. Government intelligence reports indicated that Baltimore would face a severe labor shortage and that mobilizing local women would be difficult.[19] A massive educational program, using radio, press, movies, speeches, and printed matter, was launched to apprise the city's women of the labor supply situation. A womanpower committee with representatives of twenty-three women's civic, church, and social groups helped publicize the program; a special woman's recruitment center was established by the Employment Service. The results of this barrage of publicity matched those of the more costly and time-consuming enrollment drives.[20]

In January 1943 the WMC stiffened the requirements for enrollment drives once again after discovering that the campaigns "have been conducted under various auspices, sometimes with only the most nominal participation by the War Manpower Commission." No campaign, the commission discovered, had been staged as "an integral part of an over-all plan for the utilization of local labor,"[21] and the results of the drives "from a public relations standpoint were excellent, [but] from a practical standpoint were negligible."[22] New, tougher directives made it clear that enrollment campaigns "should be [undertaken] only after every effort has been made to obtain women workers by the use of the usual recruitment devices," and outlined procedures to ensure that the WMC retained control of the drive.[23]

The Niagara Falls-Buffalo area provided an example of an enrollment drive following the new procedures. In February 1943 a womanpower center was dedicated; then radio, press, and motion picture publicity on the need for women saturated the area. Few promotional devices were ignored; even clergymen were urged to exhort the women in their congregations to take war jobs. The campaign culminated in the distribution of thirty thousand questionnaires to local women by Boy Scouts and air raid wardens.[24] Despite such intensive efforts, less than fourteen thousand of the forms were returned. A meager eighty-seven placements resulted from the drive.[25]

By the spring of 1943 enrollment drives had become a nightmare the WMC staff wished to forget. Nevertheless, during the next few months several other drives were held with equally disastrous results. A summer effort in Milwaukee involving 30,000 questionnaires resulted in the placement of 227 women; a fall campaign in Syracuse in which 60,083 questionnaires were distributed yielded sixteen placements.[26] In July the field staff was informed that "such campaigns [should] be replaced by intensive recruitment efforts directed toward filling of specific employer orders."[27]

Thus "intensive recruitment" programs similar to Baltimore's promotion became the order of the day. Such efforts usually involved a backdrop of national publicity while more active measures were undertaken locally in the hard-pressed communities. Efforts were made to halt in-migration, to encourage employers to "reserve" certain occupations for women, to improve community facilities and to deluge the local population with information on the need for women workers.[28] A formula for mobilizing women had at last been agreed upon. As a WMC report noted in early 1944, after nearly two years of experimentation, "haphazard campaigns have yielded to action better coordinated with other phases of manpower programming."[29]

National promotional campaigns were an important adjunct to local womanpower efforts, and the American public was fed a steady diet of such programs during the war years.[30] The techniques — special media presentations, announcements, advertisements, speeches, and brochures — differed only slightly, but the themes and emphases varied as war demands shifted and public attitudes changed. One of the earliest programs, the "Get-a-War Job" campaign was initiated in late December 1942. This radio campaign urged American women to fill war jobs, reminding them that "there is no other answer."[31] Two months later a special photographic exhibit on women war workers introduced a new effort. Opened with fanfare by Paul McNutt and the members of the WMC's Women's Advisory Committee at the Franklin Institute in Philadelphia, the exhibition later toured the country to acquaint women with the contributions women war workers were making.[32]

On March 1, 1943, the WMC launched a new major campaign to get women into civilian jobs. During that month and the next, twenty-seven major radio programs each week focused on the subject of womanpower.[33] Like subsequent national promotional efforts, while the goal was to persuade women to work, great care was exercised to stress "the localness of the need" and the inadvisability of moving to a new community to seek work.[34] May 1943 heralded yet another program, "Womanpower Month." Conducted by the Retail War Campaigns Committee of the OWI, this effort encouraged retail stores to emphasize the need for women in jobs and on farms.[35]

The year's most extensive national promotion, however, was the "America at War Needs Women at Work" campaign in September sponsored jointly by the WMC and the OWI, with copy prepared by the J. Walter Thompson advertising agency. The program instructed women not simply to get a job, but to get a job in an "essential civilian service."[36] "Many women are urgently needed to-day," the program plan explained, "in thousands of apparently hum-drum, unglamourous, and frequently ill-paid jobs in stores, restaurants, offices, laundries, hospitals, child-care centers, bus and street car companies, banks, public utilities, railroads and many other businesses."[37]

While as early as January 1943 the WMC had noted that "not every woman will be needed in a war factory" and that "2 out of every 3 women workers will be needed in home front jobs," the September campaign of the same year made this emphasis a major recruiting theme.[38] The new emphasis reflected fears that women were avoiding available jobs in laundries, hospitals, and restaurants while seeking more glamorous and better paying jobs in war industry.[39] Women, especially housewives not previously in the labor force, seemed the natural target for the civilian service job appeals. All subsequent national appeals for women to enter the civilian labor force reflected this growing desire for women in essential civilian services rather than in war industry. Much of the massive World War II recruiting effort directed at women by the federal government was not intended to encourage them to become riveters and welders, but to persuade them to take jobs in the service sector that had long been regarded as "woman's work." "Any job that brings victory sooner," women were repeatedly told, "is a war job."[40]

The September 1943 womanpower program featured this theme through a variety of related promotions. The campaign began with the September covers of popular magazines honoring women workers. Norman Rockwell's design for the September 4 issue of the *Saturday Evening Post*, for example, featured a woman in red, white, and blue overalls carrying, among other things, a wrench, watering bucket, dust pan, oil can, mop, and milk bottles.[41] The program included three weeks of national radio spots on women's work, the release of a special movie short *Glamour Girls of 1943* to local theaters, special news releases, and advertising and retail store tie-ins. A special insignia, an upraised torch with the words "Women War Workers" was used to identify the campaign.[42]

Government planners recognized that persuading large numbers of women to accept service jobs would be difficult. The September campaign program guide admitted that "a laundry, even with the most modern plant and equipment is still a pretty unpleasant place to work." In order to get American women to accept service jobs, the OWI suggested that the jobs "will have to be glorified as a patriotic war service."[43] In connection with this campaign, for example, the Statler Hotels had a full page ad in *Life* urging women to consider working as hotel clerks, waitresses, elevator operators, maids, and cooks. A hotel job, the ad asserted, "offers opportunity to perform a patriotic act, and at the same time earn good wages in an industry that has always attracted a fine group of intelligent workers. Today — a hotel job is a war job!"[44] Despite government efforts, the poor pay and bad working conditions associated with jobs in the service sector continued to make them relatively undesirable.[45]

The new year ushered in a new advertising program in popular magazines. Basically educational in tone, this promotion encouraged features on the man-

Beckoning women into the labor force, World War II poster. (No. 44-PA-229, Records of the Office of Government Reports, RG 44.)

power crisis in January, articles on woman's role in the war in February, and reports on community conditions which encouraged absenteeism and turnover in

March.[46] The most extensive campaign of 1944, "Women in the War," began on March 1. The program, a joint effort of the WMC, OWI, and the Army and Navy Joint Personnel Board, combined civilian and military manpower recruitment. American women were told to "get into the war effort by taking a war job in industry or joining the uniformed services," and the program was aimed at the "hard to sell" woman who had sat out the first two years of the war. The program stressed that there was *"no one feminine formula for patriotism, no one road to wartime service."*[47]

After the spring-summer 1944 womanpower program, no other major national promotions were held. For the remainder of the war, the brochures, posters, and radio and newspapers spots were used in the local areas where women were needed. By September 1944 the problem was less one of attracting new recruits to war work than of retaining current workers. This fact, coupled with the production cutbacks and layoffs that already affected some parts of the country, prompted the WMC to decide that it was "inadvisable to continue issuing national publicity showing the need for women workers."[48]

Throughout the war the national womanpower campaigns were supplemented by a variety of services designed to encourage and assist local efforts. Special women's radio program guides and fact sheets tying in with specific radio programs were prepared and distributed to program managers by the OWI's Radio Bureau.[49] In May 1943 the OWI News Bureau began preparing "The Women's Page," a fortnightly package of information on women's activities for the editors of women's sections of daily newspapers.[50] The Magazine Bureau supplied magazine editors and writers with a bimonthly *Magazine War Guide* and a magazine supplement was issued for fiction writers and editors.[51] Special programs, posters, plays, brochures, and movie shorts produced under government auspices were prepared and widely disseminated. Tie-ins by advertisers and retailers were encouraged. The effort to get women into civilian work was a war program of massive proportions.[52]

The OWI, which prepared much of the copy for the government war programs directed at the American public, insisted in its operating manual that "we deal in one plain commodity — the facts the people of this country need to win the war."[53] The womanpower materials issued by the federal government were largely of a factual nature, but their purpose was not merely to inform but to break down women's resistance and persuade them to take a specific course of action. The wartime appeal for women workers illustrates the values and unspoken assumptions the government planners held about the American woman, values that were probably shared by a large segment of the general population. Tried and true themes like patriotism were used to carry the message, but money, fear, and glamour also became important inducements. And the wartime recruiting effort continued to emphasize certain feminine characteristics and traits that were popularly assumed to have been made irrelevant by the war experience. The war emergency created a temporary demand for women in nearly all fields of work, but it did not erase many of the common stereotypes about sex roles.

From the beginning of the war, great emphasis was placed on the theme that work was woman's patriotic duty, that she must take a job as a selfless act to aid American victory. A film called *Women on the Warpath* typified this often melodramatic approach:

> Staunchly, have the women of America stood shoulder to shoulder with their men in the pioneering past. Today they take up a new burden as the Nation calls for five millions of them . . . a woman's army trained and ready to help save the homes it has been their duty to make and adorn. . . . Gone is the day of the remote battlefield, a day when war was strictly a man's job. At hand is the opportunity for women to assume a *new* responsibility. And so on they come, these housekeeping, home-defending soldiers of America to put the feminine torch to the fuse of an almighty explosion of tyranny.[54]

Efforts were frequently made to compare the woman worker's contribution with that of the soldier. A radio script prepared for the Baltimore campaign in September 1942 insisted that Americans must "treat a woman who takes a factory job as an important person, honor her as we honor a soldier;" a Signal Corps film argued that women workers were "soldiers without guns."[55]

There was little of the aggressive flag-waving of earlier wars and practically no serious discussion of the war's purpose or goals. Women were simply told over and over again that war work would hasten the war's end and the return of their husbands, sweethearts, or sons. As a typical newspaper advertisement phrased it, "Women who have already responded to the call will tell you that their job in a war plant gives them a deep sense of satisfaction — that grand feeling that they are doing their *full* part to *help speed the day of victory*."[56]

Money — the high war wages — provided another popular appeal. As an OWI newspaper spot reminded women, "Remember a production worker earns good pay."[57] The Civil Service Commission's attempt to recruit recent high school graduates for clerical jobs showed a similar preoccupation with material rewards by urging girls to "EARN GOOD MONEY, HELP AMERICA WIN, BY WORKING IN WASHINGTON."[58] Playing on the future availability of war-scarce goods, the OWI Radio Bureau suggested that a good approach to women was:

> *Save for the future while you take care of today*. You will earn more money for the needs of today, as well as for the new homes, furnishings, vacations, and other things that will be available after the war.[59]

However, since inflation was a persistent wartime problem, the OWI cautioned that "the income resulting from work in a war plant should not be talked up to the point where increased spending for consumer goods is encouraged."[60] Accordingly, a note about high wages was often followed by a reminder that "she can put her pay — and it's *good* pay — into war bonds."[61]

One common ingredient of the womanpower programs was the use of fear. Such an approach could take a variety of forms, the two most common being reminders of the tragic results of a Nazi victory and an emphasis on the personal tragedy which idle women could cause. An OWI suggestion for a pamphlet on women workers included a "Tale of Two Women." By describing the lives of two women workers, Freya Schmidt and Frieda Smith, the stark contrast could be made. The OWI proposed development of the theme that "to Freya everything is verboten and once she had been told women belonged only to children, church, and kitchen. To Frieda everything is free, always she has been told she is queen of the nation's purse, and mistress of her own destiny."[62] The *Magazine War Guide* for April and May 1944 suggested stories on the brutal and ruthless treatment of women by the Germans and the Japanese.[63] A War Production Board radio script for the popular "This Is Our Enemy" series explored the Nazi view of women:

Goebbels: The Nazi movement is a masculine movement. When we eliminate women from public life, it is not because we want to dispense with them, but rather because we want to give them back their *essential function*.

Narrator: That was Dr. Goebbels, Minister of Propaganda, speaking on February 11, 1934. And in 1936, in a new edition of *Mein Kampf,* Hitler stated:

Hitler: The German girl belongs to the State. We will lay stress above all on physical education, rather than on the spiritual or intellectual.

Narrator: In schools, in the press, on the radio, in lecture halls, this Nazi doctrine for women was proclaimed. It took time to get results. German women — like all women everywhere — considered themselves more than mere breeders. Many women rebelled — the women who were leaders in the old Germany — the teachers, doctors, lawyers. But the New Order rolled on:

Voice: 1934. 11,500 women high-school teachers.

2nd Voice: 1935. 3,000 women high-school teachers dismissed.

3rd Voice: 1936. Out of 6,000 college teachers, only forty-six are women.

3rd Voice: 1934. Dr. Gerhart Wagner, Nazi head of the German Medical Association, shouts to the leading doctors of the country:

Wagner: We will strangle higher education for women!

Sound: *Cheers*

Narrator: Yes, the Nazis cheered. Women are to be broodmares. And yet reducing women to this state still did not bring Hitler enough children for his master race. So the Nazis studied the problem of unmarried women. Why should they not have children too? And so the Nazi party went to work to propagandize a new doctrine — the encouragement of illegitimacy. Again lecturers were sent out, there were radio speeches. And young girls read in the *Arbeitsfront* journal such editorials as this one by Alfred Rosenberg:

Rosenberg: The German Reich of the future will regard the woman without children — *whether she is married or not* — as being an inferior member of the community.[64]

Fear could be used in a more personal way, as was illustrated by the title of a WMC recruiting booklet, *This Soldier May Die – Unless You Man This Idle Machine*.[65] "Every idle machine," reminded an OWI radio program fact sheet on womanpower, "may mean a dead soldier."[66] References to casualty lists were a common technique. For example, an OWI radio spot announced: "Lists of *(city)* boys who are killed, wounded or missing in action overseas make sorrowful reading for all of us. When will it stop. . . . Well, you can be sure of this — the more women at war the sooner we'll win!"[67] The message of the film *Wanted – Women War Workers* was even more direct. The beginning of the movie set the tone: "Yes, our city is a safe city — now. But so was London once." After informing women how they can help, a somber note is sounded once again:

there are idle machines in our city's war factories — and they threaten our future security. More than that — our idle machines will be paid for in death — (Sound Effect — Bomb Burst)

Your son — your brother — your sweetheart — the boy in the next block — they will pay with their lives for these idle machines. The casualty lists, the dead, wounded, and missing will be evidence of vacant places on our city's production lines — vacant places that you women could fill.[68]

At times the use of scare tactics prompted internal criticism. One series of OWI ads included such lines as

"Don't have an unnecessary gold star on your conscience — get to work today."

"Women of _____ are you making these [casualty] lists longer?"

"That's a horrible idea — women making more [of] our boys die, causing more of our men to come back crippled."

Suggesting that the messages needed revision, an OWI official recommended that "threatening women with the death of a soldier is poor psychology with which to attempt to drive them into the labor market."[69]

Glamour — in the form of excitement, adventure, and romance — offered another way to appeal to American women that was especially popular with advertisers, authors of fiction, and magazine writers. Advertisements of the "What! An Artist's Model Building a Bomber?" variety were exceedingly common in the early war period.[70] The New York Dress Institute sponsored a feature that included a pledge for women to do their "essential service" by agreeing to "avoid the mistake of drabness." Woodbury soap's "debs for defense" series focused on the exciting social life of attractive young women who did defense work. Hollander furs noted that its full length seal-dyed muskrat coats were "popular for air raid wardens."[71]

Stories of love blossoming on the assembly line offered the woman worker a glimpse of an extra bonus that might accompany war work. An August 1942 fiction selection in the *Saturday Evening Post,* for example, described a young woman's experience at national defense training school. After completing her last weld and preparing for graduation to the assembly plant, she is called aside by her riveting teacher who confesses, "I love you, rivet knocker! How about you and me getting welded." In happily-ever-after fashion they leave for the factory to help "lick them Japs."[72]

Personal testimonials were another popular tool for glorifying the blue collar life. A typical feature in *American Magazine* described the activities of a twenty-one-year-old woman who worked the graveyard shift at a roller bearing company. The article concluded that "working in war industry has made her a new more self-reliant person. She has more to spend on clothes and cosmetics than ever before, has more dates and more friends."[73] In a feature on women war workers, *Life* magazine focused on the private lives of a series of attractive young women in industry, and women, *Life* announced, were "the heroine[s] of a new order," and the woman aircraft worker was named "the glamour girl of 1942."[74] Other magazine features chronicled the lives of the "government girls," young women who made up the vast army of clerical workers who came to the nation's capital and found adventure and a well-paying job.[75]

Although the OWI and the WMC had little direct responsibility for such approaches, these agencies quickly came under attack for glamorized woman-power copy.[76] The OWI tried to curb excesses and to present a more balanced picture of war work. In 1943 the OWI program guide cautioned that war work must not be pictured as a "glorified sewing circle" and that it "takes hard work and is often quite different from the picture implied by the gay, slack-wearing beauty on the magazine cover."[77] Continued criticism and the government's increasing emphasis on essential civilian service jobs required a realistic picture of war work, and the OWI consciously tried to remove misleading statements from its woman-power copy.[78] By early 1944 the government had come to admit that in most kinds of civilian war work, there was "very little glamour."[79]

Despite superficial claims that the war experience was shattering sex role stereotypes, the womanpower literature rarely challenged traditional attitudes and assumptions about women.[80] The target of the recruiting appeal was primarily the white, middle-class housewife, "the women who have never worked before nor thought of working," and the womanpower literature was tailored so as not to offend her sensibilities.[81] Although official statements expressed a desire to recruit all women except mothers of young children, this policy was seldom enforced.[82] Relatively little effort was made to facilitate the entry of older or minority women into war jobs, and the WMC recommendation not to recruit mothers of young children "until all other sources of labor supply have been exhausted" was ignored.[83] Only two months after the recruitment directive was announced, a radio campaign indicated that additions to the labor force must "include many house-wives and even the mothers of small children."[84] In April 1944 the OWI revised womanpower copy to delete any reference to the policy, noting that "While the WMC does not actively recruit women with young children, such women are placed in jobs where their services are available."[85]

Much of the promotional literature was written in terms with which the average homemaker could identify, and great emphasis was placed on woman's patience and skill at routine, repetitive tasks. Typical of the emphasis on domestic skills was a special leaflet prepared by the Women's Bureau on the theme, "How can I, a housewife, help?" The brochure advised, "If you've used an electric mixer in your kitchen, You can learn to run a drill press . . . ," "If you've replaced blown-out fuses in your home, or repaired your electric toaster, You can learn to be an electrician's helper."[86] The literature assured women that they excelled "at fine processes requiring painstaking application," and that they had "patience and finger dexterity and [would] soon learn to make careful adjustments at high speed with great accuracy."[87] A War Department pamphlet, *You're Going to Employ Women,* concluded that "women are pliant — adaptable . . . dexterous — finger-nimble . . . accurate-precision workers . . . good at repetitive tasks."[88] Although this emphasis probably succeeded in making production work seem less foreign to housewives with no industrial experience, such an approach frequently presumed that women workers had limited talents and ambition, and it provided a subtle way to point out the woman worker's limitations. Women, wartime management literature agreed, were usually "caretakers" rather than "promoters," were overly emotional and sensitive to criticism, were jealous, and made poor supervisors.[89]

Since housewives were a favorite target for the womanpower efforts, much attention was directed toward decreasing the resistance of husbands toward working wives. A WMC recruiting pamphlet stressed that "men have to be 'sold' just as hard as women, often much more so."[90] A typical radio spot reflected this concern:

> Now — an urgent appeal to the *men* of *(city).* Is there a woman in your home with extra time on her hands? . . . *Please don't insist that she stay home.* She is desperately needed in a war job. . . . So be understanding — lend a hand with the housework — tell her you'll be *proud* if she takes a job.[91]

The programs made it clear that women were being asked to assume emergency war assignments, temporary in nature. Labor supply officials usually referred to women as a "reserve," which clearly implied that women were not expected to become a normal part of the labor force.[92] Womanpower literature often alluded to the woman worker's postwar plans, and almost without exception the ads featured women eager to return to domesticity. In a play by the Writer's War Board, *Main Street Calling,* a defense worker apprentice concludes:

> But it'll be wonderful
> After win,
> Just to keep house,

> *And take care of Bill,*
> *He's such a dear,*
> *And I miss him so.*[93]

In a similar vein, a typical WMC radio interview with a housewife-worker explored her future plans. "I'll go back to being a housewife. . . . I want to raise a family. But I couldn't live with my conscience if I weren't working toward that 'unconditional surrender' now. Most women feel that way, I know."[94]

The OWI found that much of the resistance to women workers was due to male apprehension that women would continue in industrial jobs at war's end. To answer such objections, the OWI encouraged a deliberate policy of refuting such claims, and it urged the media to "reassure men that women will be only too glad to go back home and live a normal life after the war is over."[95] Little recognition was given to the fact that thirteen million women had been in the labor force prior to Pearl Harbor, and these women could be expected to remain at the war's end. The Civil Service Commission boasted that its clerical jobs were war work "with a future," but few other employers made similar claims.[96] A War Department brochure had concluded that "a woman worker . . . is a substitute — like plastics instead of metal," and womanpower literature assumed that men and women would be happy to return to traditional patterns of work and domestic responsibility as soon as the war emergency was over.[97]

The persistence of traditional attitudes about women is especially evident in the continuing emphasis on femininity, even in descriptions of women performing traditionally masculine jobs. The women workers who are featured in the ads, newsreels, and posters are almost uniformly neat, trim, and pretty. They dress in flattering styles, and they take pains with their make-up and personal grooming. The women are either very young or very motherly, and they are most often shown doing clean jobs such as inspection in an immaculately maintained factory.

Public information on women with important roles in the labor supply program made it clear that such women were themselves very feminine. Thelma McKelvey, head of the Women's Labor Supply Service of the War Production Board, was described by *American Magazine:*

> Thoroughly feminine herself (she keeps a powder puff in her desk, loves fashionable clothes, and experiments with new coiffures), she knows that femininity is vital to a gal's morale. So she urges her sisters to work in tailored suits wherever possible, keep compacts in their pockets and wear safety caps to protect their "coifs."[98]

Margaret Hickey, who chaired the Women's Advisory Committee of the WMC, was described in her press biography as "more feminine that 'feminist,' " and she warned women not to become "pale imitators of men" and announced that "the days of the old strident feminism are over." "Women," Hickey explained, "are able to make their best contribution when they bring to their tasks the essentially feminine qualities of mind and spirit, qualities that will be greatly needed to heal the hurt and damage of the war years."[99]

In the hands of popular writers the need to assure the public of the woman war worker's feminine qualities sometimes reached extraordinary, even ridiculous proportions. Editorials in *Vogue* stressed the necessity for women to look their fashionable best as a part of their war service.[100] Popular attention was focused on a series of frivolous issues such as Veronica Lake's long hairdo completely covering one eye, which in a widely publicized move the starlet agreed to abandon for the duration in the interest of safety. Magazines devoted columns to a discussion of the propriety of wearing slacks outside of the factory, a subject upon which the *Ladies Home Journal* claimed soldiers had strong and negative views. The distractions to male workers that attractive women caused on the assembly line were the subject of countless jokes.[101]

Advertisers vied with one another to prove that their products helped prevent women from becoming unsexed by war jobs. "Her Ambitions . . . " announced a Woodbury soap feature on a worker at Curtiss-Wright aircraft, "[are] To Win The War and Romance." Pacquins hand cream insisted that "hands that do a 'man's work' can still enchant a man!" Pond's cold cream featured an aircraft instruments worker in New York who explained, "We like to feel we *look* feminine even if we are doing a man-size job . . . so we tuck flowers and ribbons in our hair and try to keep our faces pretty as you please." As part of its women-in-the-war series, Camel cigarettes published an ad showing a woman in an evening gown out with a soldier, with the caption, "Morale experts say that it's a good idea for women in the war to be 'just women' every once in a while."[102]

The editor of the *American Home* insisted that "a woman doing war work in slacks is a woman who is right now dreaming of going back to her life as a woman at home!"[103] The editors of *Nation's Business* agreed that the "veritable promised land the majority of our present 16,000,000 women workers want involves falling in love, getting married, making homes, and raising babies."[104] Even writers who assumed that the war was improving the status of women were quick to agree that the change need not alter popular views of women. Margaret Culkin Banning insisted that the woman in the war was no "breastless female warrior. She does not allow herself to become or to be considered unsexed."[105]

Such frequent reminders suggest that the womanpower effort prompted few radical changes in the ways Americans viewed women. Despite the dislocations caused by the war, the womanpower materials reflect a desire to preserve as many of the prewar values as possible. In a variety of subtle and probably unconscious ways, the literature says that though she might be doing a man's job, the civilian war worker remained very much a woman at heart.

NOTES

1. "Manpower," *Life,* 26 October 1942, p. 29.
2. Bureau of the Budget, *The United States at War,* Historical Reports on War Administration, no. 1 (Washington, D.C.: Government Printing Office, 1946), pp. 173-89, outlines the formation of the War Manpower Commission (WMC) and describes some of the difficulties faced by the agency. Eleanor F. Straub, "United States Government Policy toward Civilian Women during World War II," *Prologue: The Journal of the National Archives* 5 (Winter 1973): 240-54, focuses on some of the problems the WMC encountered in mobilizing women.
3. A directive adopted on 17 October 1942, delegated placement functions to the United States Employment Service (USES), urged use of local women before calling in migrants from other areas, discouraged the recruitment of women with young children, and insisted that age, race, and religion should not pose arbitrary barriers to women's employment. For the text, see WMC Manual of Operations, Title III, Section 2-4, "Policy on Recruitment, Training and Employment of Women Workers," 17 October 1942, pp. 1-2, Reference Records, Records of the War Manpower Commission, Record Group 211, National Archives, Washington, D.C. (hereafter cited as RG__, NA).
4. Bureau of Intelligence, Office of War Information (OWI), Intelligence Report no. 37, 21 August 1942, p. 19, Surveys Division, Bureau of Special Services, United States Information Service (USIS), Records of the Office of Government Reports, RG 44, NA.
5. For more details, see Straub, "United States Government Policy toward Civilian Women," p. 248-49.
6. In announcing this decision at his 1 May 1942 press conference, Roosevelt indicated that although WMC officials "recommend that nothing further should be done at this time," the decision was not "a permanent thing." Transcript of Press Conference no. 823, 1 May 1942, *The Press Conferences of Franklin D. Roosevelt,* 25 vols. (New York: Da Capo Press, 1972), 19: 310-11. Microfilm edition, roll 10.
7. "Enrollment Campaigns for Women Workers, 1942," *Monthly Labor Review* 56 (March 1943): 488.
8. Summary of Campaigns Conducted in 1942 for the Mobilization or Registration of Women, 8 February 1943, File "Women, Recommended Program — Accelerated Employment of," Records of May Thompson Evans, Office of the Assistant Executive Director for Field Service, RG 211, NA.
9. "Enrollment Campaigns for Women Workers, 1942," p. 488.
10. Transcript of Press Conference on Detroit Recruiting Drive, 20 July 1942, Policy Documentation File 241.11, Records of the War Production Board, RG 179, NA; Mary Anderson to Mary LaDame, 22 July 1942, File "Women's Bureau, 1942," Secretary Perkins' General Subject File, 1940-1944, General Records of the Department of Labor, RG 174, NA.
11. Draft of letter, D.J. Hutchins to All Detroit Manufacturers, 8 September 1942, Policy Documentation File 241.11, RG 179, NA.
12. Collis Stocking to John J. Corson, 21 September 1942, File "Detroit, Michigan (Women's Registration)," Records of May Thompson Evans, Office of the Assistant Executive Director for Field Services, RG 211, NA.

13. Summary of Campaigns Conducted in 1942 for the Mobilization or Registration of Women, 8 February 1943, pp. 1-2, File "Women, Recommended Program — Accelerated Employment of," ibid.

14. Summary of Statement by Bureau of Placement on Initial Program for Accelerated Employment of Women and Program for Women's Enrollment Campaigns, n.d., Records of Mary Brewster White, Information Service, RG 211, NA.

15. Program for Accelerated Employment of Women, 12 November 1942, p. 2, enclosure to memorandum, John J. Corson to General McSherry, 18 November 1942, File "Women, Recommended Program — Accelerated Employment of," Records of May Thompson Evans, Office of the Assistant Executive Director for Field Service, RG 211, NA.

16. Ibid.

17. Women's Campaigns in Critical Areas, File "Campaigns — Critical Areas," Records of Mary Brewster White, Information Service, RG 211, NA.

18. Philip S. Broughton to Glenn E. Brockway, 4 January 1943, File "Campaigns — Enrollment," ibid.

19. Intelligence Report no. 36, 14 August 1942, pp. 15, 16, Intelligence Reports, Surveys Division, Bureau of Special Services, OWI, USIS, RG 44, NA.

20. Grafton Lee Brown, "Baltimore 'Package Promotion,' " *Employment Security Review* 9 (December 1942): 24-25; Developments in the Employment of Women, 31 May 1943, p. 5, Records of May Thompson Evans, Office of the Assistant Executive Director for Field Service, RG 211, NA.

21. Glenn E. Brockway to Paul McNutt, 9 January 1943, File "Campaigns — Enrollment," Records of Mary Brewster White, Information Service, RG 211, NA.

22. Minutes of Staff Meeting of Informational Service, 12 January 1943, p. 2, File "Office — Staff Meeting," ibid.

23. USES Operations Bulletin B-63, "Planning and Conducting a Campaign for the Enrollment of Women in War Time Employment," January 1943, pp. 2, 15, 19, Reference Records, Women's Advisory Committee, RG 211, NA.

24. Leonard P. Adams, *Wartime Manpower Mobilization: A Study of the World War II Experience in the Buffalo-Niagara Area,* Cornell Studies in Industrial and Labor Relations, no. 1 (Ithaca: Cornell University Press, 1951), pp. 36-37.

25. WMC Local Office Activities — Women's Enrollment Campaign, Niagara Falls, New York, 17 May 1943, Records of May Thompson Evans, Office of the Assistant Executive Director for Field Service, RG 211, NA.

26. WMC Local Office Activities — Women's Enrollment Campaign, Milwaukee, 30 July 1943, ibid.; WMC Local Office Activities — Women's Enrollment Campaign, Syracuse, New York, 15 October 1943, ibid. The WMC Information Service staff began to refer to enrollment drives as the "monster" that never died. As White reported, "When they get desperate for women — as they undoubtedly will — they will yank it [enrollment materials] out and team it up — fancy like — with our recruiting posters, whoopee ads, etc. I no longer brood. . . . Women will work when they have to in spite of questionnaires, government officials and total hysteria." See memorandum, Mary Brewster White to Frederic W. Wile, Jr., 31 March 1943, File "Office Memoranda — General," Records of Mary Brewster White, Information Service, RG 211, NA.

27. Lawrence Appley to Regional Manpower Director, Region XI, 3 July 1943, File "Women's Enrollment Campaign, USES Operations Bulletin B-63," Records of

May Thompson Evans, Office of the Assistant Executive Director for Field Service, RG 211, NA.

28. The successful use of an "intensive recruitment" program in the Dayton-Springfield area is described in detail in an OWI press release, "The Campaign of Dayton and Springfield, Ohio, to Balance Their Manpower Needs," 26 August 1943, File "Womanpower," Records of the Program Manager for the Recruitment of Women, Domestic Operations Branch, Records of the Office of War Information, RG 208, NA.

29. WMC Program for the Mobilization and Utilization of Women for Wartime Employment — An Appraisal, 9 February 1944, p. 3, File "Womanpower Appraisal," Correspondence, Women's Advisory Committee, RG 211, NA.

30. "The purpose of the national campaign," explained the program plan for one womanpower campaign, "is to condition and 'soften-up' the public so that it will respond readily to the intensive drives to recruit women for specific jobs in specific areas as determined by the War Manpower Commission." See Basic Program Plan for Womanpower, August 1943, File "Women in War Work," Records of C.M. Vanderburg, Domestic Operations Branch, RG 208, NA.

31. Domestic Radio Bureau, OWI, Summary of Radio Campaign, 28 December 1942 through 10 January 1943, p. 17, Records of Mary Brewster White, Information Service, RG 211, NA.

32. Transcript of 11 February 1943 Meeting, p. 69, Verbatim Transcripts, Women's Advisory Committee, RG 211, NA.

33. Transcript of 14 January 1943 Meeting, p. 33, ibid.; Transcript of 11 February 1943 Meeting, p. 28, ibid.

34. Ibid.

35. Mary B. White to Philip S. Broughton, 3 March 1943, p. 2, File "Office — Weekly Reports — MBW," Records of Mary Brewster White, Information Service, RG 211, NA.

36. Supplement (A) to the U.S. Government Campaign on Manpower, 3 February 1943, p. 1, ibid.

37. Basic Program Plan for Womanpower, August 1943, p. 2, File "Women in War Work," Records of C.M. Vanderburg, Domestic Operations Branch, RG 208, NA.

38. OWI-WMC Press Release PM-4280, 17 January 1943, p. 3, Press Release File, RG 179, NA.

39. Basic Program Plan for Womanpower, August 1943, p. 2, File "Women in War Work," Records of C.M. Vanderburg, Domestic Operations Branch, RG 208, NA.

40. Fact Sheet on the Necessary Civilian Job, 1943, p. 2, File "Agriculture — Women," Records Relating to Manpower and Salvage, Domestic Operations Branch, RG 208, NA.

41. *Saturday Evening Post*, 4 September 1943, front cover.

42. Basic Program Plan for Womanpower, August 1943, pp. 7-8, File "Women in War Work," Records of C.M. Vanderburg, Domestic Operations Branch, RG 208, NA; "Huge Womanpower Campaign Set to Go in September," *Advertising Age* 14 (May 1943): 1; *Glamour Girls of 1943*, Film no. 208-166, RG 208, NA.

43. Basic Program Plan for Womanpower, August 1943, p. 2, File "Women in War Work," Records of C.M. Vanderburg, Domestic Operations Branch, RG 208, NA.

44. Advertisement (Statler Hotels), *Life*, 6 September 1943, p. 41.

45. Mary Robinson, "Women Workers in Two Wars," *Monthly Labor Review* 57

(October 1943): 666.

46. Office of War Information, Magazine Bureau, *Magazine War Guide* (Washington, D.C.: Office of War Information, 1943), p. 9.

47. Edmund C. Lynch to General White, 25 November 1943, File "Womanpower," Records of the Program Manager for Recruitment of Women, Domestic Operations Branch, RG 208, NA; Office of War Information, Magazine Bureau, *Magazine War Guide* (Washington, D.C.: Office of War Information, 1944), p. 3.

48. *What's Cooking,* 2 September 1944, File "I.B.4.h.," Classified General Records, Historical Analysis Section, RG 211, NA.

49. The *Women's Radio War Program Guide,* a monthly or bimonthly publication, began publication in June 1943 and was sent to women's program directors of nearly a thousand radio stations. Donald D. Stauffer to William B. Lewis, 24 April 1943, Women's Radio War Program Guide, RG 208, NA; report, Domestic Radio Bureau, n.d., File "Radio Bureau (Domestic) Plans and Policies," Records of the Program Manager for the Recruitment of Women, Domestic Operations Branch, RG 208, NA. For fact sheets, see File "Fact Sheets," ibid.

50. George H. Lyon to Gardner Cowles, Jr., 28 May 1943, File "Misc.," Records of C.M. Vanderburg, RG 208, NA. "The Women's Page," Domestic Operations Branch, RG 208, NA.

51. G.F. Herrick to Mary Keeler, 20 December 1943, Records of the Program Manager for the Recruitment of Women, RG 208, NA.

52. Most of these materials may be found in either the records of the OWI, RG 208, NA, and those of the Information Service, WMC, RG 211, NA.

53. OWI, Information Guide, April 1943, p. 1, Subject File, October 1941-April 1945, Division of Federal-State Cooperation and its Predecessor Units, Records of the Office of Civilian Defense, RG 171, NA.

54. Film script, *Women on the Warpath,* n.d., pp. 1-2, File "I.B.4.h.," Classified General Records, Historical Analysis Section, RG 211, NA.

55. Womanpower Script no. 19 — The Women of Baltimore, CBS, 8 November 1942, pp. 2, 4, File "Baltimore (Women's Registration)," Records of May Thompson Evans, Office of the Assistant Executive Director for Field Service, RG 211, NA; *Soldiers Without Guns,* Film no. 111-WF-9, Records of the Office of the Chief Signal Officer, RG 111, NA.

56. Newspaper Advertisement no. 4, enclosure to memorandum, Edward T. Ingle to Mary Keeler, 26 July 1944, File "Newspaper Advertising Womanpower," Records of the Program Manager for the Recruitment of Women, Domestic Operations Branch, RG 208, NA.

57. Newspaper Advertisement no. 2, ibid.

58. Civil Service Commission Stuffer for Mailing to 100,000 Female High School Graduates, 17 June 1944, File "6.2 Programs — Recruitment," Records Relating to Manpower and Salvage, Domestic Operations Branch, RG 208, NA.

59. Fact Sheet no. 218, "Women War Workers Needed Now," 10 April 1944, p. 3, File "Fact Sheets," Records of the Program Manager for the Recruitment of Women, ibid.

60. OWI, Information Guide, "Work in War Plants," June 1943, p. 2, Subject File, September 1941-April 1945, Division of Federal-State Cooperation and its Predecessor Units, RG 171, NA.

61. Fact Sheet no. 218, "Women War Workers Needed Now," 10 April 1944, p. 3, File

"Fact Sheets," Records of the Program Manager for the Recruitment of Women, Domestic Operations Branch, RG 208, NA.

62. Women on the Working Front, A Suggested Program, p. 4, File "Miscellaneous," Records of C.M. Vanderburg, Domestic Operations Branch, RG 208, NA.

63. Office of War Information, *Magazine War Guide* (Washington, D.C., Office of War Information 1944), p. 6. See also Inter-Allied Information Committee, United Nations Information Organisation, London, *Axis Treatment of Women,* Conditions in Occupied Territories Series, no. 7 (New York: United Nations Information Office, 1943).

64. The script is reprinted in Sherman H. Dryer, *Radio in Wartime* (New York: Greenberg Press, 1942), pp. 350-51.

65. Supplement (A) to the U.S. Government Campaign on Manpower, 3 February 1943, Records of Mary Brewster White, Information Service, RG 211, NA.

66. OWI, Fact Sheet, "Womanpower: War Useful Jobs," 10 February 1943, p. 3, File "Women in War Work," Records of C.M. Vanderburg, Domestic Operations Branch, RG 208, NA.

67. Radio Spot no. 15, 1944, File "Radio Womanpower," Records of the Program Manager for the Recruitment of Women, Domestic Operations Branch, RG 208, NA.

68. Film script, *Wanted – Women War Workers,* Reference Records, Information Service, RG 211, NA.

69. Edward T. Ingle to James R. Brackett, 25 April 1944, File 1.15 General Correspondence, Records Relating to Manpower and Salvage, Domestic Operations Branch, RG 208, NA.

70. Advertisement (North American Aviation), *Life,* 19 October 1942, p. 56.

71. Advertisement (New York Dress Institute), *Vogue,* 15 January 1942, p. 16; advertisement (Woodbury soap), *Life,* 4 May 1942, p. 62; advertisement (Woodbury soap),

72. Kermit Shelby, "Rivet Knocker," *Saturday Evening Post,* 1 August 1942, pp. 23, 56. See also Lucian Cary, "A Pain in the Neck," ibid., 18 September 1943, pp. 12-13.

73. "Girl on the Midnight Shift," *American Magazine,* January 1943, pp. 24-25.

74. "Girls in Uniforms," *Life,* 6 July 1942, pp. 41-44.

75. "Girl in a Mob," *American Magazine,* October 1942, pp. 33-35.

76. "Women— Now!" *Business Week,* 9 January 1943, p. 72; Program and Administrative Program in Operation to Mobilize and Utilize Women for Wartime Employment, 6 July 1943, p. 2, File "Women— Utilization of Women for War Production— Field Representative Classification," Records of May Thompson Evans, Office of the Assistant Executive Director for Field Service, RG 211, NA.

77. OWI, Information Guide, "Women in War Plants," June 1943, p. 2, Subject File, September 1941-April 1945, Division of Federal-State Cooperation and its Predecessor Units, RG 171, NA.

78. See, for example, Edward T. Ingle to James R. Brackett, 25 April 1944, File 1.15 General Correspondence, Records Relating to Manpower and Salvage, Domestic Operations Branch, RG 208, NA.

79. Fact Sheet no. 191, "Women War Workers Needed," n.d., p. 2, File "Fact Sheets," Records of the Program Manager for the Recruitment of Women, Domestic Operations Branch, RG 208, NA.

80. For a discussion of some of the popular literature about the impact of the war on woman's status, see Straub, "United States Government Policy toward Women," p. 242.

81. Merry Holt to Maj. Ernest Culligan, 9 April 1943, File "Office Memoranda — General," Records of Mary Brewster White, Information Service, RG 211, NA.

82. WMC Manual of Operation, Title III, Section 2-4, "Recruitment, Training and Employment of Women Workers," 17 October 1942, pp. 1-2, Reference Records, Women's Advisory Committee, RG 211, NA.

83. Ibid. Both older women and black women seemed eager to secure war employment, but employers were frequently reluctant to hire them. For more information on these groups, see "Older Workers in Wartime," *Monthly Labor Review* 59 (July 1944): 24-38; and Howard W. Odum, *Race and Rumors of Race* (Chapel Hill: University of North Carolina Press, 1943), pp. 73-75.

84. Domestic Radio Bureau, OWI, Summary of Radio Campaign, 28 December 1942 through 10 January 1943, p. 16, Records of Mary Brewster White, Information Service, RG 211, NA.

85. Edward T. Ingle to James R. Brackett, 25 April 1944, File 1.15 General Correspondence, Records Relating to Manpower and Salvage, Domestic Operations Branch, RG 208, NA.

86. *What Job is Mine on the Victory Line,* Women's Bureau Leaflet no. 1 (Washington, D.C.: Government Printing Office, 1943), pp. 1, 3, 5. Similarly, an OWI film, *Glamour Girls of 1943* described many war jobs in terms of common household tasks; *Glamour Girls of 1943,* Film no. 208-166, RG 208, NA.

87. The quote is from Mildred P. Crowder, *Choosing Women for War-Industry Jobs,* Women's Bureau Special Bulletin no. 12 (Washington: Government Printing Office, 1943), p. 2.
    ibid., 1 June 1942, p. 15; advertisement (Woodbury soap), ibid., 9 March 1942, p. 59; advertisement (Hollander furs), ibid., 3 August 1942, p. 75.

88. War Department, *You're Going to Employ Women* (Washington, D.C., 1943), p. 2.

89. For writings on this subject, see Gerard Tuttle, "Changes in Production Methods Occasioned by the Employment of Women," Speech, Conference on All Out War Production, University of Southern California, 21 November 1942, p. 6, File "U.S. Job De-Skilling," Subject File Relating to U.S. Women in World War II, Records of the Women's Bureau, RG 86, NA; Office of Education film *Supervising Women Workers* (1944), Title no. 003599, National Audiovisual Center, NA; Ellen Davies, radio interview, 22 June 1943, p. 2, File "Womanpower — Miss Davies," Labor Branch, Industrial Personnel Division, Records of Headquarters Army Service Forces, RG 160, NA; Conference on Employment of Women, 16 April 1942, p. 3, File "Women in War Employment," Records of May Thompson Evans, Office of the Assistant Executive Director for Field Service, RG 211, NA; American Management Association, *Supervision of Women on Production Jobs,* Special Research Report no. 2 (New York: American Management Association, 1943), p. 15; "Woman's Place," *Business Week,* 16 May 1942, p. 20.

90. War Manpower Commission, Information Service, *America at War Needs Women at Work* (Washington: Government Printing Office, 1943), p. 6.

91. Radio Spot no. 2, 1944, File "Radio Womanpower," Records of the Program Manager for the Recruitment of Women, Domestic Operations Branch, RG 208, NA.

92. See, for example, Activities of the War Manpower Commission, April 1942-April 1943, p. 22, Classified General Records, Historical Analysis Section, RG 211, NA; U.S., Congress, House, Select Committee Investigating National Defense Migration, *Hearings on H. Res. 113,* 77th Cong., 2d sess., 1942, p. 10344.

226 ELEANOR F. STRAUB

93. Ruth Wilson, *Main Street Calling,* n.d., p. 3, File "OWI 1942 Writers War Board," Records of the Chief of the Bureau, Bureau of Special Services, OWI, USIS, RG 44, NA.
94. Womanpower Radio Interview, n.d., File "W-R — 19," Reference Records, Information Service, RG 211, NA.
95. Copy "Policy for Women's Campaign," n.d., File "Campaigns — Critical Areas," Records of Mary Brewster White, Information Service, RG 211, NA.
96. Recruiting Campaign for Civil Service Commission, 12 May 1944, File 6.2, Records Relating to Manpower and Salvage, Domestic Operations Branch, RG 208, NA; Civil Service Commission stuffer, 17 June 1944, ibid.
97. War Department, *You're Going to Employ Women,* p. 2.
98. "Cappy," *American Magazine,* July 1942, p. 74.
99. Ellen Lee Brashear and Helen Morrin, "The Manpower Woman," p. 4, File "Biography Members," Correspondence, Women's Advisory Committee, RG 211, NA; excerpt from address to National Federation of Business and Professional Women in New York City, 4 February 1945, File "Release to Morning Papers, Monday, 5 February 1945," ibid.
100. See, for example, "Vogue's Eye View of Woman's Weapons," *Vogue,* 15 January 1942, p. 33; Edna Woolman Chase, "Morale . . . ", ibid., 1 March 1942, pp. 54-55.
101. "Veronica Lake," *Life,* 8 March 1943, pp. 39-40; Louise Paine Benjamin, "Orders for the Girls at Home," *Ladies Home Journal,* November 1943, p. 118; Steve King, "Danger! Women at Work," *American Magazine,* September 1942, p. 40.
102. Advertisement (Woodbury soap), *Life,* 8 February 1943, p. 103; advertisement (Pacquins hand cream), ibid., 9 November 1942, p. 90; advertisement (Pond's cold cream), ibid., 23 November 1942, p. 125; advertisement (Camel cigarettes), ibid., 2 November 1942, back cover.
103. Jean Austin, "Women, People?" *Printers Ink,* 23 October 1942, p. 22.
104. "Through the Editor's Specs," *Nation's Business,* April 1944, p. 10.
105. Margaret Culkin Banning, "A New Heroine in Literature," *Saturday Review,* 15 May 1943, p. 22.

DISCUSSION SUMMARY

Stanley L. Falk opened the discussion with a commentary from the chair, making two brief observations by way of summary about the papers.

First of all, he said, they both amply illustrate the fact that American women were never utilized to their full potential in World War II. Whatever their contributions to the military and the labor force, it is significant that American women were denied major policy-making roles in government, in the military, in industry, in the labor movement.

His second point was that while women were more involved than ever before in areas previously closed to them, things quickly slipped back to normal once the war was over. There appears to have been no real attitudinal change in the nation as a whole, including the views of most women as well as men, toward the position of women in society. Therefore the impact of wartime developments was really not as great as it might appear at first glance.

Jane Lange, an archivist who works with motion pictures in the Audiovisual Archives Division at the National Archives, told the conference that the films cited in the two preceding papers are among the holdings of the National Archives and are available for viewing by researchers. "Interesting as the wartime recruiting films were," she said, "even more interesting are some segments of the March of Time series of the late 1940s and 1950s that were trying to undo this recruitment campaign." These further emphasize the temporary nature of this campaign.

In conversations with retired Air Force Maj. Gen. Jeanne Holm, Frances Kolb of Rutgers University has found that attitudes concerning women in the army have hardened since World War II to the extent that women officers have been opposed to the increasing role of women in the military. An interesting study could be made to discover what caused women officers to become "almost reactionary" in later years.

Kolb was also interested in the question of immorality among women in the armed forces, recalling the dismay of her own family when an uncle married a woman who had been a World War II nurse, "because, after all, women in the military were supposedly immoral." She wondered whether there was any factual basis for this opinion such as records of military trials, or was it merely the result of traditional attitudes?

Susan Hartmann said that one basis of rumors of immorality among the WACS was the hostile attitude of servicemen toward servicewomen expressed in the letters the men wrote home. The director of the WAC finally persuaded the army to make a concerted effort to get army men at all levels to present a more positive picture. She called attention to a forthcoming full-scale history of the WAC now being written by Col. Betty Borden.

Later in the discussion, Miriam Crawford of Temple University returned to the question of morality in the military services. She was in the Women's Air Corps from September 1943 to February 1946 and her sister was in the WAVES. She thinks that the publicity was highly exaggerated, but that historians should realize that a very large percentage of the young women in military service were away from home for the first time, at a time when standards of traditional conduct were relaxed to some extent. She remembered one woman who was discharged from her company for pregnancy, but it was unusual, not customary. She offered a note of personal history: the reason she enlisted was because "a boy friend who had been drafted fell for the line that was being given them, that their sweethearts should enlist." She responded to his pressure.

Hartmann noted that legislators were very much interested in the question of immorality and congressional committees frequently required at their hearings statistics of the number of women discharged for pregnancy, even though it was a minuscule number.

John McLean from the Severn School at Severna Park, Maryland, brought up the possibility of women in combat duty. Hartmann was unable to predict whether women would be sent into combat, but she said, "If people have to enter combat, I think that women as well as men should assume those responsibilities. I'd prefer a volunteer army or no army at all. . . . "

Beatrice Menchaca, who works in the Legislative Branch of the Civil Archives Division of the National Archives, asked Hartmann whether there is in congressional debates any evidence of the reason for the disparities in the development of the various women's military corps — why the WAVES were created as a part of the navy while the WACS were not militarized until a year after the Corps was established and the Army Nurse Corps even later than that. Hartmann said she had seen nothing relating to this question in congressional debate. She thought the navy foresaw the legal and administrative problems that the army in fact encountered by having the women's corps in an auxiliary posture. The Army Nurse Corps had been in existence for nearly fifty years and was probably left undisturbed. The Women Marines were established in 1943 as an integral part of the Marine Corps Reserve. [Enrollment of women in the Marine Corps Reserve first took place during World War I in August 1918. About three hundred women marines enlisted before orders were issued in July 1919 for the discharge of all "female reservists." *The Marine Corps Reserve: A History* (Washington, D.C.: Government Printing Office, 1966), pp. 17, 19. The Yeomen (F) of the U.S. Naval Reserve during World War I provided approximately eleven thousand enlisted women between June 1917 and November 1918. Eunice C. Dessez, *The First Enlisted Women* (Philadelphia: Dorrance & Co., 1955) — ED.]

Ruth Oltman of Hood College, a World War II WAVES veteran, said that although the WAVES acronym officially stood for "Women Appointed for Voluntary Emergency Service," some people thought that it also meant "Women Are Very Essential Sometimes." She also remarked that she saw some of the same kinds of sexism in the problems currently surrounding the admission of women to the military academies as had occurred in the women's services during World War II. Hartmann saw little connection between events in World War II and current problems. "The women's corps," she said, "were a very small, insubstantial part of the military after the war."

Commenting on Straub's paper, Nancy Malan of the National Archives Audiovisual Archives Division said that in her work with the poster collections, she had noticed a very definite contrast in the recruiting "pitch" between the two world wars. The World War I posters appealed to women to remember Joan of Arc, "Save France," "Women of America, Save Your Country," and similar idealistic slogans. In World War II the approach was more condescending: "Come on girls, you can make a contribution as well." She thought that a study of this subject would be interesting.

Malan also spoke of the poster image of the neat, attractive, trim women working in factories, which, she said, is not supported by actual photographs of women in munitions plants. Straub amplified this idea by adding that recruiting imagery not only showed neat, trim women, but that few of the women pictured were unattractive or overweight. There were also few black women; the recruiting effort was directed almost exclusively toward whites. Hartmann told about a national contest conducted about September 1943 for the best magazine covers portraying women at work. In looking through them, she was struck by the very blond, beautiful women on all of the covers, with one exception. A union publication — it may have been a United Automobile Workers periodical — had portrayed the working woman as "strong looking and not a romantically attractive woman."

VI

TWO FIRST LADIES

INTRODUCTION

James E. O'Neill

It seems to me that first ladies in our history have occupied a position that is at once unusual, perhaps even unique at any given moment, and also paradoxical. While a first lady is in the White House, she can, if she chooses, at least, be a celebrity, a public figure who attracts attention wherever she goes and for whatever she does. But once she leaves the White House, the fleeting character of such fame very quickly becomes evident. History, I think we can all agree, has not been kind to our first ladies. Or perhaps to be more accurate about it, historians have not been too kind to most of our first ladies. A few of them have managed to secure a place of their own in their own right in our history books, but most, alas, remain relatively obscure.

This chapter deals with one first lady who, if not really obscure, was at least not well known, namely Edith Wilson, and with a second who certainly remains, even now, these fourteen odd years after her death, one of the most famous women in all of our history, and one of the most famous women of the world in our century, Eleanor Roosevelt.

Edith James, who served on the National Archives staff for two years, is well qualified to study Edith Wilson because since 1974 she has been an assistant editor of the papers of Woodrow Wilson. This project is, in my judgment, one of the best of the letter press documentary publication projects going on. That is saying a great deal, since there are a great many of them.

Joseph Lash is well known today for his work on Eleanor Roosevelt. He brings to his task as a biographer a decided advantage: he knew Mrs. Roosevelt. He met her in the 1930s when he was active in young people's movements. And it was a lifelong friendship. So he has the double advantage of having known the subject of his biography and of having worked through that very large and immensely valuable body of Eleanor Roosevelt Papers in the Roosevelt Library.

233

EDITH BOLLING WILSON: A DOCUMENTARY VIEW

Edith James

The papers of president's wives are read, usually, for what they reveal about the great men to whom the women were married — not for what they say about the women themselves. With a few exceptions, notably Joseph Lash's biography of Eleanor Roosevelt, the studies of president's wives are simply hagiographies, drawn for the most part, from secondary sources. The intent of this paper is to use a selection of the letters of Edith Bolling Wilson as an example of the variety of documentary resources available for the study of a first lady and to present a verbal portrait of the woman to whom a president was married.[1]

In 1930 Eleanor Roosevelt wrote to Edith Wilson in reference to a mutual friend, Izetta Brown Miller, who had been asked to run for Congress from the district encompassing Schenectady.

> She is a brilliant woman, very charming and a type that I think we should be proud of in Congress, therefore, I am writing to ask if you would be willing to send her a short statement saying that you appreciated the work she did nationally for the party, and that you hope for her success. She is anxious for this statement and will be most grateful to have it to use.[2]

Mrs. Wilson replied that she could not, saying,

> Were you not both so understanding, I would be embarrassed by your request in her behalf; but I know that you both, having been in public life, know how essential it is to be consistent — and I have had to decline several similar requests. So please assure her of my regret.[3]

The exchange of letters between Eleanor Roosevelt and Edith Wilson illustrates an important facet of the character of Edith Bolling Wilson. Mrs. Wilson was very much a private person, and was, essentially, an apolitical person. Before her marriage to Wilson in 1915, Edith Bolling showed practically no interest in, or knowledge of politics. Mrs. Wilson revealed this quite clearly in her autobiography. She recalled that on election day in 1912 she was in Paris and that "so little was my interest in political affairs that I could hardly have told who the candidates were." And, indeed, she declared that she had "little interest in whoever might be President of the United States."[4]

Edith Wilson and Eleanor Roosevelt were contemporaries. Born in 1872, Edith was but twelve years older than Eleanor, and she died in 1961, only one year before Mrs. Roosevelt. Their attitudes toward politics, however, seemed to be drawn from different eras.

Mrs. Wilson's letter to Mrs. Roosevelt, which is so indicative of Edith Wilson's attitude toward public affairs, was taken from the largest and most substantive collection of Edith Wilson documents, the Edith Bolling Wilson Papers at the Library of Congress. These papers are separate and distinct from the library's collection of Woodrow Wilson Papers. Mrs. Wilson's papers consist of approximately nineteen thousand items and span the years 1893-1961. The bulk of the material originated after Wilson's death in 1924, but some of the letters, such as those written to her family while she was at the Paris Peace Conference, cover the presidential period and are fine examples of her skill as an observer. The collection is composed of scrapbooks, diary notes, family and personal letters, correspondence with associates of the president, drafts of Mrs. Wilson's autobiography, and files relating to her association with such organizations as the Woodrow Wilson Foundation and the Woodrow Wilson Birthplace Foundation. Material obviously part of the president's own records was incorporated into the Woodrow Wilson Papers.

Edith Bolling was born in Wytheville, Virginia, the seventh of nine surviving children of a family impoverished by the Civil War. Her father was a lawyer and circuit court judge. Miss Bolling was educated, primarily, at home. She moved to Washington in 1890 at age eighteen. The progressive movement, which dominated the period of her early adulthood, provided the vehicle by which many hitherto uninvolved middle-class women became politicized. Edith Bolling, however, did not participate in any of the feminist reform activities of the progressive era. Her identity remained in the home. As the wife, and later widow, of Norman Galt, a wealthy Washington jeweler, her days were filled first with managing her household and later with overseeing her husband's business.

After marrying the recently widowed president, Edith viewed her primary role as helpmate, but the nature of that role was somewhat untraditional. Ellen Axson Wilson, Woodrow's wife of twenty-nine years, had been the loving and supportive wife, mother, homemaker, hostess, and adviser during Wilson's struggle in academia and in the governorship. The second Mrs. Wilson became his loving companion, unofficial secretary, and closest counselor.

A letter that she wrote in 1916 to her lifelong friend, Alice Gertrude Gordon Grayson, illustrates the way in which Edith Wilson functioned as a friend and informal assistant to the president. She wrote, "We are both perfectly well and I guess hard work agrees with us." She joyfully added the fact that she had again been running her electric car, and that, "He and I went on a real spree last night

. . . . We stole off . . . and went 'round the Potomac drive and had a beautiful time.''[5]

The letter nicely captures the spirit of their companionship and collaboration. It was selected from the Dr. Cary T. Grayson, Sr., Family Papers, which are in the possession of the Graysons's sons. Included in this collection are about sixty-five letters between Mrs. Wilson and Mrs. Grayson, who was the wife of Woodrow Wilson's personal physician. There is, as well, a diary covering the period from 1911 to 1914 that includes Edith Galt's and Alice Gordon's European tours and contains numerous references to Mrs. Galt's social activities during Wilson's courtship.

That Mrs. Wilson served as a personal adviser to the president is more difficult to document because that role usually involved only verbal communication. A poignant reminder of her advisory role was found among some correspondence in the Bernard Baruch Papers at Princeton University. In 1955 Baruch wrote to Mrs. Wilson to ask if she knew anything about the following matter.

> I think it was before Mr. Wilson went on his American trip to explain the League, he suggested to me that the Senate pass the Versailles Treaty and then in a separate Resolution to give their interpretation of views. I do not remember exactly the word, but I think it was ''interpretation.'' . . . I wonder if you can give me any information.[6]

She answered,

> I am sorry I can't help you about the other matter, as I never heard Mr. Wilson speak of it — He was so tired at that time I never spoke of serious things if I could avoid them — While before that he talked *everything* over with me.[7]

Wilson began discussing affairs of state with Edith Galt from the beginning of their courtship. When they became engaged, he had a telephone installed which connected his study directly with her home, and, via special messenger, he sent her dispatches with his notes attached or with his commentary written directly on the document.

Examples of the documents were found among the Woodrow Wilson Papers of the Library of Congress. Some reports were sent over to keep her informed of current situations. For example, on August 22, 1915, Wilson forwarded a telegram from a Mexican revolutionary war general, Jacinto B. Treviño, along with a penciled note, ''The Carranzista position stated in a very dignified way, it seems to me.''[8]

At times of such crises as the sinking of the *Arabic,* Wilson transmitted several reports a day with remarks that were obviously intended for her thoughtful consideration. On the flimsy attached to a telegram from Walter Hines Page, the American ambassador to Britain, Wilson wrote to Edith, ''I marked one sentence merely because the German authorities may claim that the submarine Commander had reason to believe that the *Arabic* was coming to the assistance of the sinking ship and might attack him (!)''[9]

We do not have written responses from Mrs. Wilson, and it would be difficult to determine the extent to which Edith's views modified her husband's course or decisions at critical moments. We know, however, from the papers and diaries of her husband's other advisers, that her comments did carry considerable weight with the president. The Papers of Col. Edward M. House at Yale University and the Papers of Josephus Daniels at the Library of Congress show contrasting assessments of the quality of her advice.

After Wilson's stroke in 1919, Mrs. Wilson assumed new responsibilities. She was no longer an auxiliary, but now performed as an intermediary between the president and the Congress, the cabinet, the executive agencies, and the people. For this she earned the reputation of "the first lady President."[10]

The popular view overstates her role. Mrs. Wilson, herself, used the term "stewardship" to define her position.[11] She viewed herself as a guardian who was faithfully using delegated authority. Documentation seems to support her claim that she did not make policy decisions on her own.

While Eleanor Roosevelt often was Franklin's proxy in politics, Edith Wilson came near to assuming this role only during the first few weeks and life-threatening phases of Wilson's stroke. During this period, she simply staged a delaying action. Virtually nothing came out of the White House in October and November. Appointments went unfilled, mail unanswered, and decisions delayed.

Later, her power became a veto power, for she determined which visitors Wilson saw and what matters were presented to him. Then, either of two procedures seems to have been followed. Mrs. Wilson informed the president of a particular issue in question in her own words or Wilson read the relevant original material himself. He dictated his reply to Mrs. Wilson or asked her to convey verbally his instructions to the responsible parties. Mrs. Wilson had good intelligence and an aloof composure and dignity. These impressive qualities enabled her to perform the difficult task.

Good examples of the manner in which Mrs. Wilson functioned were furnished from the State Department Records at the National Archives, the Joseph P. Tumulty Papers and the Woodrow Wilson Papers, both at the Library of Congress.

On November 29, 1919, Jean Jules Jusserand, the French ambassador, requested that the United States delay withdrawal of its commissioners to the Paris Peace Conference because of the German refusal to sign the protocol. Lansing requested instructions from the White House. After some delay, Mrs. Wilson responded,

> The President feels it will do no harm to delay the departure until the 9th but advices [sic] that all of the Commission leave at that date and that this be made final.[12]

In handling the question of an impending strike by the Brotherhood of Maintenance of Way Employees and Railway Shop Laborers, the Director General of the United States Railroad Administration Walker D. Hines prepared a draft statement to the railroad brotherhood and asked that Secretary Joseph P. Tumulty take up the matter with the president. Chief Clerk Rudolph Forster presented the material to Mrs. Wilson, who consulted with Mr. Wilson. She returned with the message: "The President regards this as poorly expressed — but says let it go, as he agrees to the subject matter."[13] The telegram requesting that the union withdraw its strike order went out under Wilson's signature, even though it was most un-Wilsonian in its phrasing.

Perhaps the best examples of Mrs. Wilson's stewardship are two documents that were transferred from her private file to the Woodrow Wilson Papers. One is Mrs. Wilson's own penciled draft of a statement on reservations to the peace treaty dictated by Wilson sometime in November of 1919. The other is an undated note in Wilson's shaky hand, "My darling Please read the paper to Baruch and get his impression."[14]

Mrs. Wilson married power. She did not have power. After Wilson's death, Edith Wilson retreated almost entirely from political affairs, and lived a rather quiet and unassuming existence. Her all-encompassing task was to promote her husband's peace plans and to ensure proper memorialization of his name. She played a guiding role in the development of the Woodrow Wilson Foundation,[15] in the collection of Wilson's papers, and in the writing of Ray Stannard Baker's Pulitzer-prize winning biography of Wilson.[16] Ample evidence of these activities can be found in the files relating to the foundation in the Edith Bolling Wilson Papers and in her correspondence with Baker in the Ray Stannard Baker Papers at the Library of Congress.

We see her subtle, but firm, authority in the foundation in this letter that she wrote to Newton D. Baker in 1928.

> I would welcome an opportunity to discuss with you the future policy of the Foundation. Your own mind ran so close to Mr. Wilson's in idealistic as well as practical things that I am hoping — now that you are head of the Foundation — a more definite and certain policy can be adopted.[17]

She was indefatigable in her pursuit of Wilson documents, and the result was one of the most complete collections of presidential papers that we have.

She also helped to secure an eight-volume biography of Wilson. She encouraged Baker all along the way, read every page of the manuscript closely, suggested conceptual changes, and noted errors of fact. We see her efforts in the letter that she wrote to Ray Stannard Baker in 1928. She began in a humorous vein asking to make a minor correction concerning a book Vice President Thomas R. Marshall had presented to Wilson.

> You say "He presented him with a copy" with the inscription to "Marshall, my only vice." You have that upside down, as Marshall presented *him* with a book with "From your only vice."[18]

Then she went on to more important matters relating to Baker's analysis of the Democratic convention of 1912 and to the principles involved in the presidential campaign.

During Edith Wilson's life, she appeared always to be struggling to maintain a balance between public obligation and private need. The letters of Edith Bolling Wilson, in their cumulative effect, are revealing of that enduring theme in her life. But, if a portrait of a woman can be drawn from a single letter, it might be the letter written to her mother on May 7, 1919.

> I am waiting for Woodrow to come back from Versaille [sic], where the Treaty was to be handed to the Germans. I was awfully disappointed I could not have seen it, but the room was too small to admit any body but the Delegates and . . . representatives of the Press . . . so W. felt I had better not ask to go as it would cause hard feelings with other people. After W. got back he and I went for a beautiful ride out to St. Germain, and I wished all the way you were with us to see the beauty of the Country — the fruit trees are in full bloom, and the long grey walls which surround almost every place are covered with Ivy and many have Wall flowers blooming on the top while over them wave perfect trees of both purple and white Lilac. Everybody we met had arms full of the Lilac and many soldiers had big sprays stuck in their belts. We have had three wonderful warm days, and I am so glad for Woodrow to see France in this mood, for it was so dreary here in the winter I think he felt he would never want to come back.
>
> Now I must run as it is time to go.[19]

NOTES

1. There are two full-length biographies of Mrs. Wilson: Alden Hatch, *Edith Bolling Wilson, First Lady Extraordinary* (New York: Dodd, Mead, 1961) and Ishbel Ross, *Power with Grace, The Life Story of Mrs. Woodrow Wilson* (New York: G. P. Putnam's Sons, 1975).
2. Eleanor Roosevelt to Edith Bolling Wilson, 16 September 1930, Edith Bolling Wilson Papers, Library of Congress, Washington, D.C.
3. E.B. Wilson to E. Roosevelt, 22 September 1930, ibid.
4. Edith Bolling Wilson, *My Memoir* (New York: Bobbs-Merrill Co., 1939), pp. 33-34.
5. E.B. Wilson to Alice Gertrude Gordon Grayson, 20 June 1916, Dr. Cary T. Grayson, Sr., Family Papers, supplied with the courtesy of Cary T. Grayson, Jr.
6. Bernard Baruch to E.B. Wilson, 27 January 1955, Bernard Baruch Papers, Princeton University Library, Princeton, New Jersey.
7. E.B. Wilson to B. Baruch, 29 January 1955, ibid.
8. Woodrow Wilson to E.B. Wilson, 22 August 1915, enclosed in Jacinto B. Treviño to Robert Lansing, 19 August 1915, Woodrow Wilson Papers, Library of Congress.
9. W. Wilson to E.B. Wilson, 23 August 1915, enclosed in Walter Hines Page to R. Lansing, 23 August 1915, ibid.
10. The portrayal of Edith Wilson as "Presidentress" is, today, the prevailing, common interpretation. A press release, for example, for a recent television special declared that

"during an era when women had not yet been given the right to vote, Mrs. Wilson virtually took over the reins of the White House when her husband collapsed . . . . " National Broadcasting Corporation, "Television Information Workshop Bulletin — First Ladies' Diaries: Edith Bolling Wilson," 11 December 1975, New York.

11. Edith Bolling Wilson, *My Memoir,* p. 289.

12. E.B. Wilson to R. Lansing, 2 December 1919, File 763.72119/8218 1/2, General Records of the Department of State, Record Group 59, National Archives Building.

13. E.B. Wilson to Rudolph Forster, 14 February 1920, Joseph P. Tumulty Papers, Library of Congress, Washington, D.C.

14. Draft of League Statement, ca. November 1919, Woodrow Wilson Papers, Library of Congress; W. Wilson to E.B. Wilson, ca. November, 1919-March 1919, ibid.

15. The Woodrow Wilson Foundation was established, in 1922, to disseminate the ideals of Wilson and to promote the public welfare, the advancement of liberal thought, and the furtherance of peace through an awards and a service program, and through research and publication.

16. Ray Stannard Baker, *Woodrow Wilson, Life and Letters,* 8 vols. (Garden City, N.Y.: Doubleday, Page & Co., 1927-39).

17. E.B. Wilson to Newton D. Baker, 28 November 1928, Edith Bolling Wilson Papers, Library of Congress.

18. E.B. Wilson to R.S. Baker, 25 October 1928, Ray Stannard Baker Papers, Library of Congress.

19. E.B. Wilson to Sallie White Bolling, 7 May 1919, Edith Bolling Wilson Papers, Library of Congress.

dear Mrs Roovelt the first lady

Mrs Roovelt you have helped so many

working people why dont you are the

predsint help we poor domestic working

girls cant domesti girls have a union
or not mMrs Rovelst

I am a domestic worker

making 35 dollars a mont

get ever sunday after noon off

and ever other thursday after noon off

now Mrs roseelvertdo you think that is enough

time off for a girl that work

from eight in the mori ng

till nine at night out off the 35 dolllars

i make a mont i hafter to pay 10 a day to

comute to my job 3 dollars a weea weak

room rent 50 cent a mont club dues a dollar a mont

insuare a dollar a mont on a radio i have if i was only

getting 5 dollars more i could make out so will
you please help us to get a union to get more time off

and shorter hours and get 2 holiday s off during
the year and a raise in wages we are not slaves but works
working girls likeany body else if you will ance this
lett er in your my day i will read about it
thank you please help us

Mrs Eleanor Roosevelt
Washington the White House
The First Lady

Plea to Eleanor Roosevelt for help for domestic servants. While Eleanor Roosevelt was first lady, her daily mail was filled with letters from ordinary citizens telling her their troubles and seeking her help because of her reputation for warm concern for suffering people. Some letters were fawning; others were funny, like one addressed to ''Your Royal Highness, Mrs. First Lady.'' But all writers were confident of a response, either from her directly or through her column ''My Day.'' Some of the most pathetic came from black domestic servants describing their plight. Obviously unable to answer all the letters, she sent most of them to an appropriate agency requesting that the reply be sent ''at Mrs. Roosevelt's request.''

(Unsigned letter to Eleanor Roosevelt, received April 7, 1941, Household Domestic File, General Correspondence, Records of the Women's Bureau, RG 86.)

ELEANOR ROOSEVELT'S ROLE IN WOMEN'S HISTORY

Joseph P. Lash

Writing the Biography

Let me at the outset acknowledge that I had a great advantage in writing a biography of Eleanor Roosevelt. I had had the privilege of her friendship, had kept fairly voluminous diaries, was one of the friends to whom she wrote regularly — in longhand, often after midnight — and with whom she talked quite freely.

As a consequence when Franklin Roosevelt, his mother's literary executor, asked me to go through her papers with a view to writing a biography, I came to that marvelous archive at the Franklin D. Roosevelt Library at Hyde Park with a sense of what the story was and a feeling for the personality of this extraordinary woman that documents alone could not convey. In fact, after three winters at Hyde Park going through those file boxes, my problem became one of not allowing the documents to take over and obscure the reality of the vibrant, vital "gravely gay" person whom I had known.

I had some of the same difficulty recently with Jane Alexander's portrayal of Eleanor in the ABC production of "Eleanor and Franklin."[1] It was uncanny, as others besides myself noted, the way Jane Alexander captured Eleanor Roosevelt's inner glow. And I said to Miss Alexander afterwards, "I no longer know whether I am in love with Eleanor Roosevelt or Jane Alexander." But delighted as I was with ABC's production and Jane Alexander's and Ed Hermann's portrayal of Eleanor and Franklin, I did wonder whether my children, and even more, their children, would when they thought of the Roosevelts in history, see the faces of Jane and Ed rather than of the persons whom they portrayed. But as a historian I cannot complain. As a result of the showing of "Eleanor and Franklin," there has been a vast upsurge in interest in books about the Roosevelts and the Roosevelt era.

Even with the abundance of material that I had at Hyde Park and in my own files, I did a substantial amount of collateral research, study, and absorption of atmosphere.

243

I lived at Wildercliffe, a house that was built by Chancellor Livingston[2] for his sister and was owned by the Dupees[3] who were happy to have someone in it during the winter when they were in New York. It was marvelously situated to get a feeling for those people of that part of old New York — the Livingstons, Ludlows, Mortons, Millses, Roosevelts, and Delanos — who spent the social season in the city but whose great homes were on the Hudson and especially for the stretch known as Woods Road, a Livingston enclave north of Tivoli on the Hudson.

I hastened to interview the few survivors from Eleanor's youth, beginning with a ninety-six-year-old uncle by marriage, David Gray, who when I asked him what books might give me a sense of old New York society, without hesitation sent me to Edith Wharton's *House of Mirth*. Laura Delano, FDR's cousin, a tiny but daunting woman, full of spice, lived at Rhinebeck. She was not very kind about Eleanor, but when I mentioned Mrs. Longworth,[4] promptly commented that the real reason behind Alice's maliciousness was that she had wanted Franklin. Alas, that story was quickly shot down by Mrs. Longworth and others. Then there was Mrs. Lawrance, born Margaret Dix,[5] the daughter of the rector of Trinity, a white-haired lady in her eighties, who electrified me by standing up and giving an imitation of Eleanor reciting the "Last Leaf of the Tree" with gestures according to del Sarte, and moistening of lips with the tip of her tongue. And when I talked with Mrs. Corinne Robinson Cole,[6] Joe Alsop's[7] mother, and Eleanor's cousin, about Franklin's courtship of Eleanor, she went upstairs and brought down her diary for the period. That woman could write, but she would not let me quote her: "Oh, but that's my line, Mr. Lash," she would protest.

Eleanor's Early Experiences

Arthur Schlesinger has called her "the most liberated woman of the century." She was not born that way nor did her childhood upbringing nurture traits of independence and militancy. Her mother died when she was eight and she was brought up by a grandmother[8] who was herself the epitome of Victorian female dependence and helplessness, whose husband would not allow her to shop for herself and who did not teach his wife the rudiments of keeping accounts. He chose his wife's dresses and hats, having them sent to the house for her to look at in private. Grandfather Hall[9] was a deeply religious man who maintained a resident clergyman at Tivoli with whom he discussed theological issues. Perhaps it was her grandfather's ability to cite scripture in support of his feeling that men were the "lords of creation," that led Eleanor Roosevelt on one occasion during her White House days to dictate to her secretary, Miss Thompson,[10] a column, I think it was, suggesting the scriptures might have been authored by men. It took a great deal of arguing by Tommy to persuade her that even if she were right, it was not prudent for the first lady to say so. But that was in 1940. In her youth Eleanor would have been as startled as Tommy by such a suggestion, as shocked as some of us are to discover that as late as 1910, after she was married to Franklin and had borne three children, she was still opposed to woman's suffrage, still believed, or so she would have us think, that men were superior creatures, still thought that politics were man's domain, and that women should exercise their influence upon political affairs through their husbands.

There were models in Eleanor's youth who influenced her development — women who represented strength and independence, even though they expressed their talents and potencies in ways that society — spelled with a capital S — deemed acceptable. One was Mlle. Souvestre, the head of Allenswood, a finishing school in England, to which Eleanor was sent when she was fifteen. Until then she had built her life upon identification with her father who had died when she was ten and to whose vindication by her own success she was passionately committed. But how was she to achieve success? She was the only Hall woman who was not a belle and so the road of social success was closed, even if it should have attracted her. It was Mlle. Souvestre who provided her with an alternative model and the years at Allenswood that gave her a sense for the first time that she could achieve success in her own right.

Eleanor's second model was her aunt, Theodore Roosevelt's sister, Aunty Bye,[11] at whose N Street house in Washington she was staying while awaiting Franklin's return from the Caribbean cruise on which his mother had taken him in hopes of getting his mind off Eleanor. Of Aunty Bye, Alice Longworth has said, "if she had been a man, she would have been President . . . . " Mrs. Cowles's N Street house became known as "the little White House" because Theodore Roosevelt was there so often. Eleanor Roosevelt said that "there was never a serious subject that came up while he was President that he didn't go to her at her home on N Street and discuss with her. That was well known by all the family. He may have made his own decisions, but talking with her seemed to clarify things for him."

The First Venture Into Public

Up until U.S. entry in World War I, I think Mrs. Cowles's relationship to Theodore Roosevelt represented Eleanor's conception of how women should relate to and participate in political life, and even after she emerged as a mighty champion of women's rights, she still believed that the happiest women were those who could sink themselves in their husbands' careers, serving them as companions and helpmeets, as well as mothering their children and presiding over their households.

It was symptomatic of events to come that young Eleanor attracted and was attracted by two such strong personalities as Mlle. Souvestre and Mrs. Cowles. But with her marriage to Franklin she came under the influence of another strong woman, Sara Delano Roosevelt, a dominating and quite remarkable person, but totally a traditionalist and conformist. Sara's imperial ways, together with Eleanor's desire to be accepted and approved by husband and mother-in-law, combined to keep Eleanor out of the struggle for women's rights which was then coming to a climax in such movements as the suffrage and trade union organization.

Two events triggered a renewed thrust toward public activity that had come to a stop with her marriage to Franklin — U.S. entry into World War I and her discovery of her husband's romance with Lucy Mercer.[12] Chronology here has some importance. U.S. entrance into the war made it quite proper, indeed patriotic, for women to give up conventional social duties for work with the American Red Cross. Eleanor plunged into this activity and soon was recognized as a first-rate organizer and leader. She had demonstrated her leadership qualities in Allenswood and in the Junior League, too. Her emergence as a leader in the Red Cross work before she discovered her husband's romance with her social secretary is significant: I am persuaded that even if the Lucy Mercer affair had not happened, Eleanor would never again have become a wholly private person, living exclusively for and in her family, just as I am persuaded that even had her husband never returned to political life after he was felled by polio, she would have left her mark on the times. In Eleanor's presence — as in Franklin's — you sensed greatness.

The Roosevelts returned to New York at the end of 1920 after the Cox-Roosevelt ticket, pledged to the League of Nations, had been swamped in the Harding landslide. That was the first presidential election in which women voted, and the fact that women supported back-to-normalcy and repudiation of the league in the same proportions as their husbands was a dreadful disappointment to the battle-scarred veterans of the suffrage struggle. Despite the setback they remained determined to make woman's participation in politics count for a better world. In today's terminology one would say they had been radicalized by the suffrage struggle, except that they were tough-minded, pragmatic, and liberal. But one can certainly say that they emerged from the suffrage struggle politicized: they had a feeling for organization; they were skillful agitators; they were wise in the ways and wiles of politicians. They were to be found in the leadership not only of the successor to the National Woman Suffrage Association, the League of Women Voters, but of such organizations as the Women's Trade Union League, the Women's Division of the Democratic party, and the peace and public housing movements. And one of their new recruits was Eleanor Roosevelt, who, on her return to New York not only joined but became active in these movements. She also enrolled in a secretarial course, paid for cooking lessons that she never took, and pushed and coached by Louis Howe,[13] even ventured to speak in public and became the greatest woman speaker of her time.

The Twenties – Emergence of a Leader

Throughout the twenties, the decade of prosperity, these organizations kept high the banner of reform. And many of the programs that they projected — improved working conditions for women, the abolition of child labor, collective bargaining, public housing, social insurance, prison reform — were to be realized in the New Deal.

What gave women strength in politics was their dedication to program before patronage. "One person with a belief," wrote John Stuart Mill, "is a social power equal to ninety-nine who have only interests." Louis Howe, a superb political analyst, credited women's participation in politics with the revolution in thinking that was intrinsic to the New Deal. If politics continued to divide along humanitarian-conservative lines, he wrote in the mid-thirties, and the people decided they wanted a New Deal approach to such issues as education, recreation, and labor, "it is not without the bounds of possibility that a woman might not only be nominated but elected to the office [meaning the presidency] on the grounds that they better understand such questions than the men."[14] His candidate, incidentally, was Eleanor Roosevelt, a suggestion which she firmly thrust aside.

The women of the twenties not only had convictions, they realized the importance of organization. "You must in politics have not only a scheme before you," wrote Bagehot, "but a power behind you." He thought liberals tended to neglect the latter. Not Eleanor Roosevelt or the veterans of the suffrage struggle. The power behind Eleanor Roosevelt in the twenties was, of course, in part, her relationship to Franklin D. Roosevelt, who, even after he was felled by polio, continued to be a major influence in the Democratic party, but it was also her systematic organization of the women, with New York State as a home base. It was that untiring organizational work that made her a respected figure even among the male politicos. Twice a year, sometimes with Nancy Cook[15] and Marion Dickerman,[16] sometimes with Elinor Morgenthau[17] and Caroline O'Day,[18] she got into her runabout and toured upstate New York, concentrating on the small towns, meeting with women, discussing the issues with them, persuading them to set up a women's group to represent Democratic women in the county. In the 1924 gubernatorial campaign when Smith's[19] opponent was Eleanor's cousin Theodore Roosevelt, Jr., she toured the state in her car with a huge teakettle attached, puffing steam to remind voters of Teapot Dome. That, the Republicans considered a Democratic "dirty trick," and Eleanor always spoke of the episode a little apologetically.

When money had to be raised, Eleanor raised it; when a speech had to be made she accepted the assignment, no matter how small the group, no matter how much agony making a speech still gave her; when a Women's Division newspaper was launched, she wrote for it, solicited the advertising, corrected proofs, dummied, and saw to it that the finished copies were mailed out.

By the time of the 1924 Democratic State Convention, the Women's Division was well enough organized to rebel against Boss Charles Murphy's[20] edict that he and the men leaders — and not the women — would name the two women delegates at large and the two women alternates to serve on the state committee. Mrs. Roosevelt led the protest. "We have now had the vote for four years," she told a cheering women's rally at the Hotel Ten Eyck, "and some very alert suffragists seem to feel that instead of gaining in power the women have lost." She did not like to cause "disagreement and unpleasant feelings," she went on. "But I have come to the conclusion that this must be done for a time until we can prove our strength and demand respect for our wishes."[21] Led by Eleanor the women took their case to Governor Smith. He was a candidate for president. Moreover one of his most respected and intimate advisers was Belle Moskowitz. Smith supported the women and Murphy capitulated. "A highly intelligent and capable politician," the *New York Times* said afterwards of Eleanor Roosevelt.[22]

The struggle to get the male political animal to recognize his female coworker as an equal was to last all of Eleanor Roosevelt's life, and despite the gains women achieved in the Roosevelt era, Mrs. Roosevelt at the end of her life, speaking of women's chances in politics, cautioned them that the men still were intent on excluding them from the vital decisions. Women had to be "alert to see that they are not kept from attending important meetings. Sometimes they have to be extremely insistent . . . "

I do not want to leave the twenties, the decade which saw Eleanor Roosevelt's emergence as a leader in her own right, without some reference to the drive for an equal rights amendment sponsored by the women's party. Eleanor thought the opposition of the latter to protective legislation for women on the basis of equal rights was downright reactionary. In this she reflected the viewpoint of the Women's Trade Union League and of organized labor generally. She ended her opposition to the amendment in the final years of her life. By then the trade unions were strong enough to enforce fair labor standards for all workers and the climate of opinion was favorable to such legislation for all — not just for women and children.

The New Deal Years

The years of the twenties, years when it seemed to the activists and progressives that nothing ever moved, gave way to the thirties and the depression, culminating in Roosevelt's election and the New Deal where everything seemed possible. The New Deal was youth's deal; it was labor's deal; it was the black man's deal; it was also the woman's deal. Those marvelously creative years have yet to be studied from the point of view of women's rights and women's liberation. I suspect that when they are, it will be found that during the New Deal years women achieved the largest measure of participation and recognition in government and politics from the time they obtained the vote to the 1972 Democratic Convention.

Roosevelt's victory in 1932 was in large measure a vote against Hoover rather than a vote for Roosevelt and his policies, but insofar as his majority did represent affirmation rather than rejection, it was in some significant measure a victory for women's rights. Not everyone was happy about that, as Eleanor indicated by a story that she told at a farewell dinner given to her by her fellow New Yorkers in February 1933, a few weeks before inauguration. Men turned out for the occasion as well as women, but the keynote was women's liberation, what Eleanor Roosevelt had already done, as the chairman, a man, put it, "to put out of fashion the remaining inequalities in the status of women," and the confidence that the assemblage had that Eleanor Roosevelt would prove "that even the wife of a President can live a life that will help to vindicate women's rights to intellectual and professional freedom."[23]

Mrs. Roosevelt in her reply at the end of the evening thought it wise to introduce a cautionary note. She hoped that women in government and politics would help bring about the changes and reforms that were necessary, but she did not underestimate masculine resistance. To underscore her point she read a letter her husband had shown her. "Dear Sir," it began,

> I have read a great deal and I see in the papers that you are thinking of putting a woman in the cabinet. I want you to know that my reading has taught me that sin began in the world with Eve, and woman's place is in the home. She should not speak except when her husband allows her to do so. She should work and she should never be anywhere except subject to man, for the Bible says, "Sin came with woman."

"So you see," commented Mrs. Roosevelt in her disarmingly mild way that concealed a mean hook, "women in politics have to live down perhaps a little prejudice amongst a few people." How deep-seated the prejudice was, was suggested by the chairman who pointed out that Harvard Law School did not admit women, and neither did the New York Bar Association, although it did permit ladies to use the library — one day a year. The rest of the year they were privileged to hire a room and have books brought to them.

The letter that Eleanor Roosevelt read enabled her to make her point that, committed as Franklin Roosevelt might be to equal rights for women, he faced opposition in seeking to implement that principle. And knowing Mrs. Roosevelt, I wondered as I reread the letter, whether it was not her way of alerting Roosevelt progressives that there was opposition to his naming Frances Perkins as secretary of labor. In any case, she was named, and this appointment of the first woman to sit in the cabinet signalled to women everywhere that they too were to be the beneficiaries of the New Deal.

But not without backsliding. One of the measures passed in the hundred days was the Economy Act, and section 213 of that act provided that if both husband and wife were on the government payroll, one would have to quit; and of course the one who left was the wife. The women hated section 213, but in the face of breadlines and shantytowns felt powerless to oppose it, although both Mrs. Roosevelt and Frances Perkins did protest — on economic rather than feminist grounds. It was a "very bad and foolish thing" to dismiss women because they were married, Mrs. Roosevelt told her press conference, especially as government salaries "in most cases are so small as to be hardly enough to support more than two persons and certainly not enough on which to educate and rear a family."

The women were unable to get section 213 rescinded until 1937. And even then it remained in force in the emergency agencies. Eleanor Roosevelt and Molly Dewson, the head of the Women's Division of the Democratic National Committee, protested, but they were unable to budge FDR. He and his budget director contended that since the rule prohibiting government employment of more than one in the family had been in effect when the emergency agencies were created, its enforcement had not meant the hardship of a woman having to give up her job.

That may have been true, but of course it was blatantly discriminatory in principle.

The New Deal years represented a high point in woman's participation in politics and government. This was in considerable measure due to Franklin Roosevelt who, partly because of his own openness to emerging trends, and partly because of Eleanor's teaching and prodding, had cultivated the vote of the women, had enlisted them in the party, and in the government, and his programs were responsive to the humanitarian goals that the women were more concerned with than the men.

But the appointment of women to high posts in the New Deal agencies did not happen automatically. Roosevelt's attitude was not consistent. One day, as the reporters crowded around his desk, Roosevelt showed those nearest him a new stamp issue. The men would never forgive him for issuing a Frances Willard stamp, a wire service "male chauvinist pig" remarked. The president reacted defensively, "Well, I have to grant about every one hundredth request that comes from women," he said. "That's a fact. I turn down 99 and have to give them something." "We are listening," commented Ruby Black of the United Press and a friend of Eleanor's. The appointment of Frances Perkins to the cabinet might have remained a token, except that the women, led by Eleanor would not allow it. Benignly as FDR at time felt toward the women, there had to be a transmission belt by which women's desires and objectives were translated into concrete jobs and programs. The transmission mechanism was politics — in the first place the election as president of a man who favored women's participation in politics and government, who happened in this case to be married to a woman who would press the case for equal rights at the very heart of the government.

And almost as important as president and first lady in this transmission process, was the Women's Division of the Democratic National Committee, headed by a most remarkable woman, Molly W. Dewson who has still to receive her due from historians. Molly Dewson was a no-nonsense lady from Maine whom James Farley respectfully addressed as "General" but who, for all of her toughness, was concerned with ideals and objectives. She had been superintendent of parole for girls in Massachusetts before the U.S. entered World War I, left off reforming the prisons to go to France with the Red Cross, came back to serve as research secretary of the National Consumers' League in which position she helped Felix Frankfurter prepare the economic briefs in the District of Columbia and California minimum wages cases. She had first met Eleanor in 1924 when both were active in the New York Women's City Club. In the 1928 presidential campaign when Eleanor was heading up the Women's Division and needed to send out a trouble shooter to the Midwest, she asked Molly to help out, and Molly turned out to be so good that from then on she was part of every campaign and a mainstay of the Roosevelt campaign organization.

Molly had a little list of women who were qualified and entitled to jobs, and soon after Roosevelt was inaugurated she came to Washington with her list, which she presented to Farley with a duplicate to Eleanor. Mrs. Roosevelt obtained Farley's willing agreement, for he respected what the women had done in the campaign, to clear jobs for women with Molly or herself. And in the rare instances that Farley resisted Molly's recommendations, Eleanor was there to take the matter to the boss. Molly set herself three goals as head of the Women's Division in Washington — the first two were patronage for women and fifty-fifty representation on all party committees. She obtained equal representation for women on the platform committee of the 1936 convention, a far cry from the 1924 convention when the women headed by Eleanor had to sit outside of the platform committee's meeting room and plead with a man to take in their recommendations. Molly's third objective was the clear and widespread understanding of the Roosevelt program. This tall, angular down-Easter with her patrician nose and rimless glasses deserves a book, and if I were an aspiring Ph.D. candidate I could think of no more rewarding a subject.

Molly withdrew from the Washington scene in the late thirties because of health, and though Mrs. Roosevelt persuaded her to return for the 1940 third term campaign, she left immediately afterwards. Whenever, thereafter, Mrs. Roosevelt motored to Campobello she stopped in Castine to visit Molly — and another battler for progressive cases, Bishop Scarlett,[24] "Bishop Will" as she called him. Even without Molly the women's fight for equal rights and equal representation went on, and one of the final White House conferences over which Mrs. Roosevelt presided before FDR's death had as its theme "How Women May Share in Post-War Policy Making." One of the items handed to Jonathan Daniels[25] who sat in at the conference as one of the president's aides was "a roster of qualified women."

I suspect that many feminists today would have called Eleanor Roosevelt a reactionary. As my wife has pointed out, she was a marvelous mixture of traditional and radical attitudes. In her private life she discriminated in favor of the men, especially those whom she loved. She protected them; she forgave them their sins and weaknesses more easily than she did the women. Women should not smoke; it upset her when women drank too much or dressed provocatively. The word "lady" meant something to her.

She was not only a "lady" but a great lady and because she passed this way the egalitarian concept of "women as the equal of man but different" she took a giant step forward.

NOTES

1. "Eleanor and Franklin," a four-hour special program produced by the American Broadcasting Company for television; shown on ABC channels, January 11 and 12 1976.
2. Robert R. Livingston (1746-1813), Chancellor of New York who administered the presidential oath of office to George Washington. Eleanor Roosevelt was his direct descendant.

3. Frederick Wilcox Dupee (1904-1978), author, Henry James scholar, member of the Columbia University English Department, 1940-71, and his wife, Barbara Hughes Dupee.
4. Alice Roosevelt Longworth (1884-   ), daughter of President Theodore Roosevelt, widow of Nicholas Longworth (1869-1931) who was speaker of the U.S. House of Representatives, 1925-31; Eleanor's first cousin.
5. Margaret Dix Lawrance (Mrs. Charles W. Lawrance), daughter of the Rev. Dr. Morgan Dix, rector of Trinity Church in New York City; a member of the small social circle in which Eleanor grew up.
6. Corinne Robinson Cole, a niece of President Theodore Roosevelt and Eleanor's cousin.
7. Joseph Wright Alsop (1910-   ), journalist and author, best known for his syndicated column, "Matter of Fact," which he wrote with his brother Stewart J.O. Alsop, 1945-58 and alone, 1958-74.
8. Mary Livingston Ludlow Hall (1843-1919).
9. Valentine Gill Hall, Jr. (1834-80).
10. Malvina C. Thompson, Eleanor's personal secretary from the time they worked together on the 1928 presidential campaign.
11. Anna Roosevelt Cowles (1855-1931). Her husband was Rear Adm. W. Sheffield Cowles, Jr. (1846-1923).
12. Lucy Mercer (later Rutherford), employed as social secretary by Eleanor Roosevelt in 1913.
13. Louis McHenry Howe (1871-1936), personal secretary and political adviser to Franklin D. Roosevelt.
14. Louis Howe, draft of an article, "Women's Ways in Politics," *Woman's Home Companion,* July 1935, quoted in Lash, *Eleanor and Franklin* (New York: W.W. Norton & Co., 1971), p. 390.
15. Nancy Cook, suffragist, assistant chairperson of the Women's Division of the New York State Democratic Committee, and close friend of Eleanor's. Together they owned the Val-Kill Industries established on the Roosevelt property at Hyde Park to engage rural labor to produce authentic reproductions of colonial furniture and other artifacts.
16. Marion Dickerman, Nancy Cook's close friend who became a friend of Eleanor's, principal of the Todhunter School for Girls in New York City where Eleanor was part owner and teacher.
17. Elinor Morgenthau, active participant with Eleanor in New York State Democratic politics, a presidential elector in 1924. Her husband Henry Morgenthau, Jr., was secretary of the treasury in Franklin D. Roosevelt's cabinet.
18. Caroline O'Day, chairperson of the Women's Division of the New York State Democratic Committee in mid-1920s.
19. Alfred E. Smith (1873-1944), governor of New York for four terms, 1918-21 and 1923-28, candidate for president, 1928.
20. Charles F. Murphy (1895-1924), "boss" of Tammany Hall, 1902-24.
21. Quoted, Lash, *Eleanor and Franklin,* p. 289.
22. Ibid., p. 290.
23. *New York Times,* 11 February 1933, transcript in Eleanor Roosevelt Papers, Franklin D. Roosevelt Library, Hyde Park, New York.
24. William Scarlett (1883-1973), Episcopal Bishop of Missouri, 1935-53.

25. Press Conference no. 578, 12 September 1939, *Complete Press Conferences of Franklin D. Roosevelt,* 25 vols. (New York: Da Capo Press, 1972), 14: 59.

26. Jonathan Worth Daniels (1902-   ), editor, Raleigh (N.C.) *News and observer,* 1933-70, author of many books, of which *A Southerner Discovers the South* (New York: Macmillan, 1938) was an early one that was widely read and *White House Witness, 1942-45* (Garden City: Doubleday, 1975) is the most recent; assistant director of the Office of Civilian Defense, 1942; and administrative assistant to the president, 1942-45.

DISCUSSION SUMMARY

The first question dealt with Joseph Lash's statement that Eleanor Roosevelt's position against the Equal Rights Amendment softened in her later years. Cynthia Harrison of Columbia University said that her reading of materials of the president's Commission on the Status of Women, of which Mrs. Roosevelt was chairman at her death, seemed to indicate that her opposition to ERA continued. Without notes in hand, Lash could only speculate that his source for the statement had been one of Mrs. Roosevelt's "My Day" columns, but he promised to verify this.

Trudy Peterson of the National Archives wanted to mention to the conference some of the resources on women in another part of the National Archives and Records Service, the six presidential libraries from Herbert Hoover through Lyndon Johnson. The materials that Lash had exploited so extensively, the more than thirteen hundred feet of papers of Eleanor Roosevelt, represent the kind of resources in the presidential libraries on first ladies. There are also the White House social files reflecting another kind of women's activity. In addition, the presidential papers, the core of each library, have material of interest for women's history, as do pre- and post-presidential papers. For example, as Secretary of Commerce Herbert Hoover was deeply interested in two movements of interest to women: one, better homes in America, and another, child labor laws. Material on both these subjects is to be found in the Hoover Library, waiting to be exploited.

In addition, deposited in the libraries are the papers of politically active women. For example, the Eisenhower Library would have papers of Oveta Culp Hobby and Bertha Adkins. Federal records are sometimes placed in presidential libraries; the Kennedy and Johnson Libraries have the records of the Commission on the Status of Women. And finally there are materials from the Republican and Democratic National Committees which show the activities of their women's divisions and the role of women in political campaigns. Researchers should write directly to the director of each library for conditions of access to these materials.

Someone asked Edith James about materials on President Wilson's first wife, Ellen Axson Wilson. James said that the majority of Ellen Axson Wilson's papers have been published and are available in the Wilson Papers. Actually, she said, the first Mrs. Wilson would be a very appropriate topic in women's history. She was very active in settlement work and other social work. "I think more people know about Edith Wilson," said James, "but I think it's actually Ellen that deserves a good biography."

Marcia Synnott of the University of South Carolina inquired about the positions of the two Mrs. Wilsons on women's suffrage. It is difficult, said James, to know

254

exactly how Ellen felt about women's suffrage. She died in 1914, but she made a few comments in letters to Wilson while she was on vacation in Cornish, New Hampshire, about the pressure being brought to bear on him when he first became president. There had already been a great deal of pressure during the 1912 campaign, and Wilson was sidestepping the issue throughout that campaign, trying to leave the question to a kind of local option approach. Ellen herself might have been somewhat suppressed in her feelings about women's suffrage and tried to avoid it. She always refused to appear at teas and so forth and she never came out with a direct statement.

Edith on the other hand was very annoyed with women's suffrage, although some of her close friends, people who remained her friends for life like Mrs. J. Borden Harriman, were active in the movement. But Edith herself never voted. Before the Nineteenth Amendment she was not franchised; afterwards she was disenfranchised because she lived in Washington, D.C. Although she never resorted to hostile action, she was resentful of the pressure on Wilson and the suffrage pickets before the White House. She may not have actually opposed women's suffrage, but she had no interest in pressing for it.

A matter of concern to Jo Ann Robinson of Morgan State University was the value of delving into intimate personal matters in assessing the lives of women and the effect of personal experiences on them. Noting Lash's comment that Eleanor Roosevelt's organizational ability revealed in her Red Cross work would have kept her a public person and her greatness would have emerged even without the Lucy Mercer episode, she asked Lash to comment on how scholars can assess experiences such as Franklin's relationship to Mercer in the proper historical perspective to avoid a mere appeal to prurient interests.

"In Eleanor Roosevelt's case," Lash replied, "one gets a sense of the largeness of the person and the inner drives that were pushing her toward public activity." There was no doubt that she began to do public work as soon as the war came along, providing a kind of patriotic justification for her to throw off conventional attitudes with regard to woman's relationship to her family, her home, and so forth. The effect of the Lucy Mercer affair was to show her there was no turning back for her, that if she were not to be totally dependent on a husband who had done this to her, she would have to develop a life of her own. The two streams came together. Archibald MacLeish saw the war activities as the wand that awakened the sleeping princess, but Lash thought that the Mercer affair was also rather crucial.

Would there be any value in going through Eleanor Roosevelt's papers if one were doing a study of Madame Pandit, the first woman president of the United Nations General Assembly, asked Khin Khin Jensen of Augsburg College. Lash remembered that Mrs. Roosevelt and Madame Pandit worked very closely together in the U.N. trying to increase the representation of women in the various bodies of the organization. "Documentation at the U.N. is very voluminous," he said, "and one could spend a lifetime going through the materials of the Commission on the Status of Women and the Human Rights Commission. But it's rewarding," he added.

Edith Wilson was very active in Red Cross work during World War I, James said in reply to a question from Mary Donovan of Columbia University, but she had seen no evidence that this influenced her to take a more active public role. Lash interjected material he knew of that related to the period when Eleanor Roosevelt was working with the Red Cross down at Union Station in Washington where the troop trains were coming through from southern camps on the way to ports where the men were shipped overseas. He recalled a letter from Eleanor Roosevelt to her mother-in-law talking about the impending visit of Mrs. Wilson to the station. It sounded a little bit like the sort of thing that used to happen in his barracks during World War II when they heard that a general was coming down. They had to get everything spick and span, but they knew the general was not going to stay around very long. This, he thought, was the extent of Edith Wilson's work in the Red Cross. She did nominal things that were necessary and expected, but he did not have the sense that this was something that she really pitched into. In Paris, at the time of the Peace Conference, there was considerable criticism of Mrs. Wilson for not going around to visit the hospitals where the American boys were. When word of this got to Mrs. Wilson, visits were organized.

James did not agree with all of Lash's points. She thought that Mrs. Wilson's Red Cross work was a little more genuine than perhaps the Union Station incident would indicate. Later on she gave financial support to many activities in which Eleanor Roosevelt was involved. And James felt that the criticism of Mrs. Wilson in Paris was very unfair. She has seen many letters in her papers that show that the first lady went to search out people like a serviceman from Utah who was supposed to be in such-and-such a hospital. That particular criticism of the second Mrs. Wilson is not validated by documentation, she said.

VII

AN ALTERNATIVE SOURCE: THE VISUAL RECORD

INTRODUCTION

James E. O'Neill

Nancy Malan's "paper" was delivered to the conference in the form of a slide-tape presentation set to music and narrated by Renee Channey of Washington's Radio Station WGMS. The script of the presentation has been somewhat edited to make it into a written pictorial essay using a selection of the pictures that comprised the original show.

AMERICAN WOMEN THROUGH THE CAMERA'S EYE

Nancy E. Malan

Photographs, like women, have been neglected by historians. There are many examples of their serious and effective use by other disciplines. Lawyers submit them as courtroom evidence; scientists attach cameras to their microscopes to photograph cell structure; military strategists use aerial photographs to make crucial decisions, like those which led to the 1962 Cuban missile crisis. But with very few exceptions, historians have steadfastly relied on more traditional sources. The selection of illustrations, if it is done at all, is an afterthought more frequently assigned to the publisher of a work than to its author.

This reluctance to treat photographs with the reverence accorded the written word is to some extent understandable. Clearly, Joseph Lash, for example, could not have written *Eleanor and Franklin* had he forsaken the manuscripts, diaries, and other writings of the Franklin D. Roosevelt Library for its photographic archives. Photographs simply did not suit his topic. Scholars have a traditional dependence on textual records and have been trained in the research skills necessary to use them. They have not been trained to interpret photographs. On the contrary, they generally associate them with an unscholarly, storybook approach to history. Too frequently historical photographs have been used poorly, thus reinforcing already established prejudices.

But within the framework of a basic knowledge of a historical topic or period, photographs substantially enhance our knowledge and understanding of social and cultural history. They humanize historical personalities. They provide faithful representations of dress, hairstyles, social activities, living and working conditions. By recording details, they allow us to examine the basic elements of everyday life as it once was.

260

In order to grasp and analyze the historical data contained within photographs, we need to develop "visual literacy." Too often we tend merely to glance at photographs, to look at them in the same way that we read newspaper headlines, without going on to read the story. One procedure that would offset this cursory approach is described in Howard Becker's article "Photography and Sociology." It appeared in the Fall 1974 issue of a journal with the formidable title *Studies in the Anthropology of Visual Communication.* Becker writes:

Take some genuinely good picture. . . . Using a watch with a second hand, look at the photograph intently for two minutes. Don't stare and thus stop looking; look actively. It will be hard to do, and you'll find it useful to take up the time by naming everything in the picture to yourself: this is a man, this is his arm, this is the finger on his hand, this is the shadow his hand makes, this is the cloth of his sleeve, and so on. Once you have done this for two minutes, build it up to five, following the naming of things with a period of fantasy, telling yourself a story about the people and things in the picture. The story needn't be true; it's just a device for externalizing and making clear to yourself the emotion and mood the picture has evoked, both part of its statement.

When you have done this exercise many times, a more careful way of looking will become habitual. Two things result. You will realize that ordinarily you have not consciously seen most of what is in an image even though you have been responding to it. You will also find that you can now remember the photographs you have studied much as you can remember a book you have taken careful notes on. They become part of a mental collection available for further work.

Mail bag repair shop, Post Office Department, Washington, D.C., 1907.

The interior of the Post Office Department's mail bag repair shop in 1907 is replete with telling historical details. These turn of the century workers are operating Singer sewing machines, signs of the ensuing industrial revolution. They are well covered in the high-collared, long-sleeved blouses and long skirts typical of the times. Each has her hair piled modestly atop her head. It seems likely that those who do not yet wear spectacles soon will. The only light for their close work comes from distant windows and sparse incandescent bulbs. In the event of fire or

other emergency, the ladies' rapid exit would be significantly impeded by the littered floor and crowded quarters. These conditions, along with the whirring of treadles and other industrial sounds which we can only imagine, combine in a visual and mental cacophony. The photograph captures the effects of industrialization on the woman worker. It is a historical document as applicable to women's history and labor history as any journal kept by one of the workers.

Unquestionably we cannot look at one or two photographs and draw sweeping conclusions about life during a certain time period. But we can reinforce, and make more credible and more memorable the essentials of history that we have learned elsewhere. Do we know more about the severe personal hardships of the depression by studying the face of a young woman who was suffering through it? Can we interpret more clearly the experience of Native Americans when we look at young Indian women, deprived of their native dress and sent to boarding school to learn Western ways?

Migrant mother, Nipomo, California, 1936.

Indians from a southeastern Idaho reservation, ca. 1898.

Boating in Avalon Harbor near Santa Catalina Island, California, ca. 1900.

We become a little more aware of the few acceptable amusements allowed the well-to-do ladies of the Gilded Age by looking at their very proper afternoon outing. Let your imagination supply the thoughts and concerns of a rural mother who leaves her young child alone in a mechanically rocked cradle while she labors in the fields. These images, and those in the following photographic essay of documents from the National Archives clarify and vivify the American woman's history.

Canvas house in a beet field, Caro, Michigan, 1918.

American Women Through the Camera's Eye

Sweepers with bambusa brooms in yard at Belton, South Carolina, 1898.

Look carefully at these images of American women. Look at their faces and their dress. Consider what they are doing and the details of their surroundings. These faces and costumes and surroundings capture the experiences of generations of American women.

Trimming currency, Bureau of Engraving and Printing, Washington, D.C., 1907.

269

Frank Vanderlip, assistant secretary of the treasury, and companion, ca. 1900.

Family, ca. 1900.

In 1792 Benjamin Rush, the eminent Philadelphia physician, summed up women's role with this advice to a prospective bride. "You will be well received in all companies only in proportion as you are inoffensive, polite and agreeable to everybody. Don't be offended when I add that from the day you marry you must have no will of your own. The ideal wife is kind, obsequious, uncontradicting . . ."

Elizabeth Cady Stanton

Susan B. Anthony

More than a century later, the suffrage leader Carrie Chapman Catt explained her view. "The whole aim of the women's movement has been to destroy the idea that obedience is necessary to women; to train women to such self-respect that they would not grant obedience; and to train men to such comprehension of equity that they would not exact it."

In the years between the expression of these two sentiments, change was painfully slow. Yet attitudes and conditions and opportunities did evolve. Some women focused their efforts on the specific issue of the right to vote. Susan B. Anthony, Elizabeth Cady Stanton, and Carrie Chapman Catt led the suffrage movement to its fulfillment in 1920.

Carrie Chapman Catt, 1944.

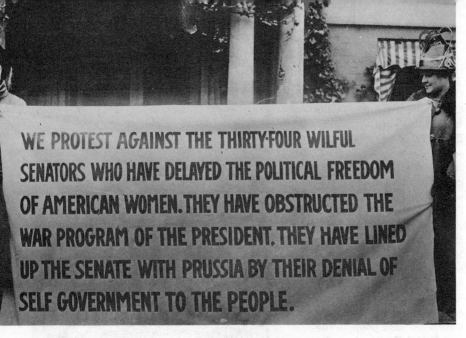

WE PROTEST AGAINST THE THIRTY-FOUR WILFUL SENATORS WHO HAVE DELAYED THE POLITICAL FREEDOM OF AMERICAN WOMEN. THEY HAVE OBSTRUCTED THE WAR PROGRAM OF THE PRESIDENT. THEY HAVE LINED UP THE SENATE WITH PRUSSIA BY THEIR DENIAL OF SELF GOVERNMENT TO THE PEOPLE.

Protesting during the Wilson administration, Washington, D.C.

Learning to use a voting machine, Chicago.

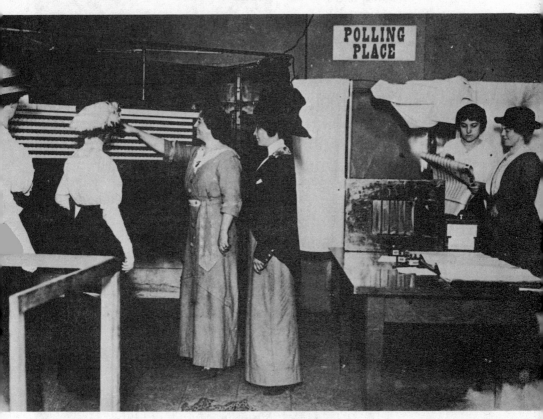

POLLING PLACE

Jane Addams, ca. 1917.

Others by their exceptional talents and accomplishments in various fields, lent credibility to the notion of equality of the sexes. Mother Jones, the activist labor leader whose life spanned a century, dramatized the plight of working children by leading them on a march from the coal mines of Pennsylvania to the Oyster Bay home of Teddy Roosevelt. Jane Addams's settlement house became a haven for Chicago's poor, and a model for social reformers in other cities. Lillian Russell lent her illustrious stage name to the World War I effort by enlisting in the Marine Corps as a recruitment officer. Frances Perkins's dedication to the improvement of industrial workers' hours, wages, and working conditions was recognized by her appointment as secretary of labor in 1933.

Mary Harris "Mother" Jones on her 100th birthday, 1930.

Lillian Russell recruiting for the U.S. Marines, World War I.

Frances Perkins, secretary of labor, appears before the Senate Civil Liberties Committee, 1940.

Farm in Haskell County, Kansas, 1941.

But what of the nameless American women whose individual lives are unrecorded in the annals of history? Throughout American history their roles quietly rivaled those of their men.

Mrs. Ettridge, ca. 1863.

Mormon family group near Moqui, Arizona Territory, ca. 1887.

During colonization they provided the household with the basic necessities of frontier life. Though tradition credits the men with the driving spirit that settled the West, the women were along with them, experiencing even more severe hardships, for they bore the children. Too often they died bearing children. Women who had to, joined the labor force in one of the few acceptable roles outside the home. They worked in textile mills and shoe factories for a third the wages of men. They became teachers, and they nursed the sick.

278

Knitting room, Mishawaka Woolen Mills, Mishawaka, Indiana, 1919.

Class from school district no. 21, Woods County, Oklahoma, ca. 1895.

American Red Cross nurses, ca. 1912.

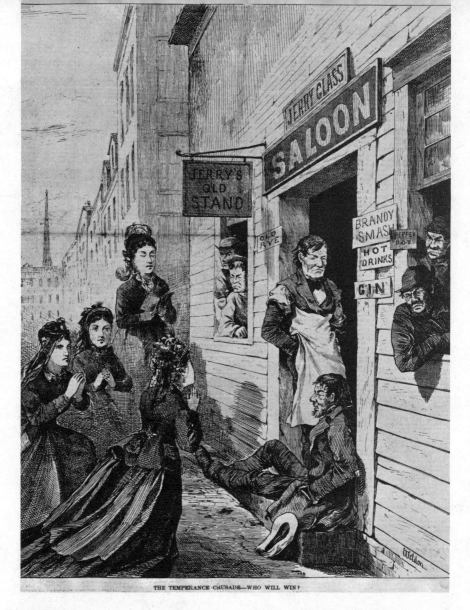

THE TEMPERANCE CRUSADE—WHO WILL WIN?

"The Temperance Crusade – Who will win?" illustration from the Daily Graphic, *5 March, 1874.*

With time and experience, they organized. The Women's Christian Temperance Union received extensive support from women who, with few legal rights of their own, were at the mercy of their alcoholic husbands. Denied the right to speak out publicly against slavery, women became more intent on securing rights not only for blacks, but also for themselves. Women of the Civil War period were active as fundraisers and field workers for the Sanitary Commission. Volunteers provided medical and other relief services to wounded soldiers and their families. Later, as members of the Red Cross, they drove ambulances, grew cotton to be made into bandages, and provided homes and health care for orphans and refugees.

"Our Women and the War," illustration from Harper's Weekly.

WAR TIDINGS!

HOME TIDINGS!

THE SISTER OF CHARITY

Canteen workers in a Liberty Loan parade, Philadelphia, Pennsylvania, 1918.

In times of war more and more women took on dual roles, still rearing families and maintaining households, but also making substantial contributions to the war effort. During World War I, the National League for Women's Service, with chapters in each state, enlisted volunteers into the Motor Corps to learn automobile maintenance and repair, the Camouflage Corps to test observers' suits, and the Home Economics Division to "can a can for Uncle Sam." The Woman's Land Army recruited, trained, and placed thousands of women for seasonal farm work. Many of them were college girls who spent their summers driving tractors, hoeing and harvesting crops. Other women made contributions to the war effort in more traditional ways, knitting socks for the boys overseas and organizing social events.

Mechanic at work in Seattle, Washington, ca. 1918.

Newton Square, Pennsylvania, and of the Woman's Land Army, 1918.

Liberty Bell chapter of the Daughters of the American Revolution, Allentown, Pennsylvania, 1918.

287

Mildred Pierce inspects hand grenades at an ordnance plant, 1943.

Working on tail cone assembly, Douglas Aircraft Company, Santa Monica, California, 1943.

More significantly, the world wars brought women in substantial numbers into the labor force, into jobs previously reserved for men. They manufactured hand grenades and other ammunition. They tested equipment. They worked in shipyards and aircraft factories. "Rosie the Riveter" became a mainstay of the home-front effort. The wartime labor shortage also opened up opportunities in civilian industries. Women joined the rank and file of light industries like food and clothing manufacture as well as the heavy steel and automobile industries.

289

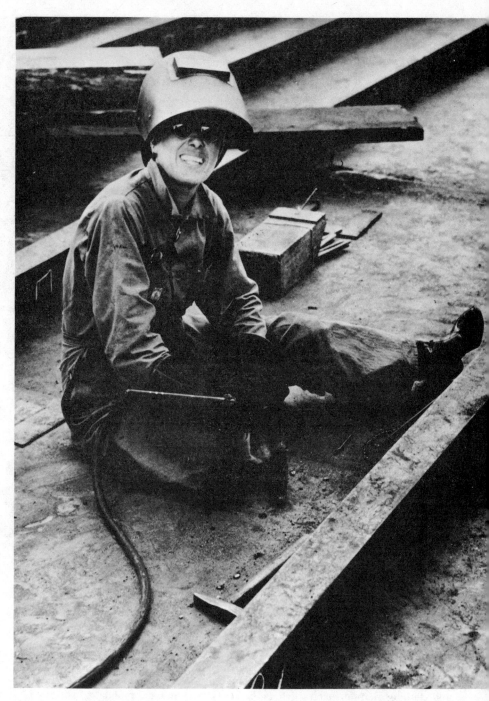

Shipyard worker, World War II.

Garment workers in a Chicago factory, ca. 1946.

*Breaking cones and knocking reclaimed sand through grate, General Steel
Casting Corporation, Granite City, Illinois, ca. 1945.*

Factory workers at the end of the day, ca. 1943.

The two world wars provided exposure of women to the world of work and of the world to working women. But peacetime brought reverses. The prevailing attitude during the depression was that the few available jobs rightfully belonged to men. Women who had demonstrated their capabilities in scores of industrial jobs were replaced by men as wartime industries closed down and soldiers returned from overseas.

What had changed, then, in the time since Benjamin Rush's advice? Socially, women were freer to have and to express their own thoughts. They were more likely to be considered individuals than spouses. Politically they had won the right to vote and were, thus, a potentially significant pressure group for politicians to deal with. Economically, more and more trades and professions accepted women and paid them wages more frequently based on performance than on prejudice. Although far from the goal of equality of the sexes, women who sought them found ever-increasing opportunities for self-development and self-expression.

Eleanor Roosevelt presents the NAACP's Spingarn Medal to Marian Anderson at the association's Thirtieth Annual Meeting, Richmond, Virginia, July 1939.

Anna Hoover votes in the
1948 presidential election,
Lancaster, Pennsylvania.

Ethel Hodell, U.S. Treasury Department official, with Assistant Secretary of the Treasury
Edward Bartelt and his assistant, Martin Moore, Washington, D.C., 1955.

Greyhound waiting room, New York City, 1947.

Preserved in these images of the past are the ordinary experiences of day-to-day life of American women. The images are important not so much for whom or what they are of, but for what they are about. They provide us with clear, vivid, sometimes humorous, sometimes painful glimpses of long-forgotten moments. They allow us to examine those moments in all of their complicated detail. Through that examination we understand better how the stage has been set for the entrance of the modern woman.

Breaking down cotton stalks, Uniontown, Alabama, 1905.

Strawberry pickers on the farm of W.Z. Raines, Humboldt, Tennessee, 1906.

Wash day, El Cerrito, San Miguel County, New Mexico, 1941.

At the county fair, ca. 1947.

PICTURE CREDITS

1. Photograph number 121-BA-420A in the Records of the Public Buildings Service. PP. 262-263.
2. Photograph number FSA 9058c Library of Congress Farm Security Administration file, Dorothea Lange, photographer. P. 264.
3. Photograph number 75-SEI-145 in the Records of the Bureau of Indian Affairs. P. 264.
4. Photograph number 79-HPA-251 in the Records of the National Park Service, Henry Peabody, photographer. P. 265.
5. Photograph number 83-FB-13426 in the Records of the Bureau of Agricultural Economics, P. 265.
6. Photograph number 83-FB-272 in the Records of the Bureau of Agricultural Economics. P. 268.
7. Photograph number 121-BA-361B in the Records of the Public Buildings Service. P. 269.
8. Photograph number 121-BA-105A in the Records of the Public Buildings Service. P. 270.
9. Photograph number 121-BA-33 in the Records of the Public Buildings Service. P. 271.
10. Photograph number LC-Z62-28195 Library of Congress. P 272.
11. Photograph number LC-Z62-46713 Library of Congress. P. 272.
12. Photograph number 208-N-25000 in the Records of the Office of War Information. P. 272.
13. Photograph number 165-WW-600A-13 in the Records of the War Department General and Special Staffs, Harris and Ewing. P. 273.
14. Photograph number 208-PR-14M-2 in the Records of the Office of War Information. P. 273.
15. Photograph number 4-G-4-1 in the Records of the U.S. Food Administration. P. 274.
16. Photograph number 262-50378 Library of Congress, P. 274.
17. Photograph number 165-WW-480A-11 in the Records of the War Department General and Special Staffs. P. 275.
18. Photograph number 208-PU-155Q-9 in the Records of the Office of War Information, Harris and Ewing. P. 275.
19. Photograph number 83-G-41934 in the Records of the Bureau of Agricultural Economics, Irving Rusinow, photographer, P. 276.
20. Photograph number 111-B-1624 in the Mathew Brady Collection, Records of the Chief Signal Officer, Mathew Brady (?), photographer. P. 277.
21. Photograph number 106-FAA-41A in the Records of the Smithsonian Institution, F.A. Ames, photographer. P. 278.
22. Photograph number 86-G-11A-4 in the Records of the Women's Bureau. P. 279.
23. Photograph number 48-RST-7B-13 in the Records of the Office of the Secretary of the Interior. P. 280.
24. Photograph number 208-LU-64F-1 in the Records of the Office of War Information, Harris and Ewing. P. 281.
25. Photograph number 262-02015 Library of Congress. P. 282.
26. Photograph number 208-LU-25G-3 in the Records of the Office of War Information. P. 283.
27. Photograph number 165-WW-599A-10 in the Records of the War Department General and Special Staffs. P. 284.

VIII

ARCHIVES AND WOMEN'S HISTORY

INTRODUCTION

Mabel E. Deutrich

It is time now to reflect on some of the things set forth in the preceding pages and perhaps to think about where we go from here. The person chosen to bring it all together is Mary P. Ryan. In her book Womanhood in America, *she has demonstrated her ability to put many pieces together to form an integrated picture and to place particular events and ideas in a wise perspective.*

Final Homestead Proof required under Section 2291 of the Revised Statutes of the United States.

WE, *S S Harriman S J Harriman*, do solemnly *swear*
that we have known *Adriennah S Harriman* for *7* years last past; that *she*
is *a single woman* consisting of _____ and *over 28 years*
of age native born _____ a citizen of the United States; that *she* is an inhabitant
of the *North ½ of the North East ¼* of Section No. *24* in
Township 26 S Range 4 East and the North ½ of the North West ¼ of Section 19 in
Township No. *26 South* of Range No. *5 East*, and that no other person resided upon the said
land entitled to the right of Homestead or Pre-emption.

That the said *Adriennah S Harriman* entered upon and made settlement
on said land on the *12th* day of *November*, 18*70*, and has built a house
thereon *12 X 14 ft Stone 1 story, One window & one door shingle roof*
_____
and has lived in the said house and made it *her* exclusive home from the *12th* day of
November, 18*70*, to the present time, and that *she* has, since said settlement, plowed, ~~fenced~~
and cultivated about *17* acres of said land, and has made the following improvements thereon, to wit:
Set out & cultivated about 60 fruit trees, about 300 forest trees
built a Hay stable 12 X 15, dug & stoned a well, built about 16 acres
of stone fences all of the value of $300 — Set out ¾ mile of Hedge

S S Harriman
S J Harriman

I, *C A James Clk of the District Court of Butler Co* *Cty of Kansas* do hereby certify that the above affidavit was taken
and subscribed before me this *5th* day of *November*, 18*77* *and that the judge*
of this District Court is absent

C A James Clerk of the District court
of Butler Co Kansas

WE CERTIFY that *S S Harriman and S J Harriman* whose names
are subscribed to the foregoing affidavit, are persons of respectability. *C A James Clk of Dist Court*

_____, Register.

_____, Receiver.

RETROSPECT AND PROSPECT

Mary P. Ryan

Although we have surveyed more than two hundred years of women's history in this volume we have given special attention to a highly selective aspect of women's past — those of her activities that have been mediated by the federal government. To the extent that these papers illustrate the holdings of the National Archives they emphasize the limited sphere of women's life that relates in some way or another to the nation state.

At first glance the archives of the United States do not seem the most promising or pertinent source of information about a segment of the population so seldom visible, audible, or even worthy of mention in the history of national politics. In fact women's historians have at times intentionally snubbed collections of political records. Some of us hastily dismissed the Nation's Capital, for example, as an outpost of male elitism, and turned instead to the more secluded byways of social, cultural, and especially family history in search of woman's past. Fortunately we are now well on the way to recovery from this particular myopia. In retrospect, these essays have established the National Archives as a treasury of documents for women's historians. We cannot overlook any longer the role of federal agencies in collecting and storing vast quantities of data on the everyday lives of female citizens. Before discussing this variety of sources, however, I would like to

Final homestead proof of a single woman. The tiny ''s'' inserted in longhand before each ''he'' on the standard Land Office form indicates that women who fulfilled all the requirements for proving a homestead were rare. The Homestead Act of 1862 provided that ''any person who is the head of a family, or who has arrived at the age of twenty-one years and is a citizen of the United States . . . [shall] be entitled to enter one quarter section or less quantity of unappropriated public lands. . . . '' Thus women were not excluded from homestead rights, and some availed themselves of the opportunity to become landowners.

Adriennah Harriman's Final Proof shows that she had not only built a house ''12 x 14 ft. Stone 1 story, one window & one door, shingle roof'' on her claim, but had ''plowed and cultivated about 17 acres'' and ''set out & cultivated about 60 fruit trees, about 300 forest trees, built a Hay stable 12 x 15, dug & stoned a well, built about 16 rods of stone fence All of the value of $300 — Set out 3/4 mile of Hedge.''

(Final Homestead Proof, Adriennah S. Harriman, November 5, 1877, Final Certificate No. 1993, Wichita District, Records of the Bureau of Land Management, RG 49.)

consider a more direct prospect that the National Archives offers to women's historians. It encourages renewed attention to the very citadel of conventional American history that we once scorned, national politics.

The current revival of interest in the suffrage movement is one example of the growing recognition of the historical significance of woman's relation to political institutions. Perhaps we had cause to sneer at studies of the suffragists ten years ago. Then the voting booth was all too often considered woman's only port-of-entry into written history. The rapid advances of our field, however, pose the relationship between women's history and the suffrage movement in quite a different way. Once the American woman has been granted a history unto herself, the campaign for the Nineteenth Amendment becomes a crucial, even poignant moment in a long and varied past. It is but one expression of woman's consciousness, an act which illuminates rather than exhausts her historical identity. Now we can discern the unique meaning of the nineteenth-century woman's movement within a larger woman's history. In this wider context suffrage represents woman's demand for a *direct, legitimate,* and *public* political role. As such the suffrage movement can be construed as the lynch-pin of a new history of women's politics.

This political history would not detail an analogous and diminished form of male politics (characterized by briefer citizenship, rarer officeholding, and less pomp and circumstance). Rather woman's political history would chronicle myriad attempts — of which suffrage is only one — to compensate for and overcome woman's alienation from the official centers of political power in America. We must also consider woman's relation to the federal government in a wider frame of reference, examining the broad sweep of sex differences as it cuts across all facets of politics; the distribution of power, the process of decision-making, the exertion of the coercive power of the state.

A review of the preceding papers can serve, first of all, to codify the variety of ways in which women have related to the government of the United States. As is so often the case in women's history, the most significant and most obvious discoveries must be read between the lines and in the missing sources. The most notable absence in this volume is a single reference to a female elected official. To state the obvious (not a meaningless gesture in this city), women have very rarely shared in the euphoria of political victory, the honor and responsibility of receiving the peoples' mandate. One woman has entered the program through a national office, but through the quieter, less obtrusive, manner of appointment. As an administrator of the National Youth Administration, Mary McLeod Bethune acquitted herself admirably, and much as we would expect, belied any invidious comparisons with male leaders. In fact, we would hope that women's historians need not follow their subjects into office, where sex differences should be quite irrelevant. Unfortunately, it will be premature to retire from this seat of women's history as long as women remain a beleaguered minority in the executive offices and the halls of Congress. Therefore, we must formulate incisive questions about women in leadership positions whether elective or appointive.

We can begin simply by trying to ascertain the special handicaps and modes of discrimination that face even this female elite. What restraints are placed on woman's power as officeholders? Are women leaders excluded from the informal circles where males resolve conflicts and make decisions — in the gentlemen's clubs and locker rooms of Washington, for example? How might women compensate for exclusion from such seats of power? Do they form countervailing female networks, or employ subversive tactics to penetrate the male sanctums? Conversely, have women officials been segregated by sex, concentrated, for example, in the Women's or Children's Bureaus? Has such segregation worked historically to the detriment or the benefit of women? Somewhere in the National Archives we should be able to locate the kinds of office communications with which to reconstruct the sexual politics of these higher circles. By assembling collective biographies, furthermore, one can begin to generalize about the distinctive career patterns and political styles of female leaders. Only by formulating and pursuing such questions can female political leadership be made a topic in women's history rather than a source for biographies or a well of anecdotes.

The same might be said about a second and still more familiar classification of women in politics, the wives of public officials, especially the first ladies. Although these American women have won their notable status by virtue of conjugal partnership, they assume national political significance upon entrance into the White House. The case of Edith Bolling Wilson seems to exemplify a very gingerly and constrained use of a first lady's potentially extensive power as agent, emissary, and confidant of the first gentleman. Eleanor Roosevelt not only used the position of first lady more aggressively, but also exploited her strategic marital alliance so as to build an independent base of power and influence. Such special cases beckon systematic analysis of the relation between kinship, marriage, and American politics. For although the wives and female relatives of public officials lack the fully legitimate power that anthropologists designate as authority, they do achieve a command over events and people which, however veiled, constitutes palpable power.

These two historical personalities, the female leader and the male leader's wife, with the addition of a few generations of voters, may seem to exhaust the female candidates for an active role in American political history. Several papers, however, have reminded us of another, perhaps more significant, and certainly more uniquely female form of politics, the reform association. Those antebellum petitioners, for example, were blessed neither with offices and votes, nor with strategic kin ties, yet collectively they may have wielded more power than many public officials. The women who mounted and carried forward petition campaigns not only registered their opinions with their husbands' representatives, but stimulated public opinion and caused considerable trouble within those public spheres to which they were denied official admission. These voluntary associations are prototypes for a long-standing tradition of women's politics, one which flexes its muscles to this day and brings women's power to bear on both sides of such issues as the Equal Rights Amendment and abortion reform. Needless to say, whoever ignores this aspect of women's politics does so at his or her peril. Yet we have hardly begun to give these groups historical recognition, much less examine the nature, sources, and method of their strength. Those reform groups composed exclusively of females expose yet another dimension of women's politics, the internal political organization of purely female groups. Do these women's organizations have a distinctive political structure, hierarchy, or modus operandi? What is the political and personal effect of this species of sex segregation?

In the nineteenth century, such associations may have been woman's chief mode of relating to governmental institutions. They are overshadowed in this century, however, by quite another political relationship, one that consumes greater energy than a petition campaign and yet entails less political initiative. I am referring to the women who play the role of servant in relation to government — that vast army of wage laborers — the low-level managers and clerical workers, who give women numerical superiority in nearly every government center. In one sense these are the women to whom historians of this century, at least, are most indebted, for they transcribed, filed, and preserved many of the documents on which conventional history is based. Yet the female government worker has seldom been made the explicit subject of history. Her power is not political in the full sense of the word: it seldom directly affects the outcome of public debate. Yet this womanpower is the fundamental driving force of the government machine: it operates the channels of written communication by which government enters the everyday lives of Americans. Surely selected records of the Women's Bureau and the personnel records of other government agencies can supply us with the raw materials for a history of this female relation to government.

The prosaic role of the government worker is not the lowest rung on the ladder that connects females to their government. We have seen women relate to political institutions in the even humbler capacity of supplicant. We have heard described the women who pleaded with the early American congresses for pensions and compensation, while similar female appeals throughout the nineteenth century still await their historian. We should acknowledge the greater proportion of women who played this obeisant role in relation to local government — as town charges, poorhouse residents, and welfare mothers. These dependent political relations are particularly relevant to women's historians. Woman's greater vulnerability to poverty with the added liability of being left the sole support of young children, place her in special need of public aid, and expose her more frequently to its attendant indignities. Moreover, a woman's recourse to government assistance can reinforce sexual domination, particularly in those cases where she begs aid directly from male officials. Again, I hope we can suggest sources, methods, and concepts which will elucidate this dark region of woman's political history.

Thus far I have classified woman's relation to federal government on a scale of power ranging from leader to dependent, and roughly sketched in the distinct and unequal pattern of women's politics. I would now like to consider a more specialized case in the history of women and the federal government, an incident which demonstrates in an extreme form the power of government to shape womanhood itself, in its economic as well as political dimensions. This case is a familiar one, the federal campaign to recruit women workers — civilian and military — during the Second World War. Eleanor Straub and Susan Hartmann have replayed portions of that campaign for us, complete with some of its most chilling sounds and insulting images of women. More importantly, by their use of the National Archives and particularly the official records of the War Manpower Commission, they have exposed the bureaucratic apparatus that conducted this propaganda campaign. Their account offers me the perfect opportunity to jump to some paranoid conclusions. First I give you, in tendentious hyperbole, my capsule summation of this episode in woman's history: the mobilization of the power of the federal bureaucracy, acting without popular representation, but in collusion with industry, advertising, and all the media of communication, so as to intervene in two supposedly sacrosanct American institutions, the free labor market and the natural order of sex roles. I ask, could we not suggest some less condescending, perhaps more effective, ways of recruiting women workers such as concrete social incentives (e.g., good day care) and specific economic rewards (i.e., good pay)? And I wonder, did this government program function as a pilot project and training ground for postwar advertisers and market researchers? To put the question as grossly as possible, did this episode in women's recent history foretell another ignominious relation between women and government, that of puppet on the bureaucrat's string?

I do not propose moral indignation as the answer to these questions. Rather I invite systematic analysis of the very complex political and cultural process they polemically identify. Tautological references to mass psychology are not sufficient to explain and describe the relationship between women's history and such sophisticated machinery of persuasion. If we are to understand the impact of these propaganda techniques on woman's behavior we will need to borrow theory and method from other disciplines. Yet our less flashy historical skills are equally indispensable. We must continue to interrogate the institutional sources of these persuasive messages. We might begin probing the documents of the War Manpower Commission even more deeply, questioning not just the general intent of the recruitment campaign but the specific calculation behind each symbol-laden message sent to women. We could proceed to dissect individual symbols, say a specific war production poster, in order to identify the intended meaning of each word and color and line. A trail of memos and minutes might lead us to conclude that certain government functionaries did regard women as puppets, and considered themselves agile puppeteers who could operate woman's psychological strings with scientific precision. Few of us, however, would accept this condescending vision of the American female. Yet we have not had much success finding a female historical voice to squelch such assertions effectively. Certainly we do not assume a direct causal relationship between expanded female employment and government's symbolic seductions during wartime. Even if we found a correlation between the two, we have little sense of how individual women translated the language of propaganda and advertising into behavior. In short, we desperately need to devise ways of interrogating the female audience of propagandists and advertisers. Did the War Manpower Commission, for example, ever survey female opinion to test the effectiveness of its techniques? Can we find among the original questionnaires and interviews data of other government agencies more precise and resonant descriptions of women's attitudes toward work during the Second World War? Can we juxtapose these with wartime propaganda in such a way as to gauge woman's receptivity to particular persuasive devices? This very knotty problem in the recent history of women illustrates how foolhearty it is to dismiss government as a focus of women's history. For it is clear that modern governments have not been indifferent to women when it suited their national purposes.

Government remains the most direct instrument of exerting social power, and as such cannot be ignored by women's historians. We must address politics from two directions; first, as the source of public decisions that directly affect women's lives, and second, as a kind of political culture, a set of common assumptions and informal governmental procedures, in which women inevitably participate and exert influence. I would like to allude to just a few of the conceptual priorities and problems entailed in this analysis of women's politics. First among the priorities is the illumination of women's political consciousness. Whenever we see a woman engaging with government we must try to identify her own perception of the power, relevance, and accessibility of political offices and officials. In the case of the presumably apolitical woman, we must find ways of measuring her alienation from government, her indifference, distrust, or scorn of power. Perhaps some of the documents reviewed in this volume contain hints of woman's political consciousness? What might be revealed, for example, by the tone, language, and style of petitions for federal compensation, letters to congresspersons, and queries of government agencies? What could we infer from the sex ratio of the government's correspondents?

Our pursuit of women's politics will undoubtedly present conceptual confusion as well as demands on our imagination. Some pitfalls lurk even in our more optimistic discoveries. For example, we can expect to uncover many hidden sources of women's informal, semipublic power. We will have to surrender, if we have not already done so, any notion of women's political history as an unremitting tale of impotence and oppression. But are we to go so far as to conclude that these female political forms are separate but equal to male dominated institutions? Or, is hidden, unacknowledged power by nature costly, tinged with wasted energy, duplicity, or diminished self-esteem? Thus, we can ill afford to retreat from such contradictions — nor from the larger context of the American political system — into some isolationist brand of women's politics. Finally, let me repeat the methodological caveat: preoccupation with national government, the most remote political forum, may tend to underestimate woman's political role, and bias any typology of women's politics. I have no doubt that we can surmount these difficulties and in so doing not only integrate women into the American political record but also revise and expand American political history.

Properly speaking we will have no history at all, however, unless we address an elemental and thus far grossly neglected concept, change. Let me introduce this concept by yet another reference to political history, considering this time politics in its violent posture during war and revolution. We might expect a comparison of the paper on the revolutionary era and World War II to illustrate the most dramatic changes in women's history. It appears obvious, for example, that woman's role in the exercise of political violence, her participation in the military has expanded dramatically, some would say progressively, in the last two hundred years. After all, can we find any eighteenth-century female roles equivalent to the WACS, the WAVES, and that vast army of female defense workers? On closer inspection, however, we can find functional analogues to each of these twentieth-century female roles. Compare those assorted revolutionary nurses, clerks, and cooks with the members of the Women's Army Corps. Did a uniform convey upon the latter a more active combatant status? Compare not the number of female participants, but the sex ratio of the two armies. Also consider the home manufactures of the eighteenth century as analogous to the production of female wage laborers in the twentieth century. In which period did women add greater value to the total amount of military stores? Actually, I would prefer not to spend any time answering this set of questions. The aim of women's history is not to indict the past with the present or measure change simply by the degree of "woman's contribution." Few of us expect all of women's history, furthermore, to descend or ascend in some linear fashion. But more important than all this is the fact that such comparison over vast expanses of time is not the most meaningful conceptualization of historical change. It is not the dimension but the process of change that has proven most interesting to women's historians. Change as a process inhabits the narrowest units of time and raises problems of explanation rather than description.

This process of change is the explicit subject matter of but a few of our papers. I would like to consider two of these, however, Judith Wellman's essay on the abolitionist petitioners, and Mary Young's study of Native American women, because they touch upon change in women's political history in a particularly evocative way. The subjects of Wellman's paper play a role familiar to political historians, perhaps rare in women's history; they are the self-conscious agents of specific changes. They set out with the intention of abolishing slavery, and engaged in political acts calculated to achieve that goal. Thus the primary meaning which a political historian might extract from this episode would be a description and explanation of any legislative or institutional change consequent upon these actions. He or she would probably seek this explanation in an analysis of the effectiveness of the reformers' tactics, their breadth of vision, and their political finesse. A women's historian, however, would most likely single out from the same sequence of events another kind of change, and seek another variety of explanation.

From this perspective, the most significant changes surround the expanding consciousness and role of an articulate group of antebellum women whose abolitionism is almost incidental. We might go even further and see these women as agents of major changes in American political history. These female abolitionists had a hand in the creation and development of voluntary reform associations, extra-parliamentary political institutions that are perhaps as significant as the political parties which date from the same period. Whichever of these changes captures the interest of a women's historian, she or he will seek to explain how *women* found and exploited the opportunity to enlarge their sphere of political action. Wellman brings the weight of her argument to bear on the decline as well as the emergence of these female political forms. She places this sequence of change in the context of a wholesale transformation of the American political system, namely the gradual surrender of a localized, moral politics to a nationally centralized, secular political order. In other words, Wellman's search for explanation in women's history goes far afield of narrow questions of procedure and policy to focus on basic structural changes in American political life.

I think I detect a similar infrastructure within Mary Young's treatment of an apparently disparate subject in women's history. Young's telescopic history of Cherokee politics intimates some curious parallels with the experience of white women in upstate New York. She outlines a progression from an informal tribal politics in which women shared considerable influence, toward a formalized political system, symbolized by an expanding constitution which disenfranchized females. Both Young and Wellman's papers seem to transverse similar territory, both span the transition from localized informal politics toward a more remote, centralized, and highly structured political system. In both instances women are restricted from access in the second, more modern sphere of power, and in consequence experience a relative decline in their political influence over time. This roughly describes the theoretical framework employed by some anthropologists to explain crosscultural variations in woman's political role. References to this particular factor in the relative differentiation of politics from the informal relations of village or class or neighborhood may prove very useful to historians of women. At any rate, it typifies the most promising general direction in which explanation in women's political history can proceed, toward the identification of structural rather than incidental change.

The search for explanation in women's history cannot stop here. Young's analysis of the Cherokee experience, for example, is linked to a maze of changes in economy, technology, education, and culture. It leads, in other words, to a complex of structures wherein and whereby women are socially differentiated from men. So at long last let me take this as my cue to break free of this political straitjacket and consider the broad dimensions of change in women's history — the transformation of the whole complex of female roles. The papers in this volume illustrate several salient characteristics of recent literature on changing sex roles. First of all, historians tend to look to change in woman's economic role as the most central and malleable aspect of her historical identity. Secondly, that role is often narrowly defined as participation in the wage labor force. Finally, and largely due to the pioneering and convincing work of William Chafe, the most significant recent changes in woman's behavior have been dated around the time of the

Second World War. The extension of this debate within this volume provides a case study for the identification and explanation of change in women's history.

Review of the relevant papers suggests, first of all, that the dating of change can set up and almost determine a whole sequence of explanation. If the greatest or most significant increase in the female labor force occurred in the nineteen-forties it will trigger a very different species of explanation than if it is dated a decade earlier. This sequence of explanation is set in motion by associating the date of change with a major historical event, the broader and more familiar the better — World War II for the 40s and the Great Depression for the 1930s. If the most significant changes occurred in the 1920s we undoubtedly would trace it to those celebrated changes in manners and mores. Dates and events can then decree an answer to another question: Who makes women's history, and how? A wartime change could be attributed to national emergency and government fiat. A rapid increase in the proportion of working women during the depression suggests the grim power of family necessity. And should the change occur in the 20s the flapper would be put at the helm as the dashing mistress of her own historical fate. For good empiricists, capable of precisely identifying and pinpointing change, this is not a bad historical method. This mode of explanation, proceeding from date to event to the mechanics of change, may not, however, be the most appropriate way of dealing with change in women's history.

Thus women's historians have proceeded, either unconsciously or purposively, to revise each of these elements in the chain of historical explanation. The most fundamental reorientation is in the method of dating changes and marking the passage of time. Time in woman's history is increasingly measured not by reference to some political calendar but to the evolving life cycle of women. The lives of individual women are then grouped together as generations, a unit of historical time which better suits our purposes than does some arbitrary decade. Life cycle and generational time allow us to intersect with changes in woman's role in a far more realistic manner than heretofore. For example, if we designate the change in the pattern of female employment as an event that occurred between 1940 and 1945, we imply a commonality of experience among women of all ages, some of whom were born before the Civil War and others who might live into the twenty-first century. Women's historians routinely assume much narrower demographic boundaries than these. In the present instance some of us may be thinking of our own or our mother's generation, or we may construct a rough birth cohort, composed for example of all women born somewhere between 1900 and 1930. Any one of these devices introduces a new sequence of explanation into women's history.

First of all, this time perspective signals a distinct set of events as the benchmarks of women's history. Black Thursday and Pearl Harbor must make room for a woman's date of birth, marriage, or widowhood. Certainly we cannot determine relationships between sex roles and such events as wars and depressions without some reference to variations in the age, marital status, and childbearing history of women. Generational shifts in the arrangement of these private events furthermore may have a more decisive effect on female employment rates than either global war or the Great Depression.

Moreover, personal and public events can come together more organically within the framework of the life cycle. When viewed through the long lens of the generation, discreet historical events blend into the continuum of woman's experience. Consider again the shift in woman's work role, not as an event dated during World War II, but as an experience of a woman born in 1910 and reentering the work force in 1945. From this perspective the decision to seek employment is informed by thirty-five years of women's history. This woman's decision to work outside the home cannot be divorced from sex role socialization that began thirty-five years before, formal schooling that may have ended fifteen years earlier, and some work experience that may have terminated shortly thereafter. The timing of a woman's work would also be conditioned by the date of her marriage and whether or not she employed some reliable form of birth control. From this perspective, change in women's history seems an incremental, unremitting process, whose causes are embedded in a personal past and evolving individual consciousness.

This revised sense of time, event, and change places women center-stage in their own history. Given this reorientation we cannot help seeing women as the most immediate and direct agents of change in sex roles. A change in the pattern of female employment is now reduced to its component parts: the individual decisions of specific women repeated in all their complexity literally millions of times. Yet here is the contradiction. If each of these decisions was completely free and perfectly individual they would occur randomly, without any pattern; there would be no women's history at all, only atomic female experience orbiting through the past.

Thus in the end the search for historical explanation ultimately leads outside the individual experience of women, and toward such specific events as war and depression, as well as the historical abstractions identified by terms like "social forces," "ideological currents," or "economic trends." Every historian can draw on a wide assortment of such generalizations and weave them together into a pastiche explanation of each event in woman's past. Unfortunately much of this predigested history has been formulated by historians quite indifferent to our subject matter, if not altogether oblivious to the women of the past. At the very least we have to adapt and remodel this body of knowledge before we can integrate it into women's history. For example, Judith Wellman did not find in all the literature on Jacksonian politics and abolitionism any ready-made theory that would suit her purposes as a women's historian. The pursuit of explanation in women's history can also uncover facets of the past that have been largely neglected by our colleagues in social and economic history. For example, three papers flirt with such a prospect. Susan Hartmann, Eleanor Straub and Mary Hargreaves all alluded to the sales and service sectors of the labor force as a major destination of female entrants into the labor force. This structural economic change, the expansion of the tertiary sector of the economy, cannot be disentangled from changes in woman's role, nor from a rippling series of effects such as the proliferation of the two-worker household, the rise in family purchasing power, and changing life styles. This single example should indicate that women's history, particularly as manifest in the sexual division of labor, is itself a force or cause in history. Accordingly, it is not enough to describe the role of women in wars, depressions, and revolutions. We must also review each of these events through the experience of women. And, finally, after we have traced the effect of sexual differentiation throughout our history we may create revisionist interpretations of all the favorite themes of American historians. Only by taking the last two steps can we move beyond the study of women *in* history to women's history.

Each dimension of change and explanation to which I have alluded could raise the prospect of metaphysical debate about such things as cause and effect, freedom and necessity, base and superstructure, materialism and idealism. The study of women may not necessitate a distinct philosophy of history, nor for that matter an exclusive custom-made methodology. All I propose is a slightly different point of entry into history, one that proceeds from the standpoint of women who have been clearly identified by generation and by social circumstances. From this strategic position we can read the past much as women experienced it, in direct and active interchange with those forces larger than themselves which we call history. The best of women's history has been proceeding this way all along, weaving in and out between the experience of women and the larger patterned relationships, the structures, of past society. Thus, in retrospect, women's history is a radical new vision. Our field of study encompasses approximately half of all the human race at the same time that it analyzes one of the most universal and obstinate of all social structures, gender differentiation. Thus it almost inevitably sharpens our understanding of the relationship between individual experience and the bold patterns of history. Prospectively, therefore, we must exploit this humanizing potential of women's history by refining our methods of recovering the experience and consciousness of our female subjects. The proof of this approach comes not in theoretical discussion but in the interaction between historians and their documents. And if my hunch is right the collections introduced by Virginia Purdy and the staff of the National Archives are particularly amenable to this approach to women's history. Certainly any one who dares to wade through all 885 feet of the Women's Bureau records will emerge with a jaundiced eye and recast the history of the twentieth century in woman's image. These records on woman's work, supplemented with published reports of the Children's Bureau, the Census Bureau, and records of agencies relating to health and education and welfare will illuminate almost every role that evolves with the female life cycle, from infant care to the widow's predicament. I suspect, furthermore, that these documents can be arranged in such a way as to resemble the sequence of that life cycle. Government statistics commonly cross-tabulate information according to age and marital status, while the original questionnaires or transcripts of interviews similarly identify the respondents. In general, government-sponsored survey research can provide massive and at the same time highly concrete profiles of women, identifying their subjects by specific time and place as well as age, marital status, and other crucial social characteristics. Specific studies, and particularly related manuscript records, can pose a graphic life-size reality (that portrait of slaughterhouse workers, for example) against the stolid background of nationally aggregate statistics.

We lose the data banks of modern government bureaucracy as we move backward in time. Yet historians of earlier America have a major compensation access to the manuscript population schedules of the federal census. Every particle of data on a census can be exploited in multiple ways by the women's historian. First of all, the queries of the census taker provoked answers to fundamental descriptive questions in women's history. They can give us a rough estimation of how many women worked outside the home, what percentage of the female population was married, and how many women lived in nuclear households. Ironically, this public document also reveals woman's most private acts. For example, because the census takers of 1900 solicited the precise birth date for every mother's child we can reconstruct a woman's fertility history and make some inferences about the use of contraception. With a little more manipulation of census data we can proceed beyond description to establish relationships and suggest causes in women's history. Virginia Purdy's arrangement of information on the women of Westown, for example, illustrated a connection between a woman's position within the family and her employment or lack thereof. She might have gone on to demonstrate the relationship between female employment and race, ethnic background, number of children, and every other item on the census. With some slightly fancier computer work she might plot a relationship between a woman's work history and her husband's occupation, or the presence of servants and other adult females in her home. Some mathematically minded women's historians may even wish to calculate a statistical estimate of the relative strength of association between women's employment and each of these elements of her social profile.

Every federal census since 1850, furthermore, supplies the basic building blocks of life-cycle analysis, the age of each female enumerated. Thus the ever-malleable census data would permit the historian to select a specific age group for analysis, for instance adolescents or elderly women. We can go further and construct an artificial life cycle out of a single census. This static age profile can describe among other things the ages at which women were most likely to leave the parental home, enter the work force, marry or bear their last child, all for a single census year. It is even feasible to follow an actual generation or birth cohort through a sequence of censuses. All in all the census remains one of the most comprehensive and versatile documents of women's history. It can be made to speak to almost any question in the field. Many will grumble, however, that this document speaks only in the lifeless, aborted language of statistics. Even if this were entirely true, the fact remains that the geographic specificity of the census invites the historian to collect all sorts of supplementary documentation both literary and archeological. One could flesh out these statistics on the women of

Westown by reading the local newspapers, entering the homes that date from 1900, perhaps even talking to some women whose names were enscribed on that census seventy-six years ago. This national document, in other words, is a major resource for local historians. It is at this local level that we can see, perhaps with the greatest clarity, women in the act of making their own history.

Finally it must be underscored that whatever geographic unit we choose as the boundary of our investigation, each one of our subjects is also a member of a specific race, ethnic group, and class — basic facts which the census schedules never allow us to forget. Each of these factors demands more attention and greater thought than they have been accorded in the past. For these terms denote more than autonomous subpopulations of women's history. They identify basic structural features of American society, which like sex, systematically set up relations of superiority and inferiority, power and subjection. Thus it is imperative that historians give concerted attention to the intersection and attendant contradictions of sex and class and race.

The enumeration of such gaps in our knowledge and thus the identification of further prospects for research in women's history could occupy us interminably and thus preclude an altogether neat ending to this volume.

In closing, I would like to make some observations on the forum in which these papers originally appeared, the women's history conference. The primary function of such gatherings has been to report on research which has been conceived, conducted, and completed by individual and often isolated historians. This particular conference, with its focus on sources and their use, goes somewhat further and brings collective wisdom to bear on individual research problems. We need more such workshop-conferences. But more than this we need permanent and systematic modes of communicating with one another and working together. This is to say, first of all, that there is much more room for joint effort among women's historians. Coordinated work is sorely needed if we are to supply the field with essential reference tools, conduct projects which entail extensive computer and comparative analysis, and comprehend the regional diversity of the United States. We can consider ways of institutionalizing women's history as a collective enterprise by developing research centers and long-term academic programs. This volume inspires this last prospect — a more broadly national and more closely federated women's history.

Biographical Sketches
Appendix
Index

BIOGRAPHICAL SKETCHES

WILLIAM H. CHAFE is best known for his book *The American Woman: Her Changing Social, Economic, and Political Roles, 1920-1970* (New York: Oxford University Press, 1972). He has also contributed to scholarly journals and anthologies. Educated at Harvard and the Union Theological Seminary, he received both the M.A. and Ph.D. degrees from Columbia University. He is now associate professor of history and codirector of the oral history project at Duke University.

GEORGE C. CHALOU taught history at Ohio State University before joining the staff of the National Archives in 1971, where he has been a specialist in military records in the Center for the Documentary Study of the American Revolution. A native of Ohio, he graduated from Manchester College and received master's and Ph.D. degrees from Indiana University. His most recent publications are two contributions to *Congress Investigates* edited by Arthur M. Schlesinger, Jr., and Roger Bruns (New York: Chelsea House, 1975). His primary research interests are the effect of federal policies on minority groups and early Indian treaties. In the fall of 1976, Chalou became assistant to the chief of the Reference Branch of the General Archives Division of the National Archives.

CLARKE A. CHAMBERS, born in Blue Earth, Minnesota, has a B.A. from Carleton College and an M.A. and a Ph.D. from the University of California at Berkeley. He has taught at the University of Minnesota since 1951 and is now professor of history. He has been director of the Social Welfare History Archives Center since its inception in 1964 and is advisory editor to the Women's History Sources Survey. He is the author of several books and many articles in the field of the history of social reform, social welfare, and the profession of social work. Among these are *Seedtime of Reform* (1963) and *Paul U. Kellogg and the Survey, Voices for Social Welfare and Social Justice* (1971), both published by the University of Minnesota Press in Minneapolis. He served on the board of editors of the *Journal of American History* and on the Organization of American Historians' Committee on the Status of Women in the Profession.

MABEL E. DEUTRICH, director of the conference, was until her retirement in August 1979, assistant archivist of the United States for the National Archives. In this position she directed the activity of the records-holding units of the National Archives and its eleven regional archives branches. A native of Wisconsin, she received a B.S. from Wisconsin State College in LaCrosse, Wisconsin, and earned her M.A. and Ph.D. degrees from American University. Almost all of her career she has been with the federal government. She began working for the Department of the Army, first as a records manager and later as historian. Since 1950 she has been at the National Archives, holding the position of director of the Military Archives Division immediately before she received her last appointment in 1975. She is the author of *Struggle for Supremacy: The Career of General Fred C. Ainsworth* (Washington: Public Affairs Press, 1962) and numerous articles. She is a fellow of the Society of American Archivists and was the first chairperson of the Society's Committee on the Status of Women.

STANLEY L. FALK, chief historian, Office of Air Force History, has to his credit a long list of publications about the military history of World War II. *Bataan: The March of Death* (1962) and *Decision at Leyte* (1966), both published by W.W. Norton, were followed by *Liberation of the Philippines* (1971) and *The Palaus Campaign* (1974) bearing the Ballantine colophon. His most recent book is *Seventy Days to Singapore: The Malayan Campaign* (London: Robert Hale, 1975; New York: G.P. Putnam's Sons, 1975). Several other works were published by the Industrial College of the Armed Forces where he was associate professor of national security affairs from 1962 to 1970 and professor of international relations until 1974. A native of New York City, he graduated from Bard College and took his M.A. and Ph.D. degrees from Georgetown University.

CHESTER W. GREGORY was born in North Carolina and studied for his A.B. and M.A. degrees at North Carolina College. Holder of a Ph.D. from Ohio State University, he is the author of *Women in Defense Work during World War II* (New York: Exposition Press, 1974). Department chairman and professor of history at Coppin State College in Baltimore, he was a member of the Baltimore Bicentennial Committee and takes an active part in civic affairs. He taught at Elizabeth City State University from 1954 to 1969 and directed the Desegregation Institute for the Albemarle Area in the summer of 1969. He has lectured widely on black history, including a visiting lectureship at Goucher College.

MARY W.M. HARGREAVES, professor of history at the University of Kentucky, is also coeditor of the papers of Henry Clay, of which five volumes have appeared. Formerly associated with the Brookings Institution and the Baker Library at the

Harvard School of Business, she holds a bachelor's degree from Bucknell University and both a master's and a doctorate from Radcliffe College. Harvard University Press published her book *Dry Farming in the Northern Great Plains 1900-1925* in 1957.

SUSAN M. HARTMANN, a native of St. Louis, Missouri, is associate professor of history at the University of Missouri at St. Louis, where she is coordinator of the women's studies program. After receiving an A.B. from Washington University, she earned an M.A. and a Ph. D. at the University of Missouri in Columbia. She received both the University of Missouri Curators Award (1971) and the David D. Lloyd prize (1972) for *Truman and the 80th Congress* (Columbia: University of Missouri Press, 1971). An earlier book *The Marshall Plan* was published by Charles E. Merrill in 1968. She has also published several articles in women's history.

ANDREA HINDING, director of the Women's History Sources Survey, has bachelor's and master's degrees from the University of Minnesota. She is curator at the Social Welfare History Archives and, as assistant professor, teaches courses in women's history and a seminar in the administration of archives. She has published articles in all her fields of interest. A member of the councils of the Society of American Archivists and the Midwest Archives Conference, she is a frequent speaker on archival subjects.

EDITH JAMES is an editor, an archivist, and a diplomatic historian. Before becoming assistant editor of the papers of Woodrow Wilson, she was acting university archivist at Princeton University and an archivist in the Diplomatic Branch of the National Archives. She has written and lectured on historical and archival subjects. Her bachelor's degree is from Marietta College, her master's from the University of Chicago, and her doctorate from the University of Maryland. She is now a historical editor in the Office of the Historian, Department of State.

LINDA K. KERBER is a native New Yorker who earned her doctorate at Columbia University and taught at Yeshiva University, San Jose State College, and Stanford University before assuming her present position as professor of history at the University of Iowa. Her book *Federalists in Dissent: Imagery and Ideology in Jeffersonian America* was published by Cornell University Press in 1970. She has published many articles and appeared frequently on programs of historical association meetings. She is a fellow of the Society of American Historians and served on the Committe on Women Historians of the American Historical Association. In September 1975 she went to London as a member of the Presidential Delegation to the opening of the Franklin-Jefferson Bicentennial Exhibition at the British Museum. She was on the History Jury of the Pulitzer Prize Committee for 1975-76, the editorial board of *American Studies* from 1973 to 1975, and is currently on the editorial board of *Signs*. Her forthcoming book, *Daughters of Columbia: Intellect and Politics in the Early Republic,* will be published by the University of North Carolina Press.

JOSEPH P. LASH is a native New Yorker, a graduate of the City College of New York, and holds a master's degree from Columbia University. During the 1930s he was active in youth and student movements and served in the Pacific during the Second World War. After the war he was one of the founding members of Americans for Democratic Action. From 1950 to 1961 he was United Nations correspondent for the *New York Post* and held the post of assistant editor of its editorial page until 1966. His first book about Eleanor Roosevelt was a small volume that he called *Eleanor Roosevelt: A Friend's Memoir* (Garden City: Doubleday, 1964). Since the publication of *Eleanor and Franklin* (1971) and *Eleanor: The Years Alone* (1972), he has written a biographical essay of Felix Frankfurter and notes to *From the Diaries of Felix Frankfurter* (1975) as well as the recently published *Roosevelt and Churchill* (1976). All four works were published by W.W. Norton.

NANCY E. MALAN was born in New Jersey and graduated from the College of Notre Dame in Baltimore. She began working with still pictures in the Audiovisual Archives of the National Archives even before she received her master's degree in American History from Georgetown University in 1970. She has written a number of finding aids and articles and has prepared several slide presentations emphasizing the evidential value of photographs in historical research. She is now an archivist in the Office of Educational Programs.

PENNY MARTELET is a young scholar who received her M.A. from Oklahoma State University in the summer of 1975. While doing graduate study she wrote a paper on the Woman's Land Army movement in both world wars. Her present position is with the Museum of Science and Industry in Chicago.

MARY LYNN MCCREE is curator of Jane Addams' Hull House, and manuscript librarian and professor at the University of Illinois at Chicago Circle. In addition she is editor of the Jane Addams papers project funded by grants from the National Endowment for the Humanities and the National Historical Publications and Records Commission of which she is a commissioner. She is coauthor of *Eighty Years at Hull House* (Chicago: Quadrangle Press, 1969), for which she received the Friends of Literature Distinguished Book Award in 1970, and of *Prairie State: Impression of Illinois, 1673-1967* (Chicago: University of Chicago Press, 1968). McCree also directs the Midwest Women's Historical Collection which conducted a Survey of Manuscript Resources in the Chicago Metropolitan Area for the Study of Women. Educated at Auburn University, she holds master's degrees from the University of Illinois and the University of Chicago. Earlier posts were director of research for the Civil War Centennial Commission of Illinois and assistant in the state archives of Illinois, her native state. She has been on the councils of the Midwest Archives Conference and the Society of American Archivists and is a fellow of the latter organization.

JAMES E. O'NEILL, deputy archivist of the United States since 1972, was formerly the director of the Franklin D. Roosevelt Library at Hyde Park, New York. A graduate of the University of Detroit with A.B. and M.A. degrees, he received his Ph.D. at the University of Chicago. Besides publishing a number of articles in scholarly journals, he is coauthor of *Episodes in American History* (Lexington, Mass.: Ginn & Co., 1973) and coeditor of *World War II: An Account of its Documents* (Washington: Howard University Press, 1976). Before joining the National Archives and Records Service in 1969, he taught at the University of Notre Dame and at the Loyola University in Chicago. He has also been a specialist in the Manuscript Division at the Library of Congress and was for a time editor of the library's *Guide to the Study of the United States of America* project.

HAROLD T. PINKETT has been since 1942 on the staff of the National Archives, where he is presently chief of the Legislative and Natural Resources Branch of the Civil Archives Division. Born in Salisbury, Maryland, he received his A.B. from Morgan College, a master's degree from the University of Pennsylvania, and after further graduate study at Columbia University, his Ph.D. from American University. In addition to many articles, his major work is *Gifford Pinchot, Private and Public Forester* (Urbana: University of Illinois Press, 1970), which, in manuscript, won the 1968 Book Award of the Agricultural History Society. He was codirector of the 1970 National Archives Conference on Research in the Administration of Public Policy and coeditor of the proceedings bearing the same titles and published by Howard University Press in 1975. Pinkett was editor of the *American Archivist* from 1968 to 1971. He is a fellow of the Society of American Archivists and has been a member of its council. He is also a fellow of the Forest History Society and a member of its board of directors.

VIRGINIA CARDWELL PURDY has been, since January 1976, women's history specialist at the National Archives. Immediately prior to her present assignment she was director of the Education Division where the last major exhibit mounted under her direction was *Her Infinite Variety: A 200-Year Record of American's Women* which was the Archives' celebration on International Women's Year. A South Carolinian by birth, Purdy graduated from the state university and took an M.A. and a Ph.D. at the George Washington University. Early in her career she was on the public reference staff of the Library of Congress. Later she was assistant historian at the National Portrait Gallery of the Smithsonian Institution and in 1968-69, keeper of the Catalogue of American Portraits. She is coauthor of *Presidential Portraits* (Washington: Smithsonian Institution Press, 1968), and has written several articles on historical and archival subjects. Since April 1978, she has been editor of the *American Archivist,* the quarterly journal of the Society of American Archivists.

MARY P. RYAN's dissertation for her doctorate at the University of California, Berkeley was entitled "American Society and the Cult of Domesticity, 1830-1860," foreshadowing what was to be her main research interest in the coming years. Articles and lectures in women's history were followed by the book-length study *Womanhood in America* (New York: New Viewpoints, 1975). With under-graduate and master's degrees from the University of Wisconsin, she taught at Pitzer College in Claremont, California, before taking her present post on the faculty of the State University of New York in Binghamton in 1972.

ANNE FIROR SCOTT graduated from the University of Georgia and holds an M.A. from Northwestern University and a Ph.D. from Radcliffe College. Now a professor of history at Duke University, she has taught at Haverford College, the University of North Carolina, the University of Washington, Johns Hopkins University, and Stanford University. A "Southern lady" herself who was born in Montezuma, Georgia, she is well known for one of her earliest publications, *The Southern Lady: From Pedestal to Politics* (Chicago: University of Chicago Press, 1970). Also on her extensive list of publications are *Women in American Life* (Boston: Houghton Mifflin, 1970), *The American Woman: Who was She?* (Englewood Cliffs, N.J.: Prentice Hall, 1970), and, with her husband, Andrew McKay Scott, *One Half the People* (Philadelphia: J.B. Lippincott, 1975). In addition to articles and lectures, she prepared six essays for *Notable American Women* edited by Edward and Janet James, 3 vols., (Cambridge: Harvard University Press, 1971). She was on the program committee and executive board of the Organization of American Historians, 1972-75, the nominating committee of the American Historical Association in 1975, and the editorial board of the *American Quarterly* since 1973. She began her career as research associate, congressional representative, and editor of *The National Voter* for the League of Women Voters of the United States in the late 1940s and early 1950s. The governor of North Carolina appointed her chairman of the Governor's Commission on the Status of Women, 1963-64, and she was a member of the President's Advisory Council on the Status of Women, 1964-69.

ELAINE M. SMITH is assistant professor of history at Alabama State University in Montgomery. Her undergraduate work was done at Bethune-Cookman College, and her master's degree is from Boston University. She has done work toward her doctorate at the University of Maryland and at Howard University. She held a Woodrow Wilson Fellowship in 1965. She has also worked at the United States Office of Education on programs for the handicapped.

ELEANOR FERGUSON STRAUB has spoken frequently on historical subjects and the concerns of women historians at national and regional professional meetings, including the first and second Berkshire Conferences. Following her graduation from Radcliffe, she earned her M.A. and Ph.D. degrees from Emory University. She has been assistant executive director of the American Historical Association since 1973.

JUDITH WELLMAN began her undergraduate studies at the State University of New York, Binghamton, and is now teaching at the State University of New York, Oswego. She received her undergraduate degree from the University of Denver. While working for her doctorate at the University of Virginia she was an educational supervisor of the Charlottesville Neighborhood Youth Corps. In her present position, she has been involved in setting up an inter-disciplinary program in women's studies and a minor in museum studies. Wellman is also a curator with the Special Collections where she has primary responsibility for oral history and for local history manuscripts. She has written and lectured in several related fields.

MARY E. YOUNG, professor of history at the University of Rochester since 1973, was born at Utica, N.Y., and did her undergraduate work at Oberlin College. She received her doctorate at Cornell University, and taught at Ohio State University for a number of years. Her most prominent work is *Redskins, Ruffleshirts, and Rednecks: Indian Land Allotments in Alabama and Mississippi, 1830-1860* (Norman: University of Oklahoma, Press, 1961). She was coeditor and a contributor for *The Frontier in American Development* (Ithaca: Cornell University Press, 1969). She has long been active in the Organization of American Historians, having received its Louis Pelzer Award in 1955 when the organization still called itself the Mississippi Valley Historical Association. She has served on the editorial board of the *Journal of American History* and on the OAH Frederick Jackson Turner Award Committee.

APPENDIX

List of Numbered Bulletins of the Women's Bureau, 1919-63

Copies of the bulletins listed below may be found in many libraries. There is also a complete set in the National Archives in RG 287, Publications of the U.S. Government. Symbols beside the number of the bulletin indicate whether or not there is material related to the bulletin in the records of the Women's Bureau. The quantity of related documentation varies from a single folder to twenty or thirty feet of research materials.

S — Survey material (raw data, reports, tables, etc., on which conclusions set forth in the bulletin were based)

C — Correspondence (often documenting the reasons for the choice of subject for study and the methods or other details of administration of the survey)

Bulletin No.

SC 1. Proposed Employment of Women during the War, in the Industries of Niagara Falls, N.Y., 1918. 16 p. 1919.

SC 2. Labor Laws for Women in Industry in Indiana. 29 pp. 1919.

3. Standards for the Employment of Women in Industry. 8 pp. Four editions, 1918, 1919, 1921, 1928.

SC 4. Wages of Candy Makers in Philadelphia in 1919. 46 pp. 1919.

S 5. The Eight-Hour Day in Federal and State Legislation. 14 pp. 1921.

6. The Employment of Women in Hazardous Industries in the United States, 1919. 8 pp. 1920.

7. Night-Work Laws in the United States, 1919. 4 pp. 1920.

8. Women in the Government Service. 37 pp. 1920.

C 9. Home Work in Bridgeport, Connecticut. 35 pp. 1920.

SC 10. Hours and Conditions of Work for Women in Industry in Virginia. 32 pp. 1920.

S 11. Women Street Car Conductors and Ticket Agents. 90 pp. 1921.

45. Home Environment and Employment Opportunities of Women in Coal-Mine Workers' Families. 61 pp. 1925.

46. Facts About Working Women. 64 pp. 1925.

C 47. Women in the Fruit-Growing and Canning Industries in the State of Washington. 223 pp. 1926.

SC 48. Women in Oklahoma Industries. 118 pp. 1926.

49. Women Workers and Family Support. 10 pp. 1925.

50. Effects of Applied Research Upon the Employment Opportunities of American Women. 54 pp. 1926.

SC 51. Women in Illinois Industries. 108 pp. 1926.

SC 52. Lost Time and Labor Turnover in Cotton Mills. 203 pp. 1926.

53. The Status of Women in the Government Service in 1925. 103 pp. 1926.

54. Changing Jobs. 12 pp. 1926.

SC 55. Women in Mississippi Industries. 89 pp. 1926.

SC 56. Women in Tennessee Industries. 120 pp. 1927.

SC 57. Women Workers and Industrial Poisons. 5 pp. 1926.

SC 58. Women in Delaware Industries. 156 pp. 1927.

59. Short Talks About Working Women. 24 pp. 1927.

SC 60. Industrial Accidents to Women in New Jersey, Ohio, and Wisconsin. 316 pp. 1927.

S 61. The Development of Minimum-Wage Laws in the United States, 1912 to 1927. 635 pp. 1928.

SC 62. Women's Employment in Vegetable Canneries in Delaware. 47 pp. 1927.

63. State Laws Affecting Working Women. 51 pp. Charts. 1927. (See Bull. 98.)

SC 64. The Employment of Women at Night. 86 pp. 1928.

S 65. The Effects of Labor Legislation on the Employment Opportunities of Women. 495 pp. 1928.

S 66-I. History of Labor Legislation for Women in Three States. 133 pp. 1932.

S 66-II. Chronological Development of Labor Legislation for Women in the United States. 173 pp. 1932.

SC 67. Women Workers in Flint, Michigan. 79 pp. 1929.

68. Summary: The Effects of Labor Legislation on the Employment Opportunities of Women. (Reprint of Chapter II of Bull. 65.) 22 pp. 1928.

C 69. Causes of Absence for Men and for Women in Four Cotton Mills. 22 pp. 1929.

70. Negro Women in Industry in 15 States. 72 pp. 1929.

71. Selected References on the Health of Women in Industry. 8 pp. 1929.

C 72. Conditions of Work in Spin Rooms. 39 pp. 1929.

SC 73.   Variations in Employment Trends of Women and Men. 141 pp. Charts. 1930.

SC 74.   The Immigrant Woman and Her Job. 179 pp. 1930.

75.   What the Wage-Earning Woman Contributes to Family Support. 20 pp. 1929.

SC 76.   Women in 5 and 10-cent Stores and Limited-Price Chain Department Stores. 56 pp. 1930.

C 77.   A Study of Two Groups of Denver Married Women Applying for Jobs. 10 pp. 1929.

SC 78.   A Survey of Laundries and Their Women Workers in 23 Cities. 164 pp. 1930.

79.   Industrial Home Work. 18 pp. 1930.

SC 80.   Women in Florida Industries. 113 pp. 1930.

SC 81.   Industrial Accidents to Men and Women. 46 pp. 1930.

SC 82.   The Employment of Women in the Pineapple Canneries of Hawaii. 28 pp. 1930.

S 83.   Fluctuation of Employment in the Radio Industry. 63 pp. 1931.

S 84.   Fact Finding with the Women's Bureau. 35 pp. 1931.

S 85.   Wages of Women in 13 States. 211 pp. 1931.

S 86.   Activities of the Women's Bureau of the United States. 13 pp. 1931.

SC 87.   Sanitary Drinking Facilities, with Special Reference to Drinking Fountains. 26 pp. 1931.

S 88.   The Employment of Women in Slaughtering and Meat Packing. 208 pp. 1932.

SC 89.   The Industrial Experience of Women Workers at the Summer Schools, 1928 to 1930. 60 pp. 1931.

SC 90.   Oregon Legislation for Women in Industry. 37 pp. 1931.

S 91.   Women in Industry: A Series of Papers to Aid Study Groups. 79 pp. 1931. (See Bull. 164.)

SC 92.   Wage-Earning Women and the Industrial Conditions of 1930. A Survey of South Bend. 81 pp. 1932. (See Bull. 108.)

SC 93.   Household Employment in Philadelphia. 85 pp. 1932.

SC 94.   State Requirements for Industrial Lighting: A Handbook for the Protection of Women Workers, Showing Lighting Standards and Practices. 62 pp. 1932.

SC 95.   Bookkeepers, Stenographers, and Office Clerks in Ohio, 1914 to 1929. 31 pp. 1932.

S 96.   Women Office Workers in Philadelphia. 14 pp. 1932.

SC 97.   The Employment of Women in the Sewing Trades of Connecticut — Preliminary Report. 13 pp. 1932. (See Bull. 109.)

S 98.   Labor Laws for Women in the States and Territories. 67 pp. Charts. 1931. (Revised as of 1934. See Bull. 144.)

S 99.   The Installation and Maintenance of Toilet Facilities in Places of Employment. 86 pp. 1933.

SC 100. The Effects on Women of Changing Conditions in the Cigar and Cigarette Industries. 184 pp. 1932.

SC 101. The Employment of Women in Vitreous Enameling. 61 pp. 1932.

SC 102. Industrial Injuries to Women in 1928 and 1929 Compared with Injuries to Men. 33 pp. 1933.

SC 103. Women Workers in the Third Year of the Depression: A Study of Students in the Bryn Mawr Summer School. 13 pp. 1933.

SC 104. The Occupational Progress of Women, 1910 to 1930. 87 pp. 1933.

SC 105. A Study of a Change from 8 to 6 Hours of Work. 14 pp. 1933.

SC 106. Household Employment in Chicago. 62 pp. 1933.

SC 107. Technological Changes in Relation to Women's Employment. 39 pp. 1935.

SC 108. The Effects of the Depression on Wage Earners' Families: A Second Survey of South Bend. 31 pp. 1936. (See Bull. 92.)

SC 109. The Employment of Women in the Sewing Trades of Connecticut. 45 pp. 1935.

S 110. The Change from Manual to Dial Operation in the Telephone Industry. 15 pp. 1933.

SC 111. Hours, Earnings, and Employment in Cotton Mills. 78 pp. 1933.

SC 112. Standards of Placement Agencies for Household Employees. 68 pp. Charts. 1934.

S 113. Employment Fluctuations and Unemployment of Women, 1928-1931. 236 pp. 1933.

S 114. State Reporting of Occupational Disease, Including a Survey of Legislation Applying to Women. 99 pp. 1934.

S 115. Women at Work. 60 pp. 1933. (See Bull. 161.)

SC 116. A Study of a Change from One Shift of 9 Hours to Two Shifts of 6 Hours Each. 14 pp. 1934.

SC 117. The Age Factor As It Relates to Women in Business and the Professions. 66 pp. 1934.

SC 118. The Employment of Women in Puerto Rico. 34 pp. 1934.

SC 119. Hours and Earnings in the Leather-Glove Industry. 32 pp. 1934.

SC 120. The Employment of Women in Offices. 126 pp. 1934.

SC 121. A Survey of the Shoe Industry in New Hampshire. 100 pp. 1935.

S 122. Variations in Wage Rates Under Corresponding Conditions. 57 pp. 1935.

SC 123. Employment in Hotels and Restuarants. 105 pp. 1936.

SC 124. Women in Arkansas Industries. 45 pp. 1935.

SC 125. Employment Conditions in Department Stores in 1932-33: A Study in Selected Cities of Five States. 24 pp. 1936.

SC 126. Women in Texas Industries. 45 pp. 1935.

SC 127. Hours and Earnings in Tobacco Stemmeries. 29 pp. 1934.

SC 128. Potential Earning Power of Southern Mountaineer Handicraft. 56 pp. 1935.

SC 129. Industrial Injuries to Women in 1930 and 1931 Compared with Injuries to Men. 57 pp. 1935.

SC 130. Employed Women Under N.R.A. Codes. 144 pp. 1935.

S 131. Industrial Home Work in Rhode Island, with Special Reference to the Lace Industry. 27 pp. 1935.

S 132. Women Who Work in Offices: I. Study of Employed Women. II. Study of Women Seeking Employment. 27 pp. 1935.

SC 133. Employment Conditions in Beauty Shops. 46 pp. 1935.

S 134. Summaries of Studies on the Economic Status of Women. 20 pp. 1935.

S 135. The Commercialization of the Home Through Industrial Home Work. 49 pp. 1935.

S 136. The Health and Safety of Women in Industry. 23 pp. 1935.

S 137. Summary of State Hour Laws for Women and Minimum-Wage Rates. 54 pp. 1936.

S 138. Reading List of References on Household Employment. 15 pp. 1936.

SC 139. Women Unemployed Seeking Relief in 1933. 19 pp. 1936.

SC 140. Reemployment of New England Women in Private Industry. 118 pp. 1936.

SC 141. Piecework in the Silk Dress Industry. 68 pp. 1936.

SC 142. The Economic Problems of the Women of the Virgin Islands of the United States. 24 pp. 1936.

SC 143. Factors Affecting Wages in Power Laundries. 82 pp. 1936.

S 144. State Labor Laws for Women. 93 pp. Charts. 1937. (See Bull. 156.)

SC 145. Special Study of Wages Paid to Women and Minors in Ohio Industries. Prior and Subsequent to the Ohio Minimum-Wage Law for Women and Minors. 83 pp. 1936.

SC 146. A Policy Insuring Value to the Woman Buyer and a Livelihood to Apparel Makers. 22 pp. 1936.

S 147. Summary of State Reports of Occupational Diseases, with a Survey of Preventive Legislation, 1932 to 1934. 42 pp. 1936.

S 148. The Employed Woman Homemaker in the United States: Her Responsibility for Family Support. 22 pp. 1936.

SC 149. Employment of Women in Tennessee Industries. 63 pp. 1937.

SC 150. Women's Employment in West Virginia. 27 pp. 1937.

SC 151. Injuries to Women in Personal Service Occupations in Ohio. 23 pp. 1937.

S 152. Differences in the Earnings of Women and Men. 57 pp. 1938.

SC 153. Women's Hours and Wages in the District of Columbia in 1937. 44 pp. 1937.

S 154. Reading List of References on Household Employment. 17 pp. 1938.

SC 155. Women in the Economy of the United States of America. 137 pp. 1937.

S 156. State Labor Laws for Women. As of 31 December 1937. 16 pp. 1938.

Part I. Summary. As of 31 December 1940. 18 pp. 1940. Part II. Analysis of Hour Laws for Women Workers. 45 pp. Charts. 1938. (See Bull. 202-I.)

SC   157.   The Legal Status of Women in the United States of America. 1 January 1938. United States Summary. 89 pp. 1941. Separate reports for each state and the District of Columbia.

SC   157.   The Legal Status of Women in the United States of America. U.S. Summary: Supplement I. 16 pp. 1943.

SC   157.   The Legal Status of Women in the United States of America (Rev. 1963)

 S   157.   The Legal Status of women in the United States of America (Rev. 1963).

SC   157- The Legal Status of Women in the United States of America. Cumula-
     A.   tive Supplement, 1938-1945. 31 pp. 1946.

SC   157- The Legal Status of Women in the United States of America. 1 January
     Rev. 1948. United States Summary. 105 pp. 1951. Separate reports for each state and the District of Columbia.

SC   158.   Unattached Women on Relief in Chicago, 1937. 84 pp. 1938.

 S   159.   Trends in the Employment of Women, 1928-36. 48 pp. 1938.

SC   160.   Industrial Injuries to Women and Men, 1932 to 1934. 37 pp. 1938.

 S   161.   Women at Work: A Century of Industrial Change. 80 pp. 1942.

SC   162.   Women in Kentucky Industries, 1937. 84 pp. 1938.

SC   163.   Hours and Earnings in Certain Men's Wear Industries.
           1. Work Clothing, Work Shirts, Dress Shirts. 27 pp. 1938.
           2. Knit Underwear, Woven Cotton Underwear. 10 pp. 1938.
           3. Seamless Hosiery. 8 pp. 1938.
           4. Welt Shoes. 9 pp. 1938.
           5. Raincoats, Sports Jackets. 29 pp. 1940.
           6. Caps and Cloth Hats, Neckwear, Work and Knit Gloves, Handkerchiefs. 22 pp. 1939.

 S   164.   Women in Industry: A Series of Papers to Aid Study Groups. 85 pp. 1938.

 S   165.   The Negro Woman Worker. 17 pp. 1938.

SC 166.   The Effect of Minimum-Wage Determinations in Service Industries: Adjustments in the Dry-Cleaning and Power-Laundry Industries. 44 pp. 1938.

 S   167.   State Minimum-Wage Laws and Orders: An Analysis. 34 pp. Charts. 1939. Two Supplements. 1939, 15 pp., 1940, 13 pp. 1941. (See Bull. 191.)

 S   168.   Employed Women and Family Support. 57 pp. 1939.

SC 169.   Conditions in the Millinery Industry in the United States. 128 pp. 1939.

SC 170.   Economic Status of University Women in the U.S.A. 70 pp. 1939.

S 171.   Wages and Hours in Drugs and Medicines and in Certain Toilet Preparations. 19 pp. 1939.

S 172.   The Woman Wage Earner: Her Situation Today. 56 pp. 1939.

SC 173. Standards for Employment of Women in Industry: Recommended by the Women's Bureau. 9 pp. 1939.

S 174.   Job Histories of Women Workers at the Summer Schools, 1931-34 and 1938. 25 pp. 1939.

SC 175. Earnings in the Women's and Children's Apparel Industry in the Spring of 1939. 91 pp. 1940.

SC 176. Application of Labor Legislation to the Fruit and Vegetable Canning and Preserving Industries. 162 pp. 1940.

SC 177. Earnings and Hours in Hawaii Woman-Employing Industries. 53 pp. 1940.

SC 178. Women's Wages and Hours in Nebraska. 51 pp. 1940.

S 179.   Primer of Problems in the Millinery Industry. 47 pp. 1941.

SC 180. Employment in Service and Trade Industries in Maine. 30 pp. 1940.

S 181.   The Nonworking Time of Industrial Women Workers. 10 pp. 1940.

S 182.   Employment of Women in the Federal Government, 1923 to 1939. 60 pp. 1941.

SC 183. Women Workers in Their Family Environment. 82 pp. 1941.

SC 184. The Occurrence and Prevention of Occupational Disease among Women, 1935 to 1938. 46 pp. 1941.

SC 185. The Migratory Labor Problem in Delaware. 24 pp. 1941.

S 186.   Earnings and Hours in Pacific Coast Fish Canneries. 30 pp. 1941.

SC 187. Labor Standards and Competitive Market Conditions in the Canned-Goods Industry. 34 pp. 1941.

S 188.   Office Work and Office Workers in 1940: Introduction. 4 pp.

   1. Office Work in Houston, 1940. 58 pp. 1942.

   2. Office Work in Los Angeles, 1940. 64 pp. 1942.

   3. Office Work in Kansas City, 1940. 74 pp. 1942.

   4. Office Work in Richmond, 1940. 61 pp. 1942.

   5. Office Work in Philadelphia, 1940. 102 pp. 1942.

   Wages of Office Workers, 1940. 31 pp. 1941.

   Chart. Women Office Workers: Salary Rates in Five Cities, 1940. 2 pp. 1942.

S 189.   1. Women's Factory Employment in an Expanding Aircraft Production Program. 12 pp. 1942.

   2. Employment of Women in the Manufacture of Small-Arms Ammunition. 11 pp. 1942.

   3. Employment of Women in the Manufacture of Artillery Ammunition. 17 pp. 1942.

   4. The Employment of and Demand for Women Workers in the Manufacture of Instruments — Aircraft, Optical and Fire-Control, and Surgical and Dental. 20 pp. 1942.

S 190. Recreation and Housing for Women War Workers: A Handbook on Standards. 40 pp. 1942.

S 191. State Minimum-Wage Laws and Orders: 1942. An Analysis. 52 pp. Charts. 1942. (See Bull. 267.)

S 192. Reports on employment of women in wartime industries:
1. Women's Employment in Aircraft Assembly Plants in 1942. 23 pp. 1942.
2. Women's Employment in Artillery Ammunition Plants, 1942. 19 pp. 1942.
3. Employment of Women in the Manufacture of Cannon and Small Arms in 1942. 36 pp. 1943.
4. Employment of Women in the Machine-Tool Industry, 1942. 42 pp. 1943.
5. Women's Employment in the Making of Steel, 1943. 39 pp. 1944.
6. Employing Women in Shipyards. 83 pp. 1944.
7. Women's Employment in Foundries, 1943. 28 pp. 1944.
8. Employment of Women in Army Supply Depots in 1943. 33 pp. 1945.
9. Women's Wartime Jobs in Cane-Sugar Refineries. 20 pp. 1945.

S 193. Women's Work in the War. 10 pp. 1942.

S 194. Your Questions as to Women in War Industries. 10 pp. 1942.

S 195. Women Workers in Argentina, Chile, and Uruguay. 15 pp. 1942.

S 196. "Equal Pay" for Women in War Industries. 26 pp. 1942.

SC 197. Women Workers in Some Expanding Wartime Industries — New Jersey, 1942. 44 pp. 1943.

S 198. Employment and Housing Problems of Migratory Workers in New York and New Jersey Canning Industries, 1943. 35 pp. 1944.

S 199. Successful Practices in the Employment of Nonfarm Women on Farms in the Northeastern States, 1943. 44 pp. 1944.

S 200. British Policies and Methods in Employing Women in Wartime. 44 pp. 1944.

S 201. Employment Opportunities in Characteristic Industrial Occupations of Women. 50 pp. 1944.

S 202. State Labor Laws for Women, with Wartime Modifications, 15 December 1944.

202-I. Analysis of Hour Laws. 110 pp. 1945. (See Bull. 250.)

202-II. Analysis of Plant Facilities Laws. 43 pp. 1945.

202-III. Analysis of Regulatory Laws, Prohibitory Laws, Maternity Laws. 12 pp. 1945.

202-IV. Analysis of Industrial Home-Work Laws. 26 pp. 1945.

202-V. Explanation and Appraisal. 60 pp. 1946.

S 203. Medical and Other Health Service Series. The Outlook for Women:
203-1. As Physical Therapists. 51 pp. Revised. 1952.
203-2. As Occupational Therapists. 51 pp. Revised. 1952.

203-3. In Professional Nursing Occupations. 80 pp. Revised. 1953.

203-4. As Medical Technologists and Laboratory Technicians. 54 pp. Revised. 1954.

203-5. As Practical Nurses and Auxiliary Workers and on the Nursing Team. 62 pp. Revised. 1953.

203-6. As Medical Record Librarians. 9 pp. 1945.

203-7. As Women Physicians. 28 pp. 1945.

203-8. As Medical X-Ray Technicians. 53 pp. Revised. 1954.

203-9. As Women Dentists. 21 pp. 1945.

203-10. As Dental Hygienists. 17 pp. 1945.

203-11. As Physicians' and Dentists' Assistants. 15 pp. 1946.

203-12. Trends and Their Effect Upon the Demand for Women Workers. 55 pp. 1946.

S 204.   Women's Emergency Farm Service on the Pacific Coast in 1943. 36 pp. 1945.

S 205.   Negro Women War Workers. 23 pp. 1945.

S 206.   Women Workers in Brazil. 42 pp. 1946.

S 207.   The Woman Telephone Worker. 38 pp. 1946.

S 207-A. Typical Women's Jobs in the Telephone Industry. 49 pp. 1947.

SC 208. Women's Wartime Hours of Work: The Effect on Their Factory Performance and Home Life. 187 pp. 1947.

SC 209. Women Workers in Ten War Production Areas and Their Postwar Employment Plans. 56 pp. 1946.

S 210.   Women Workers in Paraguay. 16 pp. 1946.

S 211.   Employment of Women in the Early Postwar Period, with Background of Prewar and War Data. 14 pp. 1946.

S 212   Industrial Injuries to Women. 20 pp. 1947.

S 213.   Women Workers in Peru. 41 pp. 1947.

S 214.   Maternity Benefits Under Union Contract, Health Insurance Plans. 16 pp. 1947.

S 215.   Women Workers in Power Laundries. 67 pp. 1947.

SC 216. Women Workers After VJ-Day in One Community: Bridgeport, Connecticut. 34 pp. 1947.

S 217.   International Documents on the Status of Women. 113 pp. 1947.

S 218.   Women's Occupations Through Seven Decades. 260 pp. Reprinted 1951. (See Bull. 253.)

219.   Earnings of Women in Selected Manufacturing Industries, 1946. 14 pp. 1948.

S 220.   Old-Age Insurance for Household Workers. 17 pp. 1947.

S 221.   Community Household Employment Programs. 70 pp. 1948.

S 222.   Women in Radio. 30 pp. 1947.

S 223.   Science Series. The Outlook for Women in:

223-1. Science. (General introduction to the series.) 78 pp. 1949.

223-2. Chemistry. 62 pp. 1948.

223-3. Biological Sciences. 87 pp. 1948. (See Bull. 278.)

223-4. Mathematics and Statistics. 21 pp. 1948. (See Bull. 262.)

223-5. Architecture and Engineering. 85 pp. 1948. (See Bull. 254.)

223-6. Physics and Astronomy. 32 pp. 1948.

223-7. Geology, Geography, and Meteorology. 48 pp. 1948.

223-8. Occupations Related to Science. 30 pp. 1948.

S 224. Women's Bureau Conference, 1948. The American Woman: Her Changing Role as Worker, Homemaker, Citizen. 207 pp. 1948.

S 225. Women's Bureau Handbook of Facts on Women Workers. 76 pp. 1948. (See Bull. 237.)

S 226. Working Women's Budgets in Twelve States. 33 pp. 1948.

226. Working Women's Budgets in Thirteen States. 41 pp. Revised. 1951.

227. State Minimum-Wage Laws and Orders, 1 July 1942-1 July 1950. Revised Supp. to Bull. 191. 65 pp. 1950. (Multilithed Supplements.) (See Bull. 247.)

228. The Industrial Nurse and the Woman Worker. 48 pp. 1949. Revision of Special Bull. 19.

229. Occupations for Girls and Women — Selected References. July 1943-June 1948. 102 pp. 1949.

S 230-I. Women in the Federal Service, 1923-1947: Trends in Employment. 79 pp. 1949.

S 230-II. Women in the Federal Service: Occupational Information. 84 pp. 1950.

S 231. The Outlook for Women in Police Work. 31 pp. 1949.

232. Women's Jobs: Advance and Growth. Popular version of Bull. 218. 88 pp. 1949.

S 233. Night Work for Women in Hotels and Restaurants. 56 pp. 1949.

S 234. Home Economics Occupations Series. The Outlook for Women:

234-1. In Dietetics. 77 pp. 1950.

234-2. As Food-Service Managers and Supervisors. 54 pp. 1952.

S 235. Social Work Series. The Outlook for Women in:

235-1. Social Case Work in a Medical Setting. 55 pp. 1950.

235-2. Social Case Work in a Psychiatric Setting. 56 pp. 1950.

235-3. Social Case Work with Children. 69 pp. 1951.

235-4. Social Case Work with Families. 80 pp. 1951.

235-5. Community Organization in Social Work. 37 pp. 1951.

235-6. Social Work Administration, Teaching, and Research. 79 pp. 1951.

235-7. Social Group Work. 41 pp. 1951.

235-8. Social Work. General Summary. 93 pp. 1952.

S 236. Women in Higher-Level Positions. 86 pp. 1950.

237. Women's Bureau 1950 Handbook of Facts on Women Workers. 102 pp. 1950. (See Bull. 242.)

S 238. Part-Time Jobs for Women: A Study in 10 cities. 82 pp. 1951.

S 239.   Women Workers and Their Dependents. 117 pp. 1952.

S 240.   Maternity Protection of Employed Women. 50 pp. 1952. (See Bull. 272.)

241.   Employment of Women in an Emergency Period. 12 pp. 1952.

242.   Women's Bureau 1952 Handbook of Facts on Women Workers. 121 pp. 1952. (See Bull. 255.)

243.   Report of the National Conference on Equal Pay, 31 March and 1 April 1952. 25 pp. 1952.

244.   Womanpower Committees during World War II: United States and British Experience. 73 pp. 1953.

245.   A Short-Term Training Program in an Aircraft Engine Plant. 11 pp. 1953.

S 246.   Employed Mothers and Child Care. 92 pp. 1953.

247.   State Minimum-Wage Laws and Orders, 1 July 1942-1 March 1953. 84 pp. Charts. 1953. (Multilithed Supplements.) (See Bull. 267.)

248.   "Older" Women as Office Workers. 64 pp. 1953.

249.   The Status of Women in the United States, 1953. 26 pp. 1953.

250.   State Hour Laws for Women. 114 pp. 1953. (See Bull. 277.)

S 251.   Progress Toward Equal Pay in the Meat Packing Industry. 16 pp. 1953.

252.   Toward Better Working Conditions for Women. 71 pp. 1953.

253.   Changes in Women's Occupations, 1940-1950. 104 pp. 1954.

254.   Employment Opportunities for Women in Professional Engineering. 38 pp. 1954.

255.   1954 Handbook on Women Workers. 75 pp. 1954. (See Bull. 261.)

S 256.   Training Mature Women for Employment. 46 pp. 1955.

257.   The Effective Use of Womanpower — Report of the Conference, 10 and 11 March 1955. 113 pp. 1955.

S 258.   Employment Opportunities for Women in Professional Accounting. 40 pp. 1955.

259.   State Minimum-Wage Order Provisions Affecting Working Conditions, 1 July 1942 to 1 June 1955. 75 pp. (See Bull. 269.)

260.   Employment Opportunities for Women in Beauty Service. 51 pp. 1956.

261.   1956 Handbook on Women Workers. 96 pp. 1956. (See Bull. 266.)

S 262.   Employment Opportunities for Women Mathematicians and Statisticians. 37 pp. 1956.

263.   Employment Opportunities for Women as Secretaries, Stenographers, Typists, and as Office-Machine Operators and Cashiers. 30 pp. 1957.

S 264.   College Women Go to Work: Report on Women Graduates, Class of 1956. 41 pp. 1958.

265.   Employment Opportunities for Women in Legal Work. 34 pp. 1958.

266.   1958 Handbook on Women Workers. 153 pp. 1958. (See Bull. 275.)

267.   State Minimum-Wage Laws and Orders, 1 July 1942 to 1 July 1958.

Part I: Historical Development and Statutory Provisions. 31 pp. Charts. 1958.
Part II: Analysis of Rates and Coverage. 1963. In press.

S 268.   First Jobs of College Women: Report of Women Graduates, Class of 1957. 44 pp. 1959.

269.   State Minimum-Wage Law and Order Provisions Affecting Working Conditions, 1 July 1942 to 1 April 1959. 141 pp. 1959. (See Bull. 280.)

S 270.   Careers for Women in the Physical Sciences. 77 pp. 1959.

S 271.   Careers for Women in Retailing. 52 pp. Reprinted 1963.

272.   Maternity Benefit Provisions for Employed Women. 50 pp. 1960.

273.   Part-Time Employment for Women. 53 pp. Reprinted 1961.

274.   Training Opportunities for Women and Girls. 64 pp. Reprinted 1961.

275.   1960 Handbook on Women Workers. 160 pp. 1960. (See Bull. 285.)

276.   Today's Woman in Tomorrow's World. 138 pp. 1960.

277.   State Hour Laws for Women. 105 pp. 1961.

S 278.   Careers for Women in the Biological Sciences. 84 pp. 1961.

S 279.   Life Insurance Selling — Careers for Women as Life Underwriters. 35 pp. 1961.

280.   State Minimum-Wage Law and Order Provisions Affecting Working Conditions, 1 July 1942 to 1 January 1961. 147 pp. 1961.

281.   Day Care Services: Form and Substance. 55 pp. 1961.

S 282.   Careers for Women as Technicians. 28 pp. 1961.

S 283.   Fifteen Years After College: A Study of Alumnae of the Class of 1945. 26 pp. 1962.

284.   Women Workers in 1960: Geographical Differences. 17 pp. 1962.

285.   1962 Handbook on Women Workers. 202 pp. 1963.

286.   Women Telephone Workers and Changing Technology. 1963.

Special Bulletins

C 1.   Effective Industrial Use of Women in the Defense Program. 22 pp. 1940.

C 2.   Lifting and Carrying Weights by Women in Industry. 12 pp. Revised 1946.

C 3.   Safety Clothing for Women in Industry. 11 pp. Supplement 4. 1941.

4.   Washing and Toilet Facilities for Women in Industry. 11 pp. 1942.

5.   Women's Effective War Work Requires Time for Meals and Rest. 4 pp. 1942.

C 6.   Night Work for Women and Shift Rotation in War Plants. 8 pp. 1942.

7.   Hazards to Women Employed in War Plants on Abrasive-Wheel Jobs. 6 pp. 1942.

C 8.   Guides for Wartime Use of Women on Farms. 11 pp. 1942.

9.   Safety Caps for Women in War Factories. 8 pp. 1942.

C 10. Women's Effective War Work Requires Good Posture. 6 pp. 1943.

11. Boarding Homes for Women War Workers. 6 pp. 1943. Supplement: Wartime Reminders to Women Who Work. 8 pp. 1943.

12. Choosing Women for War-Industry Jobs. 10 pp. 1943.

C 13. Part-Time Employment of Women in Wartime. 17 pp. 1943.

14. When You Hire Women. 16 pp. 1944.

15. Community Services for Women War Workers. 11 pp. 1944.

16. The Woman Counselor in War Industries: An Effective System. 13 pp. 1944.

17. Progress Report on Women War Workers' Housing, April 1943. 10 pp. 1944.

18. A Preview as to Women Workers in Transition from War to Peace. 26 pp. 1944.

19. The Industrial Nurse and The Woman Worker. 47 pp. 1944. Revised and reprinted as Bull. 228. 1949.

SC 20. Changes in Women's Employment during the War. 29 pp. 1944.

INDEX

352   INDEX

Wood, Peter, 23
Wood, T.A., 39
Woodhouse, Chase Going, 179
Woodrow Wilson Birthplace Foundation, 235
Woodrow Wilson Foundation, 235, 238, 240 n
Woodworth, Phyllis, 92
Work: definition, 5
Working women, 5-6, 179, 262-263, 279, 285, 289-290, 291, 292, 293, 315-316; civilian war production, 85-86, 206-219, 311; government service, 2, 182, 249, 262-263, 310; occupational distribution, 179-180; overcoming male resistance, 182, 217, 218; proportion of married women, 182-183; public opinion, 181, 184-185; records, 35-36; restrictions against, 181; rural background, 183-184; wages, 180, 181, 184, 213; (*see also* Woman's Land Army)

Works Progress Administration (WPA), 151, 152, 164, 182
World War I: women's participation, 136, 195-196, 197, 284. *See also* Woman's Land Army
World War II, 195, 202, 227; black job placement, 167, 168; civilian labor force, 181, 206-219, 289-290, recruitment, 210-213, 311

Yellin, Jean Fagan, 16, 128
Yorke Margaret, 77
Young, Louise, 10
Young, Mary E., 128, 313, 314, 327
Young, Rebecca, 86
Young-Megahy, Consuelo, 169
You're Going to Employ Women, 217

Zeimer, Linda, 29 n

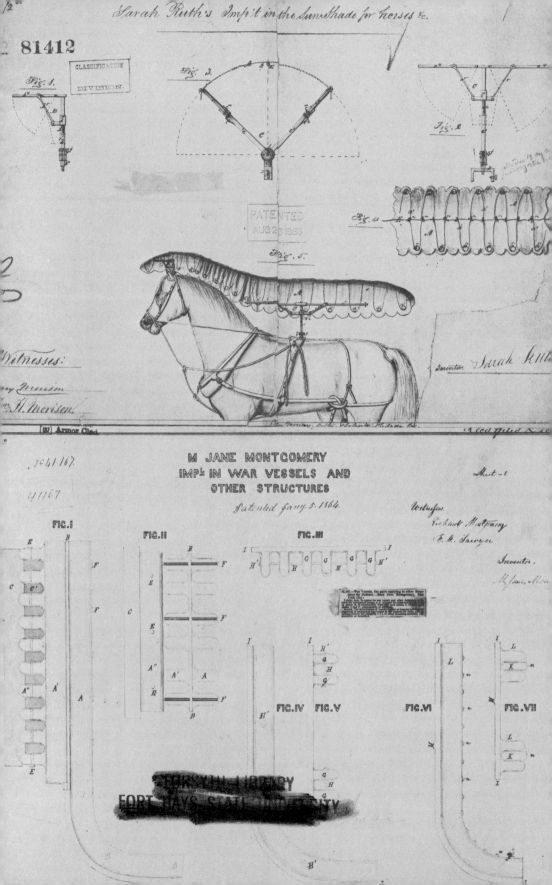

Sarah Ruth's Imp't in the Sun Shade for horses &c.

81412

Fig. 1.

Fig. 3.

Fig. 2.

PATENTED
AUG 25 1868

Fig. 4.

Fig. 5.

Witnesses:

Inventor Sarah Ruth

[97] Armor Clad

No 41167.

41167

M JANE MONTGOMERY
IMP'T IN WAR VESSELS AND
OTHER STRUCTURES

Patented Jany. 5. 1864.

Witness.
Richard Montgomery
E. B. Sawyer

Inventor.
M. Jane Mont...

FIG. I

FIG. II

FIG. III

FIG. IV   FIG. V

FIG. VI

FIG. VII